The Ultimate
GREYHOUND

Edited by Mark Sullivan

Howell Book House

New York

HOWELL BOOK HOUSE
IDG Books Worldwide, Inc.
An International Data Group Company
1633 Broadway
New York, NY 10019

ISBN 1-58245-130-3

Library of Congress Cataloging-in-Publication Data
available on request

Manufactured in Singapore

10 9 8 7 6 5 4 3 2 1

CONTENTS

CONTRIBUTORS

MARK SULLIVAN (Editor): Mark's interest in Greyhounds started with regular visits to White City Stadium, and this deepened when his family started to own racing dogs. Mark worked in racing kennels at weekends, became an owner-trainer, and at the age of 19 he took out a trainer's licence.

He enjoyed a number of successes with his dogs before going into racing administration. Spells in the racing office at Slough and Wimbledon led to an appointment with the *Racing Post* and then with *The Sporting Life*. During his time on the 'The Life', Mark earned a place in the *Guinness Book of Records* for tipping 12 winners from 12 races at Wimbledon at accumulated odds of 279, 256-1. He now works as a freelance writer and broadcaster, and with his wife Martina, runs the National Greyhound Racing Club for the British Greyhound Racing Board.
See Part II: The Racing Greyhound.

ESPEN ENGH was born into a family of Greyhound enthusiasts – he bred his first litter at the age of 13, under the Jet's prefix, with his mother Kari Engh Nylen. Since then, there have been 87 homebred Jet's Greyhound Champions, with a total of 231 Champion titles in 17 countries, in addition to World Champion, European Champion, and Champion of the Americas titles. Some 24 Greyhounds, owned or bred by Jet's, have won Best in Show at Championship shows.

As a Championship show judge for Greyhounds and other sighthounds, Espen has officiated in more than 40 countries in Europe, Africa, Asia, Oceania, North and Latin America, including many Greyhound Specialties, and the FCI World, European, Asian and American shows. By profession, Dr Engh is a vet and associate professor at the University of Oslo, Norway.
See Part I, Chapter 2: The Sighthound Family: Part IV: The Show Greyhound.

ANNE FINCH, a qualified nurse of some thirty years standing, first became involved in Greyhounds when she adopted Emma, a stray dog. Like so many Greyhounds, Emma proved to be a devoted, patient and loving companion. Emma was a former racer, and it was by studying her history through her ear-marks,

that Anne discovered the world of racing Greyhounds, and the tremendous need to find homes for retired dogs. Since that time, Anne has been a tireless campaigner on behalf of former racing Greyhounds and has been responsible for finding homes for many hundreds of Greyhounds. She has taken a special interest in Greyhounds that race in Spain, and she has organised rehoming schemes for Spanish and British dogs in a number of European countries, including Germany, as well as in the USA. She is the founder of the registered charity Greyhounds in Need.
See Part III: The Retired Greyhound.

JOHN KOHNKE BVSc (Sydney) RDA is a veterinary surgeon who has made a lifelong study of the Greyhound, specialising in diet and nutrition, and the diagnosis and treatment of racing injuries. He has written the widely acclaimed *Veterinary Advice for Greyhound Owners* and has contributed to many other books. For the past 15 years, he has written a regular monthly column in Britain's leading Greyhound paper, with feature articles in Australian Greyhound magazines as well as in the *National Greyhound Review* in America. He is in great demand to present lectures and seminars and is a world acknowledged authority on the feeding of Greyhounds.
See Part V: Health Care.

NICK WATERS has been involved with dogs since the mid-1950s. He has bred Challenge Certificate winners in Mastiffs, Standard Poodles and Irish Water Spaniels, and, with Liz Waters, he shares the Zanfi kennel, one of the most successful connected with the Irish Water Spaniel.

By profession, Nick is a canine art historian and freelance writer, and he contributes regularly on the dog in art to magazines and weekly dog papers in both the UK and the USA. For many years, his trade stand featuring canine antiques and collectables was a familiar sight on the British show scene.
See Part I, Chapter 1: Celebrating the Greyhound.

STEVE NASH, a top-class photographer specialising in Greyhounds, has taken a special collection of photos to illustrate this book.

1 *CELEBRATING THE GREYHOUND*

How dogs performed a job was, for previous generations, far more important than purity of lineage or aesthetic qualities. One of the exceptions would seem to be the Greyhound, whose looks and breeding have always been paramount.

Writing in Robert Leighton's *The New Book of the Dog* (published 1907), Frederick Gresham has the following to say: "The Greyhound is the oldest and most conservative of all dogs, and his type has altered singularly little during the seven thousand years in which he is known to have been cherished for his speed and kept by men for running down the gazelle or coursing the hare. The earliest references to him are far back in the primitive ages, long before he was beautifully depicted by Assyrian artists, straining at the leash or racing after his prey across the desert sands. The Egyptians loved him and appreciated him centuries before the Pyramids were built."

DOGS OF THE CHASE
The early depictions of dogs on bas-reliefs and tombs concentrated on dogs of the chase, which served to provide sport and put food on the table. In the main they were of two types – a heavy, powerful, yet athletic

Egyptian mural – from the tomb of Beni-Hassan, 2200BC.

Mastiff-type dog and one which would, today, be easily recognisable alongside the Greyhound. Some are shown with a feathered tail and ears heavy with a silken fringe; the ancestors, no doubt, of the Saluki from Arabia. The stele of Antefaa II (Xth dynasty), for example, shows a Pharoah being escorted by four very different types of dog, one of which is of a definite Greyhound type.

The graceful lines of the Greyhound have, throughout the centuries, appealed to artists. Greek artists were particularly fond of introducing those lines of the Greyhound as ornamentation in their decorative workmanship. In their metalwork, carvings in ivory and stone and as elements in the designs on their terracotta oil bottles, wine coolers and vases, the Greyhound is frequently to be seen, sometimes following the hare, but always in characteristic attitudes universally associated with the breed.

GRECIAN STYLE

The Greeks had a tendency to stylize or idealize their subjects and the lines of the Greyhound would therefore have had a particular appeal. A panel from a terracotta wine jug now in the British Museum features four Greyhounds in the typical stylized manner of 500 BC Greek art. One of the dogs shown is Cheiron the Centaur, fawning in front of Peleus and the infant Achilles. On another Greek vessel, this one in the Museum of Fine Arts in Boston, Actaeon is shown being attacked by three dogs, ancestors of our present-day Greyhounds. In Grecian

mythology, Actaeon was a huntsman who, surprising Diana bathing, was changed by her into a stag, and torn to pieces by his own hounds.

The depiction of Diana the Huntress has become a popular recurring theme throughout the history of art. A school of Fontainebleau study of c1540 shows the naked Diana setting forth with a white Greyhound wearing a collar from the 16th century. In Diana's left hand is a bow and in her right hand, held alluringly by her breast, she carries an arrow. In more recent years, Diana has become considerably more modest. Followers of Diana believed that she stopped hunting on the Ides of August and it was thereafter forbidden to hunt at that time. Men temporarily put away their hunting weapons and their dogs were crowned with garlands of flowers.

Another well-known surviving relic of Grecian art is a sixth century BC Attic rhyton from Felerii, now in the Villa Giulia Museum in Rome. In the form of a Greyhound's head, the hound wears an ornate collar decorated with an Apollo-like god with a lyre. Apollo had the first lyre ever made and the most wondrous music lay within it. With this piece there is perhaps an early connection with hounds making music. The rhyton, an unfooted drinking vessel, is the ancestor of the stirrup cup, such cups being traditionally offered to mounted huntsmen at the meet prior to hunting.

Another early surviving relic showing a Greyhound is a Corinthian vase decorated with scenes from a feast. In one, we see a

A panel from a Greek terracotta jug now in the British Museum. From 'The New Book of the Dog' by Robert Leighton, 1907.

*Graeco-Roman group found at Monte Cagnolo.
now in the British Museum.
From 'The New Book of the Dog' by Robert
Leighton, 1907.*

dog picking up scraps from the floor which
people feasting at the table have dropped.
This is perhaps one of the earliest
representations in art showing a hound as
part of an everyday domestic scene.

'DOG DAYS'

Old Persian manuscripts and works of art
also show the Greyhound. In a miniature in
the Bibliothèque Nationale in Paris entitled
Mad Dog, the Greyhound type is shown
attacking its owner. Early cultures feared the
appearance in the sky of the Greater Dog-
Star, Sirius, its coming each year signalling
the beginning of summer and a period of
unbearable heat, increased disease and burned
crops. The hottest days of the year were
known – and still are – as 'dog days'. The
Persians believed that Sirius's appearance
enhanced the sun's heat, causing
hydrophobia, and that dogs were more
susceptible to madness at this time. As a
result of this belief, the dog went through a
long period when it was feared, distrusted,
something to be scorned and turned away.
Does this Persian miniature represent this

attitude, or does it portray for the first time
in art a rabid dog? The dog appears very
emaciated, its tongue is hanging out and it is
obviously slobbering.

HERALDRY

The Greyhound became a symbolic creature,
never more so than where heraldry was
concerned. Heraldry, and the wearing and
issuing of coats of arms, in the form we
understand, originally had a very practical
role. It goes back to the crusading
expeditions and, in England, to King Richard
the Lionheart in the 12th century. A surcoat
– a loose robe – was worn by knights over
their armour and decorated with devices by
which heralds described the wearer. Such
coat-armour distinguished the various noble
warriors when wrapped in their complete
suits of steel. Heraldry conjures up every
aspect of upper-class life: a pedigree; a sign of
purity; of ancient lineage; of someone with
entitlement; of belonging. So when choosing
a dog for one's coat of arms – and dogs are
among the most popular of all animals –
what more appropriate breed than a
Greyhound? It was one of the first breeds to
be represented on coats of arms and has been
shown courant – running; passant – walking;
statant – standing; or rampant – standing on
its hind legs.

One of the earliest records of the breed on
arms is on those of Sir John Percival, Lord
Mayor of London in 1499, which showed
three hounds. The breed became popular
with Lord Mayors of London, with a
number of others who followed all having
Greyhounds. Sir Thomas Kneysworth also
had three, as did Sir John Allen, with Sir
William Hollis having just one, together with
a fish. Perhaps he was interested in fishing as
well as coursing, for the choice of decoration
frequently indicated the bearer's interests.

The Greyhound was not confined to
British families; the arms of the 17th and

18th century Marquis of Nicolai show one Greyhound courant and two Greyhounds rampant. Kings of Europe also incorporated Greyhounds into their coats of arms. Charles V, Henry II and Philippe VI of France and Edward VI, Henry VII, Henry VIII and James II in England, all chose the breed. Henry VII adopted the Greyhound as his personal standard and it remains the symbol of the House of York to this day.

THE WHITE GREYHOUND

By the late Middle Ages and into the Renaissance period, a white Greyhound had come to symbolise power, pageantry and majesty. Two of the best known paintings on this subject are Antonio Pisanello's (1395-1455) *Vision of St. Eustace* and Albrecht Dürer's (1471-1528) interpretation of a similar subject, *The Vision of St. Hubert*. Pisanello's painting was considered his greatest and most imaginative, and an

ABOVE: 'The Vision of Eustace' by Antonio Pisanello (1395-1455).
From 'The New Book of the Dog' by Robert Leighton, 1907.

TOP RIGHT: 'The Vision of St Hubert' by Albrecht Dürer (1471-1528).
From 'The New Book of the Dog' by Robert Leighton, 1907.

BOTTOM RIGHT: Gaston Phebus surrounded by huntsmen and dogs – from his 'Treatise on Hunting' written in the 14th century.

excellent illustration of his naturalism, his rendering of the splendour of knighthood and his joy of nature, both animate and inanimate. Dürer's painting shows the moment when Hubert was hunting in the forest one day when he suddenly saw a magnificent stag with Christ on the cross hovering between its horns. Falling to his knees, he swore never to hunt again. He was eventually named as a patron saint of animals. If not considered Dürer's greatest work, it is, nevertheless, considered to be of the finest quality.

Many other images of white Greyhounds appeared around this time, of which the following three examples, two of which are from literature, are typical. *The King's Grand White Dogs* and other illustrations from the Gaston Phebus (or de Foix) *Treatise on Hunting* written in the 14th century, with illuminations added about 1440, is now in the Bibliothèque Nationale in Paris. This work, according to Clifford Hubbard, "has become the greatest hunting book of all times, and the parent of the very earliest English contribution on venery."

A 15th century treatise on falconry and venery in the Bibliothèque de Chantilly shows a mixed pack of white and red Greyhounds, together with huntsmen bringing down wild boar. Paolo Uccello's (c1396-1475) *Hunt in the Forest,* which he painted in 1468, is considered his last important work. This highly complex composition shows mounted huntsmen, followers on foot and a considerable pack of mostly white Greyhounds in pursuit of deer in a forest at night. The picture is lit up by the white Greyhounds and the Florentine youths with their bright clothes; there is no hint of brutality or death – it is as if we are the observers of a pageant of the chase. As Kenneth Clark said of the picture: "The hounds leap in a symmetrical recession, like dancers in an animal ballet, across a carpet of flowers. Here the union of man and nature comes curiously close to the image of the Golden Age ... and the forest has the mystery of a fairy tale." The Golden Age was a time in mythology when men and animals lived together in harmony.

The image of the white Greyhound as the supreme dog of the chase was by no means confined to the classical artists of Italy and neighbouring countries. David Kloker von Ehrenstahl (1629-98) was the German-born painter at the Swedish court and is described as the 'father of Swedish painting'. His portrait of one of Carl XI's white Greyhounds bringing down a stag has far more 'realism' to it than Uccello's painting of some 200 years earlier. We are, though, now moving from a period in art which sanctified death, where the beast, amid much ritual and celebration, finally gave itself to a superior force. After a period where death in all its brutality was shown in art – as depicted by Ehrenstahl – Gustave Courbet (1819-77) was, to some extent, to reintroduce the ritual and celebration of death into sporting art in Northern Europe.

CREATURES OF IMPORTANCE
In early 'high art' when the Greyhound was portrayed outside the hunt and the chase, he continued to be shown as a creature of almost heraldic and symbolic proportions. Piero della Francesca (1410/20-92), the Italian painter and mathematician, shows clearly this approach. As Kenneth Clark comments in *Animals and Men:* "The two dogs who accompany Sigismondo Malatestra in Piero's picture of him kneeling before his patron saint are almost heraldic in their stillness and symmetry." Piero's training as a mathematician may well have contributed to the 'order' which he gave to his dogs.

A similar approach was adopted to paint the Greyhound positioned at the front of a miniature attributed to Jean Fouquet (c1425-

The frontispiece to Sir James Ware's 'De Hibernia', 1658.

An allegorical picture from 'The Book of Beasts', 1665. Author unknown.

80), an artist considered as having been the major French artist of the 15th century. The miniature, which is now in the Bibliothèque Nationale in Paris, is of Louis XI and his premier knights of the Order of St Michael. Be it as an accompaniment in portraiture, as the supreme dog of the chase, or as an heraldic beast, one thing which all these early Greyhounds display are heavy, ornate collars showing that they were creatures of importance, held in high esteem, who would have belonged to monarchs, princes and other high-ranking noblemen.

SPORTING EMPHASIS
Moving on from the Middle Ages and the

Renaissance periods, sport with hounds and dogs became the privilege of a much greater proportion of the population. The landed families were able to enjoy sports which previously had been confined to royal rulers and their families. Hare-hunting and coursing were, by comparison with fox and stag-hunting, inexpensive and easy to organise. Coursing was a most popular sport in the late 17th and 18th centuries, the Greyhound was now owned by a much wider group of people and, as such, moved away from its earlier symbolic image as that of a creature of pageantry. Numerous coursing clubs were set up from the middle of the 18th century and it was only a hundred years later that the trial of dogs and how they performed, and not the capture of game, became all-important. For the first time in sport, the death of the animal no longer held supreme position as the single most important moment of the sport.

Southern Europe had seen the birth and been the home of 'high art' but, in Northern Europe, and England in particular, the reputations of a great many artists who earned sizeable incomes from painting sporting scenes were to become firmly established. Northern Europe was home to a new school of painting which did not rely on historical, mythological, almost symbolic subject matter: that of genre and landscape painting.

One such early artist was Albert Cuyp (1620-91), whose painting of Michael and Cornelius van Meedervoort with their tutor and coachman shows them starting out for the hunt, while in the background four Greyhounds are already chasing a hare. Organised coursing or testing of one dog against another had yet to become firmly established, even though Queen Elizabeth I in the 16th century had ordered the Duke of Norfolk to draw up a code of rules. In England the landed families, who were to produce the great 'livestock improvers', wished for nothing greater than to have themselves portrayed amid their estates and the pastimes which gave them so much pleasure.

THE SPORTING ARTISTS

First of the principal British sporting artists was Francis Barlow (c1626-1704). He was born in Lincolnshire, a county known for the quality of livestock produced there. Along with Norfolk, it was also known for the quality of its hares. Referring to one of Barlow's paintings, William Secord in his book *Dog Painting*, records that: "Many of Barlow's compositions have a naive quality

Lord Rivers rides out in front of the family seat to watch his Greyhounds coursing.
An engraving by Blome from his 'Gentleman's Recreation', 1686.

which adds to their appeal. Even though the hare, further away from the viewer than the Greyhound, should by the rules of perspective be quite small, it appears rather large." Another of Barlow's paintings which includes a Greyhound, together with a couple of hounds and an assortment of dead game, is painted in the tradition of the Flemish school of still-life painters. This style of painting, made popular in Northern Europe, was a stepping-stone from the classical to the sporting art popularised in England.

Although hare-hunting and coursing were inexpensive and easy to organise, which no doubt contributed to the sport's popularity, they were still very formal and structured

The Greyhound from Buffon's 18th century publication 'Histoire Naturelle'.

occasions, as the engraving by Blome from his *Gentleman's Recreation* (1686) clearly shows. An impeccably turned-out Lord Rivers rides out in front of the family seat to watch his Greyhounds coursing hares. This same formality is shown by James Seymour (1702-52) in his oil *A Coursing Scene*. It is a highly structured painting which captures the end of a successful course. The two Greyhounds and the mounted field rest beside a tree, while a dismounted servant, who brings the two units of the picture together, shows the squire and his somewhat impassive wife the dead hare.

Although interest in coursing hares had increased enormously, Greyhounds were still used to bring down other game, even though coursing of both deer and foxes had virtually ceased in 18th century England. Charles Towne (1763-1840) shows us a Greyhound bringing down a stag in a park; the dog is particularly fit and, for a painting of this period, displays much greater freedom of

movement than was frequently the case around this time. This same subject was tackled at least twice by George Stubbs ARA (1724-1806), once in 1765 and again in 1769, being similar studies of a single Greyhound bringing down a stag.

'LIVESTOCK IMPROVERS'
Two great English sporting gentlemen and 'livestock improvers' did much to revitalise and establish the Greyhound's reputation towards the end of the 18th century. Lord Orford, who founded the Swaffham Coursing Club in 1776, and who was concerned that the breed had become too fine to take a hare, experimented with various crosses, including the Bulldog and the Norfolk Lurcher, the latter carrying half Greyhound blood.

Perhaps the most important patron, though, was the flamboyant Yorkshireman, Colonel Thornton. He was a pre-eminent breeder of dogs, in particular Foxhounds,

13

Colonel Thornton's 'Major' from John Scott's engraving of Philip Reinagle's painting. From 'The Sportsman's Cabinet', 1803-04.

Pointers and Greyhounds. He was also one of the first great collectors of sporting pictures. It was Thornton who established Philip Reinagle RA (1749-1833) as the great sporting artist of his era. Reinagle was one of a family of twelve artists whose father arrived in Scotland in 1745 as a supporter of the Young Pretender. In the dog world, he is best remembered for a series of paintings which were engraved by John Scott and which appeared in William Taplin's *The Sportsman's Cabinet*, published in 1803-04, which was the third dog book in the English language.

One of these engravings was of the Colonel's dog Major, the original painting being exhibited at the Royal Academy in 1805. It was at Lord Orford's dispersal sale following his death that Colonel Thornton bought Czarina, a bitch who won forty-seven matches without ever having been beaten. She did not breed until she was thirteen years old and her litter of eight included the dog Claret, who in turn was the sire of Major, winner of the Thousand Guinea Challenge on Epsom Downs.

COURSING DEPICTIONS

Coursing subjects became very popular, helped by the hand of the engraver, for such engravings, either as prints or illustrations in books and magazines, found their way into the homes of so many people who could never have owned the originals. Sawrey Gilpin RA, FSA (1733-1807) painted

From the engraving of Sawrey Gilpin's painting of 'Maria' and Lord Orford's 'Czarina' from the Rev. William Daniel's 'Rural Sports', 1801.

CZARINA *and* MARIA.

Czarina and Maria coursing a hare, an engraving of which appeared in the Rev. William Daniel's *Rural Sports* (1801), and Henry Corbould's (d. 1844) painting of a coursing scene at Swaffham, which was published in *The Sporting Magazine* in 1793, are two of many examples.

One of the best known of all coursing paintings is *The Waterloo Cup Coursing Meeting 1840,* which was painted by Richard Ansdell RA (1815-85) for the Earl of Sefton on whose ground the Waterloo Cup was run. The painting by Ansdell, who is the only artist to have had a town named after him, was of the fifth Waterloo Cup meeting in which thirty-two dogs ran, with Mr Easterby's black dog, Earwig, being the winner. Prominent among those in the picture are the Earl and Countess of Sefton, the Earl of Stradbroke and the Marquess of Douglas. In common with such grouped composite pictures, all thirty-two dogs are shown.

It became popular with artists to paint Greyhounds being held by boys or elderly grooms and retainers. Edward Topham's Snowball, painted by Henry Bernard Chalon (1771-1849), the dog being restrained by William Poshby, who always trained him, and Camarine, the property of J. Story Jr, painted by J.R. Ryott (c1810-60) being held by a boy, are two typical examples.

DOG PORTRAITURE

Long before it became established for the dog to be treated in portraiture as the subject matter in its own right, the Greyhound was one of a handful of breeds so honoured. Edmund Bristowe's (1787-1876) portrait of W. Adam's two Greyhounds shown in an extensive landscape, which dominates the picture, is typical of many English dog portraits of the period. To emphasise – if any emphasis was needed – that the dogs are hare dogs, a dead hare and a Beagle accompany them in the picture. At an early age, Bristowe was patronised by the Duke of Clarence, later William IV. While in Bristowe's painting the landscape dominates, in Henry Barraud's (1811-74) painting of Lydia, the dog is the focal point; the landscape is nonetheless dramatic but the dog takes up most of the picture.

George Earl (op1856-83) was one of the first artists who specialised in portraits of named dogs, something which the coming of shows was going to popularise as the years were to progress. His painting of one of the most famous Greyhounds of all time, Lord Lurgan's Master McGrath, is typical of the many head study portraits Earl was completing at that time. Master McGrath was the winner of the Waterloo Cup in 1868, 1869 and again in 1871.

It was Titian (c1487-1576) who had introduced the dog as an accompaniment in

The Greyhound 'Lydia' by Henry Barraud (1811-74).
Courtesy: Sara Davenport Fine Paintings.

The Greyhound 'King Cob' by Henry Barraud (1811-74).
Courtesy: Iona Antiques, London.

Master McGrath, winner of the Waterloo Cup in 1868, 1869 and 1871, painted by George Earl (op 1856-83).

Colonel North's brindle Greyhound 'Fullerton' is one of the most famous of all Greyhounds. He was the winner of the Waterloo Cup four times from 1889-1892, and he is now in the Natural History Museum, London. This painting by Harrington Bird (fl 1870-93) was reproduced in 'The New Book of the Dog' by Robert Leighton, 1907. The other dog is the Colonel's Simonian.

Sir Edwin Landseer's influence on the dog in art is immeasurable – this enamel is very much in the style of the great man's work.
Courtesy: Sara Davenport Fine Paintings.

Study of 'Port', a successful dog at coursing meetings, bred by Dodd, Ragley, Shropshire, by 'Wisher' out of 'Blanche'. English School circa 1834.
Courtesy: Iona Antiques, London.

Signed William Davis and inscribed 'A Gift from Dr Maguire to Mrs Davis, Fisherton, Delamere, October 1846'.
Courtesy: Iona Antiques, London.

A Greyhound Being Held by a Boy, by J.R. Ryott, dated 1840 and inscribed: 'Camarine the property of Mr J. Story Jun. In 1838, won the Caledonian Gold Cup, value 33 Soverings and the same year won the Liverpool Stake of 100 Sov's and has always shewn herself game in every point that distinguishes a high bred and superior Greyhound'.   *Courtesy: Iona Antiques, London.*

English School, inscribed 'March 1846'.

Courtesy: Iona Antiques, London.

Unsigned English School circa 1850. Inscribed 'Young Bess'. The property of W. Moffat of Mortlake.

Courtesy: Iona Antiques, London.

'Waiting For Master' by J. Valentine (fl 1884), English School.

Courtesy: Sara Davenport Fine Paintings.

Mr Dennis's 'Dendrapis', winner of the Waterloo Cup in 1909, by Thomas Blinks (1853-1910).

Courtesy: Sara Davenport Fine Paintings.

'Destined,' pastel on paper by Jacquie Jones. Exhibited at her solo exhibition, London, 1998.

Courtesy: The Park Gallery, London.

portraiture, and this appealed greatly to the 18th century landed families. Stubbs's portrait of Robert, 10th Lord Petre, which he painted in 1785, has all the elements of a portrait of a sporting squire. His Lordship rides his favourite horse over his extensive estate, in front of him stands a black and white Greyhound and he leans back in the saddle to attract the attention of a white Greyhound. It is the presence of the dogs which invites the viewer to observe the picture in detail.

Sir Edwin Landseer RA (1802-73) was at the forefront of finally establishing the dog as being the subject matter in its own right in portraiture. His pictures were frequently anecdotal and his dogs were often given human characteristics. His influence on the dog in art has been greater than any other single artist and cannot be overestimated. Landseer's portrait of Eos, the favourite Greyhound of HRH Prince Albert, is unquestionably the best known of all Greyhound pictures and one of the best known of all dog portraits. Prince Albert brought her with him from Germany and the painting was commissioned by Queen Victoria as a Christmas present for Prince

Albert in 1841. It was exhibited at the Royal Academy in 1842. In the picture, Eos is shown in the setting of Buckingham Palace, guarding her master's property and looking up with an expression of devotion. On a deerskin footstool are Prince Albert's opera hat and gloves and on top of a table, which is covered with a heavy, rich red cloth, is the Prince's cane. In January 1842, Eos was accidentally shot by Queen Victoria's uncle Ferdinand of Saxe-Coburg-Gotha in a shooting party at Windsor Castle, but she survived her wounds and died in 1844, aged nearly eleven. Landseer's picture of Eos is the largest of his single pictures of royal pets and is considered one of his finest animal studies. Eos features in several other paintings by Landseer, including *Windsor Castle in Modern Times* and, according to Richard Ormond, the leading authority on Landseer and his work, this painting and the portrait of Eos may have been intended to hang as a pair at Windsor Castle.

The Greyhound became a favourite subject in dog portraiture and many of the leading artists, as well as a good many minor ones, were all attracted to the breed's form. William Malbon's (op1834-69) study of seven dogs all belonging to Mr Brown of Mansfield, which was completed on December 21st 1853, is an early example of a study of so many dogs. The work of Robert Morley (1857-1941) is always well observed and has a certain anecdotal quality to it. He completed a number of commissions for Queen Victoria, one of which was a study of Eos and two of her offspring which still hangs in the Royal collection.

John Frederick Herring Snr (1795-1865), like Malbon, was another early 19th century artist who painted a group of Greyhounds, in his case four, belonging to John Sabine. Perhaps the ultimate picture, so far as the number of dogs is concerned, is an oil by William Henry Davis (c1786-1867) one of the most successful and prolific livestock painters of the mid-19th century. Dated 1831, it shows Colonel Newport Charlett's eleven Greyhounds at exercise with Tom Bayliss, the groom. In the background is Hanley Court, Worcestershire. In many ways Greyhounds received the same treatment from the earlier artists as that apportioned to scent hounds.

The late 19th century saw a new breed of artist arrive upon the scene, whose artistic lives centred around dog portraiture – names which include Arthur Wardle (1864-1949), Maud Earl (1864-1943) and Thomas Blinks

A Victorian spelter copy of an animalier bronze. Spelter became very popular as the 'poor man's bronze', and is now very collectable.

(1853-1910). The work of many artists is frequently characterised by their treatment of their subject's eyes; in the case of dog portraiture, this is perhaps never more true than with the work of Wardle. The look and expression which he gave to two Greyhounds being restrained by a young girl is reminiscent of his numerous studies of Fox Terriers.

Maud Earl completed many studies of Greyhounds, including Fabulous Fortune, Fearless Footsteps and Farndon Ferry, all Waterloo Cup winners for the Fawcett brothers between 1896 and 1902, the year in which Earl completed their picture. Not surprisingly, Waterloo Cup winners were popular subjects and Thomas Blinks painted Mr Dennis's Dendrapis, winner in 1909. This is among Blink's better works but unfortunately, in today's political climate, it does have one thing against it – the inclusion of a dead hare.

THE INTEREST OF SCULPTORS
Perhaps no other breed of dog has received the attention of sculptors more than the Greyhound has. From Roman times right up to the art nouveau period and beyond, the breed's form has had an everlasting appeal. One of the earliest and one of the best known images is the Graeco-Roman group now in the British Museum, which was found at Monte Cagnolo near the ancient Lanuvium. One dog sits behind another, the second dog resting one paw on the shoulder of the first dog and carefully licking its ear. Another early group in the British Museum shows Actaeon being devoured by two of his dogs. In the Vatican Museum is a carved marble group showing a rather glamorously attired Diana with a rather emaciated dog, and in the Musei Capitolini in Rome is a similar carved marble, but in this case both Diana and her Greyhound look far more able to cope with the chase.

When it comes to the work of the animaliers, dogs must surely follow horses in popularity, with the Greyhound family being the most popular. Some are unquestionably Italian Greyhounds, particularly the finely modelled groups by Pierre Jules Mene (1810-71). Some of the best known models of Greyhounds with hares at their feet are from models by Christophe Fratin (1800-64). Jane Horswell in *Les Animaliers* records him as being acclaimed 'the greatest animal sculptor of his day' at the Great Exhibition in London in 1851. His model of c1840 shows not just a Greyhound with a dead hare, but a dog with all the body language which tells us that it has just successfully coursed that particular hare.

An unusual group by Emmanuel Fremiet (1824-1910) shows two Greyhounds standing alert looking straight ahead and, in total contrast, a pair by Antoine-Louis Barye (1796-1875) shows two dogs recumbent on bases. Although their pose is very classical, there is also a dramatic realism to their posture. Barye is considered the father of the animalier school of sculptors.

A popular model, much reproduced, is Jean-Francois-Theodore Gechter's (1796-1844) study of a dog crouching on its haunches and looking back over its shoulder. In more recent years, the 20th century sculptor, John Skeaping (1901-80) completed a number of Greyhound models. He was, though, passionate about Greyhound racing and owned many of the breed. Following the introduction of Greyhound racing into this country in the 1920s, a number of clubs included models of Greyhounds on many of their trophies.

GREYHOUNDS IN PORCELAIN
Many of the early English porcelain manufacturers introduced Greyhounds into their ranges. In most cases the dogs were shown sitting or recumbent, as such slender legs would have failed to withstand the heat

Early Rockingham plate – the centre panel is decorated with a coursing scene.

of the kilns. Among the earliest are a pair of Derby Greyhounds from the late 18th century, one black and white, one brown and white, both shown recumbent on bases appliquéed with flowers. Chamberlains Worcester c1820-40 and Grainger Lee & Co, Worcester 1820-37, both manufactured

Greyhounds and in both cases the dogs are shown recumbent with the characteristic pose of one front leg across the other. This same treatment was given to the breed in a much larger model by Copeland and Garrett, 1833-47.

Rockingham, 1826-30, produced a silhouette group of two white Greyhounds, a bitch standing in front of a recumbent dog. Minton produced a Parian dog seated on a rocky base c1850-70 and at the same period a Samuel Alcock model appeared showing two dogs recumbent on a tasselled cushion. The bitch poses elegantly while the dog scratches itself! With this model, as with some others, it is arguable whether the dogs are in fact Greyhounds or Italian Greyhounds and it is always wise to let the collectors decide, for only they know. The Greyhound and coursing scenes also found their way on to the decoration of cabinet plates and tableware.

Two of the most collectable manufacturers of 20th century English ceramic dogs are Doulton and Beswick. Doulton introduced a brown, cream and white dog by an unknown

An English porcelain model of a Greyhound by Copeland and Garrett 1833-47.

modeller into its range in 1931, and Beswick in 1942 introduced Jovial Roger from a model by Arthur Gredington. In 1939, he was appointed the first resident modeller for Beswick and much of his output was essential to Beswick's continued popularity.

Second only to the Spaniel, the Greyhound is the breed most associated with the Staffordshire potters. They chose their subjects from people and events which were popular at the time. Landseer in his paintings had certainly popularised the Toy Spaniel – the ladies' comforter – and the Staffordshire potters would have been only too aware of this. As to the popularity of the Greyhound, coursing had become *the* most popular sport and was followed by all classes of society, so the modelling of Greyhounds would have been a wise commercial move.

Many of the Staffordshire potters' human portraits carried the names of the subject on their bases but a pair of Greyhounds are the only named dog figures. Now much sought after, they feature Master McGrath and Pretender. Master McGrath won the Waterloo Cup in 1871 for the third time, on this occasion running against Pretender. Both dogs were very popular countrywide, and it was odds-on who would win. The result was so close that it enhanced Master McGrath's reputation even further and made Pretender famous for posterity.

Collectors can amass quite a collection of Staffordshire Greyhounds: Greyhounds recumbent; against trees acting as spill vases; with or without hares; singly; in groups of

One of a pair of Staffordshire Greyhounds with hares, circa 1860.

two, or even three; accompaniments to centrepiece mantle clocks; with Toy Spaniels; with human figures, usually in Scottish dress, for Queen Victoria had popularised everything Scottish. There are, though, a great many copies of Staffordshire pieces and new collectors to this field should be very cautious.

2 THE SIGHTHOUND FAMILY

It might, possibly, be pretentious to claim that the Greyhound is the forefather of the other sighthound breeds, but the Greyhound is, undoubtedly, the best-known. As we have seen in Chapter One, Greyhounds have been described in literature, and been depicted in art, as the epitome of a functional hunter and a live courser, throughout the centuries. It is probably true to say that the other sighthound breeds cannot be fully appreciated or understood without having at least a working knowledge of the Greyhound, as a point of reference.

SHARED ORIGINS
It is more than likely that sighthounds originated in the Middle East and were derived from common ancestors, but the exact origins have been lost in the mist of time. It is therefore impossible to say with any degree of certainty if those common ancestors were more similar to the Pharaoh Hound, the Ibizan Hound, the Greyhound or, maybe, to the Saluki. Ample evidence, both in literature and in art, proves that sighthounds very similar to these breeds have existed for millennia. Enthusiasts of the different sighthound breeds often claim that their particular breed is the original and the source of the others, but such claims can hardly be substantiated. The concept of pure breeds of dogs as we know it was developed only in the mid-19th century with the advent of Kennel Clubs, stud books and Breed Standards.

COMMON DENOMINATORS
What do the sighthound breeds have in common? The obvious common denominator lies in their function as hunting dogs, using their sight as the primary sense for finding the game. The sighthounds will use their immense speed and turning ability to chase down and kill the game, working either alone, in pairs or in groups. But not all sighthounds hunt by sight alone; some also have very good scenting power and others also use their ears extensively, but all of them will normally survey their territory by sight.

When following the game at high speed through open fields, sighthounds will use the double suspension gallop as opposed to the common diagonal gallop performed by horses and heavier dogs. The double suspension gallop is a particularly swift gait; it is also called a light gallop. It is commonly used by the sighthound breeds but, contrary to popular beliefs, it is not entirely exclusive to them. Double suspension gallop can also be performed by other breeds such as Dobermans and Basenjis at particularly high speed. Greyhounds have even been observed to use the triple suspension or fast gallop, a gait pattern otherwise only rarely seen in cheetahs.

Crimean Greyhound.

Circassian Greyhound.

Arab Greyhound.

Greyhound of the Soudan (1897).

Portuguese Greyhound.

Balearic Greyhound.

There are a number of anatomical and physiological traits that are consistent with high speed and therefore common to all breeds of sighthounds, but to varying degrees in the different breeds. As a sprinter, a sighthound obviously has to have long legs to be able to cover ground at great speed. The muscles should be hard and fit, but long and lean, rather than heavy and bulky, and the distance between the shoulder blades rather narrow, but not so narrow as to restrict the lowering of the head to the ground when catching the prey. The neck must be long, strong and muscular to assist the sighthound both in discovering its game and in reaching down to grab it. This is when the sighthound's strong jaws and teeth are put to work. Aerodynamics dictate that the chest should be deep rather than broad, and the bone to appear somewhat bladed rather than round. In any sighthound breed, movement and construction are very important, with sound legs and feet a must. To sum up these traits that make up both the beauty and function of a sighthound, elegance and quality coupled with strength and muscularity should be readily apparent.

SIGHTHOUND STANDARDS
As the model sighthound, the Greyhound is mentioned in the Breed Standards of several other breeds, notably twice in the current Deerhound Standard, whereas the Irish Wolfhound Standard, in turn, refers to the Deerhound for general type and colour and to the Greyhound in the description of the ears. Both the current FCI Italian Greyhound, Magyar Agar, Chart Polski and Spanish Galgo Standards include references to the Greyhound as well, as did the original Standard for the Whippet. Knowing and understanding the Greyhound is, no doubt, a useful tool in understanding its closest relatives as well.

In recognition of the fact that the

THE GREYHOUND IN ACTION
Photos Steve Nash, courtesy Hazel Dickson.

sighthounds have a lot in common, the sighthound breeds form a separate group at shows in most countries around the world, the FCI Group 10. This group includes most of the breeds commonly referred to as sighthounds, including the Italian Greyhound, but excluding the Ibizan Hound and the Pharaoh Hound which, most authorities agree, should have been included. In English-speaking countries the sighthound breeds, with the exception of the Italian Greyhound, are included in the rather divergent Hound Group along with such breeds as Basenjis, Bassets, Beagles, Bloodhounds, Dachshunds, Elkhounds, Rhodesian Ridgebacks and others. In these countries, the Italian Greyhound is in the Toy Group.

There is much to learn about any sighthound breed by studying closely-related breeds. The following discussion on the different sighthound breeds will, therefore, use the Greyhound as a reference point and will start with the breeds closest in function and type to the Greyhound – which is the epitome of the sighthounds.

THE GREYHOUND

As a point of reference for the other sighthound breeds, it makes sense to recapitulate the essence of the Greyhound.

The Greyhound is a strongly built, upstanding dog of generous proportions, used for many centuries for hunting down hares and other prey. The dog should have good length of leg but should, at the same time, cover plenty of ground with long and gently flowing lines. Built for speed and hunting ability, with remarkable stamina and endurance, the general appearance is what defines type in the breed and is therefore of the utmost importance.

The Greyhound should combine substance with elegance and quality. The elegance should stem from the flowing lines, the length of neck, the beauty of the formation, the definition of the muscles, as well as from the quality of the skin and coat.

At the same time, the Greyhound is a strong dog with good bone and ample body, never to appear overly refined, weedy or weak. A Greyhound should have long, flat and elastic muscles as opposed to being bulky and heavy; correct musculature being crucial for the functional dog. The muscle tone should be hard, but not to the point of limiting elasticity or detracting from the smoothness of the outline.

All parts of the dog should fit together with a sweeping flow of lines, without abruptness, to create a harmonious overall balance, aptly described as smooth S-curves.

The free, long reaching movement enables the Greyhound to cover the ground at great speed, correct movement being very important in the breed. The Greyhound should possess a suppleness of limb which emphasise in a marked degree its distinctive type and quality.

The breed has a long head with powerful jaws. The eyes are preferably dark, bright, intelligent, oval and obliquely set. The ears are rose-shaped. The neck is long and clean, the shoulders are well laid with a good return of upper arm, a deep chest and capacious body. A slightly arched loin, powerful and muscular quarters and sound legs, slightly sprung pasterns and correct feet of moderate length, are also prerequisites of a good Greyhound.

The tail should be long, slightly curved and carried low. The coat should be fine and close. A good Greyhound cannot have a bad colour although the KC Standard lists certain colours as opposed to the American version. The ideal height for dogs is 71-76 cm and for bitches 68-71 cm.

The Greyhound should be a proud king of dogs demanding attention, but is also gentle, affectionate and even-tempered – an ideal family dog and companion as well as a fierce hunter.

THE DEERHOUND

The Deerhound is probably the closest relative to the Greyhound. The breed, as its name implies, was developed to hunt deer by sight. The writer Stonehenge, in some of his monumental 19th-century books, gave very interesting accounts and portraits of the varieties of the Greyhound, including dogs which strongly resemble the Deerhound. In accordance with the game, the terrain and the climate in the northern parts of Britain, and in Scotland in particular, the breed over the centuries developed into a dog resembling a rough-coated Greyhound of larger size and bone, as described by the Breed Standard. The Deerhound should suggest the unique combination of speed, power and endurance which is necessary to pull down a stag, and the general bearing is one of gentle dignity.

The typical Deerhound temperament is docile and good-tempered, never suspicious, aggressive or nervous. The head is long, with a slightly aquiline nose, the eyes are dark, the ears are small, folded and like a mouse's coat to the touch. The nape of neck is very prominent and is a rather distinctive trait of the breed. The loin is well arched and drooping to the tail, creating a more dramatically curved outline than that of the Greyhound. The coat is harsh or crisp, thick, close-lying and ragged.

Movement should be easy, active and true, with a long stride. The Deerhound is a self-coloured dog in blue, grey or brindle – the less white the better. Yellow or red fawns are fully acceptable according to the Standard, but are hardly ever seen. The minimum desirable height at the withers is 29 ins (76

The Deerhound: A dog with the speed, power and endurance to pull down a stag. Photo courtesy: Espen Engh.

cms) for males and 27 ins (71 cms) for bitches. As late as the 1950s, Greyhounds were bred to Deerhounds in both Scotland and Sweden, and a number of current Deerhounds can still be traced back to the former cross.

THE MAGYAR AGAR

The Magyar Agar, or Hungarian Greyhound, is another very close relative of the Greyhound both in pedigree and in

The Magyar Agar: A tough, hunting dog, also known as the Hungarian Greyhound. Photo: Gabor Szalanczi.

appearance. The Magyar Agar is, according to the Breed Standard, an old hunting breed which, from the 19th century on, was interbred with imported English Greyhounds and was changed accordingly. The breed is described as an indefatigable, tough, hunting dog, a picture of speed, power and endurance, who not only can catch hares, but also attacks bigger game. In character, the breed is somewhat reserved, but good-natured, intelligent, devoted and even watchful. The Magyar Agar should be somewhat longer than square with well-developed muscles and plenty of bone. The breed is not quite as big, but sturdier and with less obvious quality than a Greyhound, with an ideal height for males of 25-27 ins (65-70 cm), bitches being somewhat smaller. The head should be wedge-shaped when seen both from above and from the side, the ears are of medium size, not as soft as in the Greyhound, fairly high set and folded back in a V or rose shape. The neck is powerful and of medium length. The underline is only slightly cut up, the back rather straight and the loin only slightly arched, creating a less shapely outline than that of the Greyhound. The coat is close, but fairly rough, especially in the winter. All colours are permissible.

THE SPANISH GALGO
The Spanish Galgo is similar to a Greyhound in several ways, but has a number of traits separating the breed from its British cousin.

Like the Greyhound, the Galgo is used mainly for coursing the hare. The breed has also been used for hunting other game animals like rabbits, foxes and also boars. Whereas the Galgo may have played a part in the development of the Greyhound, the Greyhound is definitely an ingredient in the Galgo. Hallmarks of the breed include a long and narrow head, with the width of the skull not to exceed half of its length, rather fleshy rose-shaped ears, a long body with accentuated curves, with a concavity of the back and a convexity of the loin without abrupt breaks. The height of the loin in its central part may exceed the height at the withers.

The Galgo should have a marked prosternum, and be well cut up in the flanks, giving a look of robustness, agility and resistance, with straight and muscular hindquarters, harefeet, and a particularly long tail with a hook at the end. The muscles should be distinctly long and flat and never bulge. The Galgo should have a low, elastic and powerful trot. The breed comes in two coat varieties; one is fine and short and the other semi-long and hard. All colours are admitted, but are listed in order of preference as solid fawn, brindle, black, chestnut, cinnamon, yellow, red, white and bi-coloured and pied. The heights at the withers are 24-27 ins (62-70 cms) in males, 23-26 ins (60 to 68 cms) in bitches.

THE WHIPPET
The Whippet was established as an efficient rabbit-hunter and as the poor man's racehorse at the end of the last century. There are two different theories as to the origin of the breed. The most frequently cited theory is that the Whippet stems from crosses between small Greyhounds and several different

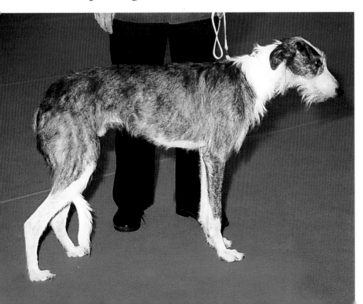

The Spanish Galgo (rough-haired): Robust and agile, this dog hunted boar as well as coursing hares.   Photo: RBT International.

The Whippet: Known as the 'poor man's racehorse'.   *Photo Courtesy: Espen Engh.*

terrier-type breeds, as shown by the fact that there existed a wire-coated variety of the breed right up until the Second World War. Alternatively, the Whippet has been selectively bred down from medium-sized, short-coated sighthounds that have existed for centuries. Most probably there is some merit in both theories, but, anyway, the Greyhound must have played a significant part in the genetic make-up of the Whippet.

The first Breed Standard made a reference to the Whippet being a small Greyhound and several leading authorities on the breed, including the influential breeder and author W. Lewis Renwick, even suggested that the breed should be called Miniature Greyhound. Over the last century the Whippet has, however, developed into a very distinct breed, still similar to, but certainly not identical to, a small Greyhound. The essence of the Whippet is a balanced combination of muscular power and strength with elegance and grace of outline, with more accentuated curves than a Greyhound, but still not exaggerated. The breed has a gentle, affectionate and even disposition with a bright and alert expression. The skull should be rather wide between the ears, differing quite markedly from the Greyhound in this respect. The Whippet's ears should be small

The Irish Wolfhound: The largest of the sighthounds.

Photo: Sheila Atter.

and rose-shaped and of fine texture. The free and supple, low over the ground, daisy-cutting movement is paramount for the breed. The Whippet coat should be fine, short and close. All colours or mixtures of colours are allowed. The size, according to the British Standard, should be 18-20 ins (47-51 cms) for males and 17-18.5 ins (44-47cms) for bitches.

Following a fraudulent attempt by its supporters to establish a long-haired variety in Whippets, the American Standard recently introduced a disqualification for long-coated individuals and such dogs may not now compete at American Kennel Club shows. Enthusiasts of this variety, resembling a cross between a Shetland Sheepdog, a Borzoi and a Whippet, are now trying to established the so-called long-haired Whippets as a separate breed, but under the name of Silken Windhounds.

THE IRISH WOLFHOUND
The Irish Wolfhound is the largest of the sighthounds, indeed the tallest of all breeds. The breed's strong and powerful appearance, but with suppleness and staying power, is in accordance with its function as a wolf-killer. The breed should not be quite as heavy or massive as the Great Dane, but more so than the Deerhound, which in general type he should otherwise resemble. Characteristics of the Wolfhound include great size and a commanding appearance, very muscular, strongly though gracefully built, movement easy and active, head and neck carried high. The head should be long and the skull not too broad, with the ears small and Greyhound-like in carriage. A scissor bite is the ideal, but a level bite is acceptable. The neck should be rather long, the chest deep and the breast wide, the back rather long than short, the loins arched. Both forequarters and hindquarters are muscular. Movement should be easy and active. The coat is rough and hard on the body, legs and head, and especially wiry and long over the eyes and under the jaw. Recognised colours are grey, brindle, red, black, pure white (genetically wheaten), fawn or any colour that appears in the Deerhound. The aim is to firmly establish a breed that shall average 32-34 ins (81-86 cms) in males, showing the requisite power, activity, courage and symmetry.

THE ITALIAN GREYHOUND
According to the FCI Standard, the Italian Greyhound is descended from ancient Egyptian Greyhounds. It further states that

The Italian Greyhound: A Greyhound in miniature.
Photo courtesy: Annette Oliver, Dairylane.

the breed resembles a Greyhound in miniature, but even more so a Sloughi, as the Italian Greyhound should fit into a square. The American Breed Standard refers to the Italian Greyhound as being very similar to the Greyhound, but much smaller and more slender in all proportions. Italian Greyhounds have sometimes been used both for coursing and racing in some countries on the European Continent and in the US. But frequently, and in other countries, the Italian Greyhound has been merely a decorative lap dog and companion. Naturally this has influenced the development of the breed and, as a consequence, general soundness has sometimes suffered.

The Italian Greyhound should be a model of grace and distinction. The temperament should be reserved, affectionate and docile, the head should be elongated and fine, and the skull flat, the length of skull being half the length of the head in total. The neck is abruptly set and the shoulders slightly oblique, with the angle between the shoulder blade and the humerus very open. Consequently, both general proportions and front construction and movement are very different in an Italian Greyhound as compared to its larger cousin, the Greyhound. Colour varies significantly between the Standards of different countries, but the country of origin insists that the Italian Greyhound should be self-coloured in black, grey, slate or isabella (fawn) in all possible shades and nuances, whereas white is only tolerated on the chest and feet. In the UK, Australia, USA and all other non-FCI countries, particolours are fully acceptable. The size according to FCI should be 12.5-15 ins (32-38 cms), whereas the British Standard only stipulates the weight.

THE CHART POLSKI
The Chart Polski, the Polish Hound, is a short-haired sighthound of great size; powerful, muscular, definitely stronger and less fine in shape than the Greyhound. The breed's sturdy frame and body, the distinct musculature and the powerful jaws show that this dog has been used in the difficult conditions of the Polish climate for hunting not only the hare, fox and deer, but also the wolf. The expressive eyes, with a lively and penetrating look, is considered important in the Chart Polski. The movement should be flowing and energetic with good extension. The Chart Polski should be confident, but reserved.

The head is very different from a Greyhound's, more like that of a Borzoi, with the strong muzzle tapering gently towards the nose to give the impression of being

The Chart Polski: The Polish Hound, a powerful dog with a sturdy frame.
Photo courtesy: Espen Engh.

pointed. Scissor bite is the norm, but pincer bite is acceptable. The ears are normally folded backwards, but can be fully erect when excited. The ideal specimen is slightly longer than high. The ribcage should be very spacious and well let down, the loin slightly arched, but in females an almost straight topline is not a fault. The tail should be in the shape of a hook curved upwards or forming a complete ring. The action of the hindlegs is unique to this breed, described as knitting (crossing legs) while on a slow trot, which is not a fault. The coat is rather harsh, not silky, and of variable length, being short on the sides, the sternum and the legs, and longer, but also harsh, on the back of thighs and underneath the tail. All colours are permissible. The size is 27.5-31.5 ins (70-80 cms) for males and 26.5-29.5 ins (68-75 cms) for bitches, but bigger specimens are permitted. The breed is strong in its home country and in Finland.

THE HORTAIA
The Hortaia is a rare sighthound breed from the Ukraine and Russia. It is very closely related to, and hardly distinguishable from, the Chart Polski, but is generally somewhat finer-built. The breed is shown at national level in some former Soviet Republics, but, even in its home country of Ukraine, the breed is only represented by a few individuals at shows.

THE BORZOI
The Borzoi, or Russian Wolfhound, allegedly descends from the old Russian Greyhound among other extinct types of sighthounds. The general appearance of the Borzoi is characterised by its height, its rich coat, the balanced proportions, and the elegance and harmony of the outline and movement, giving a distinct nobility to the overall appearance. The breed expresses noble tranquillity and reticence as well as self-

The Borzoi: The Russian hunting dog.

Photo courtesy: Espen Engh.

assuredness and calm dignity. As a coursing hound, the Borzoi is fast and enduring. In spite of the elegance of his appearance, he is basically a strong dog who enjoys a fight and is still used in Russia as a hunting dog. As a hunter, the Borzoi should be outstanding, based on his sharp sight, great speed (especially for short distances) and courage in attacking wild game.

General appearance, as well as temperament, are of primary importance when judging the Borzoi. The Standard emphasises that the general appearance should never be considered less important than singular points, no matter how important those may appear. The body length of a Borzoi should slightly exceed the height at the withers. The head is quite characteristic; long, narrow, dry and finely chiselled, gradually converging to the tip of the nose, with the muzzle somewhat longer than the skull and a highly distinct profile caused by the missing stop and a slight Roman nose. The ears are rose-shaped in repose, but can be erect or semi-erect when the dog is alert. The topline has more of a curve than other sighthounds, more pronounced in males than in bitches. The

bones should appear to be bladed and the feet should be narrow and oval. Movement should be springy and far-reaching at a trot. The coat is long, silky, wavy or curled, especially profuse on the neck, lower chest and the rear of forelegs and hindlegs. The Borzoi comes in many colours, including white, gold in all shades, red, grey, brindle, black and tan and these colours in combinations. The height at the withers is 27.5-32 ins (70-82 cms) for males and above, in bitches approximately 2 ins (5 cms) less.

THE AZAWAKH
The very distinctive Azawakh stems from south of the Sahara desert, more specifically from the present-day countries of Mali and Burkina Faso; the breed was named after the valley of Azawakh. The first Azawakhs were imported to France and Yugoslavia in the 1970s and were initially confused with the Sloughi. For hundreds of years the companion and hunting dog of the nomads, the Azawakh is a particularly leggy, dry and elegant dog and should give a general impression of great fineness. The Azawakh should be distinctively taller than long, with

The Azawakh: Companion and hunting dog of the nomads.   Photo courtesy: Espen Engh.

the height at the withers exceeding the length of body with a ratio of ten to nine.

The bone structure and musculature should be transparent beneath the fine skin and the very fine coat which befits a dog living in a very hot climate. The breed is attentive, distant and reserved with strangers, but gentle and affectionate with his owners. The Azawakh should be very moderately angulated both ends, have a nearly horizontal topline or rising towards the hips, distinctly protruding hipbones, an accentuated sternal arch and tuck-up, rounded feet and a flat skull, the width of which should be definitely less than half of the length of the head with a marked occipital protuberance. The ears should be fine, drooping and flat in the shape of a triangle with a slightly rounded tip.

Movement is an essential point of the breed and should be very supple, the whole dog being very 'up', with a particular lift at the trot and an extreme carriage. Height at the withers should be 25-29 ins (64-74 cms) for males and 23.5-27.5 ins (60-70 cms) for bitches. According to the FCI Standard the Azawakh should be fawn (all shades from light sable to dark fawn) with white stockings on all four limbs. The black brindle colour was initially not admitted, but has been fully accepted since 1994. Due to selective imports, the Azawakh is now much more homogeneous in Europe than in its home territories where it comes in several colours.

The quality of the breed is high in several countries, including Germany, France and Switzerland where the Azawakh is very competitive at Group level.

THE SLOUGHI

The Sloughi originated in the Orient, but was adapted for many centuries to the climate and desert terrain of Northern Africa and developed into the national dog of Morocco. The general appearance is that of a very racy dog with muscular leanness, but definitely more substantial and less extreme than the Azawakh. The length of body is slightly less than the height at withers, but again not as accentuated as in the Azawakh. The head is long and refined, but at the same time rather strong with a rather wide skull and barely pronounced stop. The ears are high-set and dropping close to the head, triangular and slightly rounded at the tips. The back should be almost horizontal, but the loins are slightly arched. The feet should have the shape of an elongated oval. The skin

The Sloughi: A breed that originated in the Orient.   Photo Courtesy: Espen Engh.

is very fine, close-fitting to the body, the coat is very short, tight and fine. Accepted colours are sand-coloured, fawn, sable (sand with black overlay) and brindle with or without a black mask or with or without a black mantle. Although black and tans are not specifically mentioned in the Standard, they are also fully accepted, white markings and white stockings being considered

The Saluki: Known as the 'gazelle hound', this is a dog of grace and symmetry.
Photo courtesy: Espen Engh.

disqualifying faults in the breed. The ideal size is 27.5 ins (70 cms) (with a span from 26-28 ins (66 to 72 cms)) in males and 25.5 ins (65 cms) (24-26.5 ins (61-68 cms)) in bitches. Outside the breed's country of origin, the Sloughi is of very high quality in several countries on the European Continent, notably Germany, Holland and France.

THE SALUKI

The Saluki or Gazelle Hound originates from a wide geographical area, including Persia, Saudi Arabia, Syria and North Africa. The breed may be as old as or even older than the Greyhound. The widespread origin is responsible for the large variety within the breed. The whole appearance of the Saluki should give the impression of grace and symmetry, and of great speed and endurance, coupled with strength and activity to enable the dog to kill gazelle or other quarry over deep sand or rocky mountain.

The head is long and narrow, with a moderately wide skull, the whole showing great quality. The ears are long and rather high-set. The expression should be dignified and gentle with deep, faithful, far-seeing eyes. The Saluki is reserved with strangers, but not nervous or aggressive. The breed is dignified and independent. The Saluki should be a moderately angulated dog both ends, and exaggerations are to be avoided. The feet are a distinct hallmark of the breed; strong and supple with long and well-arched toes, the two central toes being definitely longer than the lateral ones, with good feathering between the toes. At the trot, the Saluki should appear effortless, fluent, very supple and lithe, well-balanced between front and rear. The breed comes in two coat varieties; the smooth and the fringed. In the latter there is more or less abundant silky feathering on the ears, the tail and at the back of front and hind legs. The classic colours in the Saluki are white, cream, fawn, golden, red, grizzle, tricolour and black and tan. The recent FCI Standard admits all colours. Dogs should average in height from 23-28 ins (58.5 to 71 cms). Bitches may be considerably smaller than the males, this being very typical of the breed.

THE MID-ASIAN TAZI
The Mid-Asian Tazi is a recognised sighthound breed in several of the former Soviet republics with roots in the Republics of Uzbekistan, Turkmenistan and Kazakhstan where they have been, and are, used for hunting fox, hares, wolves and other animals. The breed can work independently or with golden eagles, which partnership is especially valued. Most Tazis are hard to distinguish from a Saluki, but the Tazi comes in different colours not seen in Saluki, notably white and blue, and has a rather square-shaped head and a ringed tail, carried low. The height at the withers is 23.5-27.5 ins (60-70 cms) for males and 21.5-25.5 ins (55-65 cms) for females. The breed is slightly longer than high.

THE KHALAG
The Khalag is a fascinating dog, highly reminiscent of the Bell-Murray or Desert-

The Khalag: Long-legged and elegant.
Photo courtesy: Espen Engh.

type Afghan Hounds introduced to Britain in the 1920s. As the Bell-Murray dogs were mixed with the Ghazni or mountain-type Afghan Hounds to create what today is known as the Afghan Hound, dogs of the two original types remained in Afghanistan. Recent imports from Afghanistan to Poland, and later to Switzerland, re-established the Bell-Murray Afghan in Europe under the name of Khalag. These long-legged, elegant dogs with exotic expressions and square, angular bodies possess most of the breed points of an Afghan Hound. The Khalag has a provisional Standard and is shown at national level in Switzerland. In Russia another type of Afghan Hound, more similar to the original mountain type, is shown under the name of Aboriginal Afghan or Bakhmul.

THE AFGHAN HOUND
The Afghan Hound stems, as the name implies, from Afghanistan, but the original imports also came from neighbouring countries such as India and Pakistan where the breed was reputed to have been used to hunt everything from small game to snow leopards. Two decidedly divergent strains of Afghan Hounds were imported in the 1920s and blended into the current breed that is now so popular over the whole world. The whole appearance of an Afghan Hound should give the impression of strength and dignity, combining speed and power. The breed's distinctive gait should be smooth and springy with a style of 'high order'; the head must be held proudly and the ringed tail should be raised when in action. The Afghan Hound should be dignified and aloof with the expression of a certain keen fierceness; the dog looks at and through you. The long coat of very fine, silky texture, with a peculiar coat pattern, is an attraction of the breed and a requirement for survival in the cold mountain terrain of the breed's original

The Afghan Hound: Strong and dignified, the breed has a very characteristic gait.
Photo courtesy: Espen Engh.

habitat. In sharp contrast to the smooth-flowing, continuous curves of the Greyhound, the Afghan Hound should have an angular outline with a straight and short loin with prominent hipbones. All colours are acceptable. The ideal height according to the British and FCI Standards is 26.5-29 ins (68-74 cms) for males, 25-27 ins (63-69 cms) for bitches; the American Standard is one inch lower.

THE TAIGAN
The Taigan is not dissimilar to the mountain-type Afghan Hound and was developed in the former Soviet Republic of Kirgizstan. He is an excellent hunting dog, greatly respected by the Khirghizes. The Taigan has the courage and keenness to hunt the fox. The breed is a strongly built sighthound with very powerful bones. The Taigan is, both in construction and coat pattern, more similar to an Afghan Hound than anything else, but with a less striking overall appearance. The coat is wavy and coarse, and the tail is not very long, thin, fine and spirally-formed at the end, while the ears are low-set and hanging close to the head. The Taigan comes in several colours: black, red, grey and gold, white, plain and spotted, but not dappled. The breed is quite rare, but is shown at national level in several former Soviet Republics.

THE PHARAOH HOUND
The Pharaoh Hound (Kelb Tal Fenek) is a medium-sized dog of noble bearing with clean-cut lines, graceful, yet powerful, and fast with free, easy movement and alert expression. The breed probably descends from Egyptian dogs brought to the Mediterranean islands of Malta and Gozo by

The Taigan: This breed has strong similarities with the Afghan Hound.
Photo courtesy: Espen Engh.

The Pharaoh Hound: Hunts by scent and sight, as well as making use of its large ears.
Photo courtesy: Espen Engh.

Phoenician traders, with the modern breed originating from these two islands. An alert, keen hunter, the Pharaoh Hound hunts by scent and sight using its large ears to a marked degree when working close. The temperament is alert, intelligent, friendly, affectionate and playful.

The head is an important hallmark of the Pharaoh Hound. The top of the skull should be parallel with the slightly longer foreface, with only a slight stop; the whole head should represent a blunt wedge when viewed in profile and from above. The ears are medium/high-set, carried erect when alert, but very mobile. As for construction, the Pharaoh Hound is a typical, normal sighthound with a long and muscular neck, well-laid-back shoulders, strong, well-knuckled and firm feet, strong and muscular hindquarters with moderate bend of stifle, the length of body being slightly longer than the height at the withers. The body should be lithe with an almost straight topline and a deep brisket.

The Cirneco Dell'Etna: used for hunting wild rabbits in Sicily.   Photo: RBT International.

Movement should be free and flowing with the head held fairly high; the dog should cover ground well without any apparent effort. The coat is short and glossy with no feathering. The colour is tan with very limited white, but a white tip on the tail is strongly desired. Size is 22-25 ins (56-63 cms) in males and 20-24 ins (53-61 cms) in bitches.

THE CIRNECO DELL'ETNA

The Cirneco dell'Etna, the Sicilian Hound, is in many ways reminiscent of a miniature Pharaoh Hound, but with a more Whippet-like shape. The breed has a similar origin to the Pharaoh Hound and is used for hunting wild rabbits in Sicily. The Cirneco is a medium-sized dog of elegant and slender shape, robust and strong, but of light construction. The body fits into a square. The Cirneco is a temperamental dog, but at the same time gentle and affectionate.

The muzzle is normally less than half the length of the head, but preference should be given to equal length of muzzle to skull. The cranial region is of oval shape, the top of the skull and muzzle are slightly divergent or parallel; the skull is just slightly convex, the stop is well accentuated. The ears are set quite high and close together; erect and rigid with a triangular shape and a narrow tip, their length is not more than half the length of the head. The eyes seem rather small and should be oval and not too dark, but give a soft expression. The topline should be straight, but sloping gracefully from the withers towards the rump; the underline should be smooth and well tucked-up. The tail is carried like a sabre when in repose, lifted over the back when the dog is alert. The coat is short (up to 1 in (3 cms) on the body) and close. Accepted colours are self-coloured fawns, more or less intense or diluted or fawn with more or less extensive white (blaze, mark on chest, feet, tip of tail,

The Ibizan Hound: A deerlike elegance combined with the power of a hunter.

Photo courtesy: Espen Engh.

belly), but a white collar is less appreciated. Self-coloured white, and white with orange patches is tolerated, but not very common. Ideal size in males is from 18-19 ins (46-50 cms) bitches from 16.5-18 ins (42-46 cms).

THE IBIZAN HOUND

The Ibizan Hound, or Podenco Ibicenco, originates from the Mediterranean islands of Mallorca, Ibiza, Minorca and Formentera. A hunting dog whose quarry is primarily rabbits, this ancient hound was bred for centuries with function being of prime importance. Lithe and racy, the Ibizan Hound possesses a deerlike elegance combined with the power of a hunter. The breed combines the senses of sight, scent and hearing and is a very efficient hunter in very difficult terrain, often working in packs. In the field, the Ibizan is fast and without equal in agility and jumping – the breed is able to spring to great heights from a standstill.

Strong, without appearing heavily muscled, the Ibizan Hound is a hound of moderation and, with the exception of the ears, he should not appear extreme or exaggerated. The breed is reserved with strangers, but not nervous or aggressive. The head is fine and long, the stop not well defined, the length of muzzle from eyes to tip of nose equals the length from eyes to the prominent occiput, with a slightly convex muzzle. The ears are large, stiff and highly mobile, erect when the dog is alert; drop ears are unacceptable.

The breed has several anatomical peculiarities; rather square in proportions and hard in outline, the front is rather steep and definitely narrow as compared to related breeds. The breastbone should be very prominent and create an acute angle, the chest should not reach to the elbow, the front feet may turn slightly outwards. The Ibizan Hound moves with an efficient, light and graceful, distinctly suspended trot, with a slight hover before placing the foot to ground. The coat is either smooth, wire or long, but always hard. Accepted colours according to the FCI Standard are white with red (chestnut), also solid white or chestnut. Lion colour is acceptable in long and wire-haired individuals of high quality, but not in short-hairs. Lion colour is fully accepted in both the English and American Standards. Size in males is 26-28 ins (66-72 cms), in bitches 23.5-26 ins (60-67 cms).

The Podengo Portuguese: This breed comes in three sizes – this is the medium size.

Photo: RBT International.

THE PODENCO CANARIO

The Podenco Canario is used for rabbit-hunting in the Canary Islands, but is very rarely seen outside its home territories.

Morphologically, the Podenco Canario would be classified as a sighthound, but the breed hunts by use of both nose, sight and hearing, being able to hunt from dawn to nightfall. In the highly specialised terrain in the Gran Canary Island and Tenerife, the Podenco Canario uses his nose and hearing to detect the presence of rabbits at the bottom of natural crevices of the terrain, in the heaps of stones at the edges of ploughed fields, in the volcanic tubes and in the thorny bushes.

The breed is of medium size, built on longish lines, slender and light. It is described as courageous, agitated and with an enthusiastic dynamism. The head has the shape of an elongated, truncated cone with parallel planes, amber-coloured eyes, and quite big and broad-set ears which are pricked when excited. The colour is preferably red and white and the size 21.5-25 ins (55-64

cms) in males, 20.5-23.5 ins (53-60 cms) in bitches. The smaller, but somewhat similar breed, Podenco Andaluz, is not recognised by the FCI, but is shown at national level in mainland Spain.

THE PODENGO PORTUGUESE

The Podengo Portuguese is a borderline sighthound, hunting by scent as well as sight. The breed stems from the northern parts of Portugal and comes in three varieties of sizes, the large, medium-sized and small. By far the most common is the small variety which bears little resemblance to a sighthound; the large and medium-sized varieties are much more sighthound-like. The Podengo Portuguese comes in both smooth-haired and wire-haired varieties. They are rather rare and not very homogeneous even in their home country.

There are other, and very rare, members of the sighthound family, notably in India. These are, however, not present in Europe.

PART II

THE RACING GREYHOUND

3 *UNDERSTANDING THE RACING GREYHOUND*

By and large, racing Greyhounds are the antithesis of what those who are unfamiliar with them normally expect. Perhaps it is their racing image of speed, aggression and, probably most of all, the wearing of a wire racing muzzle that makes the general public perceive these gentle creatures as being savage killers. This is an almost laughable concept to people who devote their lives to the care of the racing Greyhound.

The uninitiated, once they become acquainted with the racing Greyhound, discover him to be a gentle, honest, caring, sensitive and affectionate hound. Greyhounds are kind-hearted and have a marvellous affinity with humans, including children. They are well-meaning and non-demanding dogs, happy to idle their days away sleeping.

In my experience, Greyhounds are probably among the most loyal of all breeds. Sometimes, however, I doubt their intelligence. That is the only conclusion I can come to about an animal who suffers the physical hardship of chasing an artificial lure week in and week out with, in most cases, no reward whatsoever.

Perhaps in that respect I am underestimating the role which an overwhelming instinct to chase plays in all this. Do not forget, we are talking about a breed that will continue to pursue an artificial

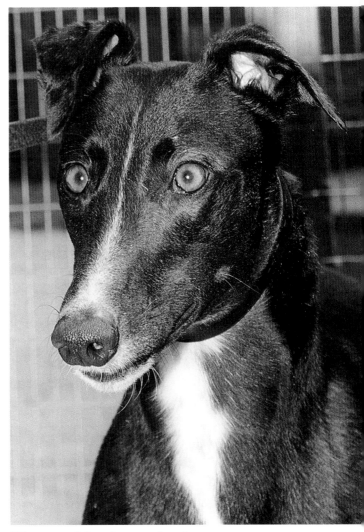

The successful trainer needs to have an understanding of what is going on in the Greyhound's mind.   Photo: Steve Nash.

lure even after breaking a limb.

Greyhounds are very proud creatures. They carry their heads high and have an admirable dignity. They are also impeccably clean. If turned out often enough, the Greyhound will keep his kennel spotless. Only when he is abandoned for a protracted period will the Greyhound soil his kennel and, in a lot of cases, his embarrassment at doing so will be almost palpable.

The Greyhounds who make the best racers are the jealous ones. They are so consumed with the determination to make the quarry their own that they will draw on all their resources and take chances others will not.

It is usually easy to identify those that have a jealous streak early in their lives. They are always first to the rag doll when at play with their littermates in the puppy paddock. That rag doll is their prized possession and woe betide anyone foolish enough to attempt to take it from them. At best, they will be sent off with a flea in their ear and, at worst, they will depart with a nip taken out of their ear.

INSTINCT

We are all born with instinct and the Greyhound, in common with any other breed of animal, displays instinct for the very first time practically seconds after he is born when he seeks out his mother's teat to suckle.

It is not long before the Greyhound puppy usually exhibits the first signs of what will, hopefully, become a finely-honed instinct to chase when at play with his friends in the paddock. Throw a ball and he will chase it. Drag a rabbit skin and he will stalk it, occasionally attacking, and displaying all his predatory perseverance.

The first time the Greyhound puppy is let

The puppy has yet to be influenced by environment or training, but he has already inherited the breed's instinct to chase that has been developed over many centuries.   *Photo: Steve Nash.*

Instincts awaken as young Greyhounds start to explore.   *Photo: Steve Nash.*

loose in the field he will investigate a hedgerow. His instinct tells him that the hedgerow is the most likely harbourer of something exciting to chase. It has also been known for Greyhounds of all ages, when at liberty, to trace the passage of rabbit warrens in order to find a point of access. That, again, is down to instinct.

It is instinct that takes control when a puppy chases the lure during his first schooling trial, or attempts to pursue a motor vehicle or the paper-boy on a bicycle. That same subliminal awareness applies when the Greyhound will short-cut the bend in a bid to head off the outside track lure as it is driven round a turn.

It is hardly surprising, given his history, that the Greyhound has this instinct to hunt, chase and run free. After all, the Greyhound has been an ever-present part of the fabric of man's sporting pursuits since the dawn of time. The instinct to hunt and chase is indelibly ingrained into the breed.

The Greyhound, the fastest of the sighthounds, has incredible powers of vision, far greater than man, and he likes to work in a pack. That ability to run in a pack is something that has served him extremely well when racing against five other dogs in Britain and Ireland, or against seven rivals, as is the case in America and Australia.

I say that the Greyhound hunts mostly by sight, but he should not be dismissed as a predator by scent. How else do you explain why a Greyhound will put his nose to the ground when he loses sight of his prey? He is sniffing out another hare, maybe. Greyhounds also have a marvellous retrieval instinct and do not have to be taught to return quarry to their masters. It is something that comes naturally – or is that instinct?

GETTING THE BEST FROM YOUR DOG

A generic understanding of the Greyhound is one thing but, to get the best from your racer, it is important for the handler to develop a close relationship.

So, to coax a full commitment from his or her charge, it is important for a trainer to identify the uniqueness of the individual at the end of his or her leash, because pandering to those little quirks, fancies and peculiarities plays a pivotal role in the evolution of the racing Greyhound. It is important that the dog is happy. A happy, contented dog will always perform to his optimum level whenever physically possible, whereas an unsettled, unhappy one will not.

The successful development of the Greyhound as a racing machine relies greatly on the trainer's ability to get inside the dog's head. It is a mission that will require lots of time and plenty of patience but it will ultimately prove a most rewarding and fruitful experience.

MAKING THE GREYHOUND FEEL AT HOME

The first contact between the trainer and his new charge is of vital importance as it will have a huge bearing on how the dog/trainer

The Greyhound is one of the most laid-back of all breeds.

Photo: Steve Nash.

relationship evolves. Some petting, and a friendly tone in the voice, can do wonders for breaking down barriers.

Generally speaking, and perhaps because of the transient nature of their lives, Greyhounds are the most laid-back individuals – most vets will identify Greyhounds as the easiest of patients. Some Greyhounds develop an independent streak and, quite frankly, could not care less about who is handling them or where they are living.

But there are others who, just like some human beings, are vulnerable and nervous and do not find it easy to adapt to change. Remember, it could be the first time they have been away from their home, the place where they were born and reared, and away from the only people they have known in their short lives.

Norah McEllistrim is contracted to supply racers at Wimbledon, which hosts the UK's premier event, the Greyhound Derby. She believes that it is important to have a close relationship with all her charges. Although she runs a big, some might say impersonal, establishment where 70 or 80 Greyhounds may be housed at any one time, she reckons she has a good rapport with her inmates.

Norah, a daughter of the late, great Irish trainer Paddy McEllistrim, said: "Greyhounds are independent to a certain degree but I believe if a dog is treated well emotionally, it can make the difference between a dog being a good grader or an open racer.

"Nervousness is one of the biggest problems and I am certain it affects a dog's ability to produce his best on a track. If you can encourage them to be more confident and independent, it can make a great

A sense of self-confidence is essential in the racing Greyhound.

Photo: Steve Nash.

difference to the way they perform on the track.

"Praise them, stroke them and generally make them feel at ease with you and you will be surprised how much of the nervousness will disappear."

Norah also warns owners not to be fooled by first impressions. She added: "You will see the occasional dog coming in who will be as quiet as a church mouse, perfectly behaved and very docile. Within days, that same animal will be the life and soul of the kennel.

"It is pretty much the same as the kid who is on his perfect behaviour the first time he visits your house. But by his third or fourth visit, he is running riot."

Norah is convinced that the temperament and character of a dog is not something that is predetermined by his genes but is more a product of his upbringing. "From my experience, there are some breeders whose dogs you will have no problems with at all. They are easy to handle, full of confidence and generally a pleasure to have about the place.

"But there are other breeders whose trademark is timid dogs, who are hard to handle and who find it very difficult to accept change. In fact, some of these dogs are simply too frightened to chase the lure and are an absolute nightmare to handle."

MAINTAINING INTEREST

One of the biggest enemies any track trainer has to face is staleness in his or her charges. It is a problem that is becoming increasingly prevalent as racing schedules get busier and busier – dogs race more often, usually at the same track; they are subjected to more trouble in running and, as a consequence, they become apathetic, lose confidence or, in some cases, refuse to chase. Firstly, how does a trainer identify a problem and, secondly, how do we address it?

We spoke earlier about the importance of a trainer getting to know his or her charges. If that has been successfully achieved, the handler will more quickly notice staleness manifesting itself in the Greyhound.

Often there will be little difference at home. The boisterous dogs will still bounce off the walls and the calmer, more reserved type will still observe the world from the comfort of his bed with an air of aloofness.

But on the track you might notice runners staying wide of the pack, not displaying the same sort of conviction at the turns (i.e. holding back), showing more interest in their racing companions than in the lure and generally not running as you would expect them to.

Most trainers believe that the most effective way of preventing or correcting staleness is by making sure that their charges' minds are kept active at all times. Variety may be the spice of life, but it has also been the saviour of many a dog who has began to lose interest in chasing.

If, as is the case in the United States and Britain, a Greyhound will spend the majority of his life racing at one, or a maximum of two tracks, a training regime that includes a regular change of scenery is of paramount importance.

WALKS

For most trainers in the four main racing nations, America, Australia, Britain and Ireland, walking plays a sizeable role in conditioning methods. Why not have a rota of walks? A new one for every day of the week, taking in different environments – countryside, urban and suburban. Introducing a dog to hitherto unexplored land with new sights, sounds and scents will send the naturally inquisitive nature of the Greyhound into overdrive.

Obviously, you are not going to have such a variety on your doorstep, but there is nothing to prevent you bundling a group of dogs into a van or station wagon and driving off to find suitable walks. Take them to places

Rotating walks is a good way of changing routine and maintaining interest.   *Photo: Steve Nash.*

where they are certain to see lots of wildlife – woodland is great because of its potential for the unexpected, especially strange noises.

Whenever possible, throw sticks and rocks into hedgerows when walking, to attract the attention of the dogs. They will automatically look for the source of the noise, suspecting it to be a rabbit, a hare, or something equally exciting. Encourage them to investigate the hedge.

Also, change their walking companions whenever possible – although, when introducing newcomers to a pack, there is always the potential for trouble, so be on your toes.

CHANGING TRACKS

You will be amazed at the results that can be achieved by just giving a dog a run at a track other than the one he usually races at. The change seems to breathe new life into the dog and very often trainers will give a dog a run away from home before he next races at his regular venue.

There are numerous schooling tracks where you can give a dog a spin, or even give him a run behind a whirly gig with a fresh skin. The track does not have to have a different lure, although it is always preferable if it does. At the pickup, always encourage the dog to play with a dummy hare, which should contain a squeaker for authenticity

A change of track will often give new zest to a Greyhound.   *Photo: Steve Nash.*

Hurdling is a popular option in the UK. Photo: Steve Nash.

and, most important of all, praise him. Let him know that by completing the trial he has pleased you.

In the case of a dog who has lost his confidence, it is always prudent to give him a couple of trials without other runners. This will enable the dog to get round the turns without bumping; that can go a long way to rebuilding confidence.

HURDLING

In Britain and, to a lesser extent, Ireland, hurdle racing, or even just a few trials over the sticks, is seen as a way of tackling a Greyhound's waning interest in racing after an artificial lure.

The hurdles keep the Greyhounds interested and the punctuated sight of the hare, which will appear and disappear with every flight, is recognised as a good way of rekindling the Greyhound's interest in the hare.

HOLIDAYS

Just as we humans like a break away from the routine of going to work five days a week, Greyhounds sometimes benefit from a holiday. If all else fails and your dog is still having problems keeping his mind on the business of racing, why not send him to a retreat. After all, if a change is as good as a rest, this is a combination of both.

There are kennels that specialise in resting dogs, whether they be bitches in season, lame dogs or those that just require a change of scenery to recharge the batteries. Very often, the dog will return with renewed enthusiasm and a totally different attitude. A month-long stay is usually enough to effect a change.

However, it is always sensible to vet carefully any new kennels you are considering using. Seek recommendations from trusted friends, visit the establishment before you make up your mind, and pay special attention to the hygiene standard and the condition – mental and physical – of the inmates.

There is nothing worse than a Greyhound returning from a rest kennel with parasites, poor skin condition, dehydration, or anything else he may have picked up while there.

COURSING

Some trainers believe the perfect remedy for a track performer who has become jaded is a run behind a live hare up a coursing field.

Coursing is becoming an increasingly rare option.   *Photo: Steve Nash.*

For trainers in Australia this is impossible, as coursing is no longer legal in any state in the country.

In America, coursing is permitted in some states but is hardly a vote winner. In the states in which it does exist, it is hardly recognisable to those used to the sport in Britain and Ireland. American Field Coursing Meetings are open to all sighthounds. Up to three dogs take part in any one course. They are scored by a judge, who, unlike his horse-riding British and Irish counterparts, carries out his role on foot.

In Britain, it used to be possible for you to pay for a trial for your dog behind a live hare after a coursing fixture had been completed. Such opportunities these days are few and far between and depend on a number of factors.

One of these is that you are a member of the respective club you approach. Secondly, when the meeting is over, if the beat is still out and hares are still around, the Club may announce over the public address system that trials are available. It is, however, entirely unpredictable and trainers should never travel to a meeting on the off-chance of getting a trial.

The situation is very different in Ireland, where coursing is undergoing something of a renaissance since the introduction of muzzling. Trials – pre-season, and pre- and post-meetings – are available and there is nothing like a long run behind a good strong hare to add that spark of enthusiasm to the battle-weary, disillusioned tracker.

THE RIGHT ENVIRONMENT

It is obvious that a Greyhound can only be expected to reach and maintain his best form if he is completely happy and at one with his conditions at home. So, creating an environment that keeps the racing Greyhound contented has a crucial bearing on his performance on the track.

We know from everyday life that happiness

Droopys Pacino – trained within the shadows of Tottenham Hotspur Football Club in London.

Photo: Steve Nash.

in our own surroundings is something that has a huge effect on how we behave. You only have to reflect on how you perform at work when things at home are not as they should be to realise that. Can you honestly say your work is not influenced if things at home are not what they should be? So it is with Greyhounds.

In the main racing countries, Greyhounds are kept in what can only be described as a controlled environment. The importance of strict discipline and routine when handling racing animals cannot be overestimated. But, while discipline and routine are extremely important, it is also vital that we allow the dog time and space to relax and enjoy his life in the racing kennels.

The Greyhound probably leads a more controlled existence in America than

anywhere else. Routine there is strictly adhered to. There is probably a little more flexibility in the other countries, although there is not a trainer in the world who would undervalue the importance of routine.

Consistency is very important. Greyhounds like to know what they are doing and when, and they perform much better when their daily life has some order about it.

Deciding on where to have your kennel is something which needs serious consideration. The majority of people, given the choice, will opt for a spot in the countryside and it is no coincidence that most kennels are away from urbanisation.

The countryside – or lesser populated areas – offers the chance for the Greyhound to develop his senses and the right sort of stimulation for the development of the Greyhound's instinct to hunt and chase.

However, not everyone agrees and English Derby-winning trainer Gary Baggs feels that it is perfectly feasible to attempt to train Greyhounds from a kennel in the most built-up of areas. There are some good examples to back him up, including the 1998 English St Leger winner Droopys Pacino, who is trained in the shadows of the floodlights of Tottenham Hotspur Football Club at busy White Hart Lane in north east London.

Tony Bullen, who trains Droopys Pacino, said: "To be honest, training in London is not something I have given a great deal of thought to. We tend to go against the rush hour in as much as we walk when things have quietened down. I don't think a Greyhound trained in the town is at a disadvantage. If he is fast enough, he will win races wherever he is trained."

Baggs, who is contracted to supply racers to the leading London venue Walthamstow, said: "Living in town shouldn't put people off training Greyhounds as long as they have access to a vehicle which, in 20 or 30 minutes, can take them out to a rural location to exercise. Walks, gallops, good food, a clean bed and kennel comfort are what is important in any Greyhound's environment and you can get those things in the town as well as the countryside."

However, Matt O'Donnell, one of Ireland's leading trainers and the winner of three Irish Derbys and one English, disagrees. He said: "A kennel in the countryside is by far the most preferable of locations. It is important that dogs are surrounded by their natural environment and that is the countryside."

THE PERFECT KENNEL

What is important is that the Greyhound has somewhere to live that is free from parasites, is easy to keep clean, and is convenient for the trainer and staff, so that they are mobile and able to carry out their daily duties concerning the wellbeing of the dog; that it has facilities that allow for the proper training of Greyhounds; and that the premises can be made totally secure.

So what are the best conditions in which to house your dog? In America the emphasis is on speed, efficiency and the economical use of space. To that end, the crate system employed in virtually all kennels in the US is perfect.

The archetypal kennels in America will be built of brick with a plaster covering. The roof will be insulated and the kennel will also have a false ceiling in order to preclude the influence of the weather on the temperature of the kennel.

A self-adjusting air conditioning unit will keep a constant temperature of around 72 degrees F in subtropical areas such as Florida. It will be slightly cooler in locations further north, such as New Hampshire, in order to mirror outside conditions.

Greyhounds in America are housed in crates, the typical measurement of which is 4 ft by 3 ft. The crates are kept on two tiers and the general rule is that bitches, being a

bit lighter than most of their dog counterparts, occupy the upper level.

Imagine a room, no bigger that say 50 ft by 25 ft, housing 60 crates. Two of the walls might be lined width-wise by 13 crates. There would be two tiers, so each of those walls could house as many as 26 Greyhounds. Any one area would house up to 60 dogs. That is something trainers from other racing continents find hard to believe.

The crates, which are approximately two inches off the ground, are on casters which means that it is easy to pull them away from the wall and clean the area behind.

The Americans are renowned for their economic use of both space and time and the kennelling system employed underscores that attitude. With the crate system, 60 dogs can be fed and watered in 20 minutes. It is as quick and effective as that.

Each kennel would have two small turn-out pens of approximately 50 ft by 25 ft and an undercover pen. Most kennels would put 20 dogs in each pen so the whole kennel could be let out in one hit.

The system is quite safe. All dogs are muzzled and supervised by experienced handlers who single out troublemakers and keep an eye on them.

When designing my kennels in Britain, one thing I placed great emphasis on was having the facility to completely evacuate the kennels at any one time. This is important for cleaning purposes as well as for safety; in the case of a fire or a similar type of emergency, it is of paramount importance that all dogs can be liberated.

We built a 10 ft x 4 ft concrete paddock for every kennel. Each paddock had its own drain and each was separated by a 6 ft wire fence. The concrete had a pitted texture in order to prevent Greyhounds slipping when it was wet.

A prerequisite of any site that is going to be used to house a Greyhound kennel is that it is well drained. The nuisance factor of having to continually clean paws made dirty by muddy paddocks is bad enough, but, in places with warmer climates, in Florida for example, a poorly drained site can prove the precursor to problems such as hookworm.

I always favour a brick kennel. Wood kennels are notoriously difficult to keep disinfected and are an obvious fire hazard. The kennel area should not be too big because of the heating difficulties larger areas present. And, while on the subject of heating, I would advocate the installation of a hot water pipe running under the beds. I have seen some good examples of this at work.

BEDDING
For bedding, I am a firm advocate of paper, and plenty of it, in the winter. In the summer, perhaps some foam covered by a carpet. Straw is something I have used in the past but it is dusty and must be changed every few days. Paper comes well wrapped, is usually quite clean and needs to be changed once every five or six days.

The carpet bedding in the summer serves a good purpose. It is sufficient when the weather is warm and discourages fleas. It must also be remembered that an ample supply of bedding is essential because Greyhounds have the propensity to develop pressure sores.

HYGIENE
Each unit in the kennel generally houses two dogs who rest on a wooden slatted bed, which can be dismantled for cleaning purposes, and is elevated roughly a foot off the ground. The area under the bed should be blocked off, although opinions differ on that point.

Retired English champion trainer George Curtis says in his book *Training Greyhounds* that the area under the bed should be accessible. One of the purposes of this,

George says, is so that it can be used as a sanctuary by Greyhounds who are being bullied by their kennelmates. However, I believe that not bricking up that area presents huge hygiene problems.

While on the subject of hygiene, it is prudent to wash down kennels completely at least once a month but be careful not to use too much disinfectant. It can burn and also make dogs nauseous.

The bed, which should be roughly 6 ft wide by 4 ft deep, ideally will be partitioned to allow each dog his or her own space. The floor should be sealed by an impervious rubber-type coating (epoxy resin with added grit to prevent slipping). This alleviates the problem of urine soaking into the concrete. The covering should also be used up to about six inches up the wall (in place of a skirting board).

I always favour a bright kennel so I advocate plenty of windows, although the security aspect does not always allow this, as each window should be fitted with bars to prevent intruders. Also, windows should be far enough away from kennels to prevent any access by projectiles.

When painting kennels it is always important to remember to avoid the use of lead paint. Otherwise, the likelihood of Greyhounds becoming poisoned is a real possibility.

Ventilation can be provided by the windows. However, when building from scratch it might be prudent to install an air conditioning unit with a self-adjusting temperature gauge if the budget stretches that far.

I prefer kennels to have brick partitions from ground level up to about five feet, in order to stop Greyhounds in adjacent kennels seeing each other. The rest of the partition should be steel or wire mesh to maximise any light that is available.

KENNEL COMPANIONS

It is usual in Britain and the Republic of Ireland to kennel dogs in twos. Some trainers favour putting a dog with a bitch because they feel that mixing the sexes is a less likely foundation for kennel companions fighting. However, George Curtis and many of the other top trainers have kennelled dogs together with smashing results.

The choice of a kennel companion can be as vital a part of a Greyhound's environment as anything else. In most cases it is pointless putting like with like – two boisterous animals would probably knock hell out of each other vying for the attention of their handler.

Careful consideration has got to be given to mixing. Putting together a dominant and submissive is not necessarily a recipe for disaster. Mixing and matching is very much a trial and error thing, but it is important that the end result is right.

The front of the kennel ought also to be steel mesh. I also like each door to fall 6 to 8

The choice of kennel companion can have a big influence on a Greyhound's well-being.

Photo: Steve Nash.

ins off the ground. This allows for feeding bowls to be slipped underneath – something that saves plenty of time at feeding. However, too big a gap would leave open the possibility of smaller dogs or bitches escaping.

TREATMENT ROOMS

A top-class kennel ought also to have a treatment room. This would include an area for the use of physiotherapy units such as ultrasound, magnetic field therapy and laser therapy. A tiled shower unit with a high-pressure shower for hydrotherapy is another desirable facility.

The treatment table should stand approximately 3 ft high and should be 6 ft wide and 4 ft deep in order to accommodate a Greyhound lying on his side for examination and for maintenance work such as nail-cutting and bandaging.

THE AUSTRALIAN-STYLE KENNEL

Some or most of the aforementioned applies to the majority of kennels in Britain and the Republic of Ireland and, to a certain extent, Australia as well. However, Down Under, kennels have a much more open-plan look.

Kennels are generally on a much smaller scale. The Australians favour a barn-type of building with an open-plan kennelling area. The partitions are mostly made from steel mesh that assists with the circulation of air when the weather is sometimes unbearably warm in the summer. The dogs' beds also tend to be closer to the floor, once again in an attempt to find cooler conditions.

The Australians prefer all kennels to have a run adjoining the kennel. Once again, concrete or cement is the favoured base for the kennel.

The Australians also have an original view on beds and many dogs can be seen sleeping comfortably on dog trampolines and canvas hammocks. Australian dogs are usually kennelled singly and they are not muzzled. That could result in problems if the dogs become bored and start chewing themselves, so it is important that their minds are kept occupied.

4 *REARING AND SCHOOLING*

It is impossible to overestimate the importance of the correct rearing and conditioning of the Greyhound as a precursor to his success on the race track. Regardless of the talent of the trainer, it is the rearer who produces the raw material that will be handed over to be turned into the racing machine. If the job is not done correctly in the first place, no amount of effort by the trainer will turn a slow dog into a fast one.

That is why proper rearing and correct pre-track education are so vitally important. To become accomplished racers, puppies must be provided with a grounding that includes a well-balanced and all-encompassing diet that contains the nutrients for them to grow properly, as dictated by their genes. They also need exercise that will allow them to fulfil the potential they have for speed and agility, and they must live in an environment that will allow them to mature into non-nervous and well-adjusted adults.

FEEDING PUPPIES
The first, and probably most important, factor is to ensure puppies have a proper diet. Their stomachs are smaller than those of the adult dogs and, as a consequence, cannot take in enough energy and nutrition in one or two meal sittings to satisfy their daily needs. That is why puppies are fed more often than their fully-grown counterparts.

Correct rearing is of vital importance if a Greyhound is to achieve his potential on the race track.   *Photo: Steve Nash.*

Puppies are usually fed from a communal bowl.

Photo: Steve Nash.

Opinions may differ but I believe that once a puppy is fully weaned from his mother he should be fed three meals a day until he is ready for schooling on the track at about 12-14 months. At that stage it is usual to feed just twice a day in Australia, Britain and Ireland, although American trainers usually introduce a one-meal-a-day programme before the puppy reaches 12 months old.

The time of day you feed your puppies is not important, but what is important is that they are fed at that same time every day. Do not forget that dogs are creatures of habit. Because of their age, puppies are more susceptible to stomach bugs, so it is also vital that all eating bowls are cleaned properly after use.

Up to 12 months of age, puppies are usually fed from a communal bowl, both from a practical point of view and also in order to instil in them, even at that early age, a competitive edge. The pups will always try to out-eat each other and some breeders use feeding time to spot determination and aggression in their puppies. However, it is always important to make sure they all get enough food and that the weaker, less forceful ones do not miss out.

If one or two are clearly struggling to get enough, it is best to take them away and feed them on their own. By the same token, it is prudent to check that others are not getting too much. It is always preferable for puppies to be well covered, but that does not mean fat and, consequently, unhealthy and unhappy animals.

Most rearers use a complete biscuit as the base material for meals. These biscuits are manufactured with varying amounts of protein. Protein is a vital part of a pup's diet because of its value as a growth promoter. It is important that puppies have a diet containing 24-27 per cent protein, which can be provided exclusively by biscuits, or by a mix with meat.

Given that the puppy will spend the majority of his first year playing and chasing with his littermates, it goes without saying that energy is an important part of his dietary requirements. Carbohydrates such as breakfast cereals, bread, pasta and potatoes are all sources of energy.

The amount of energy your puppy receives, and the exercise in which he participates, must be closely related. Otherwise the puppy will put on weight, become fat and suffer the problems that obesity brings, such as the reduction in his ability to exercise, extra stress on his limbs and the start of heart problems.

Minerals are extremely important. Less than enough of the likes of calcium and phosphorus can result in poor bone development. The correct balance of calcium and phosphorus is important, and is usually taken care of when you are using complete feeds on their own. However, an imbalance in favour of phosphorus can occur when feeding a complete meal and meat. When meat makes up half of a Greyhound's meal, a calcium supplement should be added to provide balance.

Generally speaking, most complete feeds provide the correct quantities of vitamins for young dogs. Those that are important for puppies are Vitamins A, D and E, as they are the ones that are associated with growth and development. Water should also be available at all times.

The first feed of the day should be a milky feed. I used to get five gallons of milk a day from a local farmer, enough to feed my pups (we had an average of 12 or 14) and race dogs.

For breakfast, usually fed between 8 am and 9 am, I would warm a saucepanful (six to eight pints) and mix in some of the well-known types of good cereal, some honey which would melt in the warmth of the milk, glucose and the occasional egg or two.

The second meal of the day would be around midday. At this 'sitting' the puppies would be given some brown bread, gravy and tripe. In addition, we would add bone-meal to help meet the demands of developing bones.

The main meal was fed at around 5 or 6 pm – at the same time as the race dogs would be receiving the second of their two daily meals. The pups received much the same as the race dogs: a complete biscuit (we used 27 per cent Wafcol, Kasko or Purina) which had

been soaking in water for a couple of hours at least, some brown bread, cooked beef and/or chicken, occasionally we would give them fish, and vegetables. The stock from the vegetables would be added to ensure a moist but not too loose consistency. Clean drinking water would be made available to the puppies at all times.

REARING AND SCHOOLING AROUND THE WORLD

AMERICA

Mary Butler is one of the leading breeders and rearers in America. She brings up hundreds of dogs every year on her 80-acre Greymeadows Farm in that heartland of American Greyhound country, Abilene, Kansas. Mary and her husband, Jack, employ four trainers to handler their charges at various tracks in America. One of those is Mick Darcy who is presently the most prolific trainer at the St Petersburg, Florida, venue Derby Lane, the leading Greyhound venue in the United States.

Bleach bottles, a most improbable item, play an integral part in the rearing of youngsters at Mary Butler's impressive spread. She explained: "That is all I use to bring out the instinct to chase in my puppies.

"When I have finished with the bleach bottles in the kennels, and cleaned them out, I throw them out into the paddocks. There is so much wind in Kansas, and the land is so flat, that the bottles blow all over the place. The pups go mad and chase them everywhere. After that there is no need to tempt them with skins and things to get them chasing."

Mary rears upwards of 30 litters a year. An operation that size must be well organised to function at all and Mary, in common with most American trainers and rearers, uses a system that seems to run like clockwork.

From the day they are born until they leave

The period puppies spend with their mother is extended for as long as possible.

Photo: Steve Nash.

the farm to go into training with one of the four trainers Mary and Jack employ, the pups will have everything planned for them.

Mary whelps down all her bitches in a huge brood building. The building is sectioned off into whelping suites and as many as 11 bitches have been accommodated at any one time. Four or five is a more comfortable number, however, and Mary attempts to have that number on the go at any one time.

Mary said: "I try to keep the puppies with their mothers in the brood building for as long as possible. They usually stay with her until they are roughly eight weeks old. There are some mothers that will be happy to tend their offspring for longer, while others get tired and snappy after a shorter period.

"I think the longer the pups and the mother are together the better. Although a mother may have gone past the stage of

nursing her offspring, there is so much she can teach them and the socialisation of puppies is much greater."

SOCIALISATION

The socialisation stage occurs between three and ten weeks. At this stage, the puppy begins to become aware of sights, sounds and smells. He becomes co-ordinated in his movement. He suddenly realises that there is a big wide world out of the comfortable confines of the whelping area.

Puppies at Mary's farm are moved from pen to pen in tandem with their development.

At around eight weeks old they will be moved, as a litter, from the brood building to an indoor/outdoor facility from which they will have access to 10 ft wide by 150 ft long pens on a sand surface.

Two months later they are switched to

Play helps to stimulate the chasing instinct.   *Photo: Steve Nash.*

another indoor/outdoor facility They will stay there for two months and then they go on to the last building that has pens of 10 ft wide and 200 ft long, again on sand. At this stage, Mary will split litters of eight and upwards.

At six months the pups will go to the fully outdoor grass pens. Home is a dog house and the pen is 80 ft wide and 300 ft long. Three months later the pups are switched to the longest grass pens at Greymeadows Farm, which are 80 ft wide and 450 ft long.

Mary said: "The idea is that the puppies gradually build muscle mass and lung capacity. This is the method that has worked for me but I know plenty of breeders and rearers who do things differently."

At 15 months the pups leave the paddocks and Mary begins what in America is called the 'breaking in'. This term covers the process of leaving the relative liberty of the rearing pens and getting used to life as a grown-up, becoming accustomed to wearing a collar, walking to a lead and becoming familiar with crates.

SCHOOLING

At around 15 months, Mary starts her schooling programme. She said: "We start them on the Whirly Gig. That brings out the instinct in the dog to hunt and show aggression. The dummy lure we use might be a skin or something similar with a squeaker inserted to simulate the sound of a rabbit or suchlike."

Puppies are given two goes a week on the Whirly Gig until Mary has considered that they have mastered it. She said: "By mastering it, I mean that the puppy is displaying aggression and attempting to bring down the lure. That usually takes between six to eight weeks.

"Then we go to the track. I always slip my dogs in twos when they first visit the track. I like them to compete and I only ever give solos when I am concerned that the Greyhound is not chasing properly. Slipping them together injects that bit of competitiveness, which I believe is important."

Mary is a great advocate of competitiveness

all the time. Even when Greyhounds are having their first run from the boxes, she likes them to go in twos. She explained: "After their first trial, then I put the winners with the winners and the seconds also together. That gives every dog a chance to win, which is so important for their confidence."

But before they get to the traps they will have had something in the region of half a dozen handslips. Mary said: "It is important they get a thorough schooling before I even try them from the boxes. For the first two handslips I let them go 3/16ths of a mile. I watch them to see how quickly they recover afterwards – whether I am taxing their kidneys. It gives me an idea of their fitness.

"Then they have two slips from the escape area, and I bring them to the half-mile point for their final handslip. On the sixth visit to the track I generally put them in the boxes. They go straight in. We don't walk them through or anything. They go straight in the box and it is closed. I stand in front of the box and use a squeaker to grab the attention of the dog and make sure it is facing the correct way when the hare comes along.

"First time from the boxes they complete a full circuit of the track and run with one or two kennel companions. They would probably have two months of trials. They would have up to two months of going round the track on a three times in two weeks basis.

"After that intensive education, the pups will be sent off to the trainer where the whole process starts all over again. In America a dog could have as many as 40 runs round a track before his first race."

FEEDING

"As soon as my pups start eating normally (usually around three weeks) we start making them up a soupy type of cooked meat and dry food mixture, which is mixed with milk and vitamins. In addition, we always have dry Puppy Chow available. They have free access to that until they go out in the field.

"The babies – anything up to four months old – always have a cooked meat. I rotate the type between chicken, beef, tripe and liver. The quantity I give is half meat to half dry food.

"I keep them on that (dry puppy chow is still available) and feed them three times a day until they are four months old. Puppies are just like teenagers, you could feed them their supper and half an hour later they are back in the refrigerator. So the Puppy Chow is always there as something to snack on.

"Once they are four months old I find that they waste a lot of food so I put them on a once-a-day feeding programme. They also make the transition to raw meat at this stage. A typical meal at this stage might be raw meat and raw tripe, along with dried milk and multivitamins.

"A one-to-one mixture and a dry meal biscuit provide all the calcium the pups need for correct bone development. In fact, I have a reputation for rearing a very large dog. The average size of one of my bitches is usually anywhere from 66 lb to 70 lb and my males average 75 lb to 85 lb.

"I do seem to raise a large-boned animal. I put that down mostly to my feeding programme. I have my food tested to make sure my Greyhounds are getting the correct balance of nutrients. It seems to be working.

"When the dogs go into my training programme I put a bone-meal supplement into their feed. I know the calcium to phosphorus ratio in the raw meat is wrong and the dogs need that addition to put it back."

VACCINATIONS

Mary says: "I start my vaccine program when the puppies are two weeks old. I have conducted a study with K-State University on the maternal antibodies transmitted to the puppies from the mother. We found that in a particular litter – we tested three litters – those antibodies are passed on differently in each individual case.

"It means the immune system begins to kick in earlier in some than others. I have found waiting longer is not the best option and, although in some cases you may be wasting vaccine, you should start much earlier, even if it is only a safeguard.

"I do a puppy vaccine and puppy wormer every week starting from two weeks until they are 12 weeks old. I vaccinate again at 16 weeks and then again at 6 months; after that I go on to a yearly booster.

"I worm every month and rotate three different wormers. Panacur is my favourite because it gets so many different types of worm."

AUSTRALIA

New South Wales breeder and rearer Sam Cauchi came to the conclusion a long time ago that the hot Australian summers were causing his puppies great distress. So he excavated some of his 30 acres at his home at Calga and constructed a dam for them to swim in.

He said: "The main exercise field for our puppies is 10 acres in size. The dam is smack bang in the middle. We put it there some years ago so that the puppies can go to cool down when things get a bit warm."

Puppies born and reared at Cauchi's range enjoy being able to have a paddle or, if they prefer, a full-blown swim from the age of six months old. He said: "At six months the pups go into paddocks which back on to the field where the dam is. We gallop the puppies on a litter rotation basis and find that the system works really well.

SOCIALISATION

"I love to keep my puppies in groups. Four or five pups being brought up together will benefit from the rough and tumble. They learn to use themselves and balance. When they get a bit of a knock they take it like a man. They aren't chicken-hearted.

"Plenty of local wildlife make use of the field also and they keep the puppies' instinct to chase finely tuned. Rabbits, especially, come into the field at night. Come the morning the pups know where they have

Puppies benefit from being brought up in groups.   *Photo: Steve Nash.*

been and know where they hide and they go off looking for them.

"I find that is sufficient experience for them to be really keen on their quarry once they are tried on the track. All the yards I use for older dogs back on to the paddock so they can all see what is going on out there and all become excited – biting the wire and going mad.

"We leave the puppies out there until they are 12-13 months old. It depends mostly on how warm the weather, which averages at about 85 degrees Fahrenheit (28 C) in the summer, has become."

That is the end of the first phase of the rearing process that begins when the pups leave their mother at 12 weeks.

Cauchi said: "We start weaning them from their mother at about four weeks and the job is completed by the time they are three months old. Up until that age I like to keep them on a concrete paddock. It is probably the best way to prevent them catching diseases, as it is easy to keep clean and germ-free.

VACCINATIONS
"We start inoculating our dogs at five to six weeks. At that stage they get half a ml of Parvac, for parvovirus. They get a half ml each week until they are nine weeks when they get a full distemper/hepatitis three-in-one 'jab'. They then get a half ml of Parvac for the next three weeks and then another full vaccination at around 12/13 weeks."

SCHOOLING
The first home the pups at Cauchi's range will know is a 10 ft by 10 ft yard. It has a separate kennel for mum, who needs a break from caring for a hungry and demanding bunch of youngsters every now and then. At four weeks old, Cauchi starts taking the puppies away from the mother at night. He explained: "She gets a bit snappy and cranky with them."

The very first time they leave their mother on a permanent basis, the pups will spend most of their time in a grass pen, with a dog house, that measures 100 ft by 100 ft. Then at six months they make the transition to the larger paddocks that adjoin the 10-acre field.

Cauchi likes to break in his pups at 12 or 13 months old. He said: "It is a bit harder to break them into a lead and collar at that stage and some people prefer to do it younger; occasionally the puppies will be as young as six months old.

"The first thing I do when I take them off the field is to place a collar round their necks. Then I get them used to kennelling in special training kennels. They might stay in there a few days getting used to disciplining themselves, regarding when they empty and urinate. I get them used to the routine of emptying only when they are out of the kennel.

"After a short while I will start breaking them into walking with a lead. Sometimes this will include nothing more than standing around for half an hour getting them used to the lead being around their necks. It is the same with a muzzle. I place it on the dog and, although they will initially paw at it or rub their faces on the ground, they eventually get used to it.

"I start schooling my dogs at around 14 months. I am fortunate in that I have my own straight track (400 yards/350 metres) with a running rail so the Greyhounds get used to the noise of the hare – not only the puppies I am schooling, but all the puppies on the site see what we are doing when we are schooling.

"I believe that makes the job much easier because, when it is time for a puppy finally to undergo the education process himself, he has probably seen 40 or 50 puppies already doing it and he knows what to do.

"When it comes to getting pups used to the traps I put them straight in. I think it is a simple process and if you start all that business of walking them through you are only giving the dog more to think about.

"I put them straight in and sometimes start the hare in front of the boxes. I am lucky that I have a straight here with a motorised arm. It is the way I have always done it and I have built a reputation for having good beginners (starters). I give them the chance to learn themselves. They have got to get it into their minds that they get right down and the lids are going to open."

FEEDING

"We feed our puppies four times a day from four weeks. I start them on very fine mince (chopped beef) and kibble and powdered milk. We allow them to lap as much as they want. From four months we feed them twice a day until they are six to eight months when they go on to one meal a day.

"We feed them plenty of meat and biscuit (I stick to 20 per cent protein and 15 per cent fat) and calcium, but on Sunday we don't feed at all. It helps clean them out and keeps them hungry for the coming week. I like to keep my puppies very lean. I don't like fat puppies. I don't like fat dogs that are so big they cannot even walk. I like them lean and hungry but also healthy.

"I worm every two to three months and change my wormers every time. I also give a lot of hook shots. Hookworms are a big problem out here and I like to do the dogs at least three times a year."

IRELAND

Irish breeders Sean and Michael Dunphy produce more open race winners in Britain than anyone else. Their Droopys prefix is known the world over and is synonymous with quality: quality pups from quality

The traditional method of free-range rearing is still favoured by many Irish trainers.

broods. The Dunphys are based at the 150-acre family farm in Portlaw, County Waterford. They rear around 50 to 60 pups a year and believe in the traditional Irish free-range type of rearing, with one or two concessions.

Sean and Michael Dunphy are always delighted to welcome visitors to their farm, known as Ballyvalican. They are, of course, friendly lads but there is an ulterior motive. Michael revealed: "We are a bit tucked away from passing traffic so we rely on people coming here to help socialise the pups."

SOCIALISATION

Between the ages of five and eight months the Dunphys' pups will meet virtually everybody who comes to the house, including the postman. Michael added: "We call it being 'on the Boreen'.

"The idea is that it takes the nerves out of them. If they are nervous they won't settle when you sell them. This way they will be seeing people the whole time and we get very few problems.

"From that point they can go off into the fields. We have the farm split into two and we rear a batch in each. They may not necessarily be from the same litter or the same age (although they are usually fairly closely matched in age).

"We like them to run in packs. It is important, because they get used to running alongside other dogs at speed. It holds them in good stead when they go on the track. There is plenty of rough and tumble when they do it that way and you may get the odd fella who is being picked on. But the solution is to take him away and put him with another group.

"They have the freedom to run where they like and they often stray quite a distance. There is a river about a mile away that stops them going too far.

"The furthest one has ever gone was about three miles. But that was because he was spooked by thunder and lightning one night. But generally speaking they will always come back for their food."

But this type of free-range rearing does not come without its problems. Michael added: "We lose the odd one. They could get knocked over and killed by a car or a tractor. But that will always happen when you have a batch of 12 or more dogs roaming the area the way they do here.

"Our puppies generally leave their mother at six or seven weeks. We first worm them at 14 days and continue worming every seven or eight days until they are about 12 weeks old. They are then wormed approximately once a month. The wormer we use stays the same for the first couple of doses, after that we switch them about to maintain some sort of potency."

The pups at the Dunphys' are usually considered forward enough to be kennelled at about 11 to 12 months. Michael added: "That's the usual age but I might bring them in a little earlier if the ground is hard.

"Once they get that bit bigger they are able to use themselves more and can get hurt if there is frost about. The smaller lad doesn't do himself any damage because he cannot build up a tremendous speed and he is more supple. But the big dogs fly about the place and you are taking a bit of a chance with them if the frost is about."

By the time it comes to kennelling the pups, they are already used to a collar, lead and muzzle.

Michael said: "We train them to lead and collar and put a muzzle on at 9 to 10 months. We just put them on and let them get on with it. There is obvious reluctance at first but they soon get used to it."

FEEDING

Until seven months, puppies at the Dunphys' range are fed three times a day. They keep the

PUTTING ON A MUZZLE
Photos: Steve Nash.

Step One.

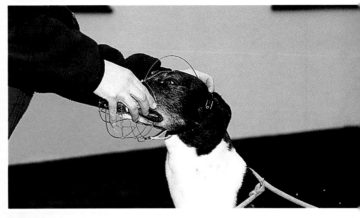

Step Two.

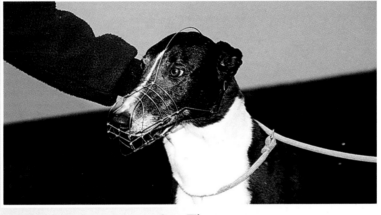

Step Three.

same feeding times of 8 am, 3 pm and 11.30 pm. Michael said: "We leave nuts (complete biscuit) with them between the second and third meals. The last meal of the day will usually be a sort of mash, a bit of tripe, milk and biscuit. We use watered-down cow's milk.

"After that they would be fed pretty much the same as the race dogs. They have a milky breakfast with cereal. The main meal is normally nuts and raw meat, sometimes fish and sometimes chicken. We believe in top-class, good-quality food. You only get out what you put in."

EARLY TRAINING

At about ten months, the Dunphys start to allow the puppies a spell on the track they have at home. Michael said: "We let them gallop round without the hare. They are only chasing each other but it teaches them to balance themselves at the turns.

"When they reach about 13 months we put them behind the drag lure on our gallop at home. At this stage we introduce them to the traps. We believe in walking them through the boxes a couple of times to familiarise them and get them used to the starting gate going up. We do that twice a week for three or four weeks. After that we take them to the track.

"The first time they visit the track they have a 300-yard solo sprint from the traps. At this stage they are used to the boxes and show no nerves. It is important that they are not spooked on their first visit, because first impressions are lasting.

"It is quite easy from that point in. The pups usually have another sprint before we give them their first trial to qualify them to race. Within a couple of more runs they are ready."

The Dunphys do not train many Greyhounds. They usually have just one or two races before the pups are bought by one of their long list of regular clients in Britain or Ireland.

ENGLAND

George Adams is based in Barnet, Hertfordshire, on the outskirts of London. He has the use of 30 acres but says he is comfortable just utilising eight acres of that land. George has been breeding Greyhounds for around 15 years and enjoyed his biggest success with Night Trooper, runner-up to Shanless Slippy in the 1996 English Derby. Night Trooper, who was an excellent starter, won the £20,000 Reading Masters and the prestigious Pall Mall, a race that has a long and illustrious history in the English calendar. George might rear up to three litters a year.

FEEDING
It is no wonder that the management of George Adams's local supermarket is delighted every time he whelps down a litter. George revealed: "When I have pups past the weaning stage I buy in all my milk from there."

That amounts to about 30 pints a day which, if nothing else, comes to a pretty penny. But George added: "It is the way I have always done it and I get good results. We use cow's milk and a little bit of lactose mixed in right up until they are five months. At that stage I switch to a very good-quality

powdered milk (SMA baby milk) which I buy in from Ireland."

Feeding is at the top of George's list of priorities. He said: "We don't like to cut corners but, because of some shrewd buying, we can do it quite economically.

"We use a lot of pasta because it is very easily digested. I am a great believer in chicken – a lot of it – and beef. We use brown bread and pasta, because it is bulkier, and we use plenty of soups. The only biscuit I have ever used is the Wafcol Racer, of which I give the dogs a small cup with their main meal every day."

George places a lot of emphasis on good feet. He said: "In their early days I like the pups to spend plenty of time on concrete. It helps their feet develop a desirable sort of box-like shape. Flat feet are sometimes inherited, but are often caused by spending too much time on muddy paddocks.

"Another benefit of concrete paddocks is that they can be washed down and are therefore far more hygienic than grass paddocks.

"We try to keep the puppies with their mother as long as possible, but it depends on her. If she is getting along okay with them, they stay. We have had cases of the bitch still being with her puppies when they are 10 weeks old.

"It also depends on the size of the litter. If it is big, we may have to take some of the pups away and hand-rear them. We do that using a special milk that our veterinary surgeon gives us.

"At our whelping den we have a sliding partition door. It is low enough for the mother to jump over to the other side where we have a bed made up for her. It gives her the opportunity to get away from the pups if she so desires."

SCHOOLING
George reckons that all his puppies need in

Exercise, food and sleep are the key ingredients for rearing strong, healthy dogs.

Photo: Steve Nash.

order to grow into big, strong adult dogs is plenty of exercise, food and sleep. He added: "That's what I believe in for bringing up children and, as far as I am concerned, dogs are no different.

"In the morning they are let out of their paddocks into the field to gallop. They run their feet off and we bring them in. Once they have calmed down we feed them, then they fall to sleep. That process is repeated three times a day.

"I know a lot of people are against this, but when they are about five or six months old we put our puppies behind the drag for 35-45 yards (30 or 40 metres). Really only to find out which ones are keen and which of them might be a problem when it comes to schooling. We do that once or twice and don't bother with it again.

"I love to watch the pups galloping. A good litter goes out into the field and almost immediately they are looking for game. They hunt and they stalk, they are such livewires. Only the other day one of our pups caught a magpie.

"We generally keep them out in the field in packs but at eight months we split them up into pairs. When we do that we try to match them with dogs they get along with but, if we find one is a bully, we will put him in with another bully. It then becomes a battle of the toughest. It all comes down to stock sense. That's why farmers make such good rearers of Greyhounds.

"At the same time as we split them into pairs, they are taken on a rope lead. They kick and buck for a while but they soon get used to having a collar and lead on. We also

SCHOOLING A GREYHOUND
Photos: Steve Nash.

The Greyhound is put in the traps, with the exit open.

As the lure starts up, the Greyhound sets out.

With a good sighting of the lure, the Greyhound is keen to chase.

A slightly tentative start, but the Greyhound is now on the lure.

The skill is to keep the lure a reasonable distance from the Greyhound, but ensuring he remains intent on the chase.

Cornering tightly, the Greyhound is already learning the skills involved in track racing.

Once the Greyhound gets to the track, he is generally raring to go. Photo: Steve Nash.

start putting on muzzles at that age. They hate them but, once again, settle down to getting used to having them on.

"To start our pups schooling we put them behind the ball hare. We get the pups used to the traps by walking them through. The traps are out in the field and the pups would normally come across them on a daily basis when out for exercise, and I always encourage them to go through them at an early age.

"It makes it easier at the track. First off, I handslip them to the first bend of the circuit, and then I go back one bend at a time until we complete a full circuit. After that we give them a few solos and before you know it they are ready for their first race."

5 PEAK PERFORMANCE

Greyhound trainers the world over have a pretty similar attitude to feeding. They make a few concessions to scientific advancements in the world of nutrition but, by and large, stick with the trusted formula of fresh meat, and vegetables on a carbohydrate base.

A BALANCED DIET

The number of meals a day may differ, but all trainers agree that feeding time should be the same time every day, ever mindful of the role routine plays in the life of the racing Greyhound.

Trainers are also consistent with what they feed and, by and large, give the same meals every day, with only slight variations to prevent that dreaded condition of boredom creeping in. Just as it is with every other aspect of their lives, the element of surprise is important when it comes to what Greyhounds eat at the end of a day.

The food has to be right or else how can the Greyhound be expected to maintain his slim, muscular appearance and perform at his optimum level race after race? After all, you would not put low-grade fuel into a Formula One racing car and expect it to convey its driver to the World Championship.

Have you noticed how the most prolific handlers in the sport always mention feeding when asked to what they attribute their success? That is no coincidence.

Most trainers agree that meat must be included in the diet. The emergence of processed dry biscuit in the late 1970s sought to make the feeding of meat a thing of the past but it never succeeded.

Complete biscuit established itself as part of the racing Greyhound's diet but, in the majority of cases, it is used in conjunction with meat and not instead of it.

These days there is a huge selection of feeds on the market. Each and every one of them is designed to supply to the Greyhound a correct balance of all the nutrients needed – carbohydrates, fats, minerals, proteins, vitamins and water – for the sustenance of the racing animal.

But, aware that the battle to wean trainers off meat has failed, animal feed manufacturers have made a concession and these days make complete biscuit with varying degrees of protein to allow for the continued feeding of meat.

For instance, feed is now available containing anything from 12 per cent protein to 30 per cent protein. In most complete feeds used by professional trainers, the amount of protein is 27.5 per cent. Soaking usually takes 15-30 minutes. Water should be available at all times when using this type of feed.

A typical main meal in America, Australia,

The canine athlete must be fed a top-quality diet in order to perform to the best of his ability.

Photo: Steve Nash.

Britain and Ireland would be a complete meal/biscuit, meat (beef, horse, chicken or, in Australia, kangaroo) and vegetables and the finished article should be a combination of foods that provide the racing Greyhound with a compact and nutritious diet.

ADDITIVES

A multimillion-dollar industry has grown around the manufacture of food supplements. There seems to be a lotion or a potion for every possible condition and some that do not even exist.

However, some have good value, one of which is Vitamin E. One of the more popular Vitamin E supplements on the market is White E. This is a natural product .

Vitamin E is essential for keeping Greyhounds in good racing shape. Not enough of it and your racing Greyhound will experience a decline in muscle function as well as a number of other things. It is worth bearing in mind that by freezing your meat you are killing its Vitamin E content, so a

supplement in those cases is essential. When giving Vitamin E, it is important to remember it is an antagonist of Iron, so avoid giving the two together.

Some trainers who offer a chicken diet may also find that their Greyhound is low on Vitamin B12. A supplement of this vitamin and Vitamin C are probably most important for the continued health and high performance of the racing Greyhound.

FEEDING THE RACING DOG

AMERICA

Leading Derby Lane and Tampa trainer Mick Darcy said: "We feed once a day – in the mornings (between 9.30 and 10 am) only – and that is typical of a trainer in America.

"When I first came to America with Pat Dalton 14 years ago we raced only six nights a week. Because of that we were able to feed in the afternoons. But in the late 1980s an additional three matinee meetings a week were introduced. Afternoon feeding was phased out because it disrupted the schedule too much and morning feeding was introduced.

"In terms of feeding racers, a morning meal for a dog running that night would be a half-pound snack.

"At the moment we are carrying 55 dogs in our kennels. With that number of dogs we would use 90 lb of raw meat every day. About 10 lb of boiled rice, 10-15 lb of macaroni, other bits and bobs and then a complete biscuit like Kasko or Purina.

"It is all mixed together in a tub and then dished out. The food is fed fairly dry but the dogs have access to water at all times.

"We don't have the same problem they have in the Northern States. There, because of the colder weather, they have to adopt a fatty feed to keep the dogs' weight up. Our biggest problem is that they put weight on because of the heat in Florida. That's why our diet is probably more protein than carbohydrate."

AUSTRALIA

Top Australian trainer Alan Britton likes to feed his charges twice a day. He said: "We start pretty early and I like to feed a breakfast. That consists of an 8 oz cup of water to half a cup of milk. Added to that are molasses, honey, a dehydration mix and half a cup of complete biscuit.

"My main feed is wholemeal bread (four slices for dogs and three for bitches), the same complete food we use for breakfast (one 8 oz cup for dogs and two thirds of a cup for bitches), raw beef (a pound and a half for dogs and a pound and a quarter for bitches). My wife makes up a vegetable soup, with barley, and that is used to soak the food (two and half mugs of soup for dogs and two for bitches).

"I favour raw beef. I have tried chicken,

fish and everything else but I always come back to raw beef, which I believe is best and produces the best results. A lot of people think I feed a very wet meal but I like to get the fluid into them because I don't consider Greyhounds to be great drinkers of water. In addition, the barley in the soup also helps the kidneys.

"Sometimes I will give dogs pasta in a fluid base after a hard race. It is very easy on the stomach and is probably better for them after the stress of competing."

IRELAND

Paul Hennessy is one of Ireland's best known and most successful trainers. He places great emphasis on feeding and is so keen on milk that he keeps six cows at his kennels in Gowran, Co. Kilkenny.

He said: "Breakfast can vary between cereal in the summer and porridge in the winter. Both are served with lashings of full-fat milk from our own cows. I especially believe in porridge in the winter when the weather is cold. We use Kennel Vite (a multivitamin tonic) in the breakfasts.

"For the main meal I give the dogs half Red Mills Racer and half brown bread. We boil our meat and then mince it. We generally use beef or chicken (one or the other – rarely both together). But the two days before a race I like to use chicken. I think they are a bit freer on it. We also use vegetables and pearl barley in the soup. The only additive I use in the evening meal is Vitamin E.

"I always cook my meat, for no other reason than I have always done it that way. They are running well on what we are giving them so there is obviously no need to change.

"As a pre-race meal I would give a smaller breakfast than normal (the same items just less of them) and then I would give them something at about 2.30 pm. That would probably be toast with equal quantities of tea and milk. I give them tea because milk on its own can make them a bit loose."

ENGLAND

English Derby-winning trainer Gary Baggs said: "Feeding is so important. We probably take more time over feeding than anything else.

"We feed a breakfast. A bit of cereal with White E (Vitamin E), honey, Vitamin C. I used to use powdered milk but these days I prefer to soak the breakfast in a bit of beef or chicken stock or diluted molasses.

"In the afternoon we feed a main meal of a complete dog food (between 6 to 8 oz depending on whether it is a dog or bitch), we add meat – cooked and raw – and I use pasta and rice every day. I am not a big believer in using vegetables, but the food is soaked with beef or chicken stock.

"I am a firm believer in occasionally

replacing the beef with fish and chicken. Some people are obsessed with giving huge amounts of meat that is not good for the dogs. It clogs up their kidneys and is counterproductive. I also use pasta as a pre-race meal because it loads up the carbohydrates which increases their energy."

"I always give them access to water and keep an eye on the amount they are drinking. If their water intake is high, it is a sign that things are not as they should be inside. Another indication that a dog is not feeling himself is if he is eating grass. It is natural for a dog to pick grass when he has an upset stomach because it will make him vomit."

Pat Norris said: "In the evening meal they get brown bread, meat, nuts (complete biscuit). I always cook my meat and I always feed beef. There is no particular reason that I cook it other than it is what I have always done and I feel safer doing it that way. I occasionally use vegetables and soak the food with stock from the cooked beef.

"I keep track dogs as well as coursing dogs

ABOVE: *Weighing the dogs is a regular part of a racing kennel's routine.   Photo: Steve Nash.*

LEFT: *Each Greyhound is fed according to its size and workload.   Photo: Steve Nash.*

Walking is rated as a beneficial form of exercise for the racing Greyhound.   *Photo: Steve Nash.*

but I feed them differently when it comes to breakfast. The trackers get a cereal that I soak with half a cup of milk and water. The coursers are working much harder and often get a smaller version of the evening meal. It is important that they keep a good back on them.

"The night before a dog is due to run in a course I will feed much the same but probably a little earlier because they will be going to slips at around 11 am. I like to think that they have cleared themselves of the previous night's meal by then. On the day of coursing, I would give them a very light meal.

"They don't have any food between courses but they would have plenty of water laced with Recharge, which is a rehydration fluid."

Feeding is very much an individual thing, even down to feeding times. Mick Darcy feeds in the morning to fit in with his schedule. Some of the bigger contract kennels in Britain like to start their feeding routine at

around 1 pm and, at the smaller kennels, where there are fewer dogs to attend to, sometimes feeding will not start until 4 or 5 pm.

Some trainers also like to give their charges a complete change on Sundays. I remember I would feed only once on the Sabbath and it would usually be something light like fish or chicken on a base of rice or pasta, with a milk and water mix to soak it down.

EXERCISE

TO WALK OR NOT TO WALK?
Walking as a form of exercise has over the years been scoffed at as an anachronism, and it is true that the amount of time Greyhounds spend on the road these days is far less than in yesteryear.

However, walking as part of a training programme for the racing Greyhound has never really totally lost its appeal and it is surprising how many of today's top trainers use walking as the foundation of their coaching routine.

How far and how often trainers walk their dogs is very much down to personal preference, but I think it is fair to say that two walks a day for anything between 15 minutes and an hour is about normal. When to walk is another thing that trainers will not agree on but it is important that, once a trainer decides on a time, he or she sticks to it.

When we talk about walking I think it is important to stress that we are referring to walking on the road and not on grass. In my opinion, the road is by far the greater conditioner. The great thing about walking is that it helps the dog develop steady breathing, assists in the breakdown of internal fat, conditions the Greyhound's muscles, strengthens his tendons and ligaments and also the toes.

Apart from the exercise aspect, other advantages of walking include the introduction of the Greyhound to new scenery (so important for keeping the mind fresh), the socialising of the Greyhound with his kennel companions and the development of a bond between the Greyhound and his regular walker.

Many trainers use walking to build their dogs up to a level of fitness before introducing galloping as the main form of exercise.

The disadvantages of walking, especially in public places and on roads, include the possibility of Greyhounds treading on glass or other sharp objects, the obvious danger of being hit by vehicles and the potential for a Greyhound to be attacked by other dogs or animals.

Leading Australian trainer Alan Britton recognises the value of walking. He said: "I walk four times a week, usually on Tuesday, Thursday, Saturday and Sunday, when the weather is cool enough. We cover about three or so miles on every outing.

"I am lucky enough to have a National Park near my kennels and I walk there. It is full of wildlife and the dogs are kept constantly on their toes by koala bears and kangaroos.

"Because of that, though, some of the dogs pull really hard and become a little stressed out. That is not good and I have to be careful, especially in the warmer weather, that they don't dehydrate."

Paul Hennessy said: "Most of my dogs would get about an hour's walking a day, split into two sessions. I gallop my dogs more than anything else and I sometimes use a circular walking machine after galloping as a way of easing the muscles back to a natural state following the intensity of galloping."

Gary Baggs said: "I am not a great believer in walking the legs off a dog. Once they reach a level of fitness, the amount of racing they have these days keeps them more than right. The biggest job then is keeping them sweet in the brain."

In the USA, walking is not part of the daily routine. Pat Dalton said: "Dogs may be walked to freshen them up, and some trainers have walking machines, but, generally speaking, it is not part of a daily routine of training dogs in the States."

Pat Norris said: "A Greyhound in training for a coursing season would have approximately 4-5 miles every day. I normally start the dog off with a mile or so and build him up to a distance of four or five miles. I am mindful of the dog going over the top and would continually monitor his progress.

"Coursing dogs must be fitter than track dogs because their job is so much more demanding and they take a lot more punishment. That is why walking, which builds such strong, durable muscle, is so important."

WALKING MACHINES
While appreciating the importance of regular

walking, some trainers are quite happy to let a machine do the job for them. Walking machines come in many shapes and sizes. The standard unit for a small kennel usually accommodates two Greyhounds who exercise on a motor-driven conveyor-belt type of machine. The Greyhounds are held in position by a collar attached to a bar across the front of the machine.

It must be stressed that exercise on this type of motorised machine must be supervised at all times. I will always remember the Irish farmer who used to put a couple of dogs on his machine and then go off to milk his cows. Needless to say, his dogs used to object in the strongest terms whenever they were being led towards the confounded thing.

Some of the bigger kennels, especially in Australia, favour a rotating walker because more dogs can be exercised at any one time. It has an umbrella appearance with as many as 12 spiders' arms to which the Greyhound leads are attached. Such a contraption is often motorised. However, Matt O'Donnell, the Irish trainer, has an innovative method for powering his.

He said: "I place a dog who fancies himself as a bit of a gigolo behind a bitch. His determination to get to the bitch would set the whole thing running and the momentum keeps it going."

The beauty of the smaller walking machines is that dogs can continue walking as part of their training programme, even when the weather outside argues otherwise. Another positive aspect is that how far and at what speed the Greyhound walks can be completely controlled. In addition, there is no danger of a stray leaping out at you and your Greyhound from a side-alley.

TROTTING
I believe this to be a marvellous form of exercise for both handler and Greyhound.

Restrict your trotting to just two Greyhounds at a time. Start walking and gradually increase the tempo until you find yourself jogging. Make sure the Greyhounds keep their legs straight at all times and do not allow them to break into a gallop. To get any benefit from this type of work, the tempo must be maintained for at least a mile or so.

GALLOPING
Galloping is probably the most popular form of conditioning the racing Greyhound and it is generally accepted that there is no better way of getting a dog fit enough to do himself justice on the race track.

In fact, many trainers appreciate the value of galloping so much that they go to the great expense of building their own gallop – a stretch of land specially designed for galloping.

Those trainers without the financial means to build their own gallop can usually find a park or golf course, for example, where they can gallop safely. Obviously permission from the park ranger or green keeper should be obtained before galloping at these places.

Whether it is behind a drag lure, controlled hand-to-hand or just free-range, galloping is an important part of preparing the Greyhound for racing. It is also a great spectacle and there is nothing quite like the satisfaction you get from watching these wonderful animals in full flight.

Putting a dog behind a drag lure or winder is a sure-fire way of knowing that he is giving the chase his 100 per cent effort. Hand-to-hand galloping involves a dog being released by one handler and called by another, who might use a whistle and drag a skin to ensure maximum effort. Slipping the dogs in Indian file with a break of approximately 35 yards (30 metres) is another method used to get the most from the gallop.

Free-range galloping is more or less just that – allowing the dogs to express

A home-gallop in Ireland – four Greyhounds are handslipped at short intervals from the bottom of the hill.
Photo: Steve Nash.

themselves in a field, either singly or in pairs. They will only do as much as they want and it is a marvellous way to combine exercise and fun. It also has excellent therapy value for the 'hyper' Greyhound who hates being confined to a kennel.

Paul Hennessy said: "I have the luxury of being able to use the nearby Gowran racecourse to gallop. It is a brilliant facility and I have full permission to use it. I don't use a winder (drag lure) but I am happier just hand galloping over about 350 yards (300 metres).

"Normally a dog in regular racing would get two gallops a week. A dog who races, say, every Saturday, would get a gallop on Tuesday and Thursday. However, there is no hard-and-fast rule. Some dogs might get three gallops a week and others might just get one. It depends on the dog.

"We believe in having our dogs as fit as possible. A good stiff gallop never did any dog any harm. I can remember an incident with Trade Union during the Champion Stakes some years back. He was a tough dog and had raced and won on six successive Saturdays on his way to the final. After the semis, I was approached by a man who suggested that rest was the only thing for Trade Union during the week leading up to the decider.

"I disagreed and galloped Trade Union three times in the five days to the final. He won the decider going away and was as fresh as a daisy afterwards."

Pat Norris said: "I assess the ability of a novice coursing dog by galloping him with proven runners. I handslip them one after the other, and note those that were gaining and losing ground. I gallop my coursing dogs 300/400 yards every day during the coursing season."

Alan Britton said: "I make a point of galloping on Monday, Wednesday and Friday. It keeps the runners sharp and is an important part of our training programme."

SWIMMING

Swimming seems to drift in and out of fashion all the time, a bit like flared trousers and the mini-skirt. It is, nevertheless, a very valuable form of exercise, especially handy when bringing dogs back from injury, in particular those dogs that have been suffering from injuries to the toes and tendons. The beauty of swimming is that it exercises every muscle in the body and does it without putting too much stress on toes, tendons and ligaments.

Swimming can also be used as another way of changing the routine slightly and keeping the Greyhound's mind fresh.

Those living in coastal areas can derive great benefits. Walking in salt water is recognised as having marvellous value in the treatment of foot and wrist injuries and, of course, the salt will also keep the feet healthy.

Swimming in the sea is not as easily done as in a pool but, by taking a dog out to your waist height, it can be achieved in relative safety. But remember not to allow the dog's head to go under water, for obvious reasons.

Greyhounds usually panic a bit when being placed into water for the first time, but they soon get used to it and it is not long before they are enjoying themselves splashing around. There are a number of purpose-built circular pools about, where the handler stands on a platform in the centre, keeping control of the dog with a rod attached to the dog's collar, and there are also straight pools.

A method I will always remember involved two large pieces of rope and a canal just outside Dublin, Southern Ireland. A special collar was made with an attachment for a lead on either side. Each of the pieces of rope had a hook at the end that was locked on to the collar. The trainer walked on the pathway on one side of the canal and his assistant was on the other. Each held their respective ropes and, with the dog in the canal, the pair walked up and down while the dog enjoyed the water in total safety.

John McGee, seven times the champion trainer in Britain, is a big fan of swimming. He said: "It is marvellous exercise for the dogs, especially in the fact that the dogs exercise muscles they wouldn't normally during walking and galloping.

"Determining how much swimming a dog needs is much like anything else. How do you know how much galloping a dog likes – it is all trial and error. I can remember one dog I trained in the eighties who swam every day and his performances showed a marked improvement on the track."

Swimming exercises all the muscles without straining toes, tendons and ligaments.

Photo: Steve Nash.

MASSAGE

They used to say you could find lengths with your dog if you rubbed him down with *The Sporting Life*. Well, the world's oldest racing paper is no longer with us but massage is still an important part of the daily routine in kennels through the world.

The firm massaging of embrocation into the muscles of the racing Greyhound increases the flow of blood through those areas, improves muscle tone, stimulates muscle growth and breaks down inflammation.

Methods of massage vary but the most used method is to stand astride your Greyhound and, starting at the front with the shoulders, rub in the embrocation with your hands via a rounded arm action. Work your way down the dog's body using the same action until you reach the hindquarters where, for effectiveness, adopt a more up and down rubbing action.

That is the most common method, but I have known trainers to lie the dog on his side on a bench and massage side-on. That means more precise finger massage to the muscle mass of the shoulders and hindquarters. It also gives the trainer an opportunity to cut and file toe nails and treat foot injuries.

FOOT CARE

The feet should never be overlooked. The emergence of sand as the primary racing surface means that foot maintenance is more important than ever before. Feet should be washed whenever necessary. Keep a close eye that sand is not allowed to gather in the quicks. Sand has an abrasive texture which does not take long to penetrate the skin if left too long.

Nails should be inspected and cut regularly. File to a smooth finish to avoid split ends.

I always favour cleaning the quicks with antiseptic and cotton wool (cotton). A lot of trainers favour a nailbrush or toothbrush but,

unless you can find one with particularly soft bristles, that method can do more harm than good.

Another type of massage that is used is the hydrobath. For instance, it is very popular in America. Submerge the Greyhound into a man-made tank where jets of warm water – the pressure is usually between 25 lbs and 30 lbs – are directed at the dog's shoulders and hindquarters.

Derby Lane trainer Mick Darcy is from the old school and prefers the manual method. He said: "I give my Greyhounds a rubdown as a matter of course every morning. I use Trainers' Choice (embrocation) which is pretty strong stuff.

"We have to keep our dogs in pretty good condition because if they don't race at least every 12 days they have to trial back. That is a national rule, although in some states dogs must race every 10 days. They allow us 12 days in Florida because we don't race on Sundays. If you don't race within 30 days you must trial twice, and if you don't race within 60 days you have got to trial three times.

"I don't like the idea of the hydrobath. The jets only hit certain areas of the dog and could miss out on vital soreness. With my hands and my eyes I know exactly where the dog needs attention and I apply it."

In Britain, the rule is that a Greyhound must race at least once every 28 days and, to keep his runners supple, a well-known trainer conducts an elaborate stretching routine with his runners prior to races. He said: "I extend their front and back legs to simulate a galloping action. There is so little done in terms of warming the dogs up before they run, but at least this helps.

"I give the dogs a vigorous rubdown at home before we leave for the track and then stretch them before the race. I find it is beneficial for the dogs. A dog knows he is going racing when in the afternoon he gets a

GROOMING AND MASSAGE
Photos: Steve Nash.

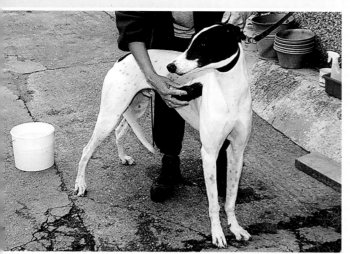

A stiff bristle brush grooms the coat and aids circulation.

This can be followed up by going through the coat with a soft bristle brush.

A comb can be used, particularly when the Greyhound is casting his coat.

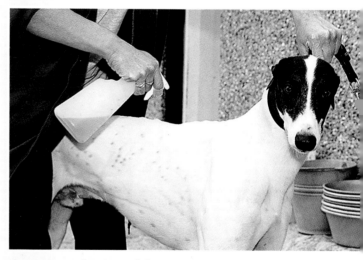

An embrocation is used for massage.

Massaging tones the muscles as well as boosting circulation.

Ears should be checked and cleaned if necessary.

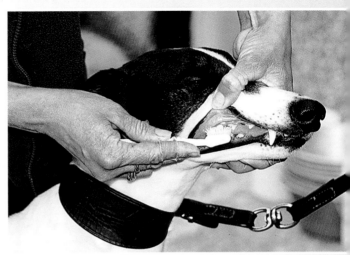

Teeth should be brushed regularly.

*If tartar accumulates on the
teeth, they will need to be scaled.*

*When Greyhounds race on sand, it is important
to keep a very close check on the feet.*

*Nails need to be kept in trim using
the guillotine type of nail-cutter.*

good rubdown and is coated up so as not to allow the muscles, warmed by the massage, to become cold and stiff before the race."

GROOMING

Although a lot of trainers no longer believe regular grooming is beneficial to racing Greyhounds, I am not so sure they are right. Perhaps trainers only think of it for its aesthetic value but they should also consider its massage qualities.

To start with, remove loose hair with either a steel comb or a hacksaw blade. Both do equally effective jobs and my personal favourite is the comb.

A stiff brush with a hard-bristled brush can do wonders to make a dog feel good and to boost blood circulation. Finish off with a grooming pad and add a shine to the coat with a piece of velvet or a towel.

Check teeth on a regular basis. A canine toothpaste and a good stiff brush or a chew on a marrow-bone are probably the most popular and best ways of keeping teeth clean.

Pat Norris said: "Mostly I groom twice a day and check for injury all the time. The biggest problems we get with coursing dogs are wrist and shoulder problems. There are certain fields which are renowned for certain injuries because of the make-up of the ground. Limestone is a big problem and fields with that as a base usually cause more toe injuries."

KENNEL ROUTINES

Kennels are always busy places and very often seem quite chaotic as the trainer and his or her staff attend to their daily chores. But, despite the mayhem, underneath there should be a routine that is closely adhered to. As we have said before, Greyhounds are creatures of habit and need that stability to perform at their best.

The normal daily routine is: let out first thing. Some trainers like to paddock their Greyhounds while kennels are cleaned.

Others, with more staff, like the dogs to be walked first thing. In the summer it is often prudent to gallop early in the morning to avoid the warmer weather in the middle of the day.

The next step is breakfast, although a lot of trainers in America do not feed it.

Greyhounds are then allowed an hour or so to digest their breakfast before perhaps the most important part of the day commences. This is the time when those racers who require machine work, treatment for injuries and grooming are attended to. In addition, a lot of trainers gallop mid-morning or give their runners a spell walking or on the walking machine. Greyhounds will then be let out prior to their keepers taking a break for lunch.

After lunch more maintenance work takes place. The dogs that need it may have more walking or galloping while others could have a free gallop. It is generally a time for topping up.

Dinner is fed late afternoon and the Greyhounds are then let out into small paddocks before locking-up a for a few hours.

There is another let-out in the early evening and again late evening. Some trainers prefer to give their charges a short walk last thing at night. It is great for relaxing the dogs, and the trainer, before bed.

RACE DAYS

The routine on a day the dog is racing will usually be very different. It is often a case of keeping the charge quiet and relaxed. Breakfast will be the same but, when dinner-time comes, the racer will be offered a much smaller meal. Just enough to keep the strength up.

The dog will be confined to short walks on the lead or let out into a small paddock to relieve himself before returning to his kennel. Conservation of energy is the name of the game.

6 TROUBLESHOOTING

It is easy to win races with good dogs, but where the trainer really earns his or her money is by getting the best from dogs who have problems, either in their attitude to racing, or with the bad habits they have inherited or developed during their rearing and/or schooling, or through their training.

FIGHTERS

The biggest problem dog any trainer will encounter during his or her career is a fighter. This is the dog who cannot resist nibbling the ear of an opponent or attacking his rival. They ruin races and, worst of all, they can badly upset the confidence of the one they have focused their aggression on. They are the real outcasts. Owners do not want them, trainers do not want them and tracks do not want them.

The ironic and sad thing is that, in a lot of cases, dogs who fight or hang – which means stopping to run with their fellow leaders once hitting the front – have more natural ability than the honest type who, despite the fact that he lacks speed, wins more races.

Sometimes there is little you can do for fighters. The problem is that, in the case of track racing, they know that the lure they are following is artificial and reckon there is more fun to be had having a go at one of their opponents.

But fighters fall into two categories. First of all there is the serial offender – the dog who, no matter what you do, will aggressively interfere with opponents at every opportunity. Mostly these dogs have inherited that aspect of their personality. You will find that their brothers and sisters also fight. They really are a lost cause and often end up on the coursing field or retired on a rug in front of some kind soul's fire.

Then there is the first-time offender who has given no indication of possessing the potential to fight in previous races. He is the dog who, with a certain amount of cunning and care by the trainer, can become rehabilitated as a respected racer.

Firstly, the trainer should check that the Greyhound is sound. On some occasions the most genuine of dogs will turn on others because of the pain of an injury and, as a consequence, the frustration of not being able to keep up with his rivals.

Once it has been established that the dog is sound, the trainer can start the job of getting him back on the straight and narrow. As I said earlier, in most cases fighters are dogs who are fully aware that what they are expected to chase is not alive. So we have to convince them otherwise.

Keep the dog who fights moving from track to track. Confuse him by running him behind different hares. The emergence in Britain and Ireland of the Swaffham hare has

Photo: Steve Nash.

made switching a little more difficult but there are numerous independents where the inside hare is still used. Also a run behind the ball hare at one of the many straight meetings is useful.

In between races, give him a go at a skin on a whirly-gig. Chopping and changing all the time keeps the dog's mind occupied and takes it off having a fight. Wherever possible, give the dog a run behind a hare on the coursing field.

Okay, it probably will not work forever but, when you sense the dog may be getting a bit bored again, give him a total break from the track for a couple of months. After that, start again, chopping, changing and keeping the dog's mind alive.

POOR CHASERS
If a Greyhound suddenly becomes a less than enthusiastic racer, it could be for a number of reasons.

Once again, the first thing to do is to get the dog thoroughly checked over by a muscle specialist and blood-tested by your vet. Injury could be at the root of the problem, or a virus may be present which may be making the dog lethargic and unable to perform with his usual alacrity.

Loss of confidence is also a factor to consider. Any Greyhound that has been in the wars may, through concern over his own preservation, question the wisdom of hurtling into the turns at something in the region of 30 miles an hour. The usual fearless tracker may suddenly become the gentleman, allowing others to turn the bend first.

In such cases confidence must be restored. A few solo trials will help, followed by a couple of runs against inferior opposition, which will often do the trick. Be careful in your selection of sparring partners. Choose only dogs that the 'patient' can easily lead, so as not to take a knock at the bend, and ones which he can beat.

Consider a change of lure. It is perfectly possible that the dog is tired of his regular quarry and fancies a different one. I can remember a Greyhound I once trained who was only moderate behind the sumner hare at the Milton Keynes track in the UK. A chance switch to an outside-make lure at the now-

Photo: Steve Nash.

defunct Wembley track in London brought out performances from this dog that I did not believe possible. He became one of the leading sprinters of his generation, set a new record for two bends at Wembley and won the coveted Sovereign Stakes at Rye House, in Hertfordshire, UK.

Another little trick is to try the dog from the trap closest to the lure – trap one in the case of an inside hare, as in America and Australia, and trap six in Britain and Ireland. Breaking on to the hare can make all the difference. Remember, very often dogs rarely see the hare during races. Dogs do not track by scent so, if there is no sight and no sound, what is it chasing?

FRETTERS

How often have you heard a trainer say: "He left his race in the kennel"? Pretty often, I would hazard a guess.

It is true that some dogs get so excited in the racing kennels prior to their races that they are in no condition to run once their turn has come. They often emerge from the racing kennels with saliva dripping from their jaws and are so obviously dehydrated that the most sensible thing to do is to put them in the van and take them home.

Placing a radio in the racing kennel with the dog often helps. Talk or music will often occupy the mind of the fretter and take it off the fact that he or she is locked up in a kennel. If that does not work, why not try the other option of placing cotton wool (cotton) in the Greyhound's ear?

The fretter will also sometimes injure himself by continually jumping around in the kennel. In such cases it is prudent to chain the dog up – using a swivel collar to prevent the dog choking himself. Once the dog realises that he is fighting a losing battle trying to liberate himself from the chain, he will usually give up and settle down.

Photo: Steve Nash.

Giving a dog a decent-sized meal will also serve to stop him fretting, although care must be taken that you do not give him too much so that his ability to race is affected.

BAD TRAVELLERS

The dogs who are poor kennellers are also likely to travel badly to the track. Once again, getting the better of the problem will result in the dog doing itself more justice on the racetrack.

If, at home, the Greyhound is kennelled with a companion, it may be prudent to take that partner along on the journey. It is a common practice in horse racing for a thoroughbred to travel with a companion such as a pony, a donkey or even a sheep, so why should Greyhound racing be any different?

The racer will associate the companion with home, safety and security. Very often, his anxiety is caused by insecurity, and the company of a partner can go quite a long way to easing that.

Once again, giving the racer a meal before departure will result in him enjoying a much more settled journey. A small portion of meat and brown bread with glucose mixed with milk is often very effective.

Restricting the racer to a confined space such as a travelling cage is also useful. When the Greyhound knows he cannot move about, he usually settles much better. And, if you are travelling in the back of an estate car or station wagon, it might be sensible to block out the windows. That is another way of keeping the racer calm.

SLOW STARTERS

I have lost count of the number of dogs who would have been Champions had they been just a fraction of a second quicker from the starting traps. Sadly, there is often very little you can do for dogs who have this

Photo: Steve Nash.

extremely frustrating habit.

While I accept that early pace is handed down to a racer by his parents, I cannot accept that poor trapping is something inherent in the breed.

I favour the theory that Greyhounds who are poor trappers are so for a reason, usually because they have had a bad experience at the boxes. They might have knocked themselves in the traps at some time, or they may have miscalculated a start and have hit their head on the gate.

In such cases, all the trainer can do is hope that a series of incident-free breaks will restore the Greyhound's confidence at some stage.

Some Greyhounds are poor beginners because they stand upright in the boxes and are totally unprepared when the lure trips the traps. To counter this, it might be sensible to give the dog some box training, blocking out the top of the gate so the Greyhound has to get down to see out.

The idea is that the dog develops the habit of getting down every time he enters the boxes and, as a consequence, is always ready to fly the lids every time the traps open.

TURNING IN BOXES

This is also a habit that the Greyhound can develop halfway through his career. Often, it will have been caused by a bad experience at the boxes but sometimes there is just no reason for it.

One trainer I was once familiar with used to bite the dog's tail as it popped out of the front of the traps after the Greyhound had turned around and was facing the back. It worked – but seemed to be a bit barbaric. However, giving the racer a reason not to turn – like the danger of having his tail bitten – is the effective way of stopping this annoying habit!

Extra box tuition, involving leaving the dog in the traps for a period of time, and keeping his attention at the front of the boxes by teasing it with a skin or a fluffy toy, is sometimes of benefit.

RUNNING ON

They do not come along too often, but there is nothing worse than a dog who will not stop, with the others, at the pickup after a race. Tracks that use a sheet at the pickup, or which have developed a catching-pen system, do not experience the problem as much as those that do not have anything in place to assist in the capture of the racers at the end of a contest.

There is no easy way to stop it happening, and the best way to prevent it is to be well staffed and extra vigilant at the pickup whenever a race includes a dog who has a history of running on.

Photo: Steve Nash.

7 ADOPTING A GREYHOUND

'Life is as dear to a mute creature as it is to a man. Just as one wants happiness and fears pain, just as one wants to live and not to die, so do other creatures.'

His Holiness the Dalai Lama

My first introduction to a Greyhound was in the 1980s with a beautiful bitch called Bambi. She was at a rescue kennels where I had gone to take blankets. I noticed sadly how many unwanted Greyhounds were there, spending their whole lives in kennels. What follows is not atypical of how someone becomes drawn into rescuing Greyhounds.

Bambi was fawn with white flecks, hence her name, and she had spent nine years in those kennels, waiting to be noticed and adopted. I could see why no-one wanted her – at least I could appreciate it even if the reason was not a good one. She was cold, unfeeling, and unsusceptible to human touch. With my nursing training, I had learned to recognise deep depression. She was lifeless and as cold as stone, and her eyes had no lustre. My heart went out to her and I travelled to the kennels as frequently as I could, to take her out for walks. She remained aloof and unaffected by my attentions. She had Irish earmarks which no-one had understood or tried to interpret. From these, I could learn her true identity,

her age, her name, where she was born and where she raced. With this information, her true history and her past glories, if there were any, would be known to us. The earmarks needed lengthy research at the Irish Coursing Club which a helpful lady undertook and which necessitated going through the archives in the basement. At last we had her name and, bursting with excitement, I rang the kennels. But it all fell rather flat. To my dismay I learned that Bambi had died the previous night alone and was not found until the morning, too late for us to greet her with the new knowledge we had about her past. I know this is all rather anthropomorphic, but the bald facts stuck with me, and have propelled me forward to working for a better deal for Greyhounds everywhere.

A GREYHOUND AS A PET?
The next true story illustrates, better than can be described, the plight, the prejudice, and the appeal of keeping a Greyhound as a pet.

Thirty years ago, Paula, a theatrical costumer, went to London's biggest rescue centre, Battersea Dogs' Home, in search of a little dog to replace her beloved Corgi whom she had just lost. There were several small dogs jumping up, barking happily, wagging their tails and generally attracting as much attention as possible. While she was petting one confident little character, her eyes were

After his racing days are over, the Greyhound deserves a loving home.   *Photo: Steve Nash.*

drawn to the pen next door. In it lay a thin, dilapidated creature looking as if it had lost all interest in living. It did not respond to her calling it.

"What is that?" she asked herself. She looked again at the sprightly little chap in front of her but was irresistibly drawn again and again to the unfamiliar, pathetic and unattractive dog in the neighbouring pen. "What chance would that poor dog have of finding a home?" she thought. She asked a kennel hand about the dog. "It's a Greyhound," he said and got the dog out of the pen. When the dog stood up he was bigger than she had bargained for. His coat was dull and ingrained with coal dust as he had apparently been kept in a coal shed. All she knew about Greyhounds was that they ran fast and wore muzzles. She had never

heard of one kept as a pet. A lady passing by stopped momentarily. "You want that dog, don't you?" she said. "But what about my cat?" Paula asked. "Just be patient, and firm and there'll be no problem – you'll see," she said and walked away. That was enough for Paula. She simply had to take that miserable dog.

What followed was remarkable. The Greyhound and his new owner first had to travel on top of a double-decker bus and then on the escalators and underground train to North London. Next day, they went back on the bus and underground train to Euston station and took the overnight train to Scotland to visit her mother who had three cats. The dog behaved impeccably and astounded his new owner with the ease with which he coped with all those challenges.

This dog was obviously something quite special. Ritz and Paula shared a good life together for eight years. Ritz sat at her feet in nearly every theatre in London and actually performed on stage as the Prince's dog in *The Winter's Tale*. For the next thirty years, Paula was never without a Greyhound. How she could have hugged that lady at Battersea who prompted her to take Ritz!

COMMON MISCONCEPTIONS

That episode did take place in the early 70s, and the last ten years has shown a remarkable change of attitude towards keeping a Greyhound as a pet, but, even so, they are still misunderstood by much of the population, even by dog lovers. I recently encountered a dog devotee who, after viewing my albums of photographs of Greyhounds tucked up with babies and kittens, actually said "But after all they are vicious animals, aren't they?"

So why are Greyhounds misunderstood? Is there any basis for such prejudice?

The first statement that is commonly made is "Oh, they always need a lot of exercise, don't they?" Curiously, the truth is nearer the opposite. As any Greyhound pet owner will tell you, they are lazy 'couch potatoes'. Maybe it is because they have run their strength out on the track, or maybe it is because they are bred as sprinters so racing for thirty seconds every five days is as much as their stamina will take. They lack fat (stored calories) and staying power, so two or three gentle walks every day is all a retired racing Greyhound usually needs to keep him happy.

The second common statement is that they need special food, and huge amounts of it! The truth is that Greyhounds can eat anything that any other dog would eat: fresh food, cooked food, canned food, wholefood. The owner can decide what is more convenient for his domestic situation and, of course, your dog will have preferences and, possibly, even 'allergies' – just as any other dog may have. Usually, he will eat as much as he needs and no more, unlike some breeds I could mention who will eat until they are sick and then start again!

The third statement about being dangerous animals is also grossly misguided. It is true that a Greyhound has been schooled while racing to chase and even kill small animals. Despite the law, live kills are still given to

The Greyhound is the archetypal couch potato.

Photo: Steve Nash.

Most Greyhounds retire at four or five years of age.

Photo: Steve Nash.

Greyhounds to stimulate the chase instinct. Yes, you must take care of your parrot, cat or Chihuahua on first introducing your Greyhound to your other household pets, but most can be detrained with patience and determination. You may have to keep your Greyhound always on a lead but the positive side, however, is that he will be very happy as your faithful companion, walking gently without pulling, by your side.

Aggression towards humans is rare. A 1996 study by Southampton University, UK, of 49 breeds of dog, rated the Greyhound the lowest in aggression. Muzzles are used by trainers to prevent accidents to their very expensive dogs, which may be worth several thousands of pounds, and are not indicative of their potential for aggression, which is very low. Rarely, they may attempt to defend you or their fellow kennelmates due to past bad experience, or a dominant, spoilt male may growl when challenged. On the whole, however, a Greyhound is gentle, even meek, and becomes nervous and timid under stress.

WHEN DO THEY RETIRE?
The racing life of a Greyhound is quite short. Greyhounds begin racing after their schooling period at about eighteen months old and are usually retired by four or five years old. During that time they may have been passed through two to three trainers and run at as many tracks. The reason for their retirement is usually due to injury which slows them up, so that their grading drops as they can no longer keep up with younger Greyhounds. The injuries they incur may be barely perceptible to the layman and may only catch up with them later in life when arthritic changes occur. A healthy Greyhound can live to 15 years old, so the retirement years are clearly the major part of his life.

Sometimes, a young dog, even as young as eighteen months, becomes available for early retirement. The reasons can be as follows: he is too slow for grading in at the track, or he is disinterested in chasing, or he is a 'fighter' which, in spite of the terminology, means the dog simply interferes or plays with other dogs while running, or he turns his head away from the lure, which disqualifies him. These youngsters are really expensive failures in the racing world but for us adopters they are gold dust because they are usually so much more trainable to live with cats or rabbits etc. They can even be more intelligent than a successful racer, having more sense than to chase a teddy bear!

The question of where and how the owner of a racing Greyhound takes leave of his dog promotes heated discussions between the racing world and animal welfare agencies. Rescuers have seen Greyhounds horribly abused when not useful for racing any more, and the racing industry suffers bad publicity from such reports. In both the UK and the USA, the racing authorities play a major part in rehoming retired Greyhounds, and a number of smaller organisations also specialise in this type of work.

GREYHOUND RESCUE

Over the last ten years, Greyhound rescue groups have sprung up all over the UK and USA. We are a devoted, persistent, overworked bunch of people, verging at times on the obsessive! We defend this lovely animal because of its undemanding, gallant, gentle, generous nature, which craves love and companionship and rarely finds it, if we look realistically at the small percentage of Greyhounds homed against the vast numbers bred annually.

The USA leads us in research and publications regarding Greyhound care and behaviour, and in the excellence of group activities, but the need is great, too, as nearly 50,000 Greyhounds are retired each year within the industry.

Interest in Europe, in particular Germany, Switzerland, Belgium and Holland is being kindled by enthusiasts. These countries do not have a professional racing industry. Some aficionados race their long-tails at weekends for fun, and, of course, there will be the occasional devotee of the sport, but on the whole we are breaking new ground in these countries with the notion of keeping a Greyhound as a pet, as the breed is so rare. A small number of people, however, who are involved in accepting and placing retired and

The adoption process is made easier if the trainer provides as much information as possible about each dog. Photo: Steve Nash.

unwanted Greyhounds are becoming as fanatical and as knowledgeable as any in the UK and USA.

THE ADOPTION PROCESS

To adopt a Greyhound, you may visit a rescue kennels, contact the retired Greyhound scheme run by the racing industry, scan the newspapers for advertisements of local societies or ring the nearest dog track. The ideal way to offer a dog for adoption is to reply quickly to the offer of a home, which may have come by letter or telephone, and to send out a 'homing' package giving preparatory information on keeping a Greyhound as a pet.

Obviously, procedures vary from country to country, and between the different organisations, but the following gives a general picture of the adoption process.

A questionnaire should be completed

which focuses the adopter's mind on the commitment of adopting a dog. It may ask about the family's previous and present pets, ages of the children, what will happen at holiday time, the family's hours of working, where the dog will sleep, and points out how much it will cost to keep a dog fully vaccinated, wormed, insured and in good health. Unless these points are considered carefully by the new adopters before they undertake a dog, then he may come bouncing back to the adoption society or, even worse, be abandoned or euthanased. When finances are borderline and domestic trouble hits the family, the dog is the first to be jettisoned. The signing of such a form, the condition of a visit by a home 'checker' who knows Greyhounds and can answer any queries the new adopters may have, and the making of a charge for the dog, will discourage the half-hearted.

When dogs are returned from homes and are relocated, this causes not only inconvenience for the hard-working volunteers but, even more seriously, causes emotional problems in the dogs, with greater tendencies towards displays of insecurity like separation anxiety and toilet training problems. The charge allows the welfare society to vaccinate, worm, sterilise, do dental cleaning, and microchip the dogs,

safeguarding their future as best as it possibly can, and usually it is a bargain considering how terribly expensive it would be to ask your home vet to do all these things. The larger societies have special arrangements with vets to carry out this work and they also benefit from donations.

It is more difficult for smaller groups to prepare their dogs so thoroughly, but as groups grow larger and stronger, they generally gravitate towards this ideal. Many Greyhound rescue groups, in addition, supply a collar, identity disc, lead, muzzle and coat because specialised Greyhound accessories are difficult to find in pet shops.

In North America, a directory exists of adoption groups in every state. The Internet also is a common way of finding out about your local group, and sites such as 'A Breed Apart' give valuable information on all aspects of Greyhound care.

In the UK, the Retired Greyhound Trust, and individuals working from within the industry, have an invaluable function as they are closely linked with trainers, owners, and National Greyhound Racing Club (NGRC) officials who are committed to taking a part in the sunset years of a racing dog when it is of no more use as a sporting dog. I have no problem in working closely with trainers over the homing of a retired dog. I can see only

Homefinders are a dedicated band of people who work unstintingly for the welfare of Greyhounds.

Photo courtesy: David Higgs.

Environmental
PRESS AGENCY

advantages in the mutual exchange of information.

It is unfortunate that we cannot always find homes for 'urgent' cases. This can be as painful for the trainer and owner as it is for us. It is right we should all share this pain and wrong that the onus falls solely on one or the other. Trainers can help us enormously with information: Is the dog a non-chaser? In other words, might he or she live with a cat? Is the dog clean in his kennels? What are his eating habits? Are there any injuries or medical problems we should know about? Is there a vaccination record? When was he last wormed? Does he get on better with bitches or dogs? When were a bitch's seasons? Is the dog noisy when left alone?

THE HOME CHECK

It should be put tactfully that someone will come and talk about what it is like to keep a Greyhound. Nobody likes to feel inspected and the very idea can be an insult to highly experienced dog owners (there is a saying about not teaching your grandmother to suck eggs...!). However, it is useful to look at the fencing, because Greyhounds do have a habit of wandering off absent-mindedly or following up a movement in the far distance! They can also jump six feet (2 m) high but they usually need to be stimulated to do this, for example, by the sight of a cat on the other side of the fence. If the fence is opaque, at least at the dog's eye level, this reduces the chances of a quick hop over. If someone's fence is about three or four feet high and the family is not keen to close themselves in completely, then trellis fencing with batons fitted to the existing fencing, which can be bought fairly reasonably and looks decorative too, can be adequate.

A Greyhound can live until 15 years old and the home-checker must stress that adopting a Greyhound is a ten-year commitment. Patience, love and

understanding are prerequisites for adopting any dog. Sometimes these are in short supply in this disposable society. Hence careful education, reassurance and the promise of support from the group will go a long way to making the homing successful.

A contract is usually presented and signed by both the homefinder and the adopter. It might say (depending on the rescue group involved) that the temperament cannot be depended upon as the history of these dogs is often barely known; that the society cannot be held responsible for veterinary care from the moment of adoption, and that, being a retired racer, there may be racing injuries which may present a problem on vigorous

It is hard to appreciate how traumatic the move from racing kennels to a family home can be.
Photo courtesy: Anne Finch.

Retired racer 'Paloma' from Spain, rehomed in Holland. The gentle nature of a Greyhound is a most endearing characteristic.

Photo courtesy: Anne Finch.

exercise; that the new owners will vaccinate the dog annually and worm their dog regularly with the correct medication; that, if the dog goes missing, the rescue society as well as the police and dog wardens should be informed; that health insurance is highly recommended; and that, in the unfortunate event of the dog not being wanted, it should be returned to the rescue society.

FOSTERING GREYHOUNDS

Some societies encourage the idea of fostering Greyhounds for a period prior to permanent adoption. This serves the purpose of providing a safe place for the dog to go, especially helpful in an emergency situation, and also avoids the necessity of expensive kennelling. Fostering can even be run on the lines of 'puppy walking' for guide dogs and hounds, using the period usefully for toilet-training, teaching the stairs, introductions to other breeds, to cats, to children and to the hubbub of family life with its noisy kitchen gadgets and electronic devices. This 'preparatory schooling' period may reduce the risk of dogs being returned once they are adopted.

Some societies feel that the upset of being 'homed' twice is too upsetting for the dog. It certainly brings a tear to the eyes of the fostering family when the dog leaves for its

new home but there is the comfort of knowing that a good job has been done.

THE GREYHOUND MEETS THE FAMILY

For a Greyhound entering the home it must be like landing on the moon. Greyhounds are born in kennels and have to be taught, bit by bit (not all at once, or the dog will have a nervous breakdown), that the floor is not for the toilet; that he does not have to scrounge for food (if he was a stray); that he may have to be left quite alone occasionally and is not surrounded by 70 other dogs; that he has a name and can be bidden to come and be talked to and caressed and regarded as an important member of the family.

Some dogs who have been treated harshly in their past are frightened of men. If this is the case, ask the man in the family to feed him and do the walking. A dependency will grow, but he may always be a bit wary of male strangers; dogs have long memories. Children will be a novelty to a Greyhound. Some are curious and thrilled to meet a little human; others may be troubled by their unpredictable movements and noise. Some rescue societies will not allow families with children under 14 to have a dog. I can see what they are afraid of, but there can be a very special relationship between a child (I

As the Greyhound settles, his personality will start to emerge.

Photo courtesy: Anne Finch.

am talking of a school-age child) and a dog, and it is a pity not to encourage this with the care and time it deserves.

Some families are brave enough to consider a dog when they have a baby coming into the family. Of course it can work. We know many families where Greyhounds and babies live side by side. For a Greyhound fresh from the track, care must be taken over a crying baby. It is very similar to the cry of a wild animal and the Greyhound is schooled to chase and respond with action to the cry of the wild, and may attack. A baby should never be left alone with an unmuzzled dog. Be aware, too, of the changes in routine which will happen when a new baby arrives and whether the dog, who used to be the centre of attention, is going to be relegated to the kitchen or away from the living areas. This is bound to provoke insecurity and jealousy in the dog, as it might too in an older child, for instance, when a new baby comes to steal the limelight. Involve the dog in the care of the baby. Do not forget to greet your dog as you always did before. Eventually, he will relax and know that the baby is no threat to his existence but is, in fact, an asset in his life.

Certain dog personalities suit different people. A confident, happy, secure dog would survive a noisy, chaotic family, whereas a more timid, quiet character would suit a more tranquil setting. Beware, however, of the dog with one of those amazing tails which go round 360 degrees whipping everything in sight. This can be just the height of a child's eyes.

We all know how little children can torment a dog. Some dogs have more patience than others. Male dogs may be more tolerant, as bitches instinctively know how to check their pups when they get fed up with them. Every dog needs to have a safe place to rest away from the children, which can be access to upstairs, or a den in the form of a large crate, or an absolutely no-go area for children. Noise itself can upset dogs, whose ears, of course, are infinitely more sensitive than ours. I have noticed that loud beat music can cause our sensitive Greyhounds to tremble. Children should be taught never to touch the dog when he is lying still – they do not always close their eyes when they are sleeping – and not to touch him when he is eating. Once startled, the dog can only respond with his mouth and this can be a death sentence for a dog who acquires the label of having bitten a child on the face, which is at his height.

THE THIEVING GREYHOUND
This can cause great hilarity or provoke anger according to the timing of the crime! Why

Relationships can take a while to cement themselves, but they can be very rewarding. Retired racer 'Mini-Chip' is pictured in Switzerland.

Photo courtesy: Anne Finch.

do they do it? I always say it is a sport and not done out of greed or, pathetically, because they had to scrounge when abandoned! I remember preparing a turkey breast for a dinner party for diplomats. The turkey took 24 hours to marinate and prepare and, thirty minutes before my distinguished guests were due to arrive, it went missing from the kitchen work surface. Emma had it somewhere in the house. I tracked her down to the sitting room downstairs where she was busy eating it as if it was her birthday. It was dragged from her mouth and served up to my guests, slightly tidied up. It did not seem to do any harm!

Crates can be an Aladdin's cave of items gone missing from the house: screwdrivers, remote controls, keys, wallets, mother-in-law's hat etc. Remember to call on the Greyhound crate first when you embark on a search for the missing item.

THE GREYHOUND AND THE ELDERLY

A Greyhound can suit an elderly person very well. These dogs walk gently beside you and move slowly and gracefully in the home. Greyhounds consider sleeping on the sofa all day their maximum form of exercise, and as for going out in the rain....forget it! It is sad to hear an elderly person say that he or she would not dare undertake keeping a dog in case of illness, disability or having to go into a nursing home. There are elderly Greyhounds in kennels up and down the country who deserve love, warmth and comfort for their remaining years/months. Why not? They would demand very little and give so much joy to a lonely elderly person. There is a UK organisation, for example, which takes care of pets who are left behind when an owner has to go into care or dies. It is The Cinnamon Trust based in Cornwall (01736 757900). This helps to make it possible for the very elderly to keep pets; after all, they are the most perfect owners, as they can give undivided attention to their pets.

GREYHOUNDS AND THE UPWARDLY MOBILE

For working couples, a Greyhound is maybe slightly more adaptable than other breeds. Not all Greyhounds would tolerate being left, but many do because they demand so little and have been used to being left for long periods in kennels. Two Greyhounds may, in fact, be easier than one in this respect, and you will feel happier about leaving them in each other's company. We say five hours is the maximum time to be left, but I have known Greyhounds left even longer than

If you take on more than one Greyhound, they will be company for each other. These three retired racers live in Germany.

Photo courtesy: Anne Finch.

this. Obviously some provision should be made for toilet requirements. There is an excellent dog door made by an American firm which I have seen used very satisfactorily. If couples are working, they must get up early and walk the dog well before they go to work and, maybe, even feed the dog so he can rest and sleep. A neighbour popping in at lunchtime to open the door and feed your dog again would settle him nicely for an afternoon's long siesta. Daytime boarding kennels is another solution if they are fun enough and comfortable.

HOUSES OR APARTMENTS
Some rescue organisations refuse to home dogs in apartments. I do not see a problem as long as, again, the owners will be dedicated to getting up and dressed in the morning early to walk the dog before doing anything else, and to do this last thing at night too. High flights of stairs can be a problem if a dog suffers from a bad racing injury, but, on

the whole, a Greyhound will remain more agile, than, say, a Labrador in its last years. Ann Shannon, who has been homing Greyhounds since 1956, probably longer than any person today in the UK, kept six Greyhounds herself in her apartment in London. No-one could have been more dedicated. She and her family had Hampstead Heath on their doorstep. Ann, incidentally, has homed 8,500 Greyhounds in 42 years of dedicated work for Greyhounds and won an award from the National Greyhound Racing Club for her stupendous efforts.

CARING GREYHOUNDS
The occasional Greyhound has even been adopted with great success by senior citizens' residences. The elderly often miss their pets in institutions and I do observe an increased love of animals among the elderly as material and other temporal attractions fall away in favour of more lasting natural values.

A Greyhound is exactly the right height for

placing a gentle, affectionate head on the mattress of a bedridden patient or the lap of a chair-bound patient, bringing warm solace to the recipient.

YOUR OTHER PETS

Other pets in a prospective household should be discussed with the homefinder before the dog enters the door. A Greyhound homed directly from the race track at four years old will take with him his chasing background, which has been cultivated in him since he began being schooled at 14 months or so. Young puppies in Ireland are often left in the open country to chase and fend for themselves and may be given only fresh carcasses to ravage and feed on communally. On the other hand, some Greyhounds will not chase at all and are deemed failures at two years old and are ready for immediate homing. Somewhere between these two extremes fall most Greyhounds. Some can never be trusted with small furry animals, while others soon learn on what side their bread is buttered and are only too anxious, if a bit bewildered at first, to please you and learn that chasing, or doing even worse things to the family cat, are simply not good etiquette any more.

To detrain, first find your cat and have him held firmly in someone's arms. Prepare the dog first, making sure that the collar is reliable and tightly buckled just behind the ears, which is the narrowest part of the neck. Attach the lead, or even two leads if you wish, and then put the muzzle on the dog. Have ready an empty soft drink can with pebbles in it and a squirt bottle with water which is sharply cold from the refrigerator. Let him see you caress and kiss the cat. The object of the exercise is to apply shock tactics when the dog lunges at the cat. Squirt his face with the water each time he makes a lunge, shouting a loud "No!". If he is trainable, he will look at you bewildered,

thinking he has dreamed it and he may lunge again. This time, throw the rattle tin on the ground next to him to shake him out of his 'possession' and watch for those eyes of his turning away from the object of interest. When he desists from his aggressive posturing, praise him and fuss him and tell him how good he is. A 'rape' alarm can be used instead, if your eardrums can stand it. A minority of dogs will remain rigid, trembling and with a fixed stare on the cat and would probably not be distracted even by the appearance of a thunderbolt in the room. These types may need a lot of work and much care and may never be safe with a cat.

The next hurdle to overcome is to break the instinct to chase a small animal which runs away from him. You need to go into

The Greyhound has to learn to live alongside all the family pets. Photo: Steve Nash.

With supervised introductions, there are rarely problems with other dogs.

Photos: Steve Nash.

your garden for that exercise. The same principle applies. Remember too, however, that your dog may learn to cherish your own cat but next door's cat could still be fair game. Do always be sensitive to other people's pets. If other people's cats come into your garden, be very careful, especially in the early days when the cats have not learned that there is a new dog in the neighbourhood. Take your dog into your garden on a leash or put a muzzle on him. If we want to keep a high profile as Greyhound owners we must show consideration to other people's loved ones, and that may mean paying their vet bills if an accident happens. Pet insurance may help you in this respect,

Learning to live in peace with the family cat may take a little longer,
but a programme of detraining will generally achieve results.

Photos courtesy: Anne Finch.

though I gather it depends on which side of the fence the victim was. Do not forget, too, that your parrot is also vulnerable. I know of two tragedies abroad which occurred within minutes of the dogs entering the homes. On both occasions the new owners, who were devastated at the loss of their parrots, forgave their new dogs. That takes a lot of loving.

As for getting on with other dogs, there is generally not a great problem. Matching male to female reduces the possibility of fights, and homes with multiple Greyhounds are not uncommon! They are something of an addiction.

8 THE RETIRED GREYHOUND AT HOME

So you proudly place your new dog into the back of your car, all touchingly prepared, and bring him home. You will generally find no problems with Greyhounds and car travel – they love it. Some insist on standing up and, mutely, will back-seat drive, watching every minute happening through the front windscreen. I sometimes wonder if they are waiting with eager anticipation to reach the dog track for a spin, as racing dogs commonly travel by private car with their trainer on race evenings.

Do not despair, however, if there is a mess in your car after even a very short journey. Your dog may have been fed a big meal that day and the combination of motion travel and nerves might make him vomit or defecate. Please do not scold him. If you did not discover it until you finished driving, he will not connect the reason for your aggression against him with the action and he will always live in fear of unpredictable scoldings from you. This is true of all house-training.

A COLLAR AND LEAD

Some dogs are frightened of entering a front door. Be careful, since pulling on the collar may cause it to come off. Greyhounds have a habit of contracting backwards and wriggling out of their collars, so it must be tightened really cosily round the narrowest part of the

Retired racer 'Cara' from Spain, rehomed in Switzerland. The retired Greyhound will need time to settle into his new home.

Photo courtesy: Anne Finch.

neck, that is, just close behind the ears. Often, you need to punch more holes on the collar; they never seem to tighten up enough for small bitches. I always insist too that a disc, with at least a telephone number on it, is put on a travelling dog; being in transit is their most vulnerable time, because of the fear and the unfamiliar territory.

Some people prefer a martingale-type collar which tightens as the dog strains against it. Some are half-chain and half leather/nylon. You may prefer a harness which goes round the shoulders and gives good control. Some harnesses will tighten over the shoulder when a dog pulls and give you control over a boisterous, lively dog. The Halti, the narrow version, controls by tightening over the nose of the dog when he pulls. The advantage here is that you can pull the head aside away from the object of desire. Care must be taken to fix these properly. Trainers commonly loop their long leather leads back down under the chest and they hold both ends either side over the back of the dog.

The traditional leather coursing fish-shaped Greyhound collar is still widely used. The leather may seem hard at first, but softens with wear or with soaping. A 44-inch webbed cotton lead, which you can loop comfortably over your hand for good control, is about the right length for making sure your dog does not fetch any wildlife out of the hedges. The dog must always wear some sort of collar at all times, in and out of the house, with identification. I have known Greyhounds that run out of a new house at the first available unguarded moment (when a child leaves a door open, or when someone puts the milk bottles outside), so do be prepared, even if it means putting a double door or child's gate across your doorway.

HOUSE TRAINING
Your dog may be more nervous in his new situation than he appears, and this may show

The affectionate Greyhound is soon ready to give his trust.   Photo courtesy: Anne Finch.

in frequent loose stools, flatulence, even in an apparently confident dog. Be patient, and do not scold him. Never hit your dog, nor rub his nose in it. All his life he has been trained to believe that the floor is his toilet. Many dogs are meticulous and will 'hold' themselves for hours. We are amazed when we transport our dogs from Spain to northern Europe, a journey of 19 hours, that the bedding often arrives absolutely dry and clean. Dogs will not soil where they sleep if they can help it. Others get 'intestinal hurry' and a nervous bladder and cannot stop going. In the end patience, tolerance and kindness will win.

It helps if there is already another dog in the house to mimic. Importing two or three new dogs at once can have the effect of maximising the accidents and a stronger line may need to be taken to train all of them at once. One owner solved her problem of six weeks' of accidents by spraying her bitches' hind parts with cold water every time they squatted on her carpet. It worked almost immediately.

Do not be neurotic about hygiene and urine; it is, or should be, sterile. It is best to blot up the wet patch with a towel, dilute the patch with water, and carry on blotting it up. Your carpet could stain more with disinfectants than with the original problem. Faecal stains can be removed with a biological detergent solution from a ready-prepared spray bottle and again blotted up. You will understand, of course, that vigorous scolding will only make your dog more nervous and more inclined to perform inappropriately again. Watch for the circling, sniffing and crouching and speedily remove the dog outside, even if he dribbles all the way, and praise him when he performs there. If you are nervous and house-proud, in the first few hours of adopting your dog, take him outside every hour, and praise him well when he goes. Some tickling of his rear parts with grass can even stimulate emptying (you may notice how some dogs prefer long grass for this activity). It will be almost impossible to stop a male dog marking his territory when he first enters your house or any other new house. Be happy! You cannot be a dog lover and not forgive his instincts! Owners of bitches will notice that near their season they urinate more.

If a dog has been clean for a while and relapses, you might ask yourself whether the dog is upset or seeking attention in any way. Of course you will have checked out whether there is any blood in the urine, signs of straining and passing small amounts, or exceptional urinating in the night. Take a sample in a paper cup or very clean container to your vet for testing in case your dog has a urine infection.

Most Greyhounds do not present major toileting problems but occasionally we meet a stubborn one. I have known of nappies and jockstraps being used out of desperation! Some dogs drink and urinate excessively out of a sort of nervousness. This should be checked out first by a vet to eliminate diabetes mellitus or insipidus. In the absence of either, reduce the water intake sensibly to control input and output. I will not give an amount because this would vary according to the weather conditions.

STAIRS AND SLIPPERY FLOORS

Most Greyhounds have never seen stairs before, and are petrified. Again, watching another dog in the house going up and down helps. Otherwise, I have found the problem can be overcome. I force him up, then down, wrapping a towel (or a Greyhound weighing harness available from a Greyhound shop)

*Retired racer 'Duke' in Germany.
The domestic environment takes a bit of getting used to, but the Greyhound is quick to appreciate his creature comforts.*

*Photo courtesy:
Anne Finch.*

under his tummy, and move his legs one by one to show him that he can do it and there is nothing to be afraid of. He usually grasps the ascent first time. Descending often takes a couple more times. Very soon, stairs become a novelty and a good game and there is no stopping him after that.

You may not, of course, want your dog upstairs, in which case leave things as they are.

Open staircases, without carpet, are a hazard and, quite rightly, are frightening. I would not encourage negotiating these because of the possibility of panic, sliding and falling through the stairs. Carpet pads can be purchased to fit each step and then there is no problem. I must admit I have only seen these advertised in Germany but purchase can always be arranged. Encouraging him up and down an open staircase will be more difficult even with stair pads. Your dog may not love your slippery tiles or linoleum in your kitchen – but it is amazing to what lengths owners will go in order to accommodate their pets! Need I say more? One very tolerant owner simply commented, after her new dog started to eat her kitchen cupboards, "Hello dog! Goodbye house!"

For dog-visiting to residential institutions with their highly polished floors, you may need to make leather bootees, maybe even with powdered resin rubbed on the soles such as ballet dancers (not a dissimilar analogy) have on stage!

WHAT ABOUT FOOD?

If you have another dog, then you are used to a certain regime, and there is no reason why your Greyhound need not eat likewise, except in the case of rich canned food which will cause loose stools. In the racing kennels, they are fed either whole food, sometimes with an egg or broth, or often a soup of horsemeat and vegetables made in a huge boiler and eaten with brown bread. This is usually only practical for large numbers of dogs, unless you have hours to spend on your dog each day.

I have known almost every form of dog food being successfully fed to Greyhounds. But, as is common with all dogs, their intestinal systems take one to three weeks to adapt to a new food – initial diarrhoea does not necessarily mean it is unsuitable. When the tummy becomes irritated or there is diarrhoea for other reasons, then boiled rice, fish, chicken and brown bread are usually tolerated well. Milk can cause diarrhoea in some dogs but is loved by many. Tea, believe it or not, is often drunk post-racing at the tracks. They seem to prefer it to water and hence it aids rehydration.

Greyhounds are best fed in two to three smaller amounts each day rather than in one large meal at night. Be guided by the chart on the side of the packet as to how much the overall amount should be for a dog between 55-77 lbs (25 kg-35 kg). To give some idea, the amount may fill a small washing-up bowl. There are other advantages to splitting the meals into smaller amounts. Defecating is more predictable and less urgent and some food at lunchtime encourages a siesta which is useful if you must go back to work.

As for additives, I believe most good dog foods contain a balance of what your dog needs but there are one or two things which can be mentioned. Fats and oils, particularly fish oil (like a teaspoonful twice a week) of cod liver oil or a tin of sardines in oil per week, can improve the coat and encourage hair growth on bald patches. I am told also that Vitamin E capsules with linoleic acid do wonders for bald thigh syndrome. Some people swear by garlic tablets for health and parasite prevention.

If you are feeding dry food of any sort, do soak it in warm water or broth first. It does nothing for the teeth to be crunching it and it can dehydrate or, even worse, cause bloat in some circumstances. Furthermore, I have seen dogs become very thin on dry food because it is simply so unpalatable and so slow going down that long gullet.

Your dog should weigh on average between 52-61 lbs (24-28 kg) if female and between 64-77 lbs (29-35 kg) if male. The outline of the lower three ribs should just be visible and the pinbones on the back should be well covered and not protruding. It grieves me to see thin dogs always searching for food in people's pockets and bags or eating fruit, or even alcohol, out of desperation. Some owners, it seems, become blind to their dog's loss of weight. He will feel the cold and become vulnerable to illnesses. My Greyhounds have always regulated their own intake and eaten until they want no more, which has met their needs perfectly, in contrast to the Labrador who will gorge. Maybe I have just been lucky. As Greyhounds age, and I mean reach twelve years and above, they can naturally lose weight as humans do, and milk and milk substitutes like cheese and brown bread and pasta may keep up the weight.

It is customary to give an elderly dog a lower-protein diet. I am not so sure that this suits Greyhounds, however. They can become very lethargic and depressed on such a diet and perk up immediately with a higher-protein diet. On the other hand, a young, lively Greyhound may become hyperactive and destructive on a high-protein diet, and will settle and calm down when the protein content is reduced.

WHERE WILL YOUR GREYHOUND SLEEP?

It always saddens me when a new owner rings us within 24 hours of adopting a dog wanting to return it because he kept everyone up all night with his whining. I do try to prime new owners that the first three nights are the worst. The dog has been uprooted

Diet may need to be adjusted as a Greyhound grows older. *Photo: Steve Nash.*

Retired racer 'Bambi' from Spain, rehomed in England. Given a choice, the sofa will always be preferred.
Photo courtesy: Anne Finch.

from his simple secure kennel life with 70 other kennelmates, the only life he knew, and thrown into an environment called a house, with all its noisy, sophisticated gadgets and frightening obstacles and strange rules, and with creatures called humans of all different ages and sexes whom he knew only sketchily before. The equivalent must be like you or me being kidnapped and incarcerated in a family of aliens where nothing smacks of the familiar, and where every minute brings with it terrifying punishments for doing what you have been doing ever since you were born.

The easiest way of accommodating to the unfamiliar is to be allowed to observe the first 24 hours; not to be left alone and not to have to cope with anything extra than adapting to the new regime as he sees it. I am trying to say, do not swamp your new dog with too many new experiences all at once. Introduce one at a time: the three-

bedroom semi, the stairs, the vacuum cleaner, the television, the electric mixer, the kids' remote-control car, other pets, the new toilet arrangements, the new food, the "terrible two-year-old" – now do you get the picture?

Are we surprised that the Greyhound is at sixes and sevens on his first night? It is always a little better if he arrives in the morning and has a day to adjust, but this is not always possible. I find it is easier to sleep downstairs on the sofa in the same room with him the first night or two. We all get more sleep that way and we are all in a better temper the next day. After the first 24 hours he may settle completely.

IN THE BEDROOM OR NOT?
Not everyone is at ease with having dogs in the bedroom. In my experience it is comfortable and natural to do so. Wherever your dog sleeps he must have a soft, warm

bed to protect his thin skin or he will suffer from sores and bruising. Extreme examples of this are shown in the dogs rescued from the Spanish kennels where they lie on hard pallets, or on concrete, and develop large bursae (like balloons) on their elbows, and envelopes of skin containing bruising hang from their breastbones. It is all so unnecessary, as soft bedding is elementary and easily obtained. For a pet dog, you can use a double duvet folded over with covers, or a pair of settee cushions, both from second-hand markets. Changeable and washable curtaining or blankets over the top complete the bed. Best are those lovely dog beds with 2-inch thick foam walls and with a removable cover. Those beds look small to start with until one realises that, of course, the head and chin come to rest naturally on the firm walls, with eyes rolling round scanning everything without ever having to move one inch of one's body!

Your dog should have a protected place, a corner, a place under the stairs, or a crate where he can retreat, away from the hubbub of the family.

The nocturnal whining of the first three days will pass when your daily routine is known and predictable in the eyes of your dog. The more you keep to a routine, the happier your dog will be.

Some dogs are happier in a confined space, rather than being given the run of the whole house when left alone. They experience a sort of agoraphobia. Small space means safety and security and subsequent relaxation. In the wild, or when a dog is straying, he seeks a sheltered nook protected from predators, sometimes low in the ground or hidden under some sort of natural protective shield. Be sensitive to their natural instincts.

GROOMING
The physical care of a Greyhound is not onerous, and you will not have trouble

handling your dog as he will be used to this from racing days. Some Greyhound trainers groom their dogs by placing the front legs on a raised box like a plinth which enables the 'undercarriage' to be reached. Grooming is obviously enjoyable for a dog and I have heard of Greyhounds placing themselves in this position waiting for their master to oblige! I am afraid that the average dog owner would not know what was expected of him. How ignorant we are! Greyhounds have short coats which require the minimum of brushing. A hound glove, which massages as well as takes out loose hair, is ideal. It is not a fallacy that white Greyhounds moult more!

Coats vary slightly according to their colour; for example, the brindle coat is a double coat and thicker than the other colours. Although it is an advantage from the point of view of grooming work, the sparse hair and thin skin are a great disadvantage if your Greyhound becomes involved in a scrap or runs into barbed wire, for instance. They

Racing Greyhounds are used to a routine of grooming, and will rarely make a fuss about being handled. *Photo: Steve Nash.*

very easily injure themselves and need stitching, whereas a dog with a longer, thicker coat would be better protected.

BATHING

New owners will be pleased to know that Greyhounds do not have a doggy smell! Dare I say that they smell as lovely as a cat? Once-yearly bathing is all that is necessary, with a gentle puppy shampoo. Lift him into the bath on to a towel or non-slip mat and into about 5 inches (12 cms) of lukewarm water and, using a spray head, wash and rinse him well. He may sink into the warm water and really enjoy the experience. Wash his face only with water using your hands. Take care to dry him quickly and well to prevent chilling.

NAIL CARE

Nails need attention, more in some dogs than others, depending on the formation of the toes themselves and on the type of surfaces

Problems may occur if nails are allowed to grow too long. *Photo: Steve Nash.*

on which they are accustomed to walking. You will notice that some Greyhounds have toes well curled over like a cat's, which keep themselves short by virtue of being in contact with the ground. Others, on the other hand, may have toes which project forward instead of over, and the nails are inclined to grow long. Furthermore, if nails are allowed to grow very long, the foot inclines backwards away from the protruding nails, on to the heel of the foot and the problem worsens.

TEETH

Teeth should be attended to every one or two days. Your dog may well come to you with appalling brown crusted teeth – do not forget to pull the lips backwards to look at the very back teeth. If your dog is being spayed or castrated, then ask for the teeth to be cleaned under the same anaesthetic. Good dentists nowadays use ultrasonic cleaning methods which harmlessly remove the tartar with high-pressure water. Then the teeth are polished to deter tartar from forming so easily again. Using a dental tool involves the risk of removing the precious enamel and leaving a rough surface on which tartar forms too easily again. A curved toothbrush with doggy toothpaste, attending well to the back teeth, is all that is needed and your dog will accept this. Alternatively, a swab, soaked in 20 vol. hydrogen peroxide, and wound round your finger, can be used in his mouth.

Neglected teeth can have serious consequences and can, for one thing, affect the heart valves. There was a sweet dog in Mallorca called Solitario, who was blind. We exported him to Switzerland. He was found to have very bad teeth and went to the vet to have them cleaned under anaesthetic. It transpired that his jaw was also badly infected and was disintegrating. The reason for his blindness then became apparent. The severe infection had spread to his skull and had attacked the optic nerves.

EARS

Ears are not usually a serious problem with Greyhounds. Meddle as little as you have to. Do not use cotton buds enthusiastically as they are too intrusive. Better is a large pad of cotton wool (cotton) with olive oil to clean the inside of the pinna. If the discharge is black and smelly, then this may indicate the presence of mites, which would need treatment from a vet.

EXERCISE

We have already said that your dog will be easy to walk on the lead. One owner in Ireland, Sybille, was out walking with her Greyhound who started to pull uncharacteristically. She was pulling back the way she had come, also rather odd as she loved her walks. Sybille gave in out of curiosity and as they approached her house she saw why. Smoke was coming out of her kitchen window. She had left something on her stove!

Always keep your new Greyhound on a lead in the early days. Do not be lulled into complacency when, 99 per cent of the time, the lead is so slack. Your dog is a sprinter and has been taught to take off like a jet engine at the sight of a lure, so always be prepared and keep the lead firmly wound round your hand. In time, your dog will unlearn his previous schooling but, meanwhile, it is sensible to know his potential. A minimum of three walks a day will be sufficient for most ex-racers who are at least four years old, and who sometimes carry strained joints and tendons from their racing days. In time, you will be able to tune in to the amount of exercise your dog needs.

My first Greyhound used to look wistfully behind her as we approached our front door, if she felt she would have liked a longer walk that morning. Try to find an enclosed piece of even ground, like a playing field, where your dog can run out his 30 seconds of wonderful athletic display without the fear of

veering off into the blue. Greyhounds vary in their fidelity when free like this. They can go very deaf when you call them or play that awful game, catch-me-if-you-can, which makes the human in the game feel such a fool in front of amused dog walkers!

Training exercises are valuable in this instance, in particular, teaching your dog to come to you. Start by taking your partner or friend with you and have him walk a few paces away. Hold your dog and face him towards your companion. Your friend calls him and you let him go and congratulate him heartily on his arrival. Tidbits can help to encourage him. Repeat this procedure two or three times and, next day, extend the distance between you both slightly. This way your dog builds up a bond with you and learns to respond to his name and your voice, whereas before he had been schooled to respond only to a mechanical 'hare' being pulled away from him.

Do be aware that Greyhounds, with their deep chest cavities, are vulnerable to bloat (when the stomach twists and causes serious obstruction). This can happen when a large meal is given too close to vigorous exercise.

Some dogs will play with a ball, though a Greyhound's jaw is so fine and pointed that a ball can be difficult to grasp without losing it straight away. Try a softer, bigger ball, or even a tennis ball, which can be squashed and gripped. Greyhounds are not natural retrievers but some can be trained. Some Greyhounds love playing with soft toys and tossing them into the air. Do not be frightened of this! One dog whom I rescued from Spain and brought to Germany frightened the family she was with because, after six years of racing and chasing a stuffed hare in Spain, she 'killed' a toy rabbit after having been retired only two weeks. The family, tragically, euthanased her.

There is something that nearly all Greyhound owners have had to live with. We

EXERCISING YOUR GREYHOUND
Photos courtesy: Anne Finch.

LEFT: Lead exercise is a pleasure with a Greyhound. This retired racer lives in Sweden.

Two Greyhounds will help to keep each other fit. This pair live in Italy.

A Greyhound will need to maintain a good, steady pace to keep up with a bike

Exercise for all members of the family...These Greyhounds live in Belgium.

call it Mad Greyhound Disease! This consists of sudden spurts of terrific spirits and energy when your Greyhound uses your house and garden like a race track and runs at top speed round both, cutting an oval track cleverly through the garden shrubs and lawn, leaving your dedicated, hard-working gardening partner with his head in his hands. It only lasts thirty seconds or so, after which follows several hours of rejuvenating sleep!

TRAINING CLASSES

Exercise and training go closely together and help to forge the bond between you. Greyhounds do not usually sit naturally. It is a design fault! Their back thighs are so developed and hard with muscle that folding them into a sitting position looks quite uncomfortable. The length of spine of a Greyhound does not seem to correlate with the length of the front legs supporting it and the shoulders have to accommodate awkwardly. I notice that the Whippet and Spanish Greyhound (the Galgo) sit naturally and comfortably. The Galgo does not have the highly developed hind muscles which have been bred into the Irish oval track racing dog, which needs more early pace and sprinting power and less long-term stamina for its 300/400-yard runs.

Taking a Greyhound to classes helps your dog to socialise with other breeds, and teaches you, as well as your dog, about handling him to the best of your ability. Your dog will probably not be the star performer, but he will be admired by all for his quiet good manners, gentle ways and his devotion to you.

Your dog will excel in the Downstay as he is so lazy anyway and will be the last in the class to budge. He will probably not be the quickest in the class at obeying vocal commands, as he has reached adulthood without any previous training and probably without even being called by name. Do not force your dog into a Down position or you could injure his back. Rather, draw him down under a chair with a treat, and then use

The Greyhound is not a natural retriever, but old dogs can learn new tricks.

Photo courtesy: Anne Finch.

the word "Down" so he learns positively to associate the word and the position.

If there are small fluffy Poodles in your class, it would be wise to use a muzzle in the early days, until your Greyhound recognises this ball of fluff as another of his species. A slippery floor is a problem for a Greyhound. He may get used to it. I carry a mat over my shoulder for him to lie on in the Downs to protect my dog's vulnerable bony prominences from a hard floor.

Do select a teacher who is not slavishly competitive or going to make you and your dog feel terrified. Your dog will pick up your tension and be anxious too, and even go to pieces. Greyhounds are not robust in the face of a hard taskmaster and being scolded. Look happy; do not forget to smile at your dog in the class despite your own inner fear of doing something wrong or silly. Hopefully, your teacher will not take the business of Obedience too seriously. There should be plenty of lightness and laughter.

Agility classes are fun in the summer outside on the lawn; they will exercise your dog's brain and some Greyhounds succeed. Mine were hopeless, despite their reputations as athletes!

Despite not winning all the rosettes, I strongly recommend training classes. As well as official training, as a club they offer support with any other problems you might encounter in connection with being a dog owner, especially for the first time.

SWIMMING
Some Greyhounds are exercised in special warm pools at Greyhound training establishments. These build up muscles while the dog does not have to weight-bear. As therapy for recovering after injuries, swimming is superb. Greyhounds may not take to the water naturally and may need to be encouraged. There are some dog-physiotherapy pools where you can pay a

small sum to exercise your dog. Possibly even your local friendly Greyhound trainer will allow your dog to swim in his pool. Greyhounds do swim in the sea. One bitch I bought back from Spain had multiple muscular tears and hernias and a badly-healed fractured hock, but she swam in the sea in Devon and built up strong muscles which compensated for the injuries.

FIELD COURSING
This is a weekend activity, better known among owners of other sighthounds in the UK than Greyhound pet owners. In the USA it is a more popular pastime than in the UK for Greyhounds. Along with the Greyhound fraternity, owners of Whippets, Afghans, Salukis, Lurchers etc. gather together to take their turn offering their dogs to run chasing an artificial lure (usually a white plastic bag) over a set course which turns corners and zigzags over the terrain. Greyhounds can be almost too fast for these runs; the cornering can be a bit hairy and the 'lure-operator' may have difficulty keeping the lure ahead of the hound.

If you are contemplating introducing your dog to this activity, do make contact first with the huntmaster to learn the conditions, and inform him that you are new to this. Usually two dogs run competitively at the beginning of the meeting. The dogs are judged on five merits – speed, enthusiasm, follow, agility and endurance – and earn points and at the end of the meeting there is a winner. In wooded areas, it would be wise to look at the course first to make sure there are no trees which would be dangerous for your high-flying Greyhound who would be unfamiliar with the sudden turns of the lure. Also, make enquiries about where the nearest emergency vet is in the area, in case of a fracture or other serious accident. Your bitch in season would not be terribly welcomed, and remember that, during the nine weeks following a season, her ligaments are loosened as if for a pregnancy, and she is more vulnerable to injury. Hot weather is also a problem. Your dogs should not run if the temperature is higher than 80 degrees F.

Other commonsense advice is, of course, that your dog must not be fed a large meal just before or too soon after racing, nor should he be allowed to quickly drink a lot of water immediately afterwards. Wait a few moments until he has stopped panting. Remember that you are cultivating his chase instinct if you are worried about him chasing small furry creatures. Make sure your constraining collars and leads are well fastened while you are being a spectator. Your dog will go ballistic with excitement while the other dogs are running. There is no doubt that your Greyhound will love this day out.

TEMPERATURE MANAGEMENT
In the summer, be ready with pails of ice-cold water to put over him and rub into his coat (so as not to create a blanket of water over the coat) and use a wet towel over him while you are waiting for his turn at coursing. If you are carrying several dogs in a trailer, however, dry them down before placing them back in the vehicle so as not to cause a Turkish bath effect with so much heat and moisture. A paddle in a cool river or lake is a perfect way to cool your dog. It is typical of the lazy Greyhound that instead of swimming, he may choose simply to lie down in the cool water.

Cold temperatures are somewhat easier to deal with. Coats are essential, waterproof or other, of which there are many for sale in Greyhound accessory 'shops' attached to rescue groups, or in racing shops. Clever dressmakers, and knitters, both women and men, can be encouraged to make coats for retired Greyhounds in kennels and this is one of the helpful contributions that carers can make to rescue groups who have numbers of Greyhounds waiting in kennels for homes. It is extremely difficult, almost impossible on our tiny budgets, to keep such establishments warm, and the dogs, when confined in cold weather, are not able to run around and keep warm. Look at the way a professional coat is made and copy it. It is important that the ties are long and can be secured under and over the abdomen, otherwise the dog loses his coat or gets in a tangle, somehow getting his leg through the neck hole, and immobilising himself!

THERAPY DOGS
I list this under activities because it constitutes one useful function of the Greyhound which has proved very successful. The Greyhound is tall, a good height for beds and wheelchairs, placid, rarely barks, has sad, soulful eyes and craves affection. I even feel the Greyhound has a special affinity with the suffering, the confined, and the abandoned. If a Greyhound can bring solace and comfort to just one disadvantaged human, then all is worthwhile. The dog should qualify by being able to respond to his name and calls for attention, and by being placid and patient. These are commonplace qualities of a Greyhound. The elderly, the disabled, the disadvantaged child and the confined look forward to these visits, and the warm, velvety, generous head and ears of a Greyhound with his placid, loving temperament, provide a wonderful source of solace.

GREYHOUND LANGUAGE
Owners and lovers of Greyhounds get to know the characteristics of the breed and it is touching and amusing to read of the same responses from our Greyhound friends from all over the world. There is the grin – not to be confused or misunderstood – when the lips are curled upwards and the teeth are

The Greyhound owner learns to understand every nuance of his dog's behaviour. This is retired racer 'Sheeba'.　　　　　　　　　　　*Photo: Sally Anne Thompson; courtesy: Anne Finch.*

bared! It really is a smile and brings delight to those who witness it.

Then there is the bow when the elbows rest on the ground and the rear is in the air. This can be combined with pounding of the front feet when anticipating something pleasurable. Greyhounds seem to know this is attractive and use it accordingly to stir up admiration. Other signals like yawning, licking, and sniffing are calming signals when your dog is trying to tell another dog, with these distracting gestures, that he is not interested in attacking.

Although Greyhounds are not great barkers – some never bark at all – there are other characteristic sounds which they make, like the long groan of satisfaction when your dog settles into a comfortable bed; the quick snaps of the teeth, often coupled with the bow, when excited; and the amazing singing which Greyhounds indulge in when a group of them are together.

I am told that it is the alpha dog who starts the chorus, raising his head into the air and letting out a loud wail when all the others join in. They end abruptly and, curiously, all at the same moment, followed by absolute silence. How they achieve this, without a maestro, I do not know. It signifies contentment and solidarity.

9 SOLVING PROBLEMS

I hesitate about having a chapter under this heading but we must be realistic, and there are times when some humans and some dogs are not wholly compatible, through no fault of their own. Everyone knows that psychological trauma affects behaviour. This is very true about the dog, who is extraordinarily sensitive, being conditioned by experience. Remember Pavlov's dogs?

I do believe, too, that there is genetic influence in the personality and behaviour of dogs, in spite of the fact that Greyhounds are possibly the most soundly bred dogs of all pedigrees. Their breeding must, of necessity, be public on race-cards, and is governed not by colour or physique, but by performance on the track. I mean by this that closely related parents cannot interbreed and be accepted by the racing club. The breeding of our adoptees is superb and can be depended upon. It is extremely rare that we, as homefinders, have a severe personality problem to deal with. This is why we can do so much of our homing by phone. We can almost guarantee 100 per cent the good personality of our adoptees, without even meeting them.

Not so easy are our human adopters. I wonder sometimes how children survive their intolerant, impatient, uncompassionate parents! Conversely, I have met the most

Patience when overcoming problems is generally rewarded with many years of fulfilling companionship.   Photo courtesy: Anne Finch.

wondrous love, patience and understanding from humans towards their dogs, and these people become our allies and friends in love and compassion for all animals. Always, their patience is rewarded by the many years of devotion from their damaged adoptees who need them so much.

A dog bestows his heart on anyone who accepts him, and to be rejected causes behavioural problems for subsequent adopters who cannot understand why the dog fears so much and claims so much from them in terms of reassurance and reinforcement. It does not take much in the way of basic psychology to understand why a creature who fears abandonment exhibits stress symptoms in his own canine way.

STRESS SYMPTOMS

So what are these symptoms? Destructive behaviour and panic in their dogs when they have been left for a short time, and inappropriate toileting, are the two main symptoms of stress. You or I might experience such panic and terror if we were deposited on a deserted island or extra-terrestrial situation. We may or may not be able to cope, according to our learned maturity, but a creature with a brain equivalent perhaps to that of a child of subnormal intelligence, is simply not equipped to apply reason to overcome such great fear, which brings pain with every minute. I have known owners who have coped with the most horrendous displays of antisocial behaviour and have overcome them with patience, skill and understanding. There are professional animal behaviourists nowadays who can give sound advice. We are the lords of the domain. May we understand, guard, and cherish those over whom we have dominance, and exercise our privileged brains to this end. So let us come to behavioural problems.

PROBLEMS OF ATTACHMENT

Dogs who destroy when the owner leaves the house usually commit their worst crimes within the first five minutes of their owner's departure. The curtains are torn down, doors are gnawed and toileting becomes haphazard. The dog can actually do harm to himself in this massive frenzy. So, what do we do about it? Strangely enough, the answer lies in minimising the amount of fuss made on your departure. In fact, ignore your dog, making no eye contact for thirty minutes before you leave, so the dog gets fed up with you and is pleased to see you go! Then, on your return, be cool and calm and do not greet your dog rapturously so that he does not start to anticipate your homecoming. Do not be angry with any damage done. He has not done this out of spite. If you scold him he will get worse, fearing your return which precedes random punishments. Your dog lives in the present and cannot associate your responses with events which are even minutes old.

Retired racer 'Emma'.
Photo courtesy: Anne Finch.

Crating your dog, or confining him in a small area, both reduce the potential for damage and give security to your dog. You can start by closing the crate door and, when the dog becomes used to his comfortable and comforting crate, you can leave it open and he will enter it voluntarily. Americans are more used to crating than the British. I see both aspects of it. I love to see dogs in freedom lounging on sofas, but this is sometimes not what your dog needs for comfort just yet if he is timid or unsure of himself.

One rescue kennel advises the following; that for the first 72 hours after initial adoption, you do not bond closely with your dog, but mainly leave him alone to settle and observe you, without being allowed to cling and follow you everywhere. I would draw the line at leaving him the whole night and would probably encourage sleeping in the same room, so that the stress does not spiral into a state from which there is no return.

Desensitize your dog gradually to your absence. Casually leave the room and go to another, closing the door. Make mock departures from your house, picking up your keys, putting on your coat and walking down the path and even starting up the car, and then coming back, keeping it all below his fear threshold so the dog does not lose control. Your neighbours will start talking,

but do not worry, they will be grateful for a silent dog next door! When you go, leave your dog exercised, fed, warm and comfortable with the radio or television on quietly, and unwashed clothes in his basket. Incidentally, do remember to coat up your dog in winter if you leave your heating off at night or when you are out.

THE TIMID DOG

We all know the timid dog who tries to flatten himself into imaginary obscurity against the kennel wall. In Spain we were asked to pick up 39 unwanted, Greyhound adults and pups whom we found in a breeder's yard. They were exceptionally beautiful, fine specimens, but I have never seen such a bunch of terrified, wild, uncontrollable dogs. We had to catch each one with a loop, tranquillize them, then vaccinate each one before putting them into our vans. Goodness knows what they had seen or suffered to make them behave like that. One bitch had a distinct scar round her neck as if she had been hanged. They lived in our refuge in piles of tens or so, burying their faces in each others' bodies. We have brought some to Europe and into quarantine. Those in homes are making very slow progress but I feel it will be a year before we see a significant difference. One family in Holland who adopted one of these dogs made the

Retired racer 'Timmy'. Photo courtesy: Anne Finch.

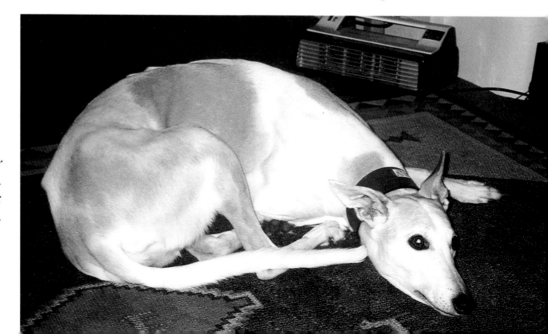

comment that their dog allowed their children to leap all over her but she hid again when adults came into the room. A timid dog may not feed or defecate in front of you. Animals are at risk from prey at both activities, hence their hesitance. Leave his food bowl accessible at nights. You will probably find it clean in the morning. If your dog is frightened of men, ask your husband always to prepare and give the food to your dog and take him for walks.

One timid dog I know went into a classical depression a few weeks after being adopted. Fortunately, the mother in the family recognised it and realised it was because of her children. I do not know if the children were noisy or whether they tormented the dog, but I doubt it. This poor dog simply could not cope with young children. I remember her drooling with terror in the car when we met her to rehome her. In the new adults-only home she was a changed dog and regained her peace and happiness.

When dealing with a timid dog, do not be tempted to fuel his terror by fussing him too much and thereby making him feel that something is wrong after all. Be cheerful, bold, confident and firm and pretend to treat him casually without eye contact at first. Smile frequently and do not transmit your concern to him. I still believe in giving a timid dog a firm hug despite his fear of such contact. Then he learns that he does not actually come to any harm and that it is actually quite nice. For a timid female dog, a male companion dog can do wonders and vice versa. Offering cubes of cheese or cooked liver can entice the dog nearer you if the dog has not already eaten.

When walking out with a timid dog, do not expose him to more than one mental obstacle at a time. Make sure the collar and lead are very snugly fastened. If he is fearful of loud traffic noises, avoid them for months, or however long it takes him to gain confidence, and not be affected by it. If he is afraid of other people, then introduce him to a friend first who will offer bits of food, but will not stare at him and will smile and be unaffected by his terror.

EXCESSIVE BARKING

Another behavioural problem is excessive barking, especially early in the morning. I cannot believe that there is no reason for this. Is it hunger, the need to relieve himself, the need for company, or is he cold and uncomfortable, or is he in pain? Barking is not common in a Greyhound. It can become a habit. This needs to be broken immediately by a change in routine. Positive training means that you do not go to him when he is barking, only when he is silent. You can try banging on his door but not entering when

Retired racer 'Malicia', rehomed in Germany. Photo courtesy: Anne Finch.

he is barking. Go in and fuss him when he is quiet. Company is what he needs. I cannot help feeling that this is the wrong way round of dealing with the problem, but families may have their reasons for excluding the dog from their bedroom or living rooms when the dog needs them most after a long night alone. The company of another dog, especially of the opposite sex, sterilised of course, also helps to give security and a distraction from isolation.

INAPPROPRIATE TOILET BEHAVIOUR
We have already covered the routine questions about house training. There is the dog who walks around with his owner for an hour, then comes indoors and relieves himself inside. Why? Is it due to a need for security, as squatting makes the dog vulnerable as prey? Is it that concrete pavements are not conducive to toileting? Does the dog need more time to sniff? Try exercising your dog (gently walking him) after a meal. Say "Busy, busy" and take him to an area of tall grass and say "Get busy" or whatever your favourite word is going to be. Concrete does not always appeal. Too much freedom can slow up a dog's house training. A constant open door gives no guidance for toileting.

Relapses in house training often reflect some change or imminent change in routine. I was not surprised when one young couple rang to ask me to find another home for their dog, whom they had had for a year but could not keep because a new baby was due and the dog had become too big. Surprise, surprise, he started urinating on the carpet.

One phenomenon is that new adopters who take on a 'problem' dog find no problem whatever, when previous owners despaired of inappropriate toileting. Dogs sometimes have devious minds. When they are happy they behave! When they are not so sure (hours left alone, noisy children, not enough exercise) they may not behave. It is a dangerous philosophy on the part of the dog, but dogs are not university material! But your dog will know your name, and the names of members of your family, and will understand much of your daily routine, in some ways, better than you do. Have respect for your dog. Respect cultivates good, responsible behaviour on the part of the dog.

COPING WITH AGGRESSION
There is aggression towards other dogs and aggression towards humans. As we have already said, Greyhounds are one of the least aggressive of dog breeds. Some people say they make good watchdogs; they will watch burglars take your TV, video, microwave, three-piece suite – and they might only yawn.

The type of aggression which you may find is associated with attachment problems, jealousy and the canine hierarchy.

I have handled literally thousands of Greyhounds and been bitten only once, and that was really hardly more than being mouthed by an absolutely terrified, abandoned bitch in Spain whom we were trying to lift up forcibly and put in a car. It is true to say I have only seen a Greyhound bite out of fear, not aggression.

Growling may occur, especially in male dogs and, again, uncastrated dogs. Castration curbs some macho instincts, but is not always successful if the dog is of mature years, say seven or upwards. I would say, however, that it is always worth trying if a dog exhibits unsocial dominant characteristics like growling when you sit on 'his' sofa or bed (even though it was yours!) or growling at strangers who visit. Remember that the hormonal changes after castration do not become fully complete for eight weeks and that, in some rare instances, a male dog may become very disturbed immediately after castration. Be patient. His emotional reactions are not entirely under his control until the hormones have settled.

Males together can cause problems of jockeying for position in the hierarchy. Unless the confrontation is serious, it is probably best to let them sort this out themselves without interfering because, once the pecking order is established, the dogs will adhere to this and the 'pack' will be at peace. If you have more than two dogs or bitches, observe who is the alpha ('top') dog and who is at the bottom (the omega). The worst bites I have received were when I went to the aid of a timid Greyhound called Harry, an omega, who was being tormented by the rest of the pack in the refuge in Spain. As I led him to the safety of a pen, a dominant Husky bit my right hand and then an hour later entered the pen and attacked the other hand! I doubt if a dominant Greyhound would be so demonstrative, but it illustrates a point.

The moral is that we humans should collude with the pecking order; for example you should feed and attend to your dominant dog first and he should have the preferential place of sleeping, which in canine terms is high up on a bed or sofa. Because of our tradition of democracy, such inequality of treatment goes against the grain, but our superior intelligence should teach us to manage our canine companions sensitively and with understanding. Furthermore, your alpha dog should be mastered by you, or there will be trouble in store. Again, the problem will be with males, especially if you are a doting female! This means insisting that your pooch obeys you and does not get privileges unless you grant them, not the other way round.

Bitches are another story. When bitches fight each other it can be to the death and this time I *am* talking about Greyhounds. Every Greyhound trainer will have an horrific story of a bitch attacking another bitch. The problem is, usually, that an omega bitch is in season, causing rivalry from an alpha vying for attention from the males. Even without the presence of a male, the bitches may fight.

If a fight breaks out, you risk getting badly bitten by trying to separate them with your hands. Try sounding a loud noise like a rape alarm, or throw over a blanket or bucket of water, use a CO_2 fire extinguisher or force them apart with a board.

Some owners notice that their dogs get on with other Greyhounds but not with other breeds. If your dog is inclined to be snappy when approached by other dogs who may be off the lead, then it may be necessary to muzzle your dog, even if he is on the lead, to prevent confrontation, and it would be wise to avoid busy parks where many dogs are running free. One way to train your dog to accept other breeds is to take him to Obedience classes where he will encounter all types of dogs and will be disciplined.

To minimise problems then, spay and castrate your dogs. If this is not possible,

Retired racer 'Wanda'.
Photo courtesy: Anne Finch.

then separate a bitch in season from the others when you are out of the house. Devalue beds, toys, food bowls, etc. by providing them in multiples so there is no squabbling over a trophy. Be careful about leaving an old or infirm dog with a 'pack' because, tragically, the stronger dogs have been known to turn on and kill a weaker member as they might do in the wild.

As pet owners we may never in a lifetime experience such tragedies. It is wise and incumbent on us, however, to learn as much as we can of the minds and instincts of our charges, as responsible, respectful carers.

BEING SOCIALLY ACCEPTABLE

Clearing up after your dog is very important for you, your dog and the public image of both. To run free in your garden, if it is absolutely secure, is obviously best and most dog owners do not mind cleaning up the mess afterwards. If you have a manhole in your garden, this can be a neat way of disposing of droppings, having used paper to

Retired racer 'Nelson', rehomed in Switzerland. Photo courtesy: Anne Finch.

collect it up. Alternatively, a plastic bag turned inside out over your hand is an easy quick way to pick it up, tying a knot in the bag and disposing of it in the dustbin. I have not found dog loos at all successful. It is the responsibility of every dog owner to clear up after his dog. Coprophagia, eating faeces, is a habit learned from the past and can really only be overcome (once food nutrition has been examined and found to be satisfactory) by picking up the droppings quickly.

COPING WITH DISABILITY

A Greyhound can live until 16 years old. Unfortunately, many do seem to succumb to bone cancer, in particular, much earlier than that. I wonder if their large bone mass, and the frequent knocks they receive while racing, do contribute to this tendency. Bone cancer is very painful, as is prostate cancer, and mood changes in your dog and unusual behaviour may indicate underlying pain. All of us at some time have seen a Greyhound amputee. Most commonly, amputation may follow a bad injury and/or osteomyelitis. It barely seems worthwhile for cancer, when there is a strong chance that it has already spread.

The Spanish animal welfare organisation with whom we work rescued a beautiful fawn Greyhound who has only 2 legs. This was the result of her hunting owner trying to kill her by shooting her and bungling it. Her skin is still full of lead shot. She lived for six months in the street in Cuenco, Spain, and even had a litter of puppies. Amazingly, she is a happy girl and accepts her disability as if it were normal for her. She was pregnant again when she was rescued and delivered another litter. It would be inconceivable to ever consider euthanasia because of the strength of her personality. She can jump up on to the sofa, and she adores her food, which she eats lying down. She could run in the paddock with the others! She has now gone to a home in Belgium where she was desperately wanted.

Retired racer 'Stevie', rehomed in the USA.

Photo courtesy: Anne Finch.

I was handed a blind Greyhound to take to a pro-dog demonstration recently and was amazed how courageously this dog coped with what must have been a terrifying experience, with loudspeakers, several hundred people and their dogs – and a brass band! He was aware of the second dog we brought, a Greyhound bitch, and I kept them close together by my knees, but what a wonderfully brave little dog! Maybe blindness in a dog, with his amazingly enhanced sense of smell, is not so disabling as in a human.

I heard of another blind dog who successfully attended Obedience classes and even managed to chase chickens!

Other disabilities include deafness which can creep up unawares in later years. It is one thing to look out for if your dog changes in behaviour, especially when left alone, and he suddenly becomes agitated and needing reassurance.

Epilepsy is not uncommon with any breed of dog. It may have been present before adoption but not observed in kennels because it commonly happens on going to sleep or waking. It is more frightening for the owners. The dog only 'blacks out'. Remove all objects which can harm him during a seizure. Do not touch him. Remove all stimuli by darkening the room and let him sleep afterwards. His behaviour following a

Retired racer 'Jo'.
Photo courtesy:
Anne Finch.

seizure can be strange. It is not entirely under his control. Do not fuss him or give the impression you are anxious or he may think something is wrong and go into another seizure. These episodes can be cyclical and may be anticipated. If so, and if they are not frequent, then it may not be best to medicate. Greyhounds in particular are oversensitive to the medication and may suffer some side-effects and these have to be weighed against the benefits.

UNHOMEABLE GREYHOUNDS

Some dogs who are aggressive with other breeds, or simply too timid for domestic life, or have continence problems, may be happier staying in the kennels with which they are familiar, with their mates of many years. There are some rescue associations who keep kennels for difficult dogs and they receive plenty of love, attention and comfort. Some people who would be otherwise unable to keep a dog at home due to their work hours or accommodation may be pleased to 'adopt' a dog in kennels and take him for walks at the weekend and might even pay for his keep and veterinary care. This is true charity work.

THE LAST YEARS

If your Greyhound has raced a fair amount, then arthritis in the mature years can be a problem. There are anti-inflammatory medicines which can help this condition, and keeping your dog warm and dry will make a lot of difference. Obviously a soft bed and warmth at night are essential, as they would be for us with our aches and pains. Observe your dog well when exercising and do not let him strain joints and muscles even further. Gentle mobility is enough when arthritis sets in.

Some people swear by special collars which give magnetic therapy to the dog. These alter the viscosity of fluids and facilitate flow. Greyhounds tend to get thinner in their old age. They retain some measure of agility, rather more so than other heavier breeds such as a Labrador.

Senility is not unknown in dogs, as in humans, in the latter years. It may show as unusual aggression or phobias like a new fear of thunderstorms or of being left alone. There are new medications which can be tried in these instances, as these problems have been of particular interest to the

Retired racer 'Tania' from Spain, rehomed in Germany.

Photo courtesy: Anne Finch.

Retired racer 'Dea'.
Photo courtesy: Anne Finch.

questions. Does he still enjoy his food? Is he continent and still able to retain his dignity in keeping clean? Does he still enjoy going out? Does he sleep at night or does he appear to be kept awake by pain? Talk it over with a friend who understands dogs and who can see things perhaps more objectively than you. Your vet may be your best adviser. My experience has been that most vets handle such situations with the utmost sensitivity and good judgement.

When the time comes for making the decision, think carefully about how you would like it to be done and talk to your vet first. We tend to rush such unpleasant tasks and then regret later that we did not do it with more thought. I feel it is kinder for the vet to come to your house and that your dog slips away in his own basket without the fear and terror of going to the surgery. This is not always possible, so try to arrange a time outside surgery hours when you do not have to face coming back into a waiting room full of people, though some clinics have a side door. If you are there to hold him in your arms, and you smile and speak reassuringly and happily, then he will not fear what you are fearing.

If children are involved, let them say goodbye to your pet and afterwards help them in their grief by having a little memorial service in the garden with a monument of some kind. They can create an album of the life of their pet in photos to occupy their minds and help them come to terms with the loss of a playmate.

It will be harder however for you. Remember that a dog's life is shorter than ours and we must experience maybe several losses in our lifetime. There is some moderation of suffering when there are multiples of dogs. The pain of the loss of one sole companion can be almost unbearable. If after several weeks you are still suffering, then do consult your doctor who may be

veterinary world of late. Always check your dog with your vet for hidden pain like toothache, earache or prostate pain. Brain tumours are not unknown and can cause a change in the personality.

If another pet dies, or even if a human member of the family departs, your Greyhound may grieve as you do and may show signs of depression and loss of interest in food and walks etc. The passage of time, anti-depressant medication or the procuring of another companion for him may help. It has even been known that a new household gadget can provoke discomfort, like an overhead fan, a noisy kitchen appliance or the arrival of a loud stereo system!

When the last days come, it is always hard to know when to make the right decision to euthanase, relieving the dog of pain and misery at his end. Infirmity and old age creep up on our dogs and we forget that they have not wagged their tail for a long time, nor enjoyed going out. Ask yourself these more understanding than you think.

Owners inevitably find happiness in a new dog, but not everyone can cope with this straight away. I personally see the gap as an opportunity to offer another needy dog a loving home and we should demonstrate, to those whom we hope will adopt for the first time, that a Greyhound is worth adopting for the second time.

There are many advantages in keeping a pet and it is said that our health, both mental and physical, improves. Dogs keep us fit, lower our blood pressure, fulfil our caring instincts, give us laughter, encourage comradeship with those who share the same hobby, and, I believe, genuinely improve the quality of our lives.

The following was quoted by Americans who lost a dearly-loved bitch from Mallorca whom they generously took to their hearts from us when they were in Germany serving in the military.

"We who choose to surround ourselves
with lives even more
temporary than our own
live within a fragile circle,
easily and often breached.
Unable to accept its awful gaps,
we still would live no other way."
        Irving Townsend

Retired racer 'Judy'.
Photo: Steve Nash.

PART IV
THE SHOW GREYHOUND

10 *ANALYSIS OF THE BREED STANDARDS*

Breed Standards are our most important tools in understanding any breed in depth; they are often referred to as the blueprint of the breed. Standards, like most things, are not perfect. They can be good, bad and indifferent. You can agree with them or not, but nevertheless, they provide the all-important rules of the game, a common platform which breeders, exhibitors and judges alike can use to assess the merit of the dogs. As with any set of rules, the Standards should not be changed frequently, and only when, or if, it is truly necessary.

It is extremely difficult to paint a word picture of something which is not only as beautiful, but also as complex as a Greyhound. The word pictures that we refer to as Breed Standards will be interpreted differently by different readers, and without a basic knowledge of anatomy, movement and dog terminology, the Standards mean very little. Neither does the text itself spell out with any exactness the priorities among all those important traits that make up a dog. It takes a great deal of experience and knowledge to interpret the Breed Standards correctly.

Fortunately we have available a couple of important tools to assist us in interpreting the Standards: the breed's function on one hand and the breed's history and tradition on the other. In other words, the Standards

should be studied and understood in the light of function and history. Extensive knowledge of both will help us to decipher the true meaning of the Standards; without such knowledge the Standards are more or less just meaningless collections of words.

The Greyhound has, through many centuries, been an incredibly efficient hunter; the breed's very *raison d'être* is the live coursing of hares and other game. Please observe that throughout this discussion the word 'hare' will be used as being synonymous with game, while fully realising that Greyhounds also have been used to hunt and course several other species, including rabbits, as well as gazelles and other large game.

It would be foolish to overlook the reason for the breed's existence in the first place, as much can be learned from studying the breed performing its proper work. Other and more recent activities of the breed, in the show ring or at the racing track, can be considered merely secondary or corrupted functions.

Throughout the centuries more or less detailed descriptions of the ideal Greyhound have appeared, the most famous of which are probably the ones attributed to Flavius Arrianus (1st century AD) and Dame Juliana Berners (late 15th century). However, it was not until after the advent of the first recorded British dog show (in Newcastle-on-Tyne in

Norw. Swed. Ch. Moyem's Chara Chanel: The breed's original function as a hunter must lie at the heart of the Breed Standard.   *Photo courtesy: Espen Engh.*

1859) that the need for Breed Standards as we know them was recognised. One of the judges at that very first dog show was Dr John Henry Walsh, better known under the pseudonym of Stonehenge. Stonehenge was not only the father of the concept of dog Standards as we now know them, but was particularly interested in and knowledgeable about Greyhounds. His books *Dogs of the British Islands* and *The Greyhound* have been much studied and admired, and they both ran into several editions. In his works Stonehenge included "the points of the breed" for Greyhounds. Many of these points are still considered valid, and several of his phrases are still found in the current Standards of the breed, but much more so in the American than in the English Standard.

Perhaps unfortunately, the "points" differ noticeably from book to book and edition to edition as Stonehenge's own experience increased.

Greyhounds are judged by the Kennel Club (London) Standard in almost all countries of the world, including Great Britain, Australia and all the countries of the Fédération Cynologique International (FCI). This Standard is referred to as the KC Standard in the following analysis of the Breed Standards. In the USA and Canada, Greyhounds are judged by another Standard, referred to as the AKC Standard below.

THE ORIGIN OF THE AMERICAN STANDARD
The current AKC Standard is in essence a

Am. Ch. Aroi Talk Of The Blues: The top winning Greyhound of all time in the US.
Photo courtesy: Espen Engh.

highly condensed and refined version of the points of the breed put forward in different works by Stonehenge. A similar, but not identical, text to the American Standard was published as early as 1912 in Leighton's *The Complete Book of the Dog*.

The Greyhound Club of America was founded in 1907 and admitted as a member club to the American Kennel Club in 1909.

The current Standard has its roots back in the early days of the club and has remained virtually unchanged ever since, the only exception being that the reference to the back being well arched has been replaced by the more appropriate well arched loin. The old, outdated phrase remains in the Canadian Standard, which is otherwise identical to the American.

The American Breed Standard is the property of the GCA, and it is entirely up to the members of the breed club to decide on the contents of the Standard. The Greyhound Standard is one among only four Breed Standards never to have been formally approved by the American Kennel Club, but it is, nevertheless, used as the yardstick against which Greyhounds are judged in the US.

THE ORIGIN OF THE BRITISH STANDARD

The current British Standard is of much more recent origin than its American counterpart. Prior to the Second World War, several Greyhound Standards were in existence. This caused considerable confusion; indeed, a leading breed authority, Edward A. Ash, wrote in Hutchinson's *Dog Encyclopaedia* (mid-1930s), that "attempts have been made to describe the perfect Greyhound as other breeds are described, but these attempts have not helped matters at all".

One of the principal tasks of The Greyhound Club after its formation in 1946 was therefore to set up a Standard for the breed. The process leading up to the present British Standard has never before been published in any detail, but has been made available by courtesy of Mrs Daphne Gilpin, past secretary of The Greyhound Club.

According to the minutes of the meeting to form the club on September 18th, 1946, it was decided that "the question of a Standard of points be left to a later date".

UK Ch. Ballalyns Foggy At Mistweave.
Photo: Steph Holbrook.

The meeting elected Mr A.H. Opie (prefix Trevarth) as president and chairman and Mr B. Stevens (Barnaloft) as secretary of the club. Mr Opie had been a noted Greyhound breeder before the Second World War; he was also among the most experienced judges of his time. It was left to him to draw up a suggested Standard for the breed.

Then, from a meeting on March 26th 1947, the minutes read: "Standard of Greyhounds – Mr Opie then read his idea of what the Standard of Greyhounds should be, with which the meeting were more or less agreed. An interesting discussion on the maximum and minimum heights and sizes for the breed then took place, and it was agreed that the ideal height was 29 ins for dogs and 27 ins for bitches." Among those present at the meeting were leading breeders such as Mr Opie, Mr Stevens, Mr J. Prowse (Carnlanga), Mr W.J. Searle (Venton), Mr W.R. Bennetto (Canfield) and Mr W.J. Hodge (Treleigh).

At the next meeting on May 27th, 1947, "Mr Opie read his definition of the Standard of the show Greyhound. All points were agreed on, with the exception of height, which caused a spirited discussion."

From another meeting on August 19th, 1947, which was additionally attended by further authorities such as Mr P. George (Parcancady) and Mr A.G. Boggia (Boughton) the minutes read: "Completion of Standard of Points – Mr Opie read his suggested Standard for Greyhounds which was agreed upon at the last meeting, with the exception of one point, namely the height. After a lengthy discussion it was proposed, and carried unanimously, that the ideal height for dogs should be 28 ins to 30 ins and bitches 27 ins to 28 ins. Mr Boggia suggested that certain words be inserted in the original Standard composed by Mr Opie, and then copies be sent to all members."

According to the minutes of a committee meeting of the Greyhound Club on July 19th, 1948, "the secretary reported receipt of a letter from the KC enclosing their proposed Standard for Greyhounds, and requesting the opinion of the Club on it. This Standard was then compared item by item with that of our Club, and it was generally agreed that we retain ours with a few alterations. A sub committee comprising Mr Opie, Mr Stevens and Mr Prowse Jun, was formed to deal with further correspondence etc. on the Standard." A compromise must obviously have been reached in the shape of the KC Standard published in the 1951 edition of Croxton Smith's *The Complete Book of Sporting Dogs*.

With the exception of a later addition of characteristics, this Standard remained unchanged for more than three decades. Then, in 1982, the KC sent a notice that it wanted the Greyhound Club Committee to go over the Standard with a view to making it more concise and requested the addition of a temperament clause. In the name of standardisation, all the British Breed Standards were reformatted, leaving out most of the verbs. Unfortunately, the Greyhound Standard was one of many Standards which suffered from this. Although basically unaltered in content, the resulting telegram style does nothing to enhance the readability, and important links between the description and the reason for the requirements of the Standard were more or less lost in some instances.

With its reply, the Greyhound Club submitted to the KC under the heading 'temperament': "intelligent, gentle, affectionate and even-tempered", which was accepted. The committee also unanimously decided to ask for a change in the description of the eyes, which was only partly accepted by the KC. As a consequence, the eye colour is no longer "dark", but "preferably dark". The resulting current Standard was approved and published in 1986. In a couple of instances I have made references to the pre-1986 Standard where this helps in clarifying points.

GENERAL APPEARANCE

KC: **Strongly built, upstanding, of generous proportions, muscular power and symmetrical formation, with long head and neck, clean well laid shoulders, deep chest, capacious body, arched loin, powerful quarters, sound legs and feet, and a suppleness of limb, which emphasise in a marked degree its distinctive type and quality.**

The Greyhound is a breed with relatively few breed-specific traits. As opposed to some other breeds of dogs, notably Toy breeds, Greyhounds are not much about details at all. On the contrary, Greyhound breeders should rather strive for the optimal general appearance both standing and moving, and judges should, above all else, strive to recognise and reward this. The general appearance, much more than anything else, is what defines type in Greyhounds, and thus the overall impression is paramount. Consequently, much of this discussion on the Standards will focus on this all-important general appearance, a description of which is, strangely, not included in the American Standard.

As can be deduced from the introduction to this chapter, the British Greyhound Standard was written by experts on the breed for the connoisseurs of the breed, not by amateurs for amateurs. Quite a few things go without saying, the word Greyhound itself being a household name for every person on the British Islands, although not always so for people from other nations. To an Englishman, the word Greyhound instantly

Assessing show potential: This is Ch. Jet's Mrs Dalloway, pictured at eight weeks.
Photo courtesy: Espen Engh.

Am. Ch Gallant Late Arrival pictured at six months.
Photo courtesy: Espen Engh.

The family line: Int. Nord. Ch. Gulds Choice Cimone with her son, Int. Nord. Ch. Jet's White Christmas. *Photo courtesy: Espen Engh.*

brings about an image of a fast, long-legged, long-necked and elegant dog. That a Greyhound should possess elegance is taken for granted, and has not even been deemed necessary for inclusion in the description of the general appearance. The word elegant, when describing a Greyhound, should not at all equate with weedy or delicate, but elegance should be stemming from the flow of the lines, the length of neck, the beauty of the formation and the definition of the muscles, as well as from the quality of the skin and coat. The sum of these traits is a high degree of thoroughbred quality, where nothing at all has been left to coincidence.

Elegance is of great importance, but equally the Greyhound is a strong dog with good bone and ample body, never to appear too refined, weedy or weak. Strength and power are important qualities to look for in a stud dog and equally so in a good brood bitch, even though the bitch should, of course, be a feminine version.

One of the main challenges of breeding

Greyhounds is to obtain that exquisite balance between strength and power on the one hand and elegance and quality on the other. The Standard of a closely related breed, the Whippet, beautifully describes the general appearance as a balanced combination of muscular power and strength with elegance and grace of outline. This could just as well have been a description of a Greyhound. An overly big and strong, chunky or clumsy dog would not be able to hunt hares, nor would an overly refined, delicate dog be able to do a day's work. Both these extremes are relatively easy to breed; combining the strength with the quality and elegance takes much more skill.

Judy de Casembroot, the breeder of the famous Treetops Greyhounds, used to give the following advice: if you look into the ring and the strongest dog and the most beautiful dog is one and the same, that is more than likely the best Greyhound. In her clever way, Mrs de Casembroot was stressing

Int. Am. Mex. World Ch. Gerico's Chasing The Wind: Top Greyhound 1996-1999.

Photo courtesy: Espen Engh.

the importance of the combination of strength and quality above everything else.

The Greyhound should be an upstanding dog of generous proportions, meaning that the breeder should strive for a dog with good length of leg but, at the same time, a dog built on long and flowing lines, covering plenty of ground. This is another difficult balance to achieve, but such a joy to behold when present. It is relatively easy to breed a high-stationed, long-legged, but short-coupled dog without the required depth and length. Unfortunately there are, and have always been, plenty of these dogs in the show ring. Much too often they have been richly rewarded, frequently not being recognised as the caricature of the breed which they truly are. At the opposite end of the scale, a long and low-stationed Greyhound is certainly not to be encouraged either and is, again, easy to breed, although not quite as common. The goal of the breeders should be to achieve that ideal balance of being up on legs and covering plenty of ground at the same time. Again,

this is a most essential part of breed type.

Additionally implied by the term upstanding is a proud dog with regal bearing. A Greyhound should be a king of dogs, demanding attention, and never merely a commoner.

The reference to musculature is repeated several times both in the British and the American Standards. Perhaps needless to say, correct musculature is crucial in creating a functional dog. A Greyhound should have long, flat and elastic muscles as opposed to bulky and heavy ones. The muscle tone should, nevertheless, be hard, but not to the point of limiting elasticity or detracting from the smoothness of the outline.

Symmetrical formation refers to the all-important overall balance of the dog and how the parts fit together to create a harmonious overall impression. The sweeping and beautifully rounded flow of lines, without abruptness, from the tip of the nose through the neck and body to the tip of the tail constitutes the epitome of Greyhound type.

The smooth flow of lines, including both the topline and the underline, has been aptly described as a series of beautifully blended unexaggerated S-curves. The correct outline is further highlighted under the headings 'neck' and 'body'.

How could the Greyhound Standard possibly denote the importance of a functional dog in a better way than insisting on a suppleness of limb, which emphasises in a marked degree the breed's distinctive type and quality? This is another very cleverly worded key phrase in the KC Standard (although somewhat ruined by the current telegram format and better expressed in the pre-1986 Standard), providing an important link between the ability to manoeuvre and the distinctive type and quality of the outstanding Greyhound. Suppleness, above anything, is just what a Greyhound needs to be able to catch the prey, or to cut it off if working in co-operation with a fellow hunter. Speed itself is of lesser importance as the dog is far quicker than the hare anyway. The dog that will be able to catch or cut off the prey is the one that has the ability to turn on a dime, enabling it to follow the very quick manoeuvres of the game. Without that extreme suppleness of limb, and, we may like to add, of the loin, the dog would be helpless against the hare. Thus suppleness is another key element in Greyhound type. The Greyhound should definitely be muscular, but his muscles should enhance rather than restrict his elasticity and freedom of movement. This will be further discussed under loin and movement.

Also included in the description of the general appearance are the references to a long head and neck, clean and well laid shoulders, the deep chest and capacious body, the arch of loin, the powerful quarters and the sound legs and feet, all important in the breed. The inclusion of these traits in the general appearance section serves to attract special attention to these features at the expense of other and less important traits. However, they will all be discussed in more detail under their respective headings.

CHARACTERISTICS:

KC: **Possessing remarkable stamina and endurance.**

Again, the Standard stresses the importance of considering the function for which the breed was originally bred, stamina and endurance being of the utmost importance to enable the dog to hunt down hares. Not even the cleverest of Greyhounds will ever be able to catch all the hares that are encountered during a day out in the fields. The hare may escape into holes in the ground or over or behind natural barriers. Furthermore, when out in the fields, the Greyhound is required not only to be able to catch one hare, but several. This makes for a major difference between the hunting or coursing dog on one hand and the modern racing dog on the

Int. Am. Nord. Ch. Gallant Major Motion.

Photo courtesy: Espen Engh.

other. The latter is asked to perform twice or, at the most, three times in a day and over a relatively short distance only. The same degree of stamina and endurance is thus not needed in the racing dog.

The pre-1986 version of the Standard reads: "The Greyhound possesses remarkable stamina and endurance, its straight through, long reaching movement enables it to cover ground at great speed." Most of the omitted words have been included elsewhere in the new Standard, but the fact that the long reaching movement and the ability to cover ground was mentioned among the characteristics of the breed definitely put more emphasis on movement in the old Standard. Maybe the shifting of focus away from movement as a characteristic of the breed to now merely being mentioned under its own headline, has decreased the emphasis on this most important trait. It has been suggested that this omission has contributed to the deterioration of movement in recent years. If that is the case, it is a great shame.

TEMPERAMENT:
KC: **Intelligent, gentle, affectionate and even-tempered.**

Many different breeds are perceived by their fanciers as being particularly intelligent. It is doubtful that Greyhounds are any more intelligent than most others, but there are different forms of intelligence, and maybe the Standard is referring to working intelligence and ability. Anyway, intelligence is very hard, probably impossible, to assess in the show ring. Certainly we do not want a blank or stupid expression, but rather one indicating spirit.

Most Greyhounds are indeed very gentle and affectionate, often more so with their owners than with strangers. But even a complete stranger should have no problem making contact with, or going over, a Greyhound. Young Greyhounds can sometimes be very exuberant and difficult to assess in the show ring and may sometimes need to be handled and moved repeatedly. Nervousness or shyness should be penalised

Ch. Krinolin.

Photo courtesy: Espen Engh.

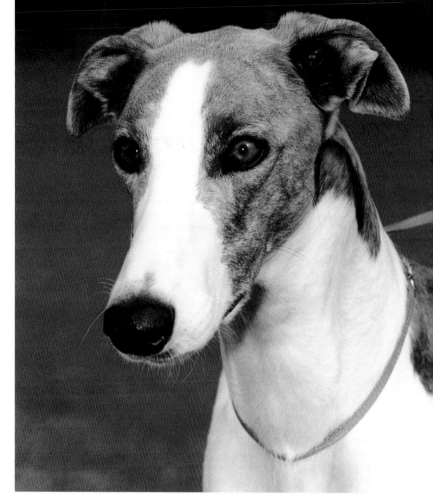

UK Ch. Windspiel Northern Pearl of Seeswift.

Photo: Steve Nash.

in relation to the degree, whereas aggressiveness is totally untypical of the breed.

HEAD AND SKULL:

KC: **Long, moderate width, flat skull, slight stop. Jaws powerful and well chiselled.**

AKC: **Long and narrow, fairly wide between the ears, scarcely perceptible stop, little or no development of nasal sinuses, good length of muzzle, which should be powerful without coarseness. Teeth very strong and even in front.**

The Greyhound is not a head breed, implying that the head is considered to be of relatively minor importance when compared with many other, if not most other breeds, including among them related sighthound breeds such as Afghan Hounds, Borzois and Pharaoh Hounds. Remember that the essence of the Greyhound is in its proportions, in the combination of substance with elegance and quality, the flow of lines and movement. Consequently, the head would have to be quite unattractive and significantly detract from the general appearance of the dog to be of much consideration when grading a Greyhound under the FCI system, nor should it normally be a major factor for placing a dog down the line. Excepted from this may be irregular or incorrect bites. A wonderful head cannot compensate for lack of the key elements of the breed, but, when all this has been said, a beautiful head can be the icing on the cake and a mark of great quality, and should be recognised as such.

The head should fit the body, i.e. the long head should reflect the long neck and elongated body of the dog. Again, overall harmony and balance should be readily evident. The head should be moderately or fairly wide, implying that both an overly narrow head and a coarse or broad head are considered a deviation from the norm. The head should reflect the balance between strength and quality.

Int. Ch. Jet's Miraculit.

The stop is described in the British Standard as slight and in the American as scarcely perceptible. The result of this difference in wording is not infrequently noticeable in the dogs themselves, some American heads tending towards a lack of stop, often with a somewhat convex or Roman profile. In contrast, dogs bred to the British and FCI Standards tend to have a noticeable stop, creating two distinct, but almost parallel planes between the skull and the muzzle. Although not mentioned in the Standards, the length of the muzzle (as measured from the tip of the nose to the stop) is somewhat shorter than the length of the skull (as measured from the stop to the occipital prominence).

As required by a dog who catches prey by his teeth, the jaws and muzzle should be powerful. A lack of underjaw is not only visually unattractive, but also a sign of weakness and lack of functionality. This is outlined in both Standards, but with different words.

The reference to well chiselled jaws implies clean and lean lines of the head, free of excess skin or lips. However, a Greyhound head will often take years to develop fully, as the chiselling and veining will gradually become apparent, and the lips may dry out up until the age of three or even four years old.

EYES:
KC: **Bright, intelligent, oval and obliquely set. Preferably dark.**
AKC: **Dark, bright, intelligent, indicating spirit.**

The descriptions of the eyes are similarly worded in both Standards and really self-explanatory. Both Standards ask for a bright and intelligent expression, and both give preference to dark eyes, the American Standard more strongly than the British.

Int. Nord. Ch. Jet's Kerrs Pink.

Photo courtesy: Espen Engh.

Perhaps surprisingly, light eyes are quite widespread within the breed, and nowhere more so than in the US. As with most traits, there are degrees of deviation from the norm, but most breed authorities find it hard to accept blue or wall eyes. Some breeders, particularly in the US, advocate yellow eyes and can point to references all the way back to Arrianus. This is, however, contrary to either Standard.

Unfortunately none of the Standards allow for the fact that Greyhounds with blue-diluted coat colour (blues, blue brindles and blue fawns or particolours with markings of any of these colours) normally have lighter eyes, which should be accepted to a degree. Although never as dark as in a dark-eyed dog with black pigment, there are equally different shades of eye colours within the blue-diluted dogs.

The eyes should be oval as opposed to round or triangular or squinting. Eye shape in the breed is generally not considered much of a problem.

EARS:
KC: **Small, rose-shaped, of fine texture.**
AKC: **Small and fine in texture, thrown back and folded, except when excited, when they are semi-pricked.**

The neat and small, rose-shaped ear of fine texture is another crowning glory or icing on the cake, but their neatness has little functional importance.

Prick ears are considered unattractive, as are big, thick and fleshy or drop ears, sometimes referred to as hound ears.

According to Spira's *Canine Terminology*, semi-pricked ears are "basically erect ears, with just the tips drooping forwards, as exemplified by the Collie and Shetland Sheepdog." These ears frequently appear, but folded much lower than in the Collie, in Greyhound puppies around the age of three to seven months and will more often than not correct themselves. However, the correctly shaped rose-ears are just that, whether the dog is excited or not.

Greyhounds are not normally required to bait or show their ears in the show ring, and this is never encouraged in Britain, only very rarely in the rest of Europe, but more frequently in America. Sometimes this serves to attract attention to perfect ears and a lovely head and expression, which is fine. However, judges should never penalise a Greyhound at any level for not using his ears in the show ring.

MOUTH:
KC: **Jaws strong with a perfect, regular and complete scissor bite, i.e. the upper teeth closely overlapping lower teeth and set square to the jaws.**

Again the strength of jaw is highlighted. The Greyhound should have a typical scissor bite. This is, however, not mentioned in the American Standard. Overshot mouths are a problem in some lines, even to the point of shark or parrot mouths; these dogs are, however, normally not exhibited nor bred from. Level or undershot bites are very rare.

Irregular or incomplete bites are generally not a problem in the breed.

NECK:

KC: **Long and muscular, elegantly arched, well let into shoulders.**

AKC: **Long, muscular, without throatiness, slightly arched, and widening gradually into the shoulder.**

A long neck is an important attribute of the breed both from a functional as well as from a purely aesthetic viewpoint. In harmony with the rest of the dog, the neck should show a balanced combination of length and strength, being long and muscular at the same time. The length of neck is essential for reaching the prey, and strength of neck is needed to hold on to it. A long neck goes with a well-placed shoulder blade, as does the smooth neckset which is essential in creating the streamlined, flowing outline of an outstanding Greyhound. The elegantly arched or crested neck is the mark of a well-constructed and well-exercised Greyhound and does a lot to enhance the general impression of the dog. A long, but narrow and weak neck is both ugly and dysfunctional, as is a short and coarse neck.

The neck is often the feature which separates the outstanding Greyhound from the merely very good one. Ewe necks and abrupt necksets are both quite serious faults which are sometimes encountered in the breed.

FOREQUARTERS:

KC: **Shoulders oblique, well set back, muscular without being loaded, narrow and cleanly defined at the top. Forelegs, long and straight, bone of good substance and quality. Elbows free and well set under shoulders. Pasterns of moderate length, slightly sprung. Elbows, pasterns and toes inclining neither in nor out.**

AKC: **Shoulders: Placed as obliquely as possible, muscular without being loaded. Forelegs: Perfectly straight, set well into the shoulders, neither turned in nor out, pasterns strong.**

The Greyhound should be able to reach out well in front both at the trot and at the gallop. This is facilitated by a well-placed and

Am. Ch. Suntiger Traveller: The USA's top winning male Gtreyhound.
Photo courtesy: Espen Engh.

Int. Ch. Jet's The Sting: Finland's top winning Greyhound of all time.
Photo courtesy: Espen Engh.

well-angulated shoulder blade coupled with a good return of upper arm.

The well-laid shoulder is very important in creating the beautiful streamlined curves from the crested neck into the withers, as well as the anterior line of the neck into the chest. Insufficient layback of shoulder instantly upsets this harmonious flow of lines, resulting in an abrupt neckset.

Both Standards again focus on the all-important musculature when describing the shoulders. The top of the shoulder blades should be rather close together, approximately two fingers breadth, allowing for those typical smooth and long muscles as opposed to the round and bulging. The latter give rise to loaded shoulders, often associated with too much width in front, upright shoulders and a tendency to barrel chests. On the other hand, an even narrower space between the shoulder blades would prevent the Greyhound from lowering his head to grab the hare.

The upper arms are not directly mentioned in either Standard, but are implied by the reference to the elbows being well set under the shoulders. Straight upper arms are a serious and common fault in the breed and one that throws the dog off balance. Insufficient layback of upper arms will invariably result in the elbows being placed in front of the deepest point of the brisket, creating an illusion of lack of depth even if

the brisket, in actual fact, is deep enough. The dog will look higher on legs and lack forechest as well as support for the front legs both standing and moving, often leading to a weak front. Another adverse effect of straight upper arms is restricted extension in the front movement. As straight upper arms influence the balance of the dog both standing and moving, it must be considered a very serious fault. Unfortunately, it is also a widespread fault.

The requirements for legs to be long and straight should be self-explanatory. Bone of good substance and quality has been focused on before. As is consistent with speed, the Greyhound should be free, and not tied in, at the elbows.

The pasterns should be slightly sprung and of moderate length. They are the main shock-absorbers and, as such, contribute a lot to the suppleness at any gait. A short and completely straight terrier-type pastern is a serious functional flaw in a Greyhound, and is more often than not associated with very short cat-like feet. At the other end of the spectrum, overly long and weak pasterns have already spent some of their capacity to absorb the shock even before hitting the ground and are therefore also incorrect. Breeders and judges should aim for a slightly sprung pastern, nothing more and nothing less.

The elbows, pasterns and toes should incline neither in nor out. The immature

Int. Aus. Norw. Ch. Rovaleco's Double Step Tango (imp. Norway) in Australia.

Photo courtesy: Espen Engh.

Greyhound will sometimes toe slightly out. This will often correct itself, whereas toeing in is a more serious fault in a sighthound, and one that will never correct itself.

BODY:
KC: **Chest deep and capacious, providing adequate heart room. Ribs deep, well sprung and carried well back. Flanks well cut up. Back rather long, broad and square. Loins powerful, slightly arched.**
AKC: **Chest: deep, and as wide as consistent with speed, fairly well-sprung ribs. Back: muscular and broad. Loins: Good depth of muscle, well arched, well cut up in the flanks.**

As stressed under general appearance, the Greyhound should be a rather long dog. This generosity of outline should be evident both in the back, the loin and in the croup.

As for the rest of the Greyhound, the ideal body also combines substance with elegance and quality. In our breed, as in almost all other sighthounds, the chest should be deep rather than broad, but should be capacious enough to provide room for the heart and lungs.

The deep chest must be of good length. Long posterior ribs are important in creating the smooth-flowing, curvy underline, again without any hint of abruptness. This is indicated by the British Standard insisting on ribs to be carried well back. A rather common fault is short posterior ribs which create an unsightly, abrupt underline. The flanks need to be well cut up, again to emphasise the beautiful underline. Many Greyhounds are lacking in tuck-up, but have a deep and fleshy loin resulting in a rather straight underline. This sometimes, but not always, can be improved with proper exercise, but it detracts a lot from the overall impression of curvy elegance.

The ribs should be fairly well sprung; the

Greyhound should be neither slab-sided nor barrel-chested, but a happy medium. Too often the bottom part of the chest is very narrow and almost sharp.

When viewed from above, the back of a well-exercised Greyhound is surprisingly broad, but it does not get much wider over the ribs. The reference to a square back is again as seen from above and not from the side, meaning that the back should be of even breadth. This should also include the loin, implying that the Greyhound should have no waist as seen from above.

For a breed where balance is the overriding consideration, the Standards unfortunately leave a lot of room for interpretation concerning the topline. The correct balance can best be assessed visually, or manually by laying one hand on top of the shoulder blade and the other hand on the haunch bone when the dog is standing naturally or properly stacked. The haunch bones should be only marginally lower than the shoulder blade, but the hips should be well covered and just barely visible so as not to cut off the flow of lines.

The Greyhound needs a supple and powerful loin to fulfil its function, which is most evident during several of the phases in the breed's double suspension gallop, and in particular in the suspended phase when the dog tucks up completely and the hindlegs reach forward far beyond the front. A dog with a weak loin will tire quickly or not be able to run at all. The loin should be slightly arched according to the British Standard and well arched according to the American, but in practice the dogs are similar on both sides of the Atlantic.

The gentle arch of loin should be harmonious and blending smoothly with the rest of the topline. It should consist of strong muscle only; under no circumstances should the spine itself be arched. A roached or inflexible back and/or loin is a most serious fault in a Greyhound, whereas a dog with only a very moderate arch of loin may still be a top contender, as shown by some of the top-winning British Greyhounds over the years. A completely flat, or even worse, a sagging topline, is, however, not acceptable.

HINDQUARTERS:

KC: **Thighs and second thighs wide and muscular, showing great propelling power. Stifles well bent. Hocks well let down, inclining neither in nor out. Body and hindquarters, features of ample proportions and well coupled, enabling adequate ground to be covered when standing.**

AKC: **Long, very muscular and powerful, wide and well let down, well-bent stifles. Hocks well bent and rather close to ground, wide but straight fore and aft.**

The hindquarters are another most important part of Greyhound anatomy. Again, the word 'generous' applies, as witnessed by the Standard asking for features of ample proportions enabling adequate ground to be covered. Consequently, both Standards focus on long, muscular and powerful hindquarters. In particular the thigh, but also the second thigh, should be remarkably wide and muscular, as the major propelling power of the dog stems from the muscles in the loin and hindlegs.

The Greyhound should have generous rear angulation, applying to both the stifle and the hock. The corresponding bones, the femur and the tibia and fibula, must be of good length. Most importantly, balance must be retained with the rest of the dog, and with the angulation in front in particular. Again, the importance of how the parts fit together is stressed by the Standard's insistence on the Greyhound being well coupled. The connection between the muscular and powerful hindquarters and the well-angulated front must be just as strong as the two parts it connects. Not only must the front and rear match each other, but the coupling must match as well.

Rear angulation should be judged when the dog is standing naturally, or when properly stacked with the hocks perpendicular to the ground. Overstretching the hindlegs or pushing down on the rear quarters will alter both the angulation and the overall balance.

The distance from the hock to the ground should be short, as implied by the reference to hocks well let down. A cowhock (a hock inclining inwards) or a bowed hock (a hock

Am. Ch. Heathero Gallant Goblin.

Photo courtesy: Espen Engh.

inclining outwards) are serious faults, particularly if evident on the move.

FEET:
KC: **Moderate length, with compact, well knuckled toes and strong pads.**
AKC: **Hard and close, rather more hare than cat-feet, well knuckled up with good strong claws.**

Breeders and judges alike agree that good feet are very important for a Greyhound. But the correct feet have been a topic for discussion since the middle of the last century, when Stonehenge himself had difficulty making up his mind, or even before that time.

It is beyond question that the foot should be strong and well knuckled, always well knit as opposed to splayed, and never flat. However, that is as far as the breeders and judges can agree.

The Cornish breeders that profoundly influenced the breed favoured a very tightly knuckled cat-foot, which might seem to be in accordance with the British Standard's requirement for a compact foot. However, the words 'moderate length' should be interpreted as working both ways; the foot can be too long, but also too short. Breed authority Dagmar Kenis has aptly compared cat-feet in a Greyhound to a lady running with high-heeled shoes.

Most breeders in America and Scandinavia, as well as some British and Continental breeders, have favoured the foot described by the American Standard. The AKC Standard asks for neither a hare or a cat-foot, but one that is closer to the first. A hare-foot is a foot where both centre toes are appreciably longer than the associated outer toes and those centre toes create an open angle to the ground level. Combine these distinctive features of the hare-foot with the height and solid knuckling of the cat-foot, and you have a typical Greyhound foot which is ideal for absorbing the shock when the foot hits the ground at great speed.

Bad feet in one way or another are among the most common faults in Greyhounds. Frequently encountered are flat, splayed or thin feet as well as overly short feet or feet that knuckle over in the distal joint, a very bad fault in a running dog.

TAIL:
KC: **Long, set on rather low, strong at root, tapering to point, carried low, slightly curved.**
AKC: **Long, fine and tapering with a slight upward curve.**

The long Greyhound tail is not only a sign of quality and adds the finishing touch to the dog, but it is also a very important steering tool when galloping. The tail should be low-set, a high-set tail being both dysfunctional

Am. Ch. Quail Roost Cameo.

Photo courtesy: Espen Engh.

Aus. Ch. Jet's Snakes and Ladders.

Photo: Narelle Robinson.

and ugly. A flexible tail is one that is strong and muscular at the root and gradually tapering to the end.

The tail should be carried low, both standing and on the move, finishing off those continuous smooth and flowing lines at the tip of the tail. A high tail carriage is very unattractive. This may be due to exuberant temperament, but is just as often connected with stilted and inflexible movement or overall lack of balance on the move.

The tail should have a slight upward curve, not a sickle and never a ring. Be aware that Greyhounds have a great tendency to harm their tails, indeed this is probably the main health problem within the breed. These accidents, whether they are honourable hunting blemishes, or caused at home by the dog whipping its tail against the walls or furniture, or by the tail being trapped in the car door, will frequently leave kinks or thickened areas, often near the end of the tail. On the other hand, kinked tails are probably the most common congenital defect in the breed. It is very difficult indeed to determine, without the use of X-ray, if a kink has been caused by accident or is a congenital defect. Judges are advised to use their discretion and not penalise a kinked tail unless it is affecting the general appearance of the dog.

GAIT/MOVEMENT:
KC: **Straight, low reaching, free stride enabling the ground to be covered at great speed. Hindlegs coming well under body giving great propulsion.**

It should be noted that the American Standard does not include any description of or even a reference to movement. This should not be interpreted as meaning that movement is of little importance in America, but rather that the ideal movement is left to individual opinion.

The British Standard describes well the typical movement. It should, however, be borne in mind that the Greyhound is really a galloping breed and not a trotter. The question should be – how do we recognise the traits that will enable the dog to gallop while assessing the dog at a trot? We should be focusing on economy of movement as opposed to wasted effort, as well as on signs of the high degree of suppleness needed in a successful hunter.

The movement should be straight as opposed to sidetracking or crabbing; this is a sign of general symmetry which is valid for all breeds. The Standard further insists on low-reaching movement as opposed to high, short-stepping or ineffective movement, but also as opposed to the lift and suspension seen in several closely related breeds such as Afghan Hounds and Ibizan Hounds. This kind of movement would simply be wasted effort for a Greyhound whose prey is close to the ground and whose hunting terrain is relatively flat.

As for the emphasis on great propulsion, it should always be kept in mind that this is a galloping dog whose reach and drive should never be compared to that of a trotting dog. It is, however, important that the dog has a powerful rear action which starts from well under the body and carries well through, never looking stilted or restricted in any way.

When assessing the dog in movement from the side, it is important to focus on the entire dog and not only on what the legs are doing – which is important enough, but, again, not as important as the general appearance. How do the parts fit together? How does the dog keep his outline on the move? How does he carry himself? Co-ordination is, of course, of great functional importance, with all four legs moving at exactly the same speed. The free and ground-covering strides should testify to the extreme suppleness needed for cutting off and catching the prey at full gallop. The key element in Greyhound movement is the suppleness of limb as denoted under general appearance. This can only be assessed properly while moving around the ring. Observe the ability to make the turns, how all four limbs and the loin work in unison to make it all look so easy and unstrained. An outstanding mover should be able to bend over and make the turns easily without having to compensate by using extra steps or changing pace.

A well-constructed Greyhound will not have an extreme neck carriage on the move, but neither should his head seek to hug the ground. The ideal head carriage is just slightly higher than the extension of the topline, never as upright as in an Afghan Hound or Ibizan Hound and again reflecting the differences in hunting terrains.

Side movement is of paramount importance in the Greyhound, but that is

Am. Ch. Arborcrest Skyracer O'Kinnear.
Photo courtesy: Espen Engh.

not to say that movement coming and going is not important as well. Again, the focus should be on minimal effort, which implies clean movement both coming and going with no looseness or breaking of the axis of the legs. However, there are two different schools of thought when it comes to what constitutes correct movement coming and going. One school prefers the legs to move in a perfect parallel fashion. The other school prefers the legs to converge towards a centre line when increasing the speed, known as single-tracking. Several authorities on sighthounds have made very strong points in favour of the latter.

Excellent Greyhound movement is truly a joy to observe, but unfortunately not a very frequently seen commodity.

COAT:
KC: **Fine and close.**
AKC: **Short, smooth and firm in texture.**

The Greyhound coat is short and smooth and rather firm in texture, not overly soft, but still very pleasant to touch. The coat should generally be very close, but is usually less so under the belly and on the inside of the hindlegs. Quite a few Greyhounds have rather thin coats, especially on the thighs. This is sometimes, but not always, due to hormonal deficiencies.

An undercoat is usually almost nonexistent in Greyhounds, but may sometimes be apparent in the winter and early spring, notably in adolescents and dogs with red coat colour.

COLOUR:
KC: **Black, white, red, blue, fawn, fallow, brindle or any of these colours broken with white.**
AKC: **Immaterial.**

It has often been stated that a good Greyhound cannot have a bad colour, and the American Standard fully accepts all colours. The British Standard lists most of the traditional colours, but on the other hand does not mention unacceptable colours.

Liver colours in Greyhounds have been a topic of some discussion. Red livers, brindle livers (both of which can be claimed to be just as much varieties of the accepted red and brindle colour as are the blue fawns or blue brindles, none of which are specifically mentioned in the British Standard) and even chocolates have successfully been shown in Scandinavia since the early 1970s, but have never been shown in Britain. The liver colours have been fully accepted by the vast majority of judges from all over the world. However, liver-coloured dogs always come with liver-coloured noses and eye rims and more often than not with light yellow eyes. It would be fair to say that most breeders in Scandinavia accept the colours, but nobody actively sets out to breed them.

Sometimes the markings of particoloured dogs, or the stripes of brindles, can create optical illusions of the head properties, shoulders and toplines. Markings that can be considered by some to be unattractive should have no influence on the rating or placement of the dog. Similarly, solid white Greyhounds will often appear to be stronger, and solid black or blue dogs more refined, than they actually are.

Am. Ch. Crestfield Sky's Sunstation.
Photo courtesy: Espen Engh.

SIZE:
KC: **Ideal height: dogs: 71-76 cms (28-30 ins); bitches; 68-71 cms (27-28 ins).**
AKC: **Weight: Dogs, 65 to 70 pounds, bitches 60 to 65 pounds.**

The height of the Greyhound, which caused such a spirited discussion when the British Standard was drawn up in 1947/48 and, indeed, long before that time, is still the matter of some discussion.

Greyhounds are never measured in the ring. Additional height to that which the Standards require is at best difficult to justify from a functional viewpoint. Very big dogs tend to be either too upstanding and gangly, or heavy and lacking in suppleness. Nevertheless, several of the leading breeders over the last 50 years have been advocating bigger dogs. It can be claimed to have become part of breed tradition that dogs above the size requirements of the Standard are rarely, if ever, penalised for it as long as type, proportions and soundness are retained. On the other hand, dogs at the lower range of the Standard should not be penalised for conforming to the Standard.

Bitches at 27 inches (68 cms), or even somewhat smaller, can still do well in the show ring. But males below the Standard size will appear to be insignificant, feminine and/or not upstanding and are rarely, if ever, seen at shows.

151

Ch. Kingsmark Queen Ann's Lace.
Photo courtesy: Espen Engh.

The American Standard does not have a height clause, but merely describes the weight. The height clause in the British Standard does not correspond well with the weight clause in the American Standard; a full grown male of 30 inches (76 cms) weighs a good deal more than 70 pounds unless in skin-and-bone condition. Still, there is in practice little, if any, difference between the size of British and American Greyhounds.

FAULTS:
KC: **Any departure from the foregoing points should be considered a fault and the seriousness with which the fault should be regarded should be in exact proportion to its degree.**

This phrase is included at the end of all the KC Standards. This is a clever wording, avoiding a long list of faults that is frequently included in Continental Standards. The Standard reminds us that no dog is perfect and that most imperfections come in degrees. Quality in dogs, with few exceptions, does not come in black or white, yes or no, and most important traits can rather be measured on a continuous scale. The absence of a fault in no way guarantees the presence of the corresponding virtue. The aim should never be just to avoid obvious faults, nor to settle for mediocrity, but rather to strive for perfection at the other end of that scale.

Judges should recognise and reward the outstanding as opposed to the middle-of-the-road, for mediocrity in itself is perhaps the worst of all faults in a Greyhound, or in any other breed for that matter.

Similarly, it is most important to learn to be forgiving when evaluating a Greyhound. The presence of outstanding virtues often may more than compensate for the presence of faults. Make sure not to throw the baby out with the bathwater.

NOTE:
KC: **Male animals should have two apparently normal testicles fully descended into the scrotum.**

In most countries the lack of one or both testicles would disqualify the male from being shown or bred from. However this is not the case in the UK.

The American Standard is followed by a scale of points. A remnant of times gone by, this gives twice as much emphasis to head and neck as to general symmetry and quality. Not included at all is movement, tail or coat. Clearly, this scale of points is of little value in assessing the importance of different traits and has deliberately been omitted from this discussion.

THE JUDGE'S VIEW
Photographs offer only a limited view on dogs in general and Greyhounds in particular. Often the photo will distort the true qualities of a dog, and the all-important movement cannot be assessed from a photo.

It is also true that you cannot evaluate temperament from photos, and most dogs appear different when you meet them 'face to face'. However, bearing these limitations in mind, the following critiques are based on pictorial evidence.

WHITE MALE (5 years)

ABOVE LEFT: Very substantial and powerful, a decidedly masculine dog. He needs more elegance and quality throughout and appears rather low on the leg for optimum balance. Strong and rather thick neck, well-muscled, but not very elegant and could be more smoothly set into the shoulder. Rather extreme layback of upper arm with a very prominent forechest. Very deep brisket, reaching below the elbow and contributing to his rather low-to-the-ground proportions. Loaded shoulders, prominent withers and rather pronounced dip, but a pleasing balance regarding the height at the withers compared to the height at the hipbones.

ABOVE RIGHT: A strong, masculine head, fitting his body. Pleasing head planes but rather deep in profile. A strong muzzle, but his underjaw appears not as strong as the rest of the head. Dark eyes with good pigmentation, particularly for his colour. Acceptable ears, although they appear somewhat fleshy and heavy.

Well filled-in as seen from the front, very well-boned all the way down, but appearing round in bone. Standing firmly on his front feet which turn neither in nor out. Short pasterns that may appear rather inflexible, but this is hard to tell from the photo.

Very strong, muscular thighs with balanced angulation of hindquarters. Hocks well down inclining neither in nor out. Not in optimum coat condition, being rather bald on his thighs. Tail long enough and well-shaped from the side, although appearing slightly skewed from behind.

BRINDLE BITCH (2 years)

ABOVE LEFT: Sweet, feminine and elegant quality bitch, but needs some more strength and substance, and could cover more ground. Tucks herself up and looks like she is freezing in her photos.

Quite a long and elegant neck, well set into the shoulders, balanced front angulation. Moderate length of body, could be somewhat more generously proportioned, but pleasing, smooth flowing underline and topline, with arched loin.

ABOVE RIGHT: Elegant, feminine head, needing some more underjaw and overall strength in profile, Very dark eyes with excellent pigmentation. Thin and small ears, neatly folded in a rose shape.

Needs to develop some more depth of brisket and a little more forechest, but appears to be a young bitch with the potential to improve. Very pleasing head and expression as viewed head-on. Very good, flexible pasterns, knuckled feet of moderate length. In this photo, she is turning her feet slight outwards.

Tends to stand with hindquarters tucked in under her body, but her angulation appears to be balanced and her thighs strong enough. I would prefer some more bone overall. Square back as viewed from behind. Long, sable-shaped tail. Very good coat quality

WHITE AND BRINDLE BITCH (5 years)

ABOVE LEFT: High-quality bitch with excellent substance and covering a lot of ground. Her neck could be longer and somewhat more elegant. which would add the finishing touch to her overall appearance. Moderate lay-back of shoulder, but with good return of upper arm. Smooth flowing topline, generously proportioned and with a slightly arched loin, although somewhat sloping in her overall balance. Her most serious imperfection is the lack of shape to her underline, which does not have a proper tuck-up. Long tail that appears rather straight in profile.

ABOVE RIGHT: Classical, feminine head profile with excellent planes, and strong underjaw. Excellent pigmentation with very dark eyes and beautiful small, rose-shaped ears.

Deep brisket and good forechest. Strong, well-muscled thighs, good angulation behind. Well-boned with a slightly sprung pasterns. Feet are well-knuckled and of moderate length. Standing parallel in front.

Very good body volume, and square back as viewed from behind. A little wide behind, but this may be due to stacking. Excellent coat quality.

11 *A-Z OF COMMON DISEASES AND HEALTH PROBLEMS*

Greyhounds are among of the world's finest natural athletes. They have been bred and selected over hundreds of years for speed and agility as competitive coursing dogs. During the last 150 years their physique and athletic speed has been refined for lure racing. The preparation and training of a racing Greyhound can be a challenging and rewarding experience. After the completion of their career, many Greyhounds become gentle companion animals and family pets.

In common with other breeds of dogs, Greyhounds are susceptible to many of the same diseases and health problems. However, the physical stress imposed by racing increases the risk of injury to the musculo-skeletal system. Muscle, joint and toe injuries are the most common cause of downtime or lay-off training, or lost racing opportunities. Greyhounds are expected to travel long distances, race twice weekly and maintain their fitness and form for extended periods of time.

Any athlete is prone to physical injury and whilst Greyhounds have been selected for strength and stamina, injuries due to changes in track surface, collisions and falls account for the majority of problems. In retirement, many Greyhounds carry the legacy of race injuries but, remarkably, most cope and lead active lifestyles.

This chapter has been written to provide a comprehensive overview of the major hereditary or injury problems. As Greyhounds age, other metabolic and arthritic problems develop in their greying years.

A

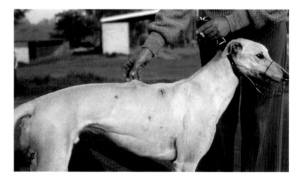

Small skin abscesses are commonly referred to as 'milk sores' or 'staph hot spots'. This Greyhound is also dehydrated, as shown by the pinched up skin and slow return, due to the loss of moisture reserves under the skin.

ABSCESS: A collection of pus consisting of serum, white blood cells, viable and dead bacterial organisms.

Common Sites: The most common sites for abscesses in Greyhounds include small boil-like eruptions referred to as milk sores or hot spots on the skin, and other localised infections of the webbing and under the pads introduced by prickles, glass or penetrating objects. Abscesses under the molar teeth can occur in older Greyhounds and infections under the cuticle and nail bed (Paronychia) can result in low grade chronic abscesses. Refer to individual conditions.

Signs: A warm, painful swelling usually takes up to 1-3 days to develop at the site of the abscess. Abscesses often form in the tissues under the skin and remain closed initially as a pustule or boil-like eruption. They may burst to the skin surface as pus accumulates and the overlying skin devitalises and softens as the abscess matures and forms a point of discharge.

Cause: Skin abscesses are usually caused by Staphylococcus organisms (Golden Staph bacterial spp.) that are introduced to the area just below the skin surface by penetrating objects, cuts, abrasions or use of contaminated needles. Greyhounds housed under dirty conditions, those stressed by hard racing or concurrent disease, may have lowered immunity against infection, especially as the Greyhound ages. Some abscesses develop as a result of blood borne infection. Occasionally one or more abscesses can form in the liver or lungs following such an infection.

Management: Small, deep-seated, developing or closed abscesses may be controlled by a course of appropriate antibiotics under veterinary supervision. Larger, more mature abscesses under the skin surface are best surgically drained, cleansed and managed by a vet. Open abscesses, such as milk sores or staph sores are best cleansed with antiseptics and treated as an open wound. Refer to Hot spots, Milk Sores.

ACIDOSIS: A term to describe the build-up of L-lactic acid in rapidly contracting muscles during anaerobic metabolism (no oxygen) at maximum speed.

Common Sites: The accumulation and retention of L-lactic acid occurs in the major muscle groups along the backline and hindlimb muscles of Greyhounds within a few minutes to 24 hours after a hard gallop.

Signs: Swelling and pain within the affected muscle groups, with reduced speed and stride length during and following a trial or race, often associated with the onset of muscle soreness, rigidity or knotting, with outward symptoms of cramping and muscle seizure.

Cause: Acidosis is most common in Greyhounds that are not fit enough for the speed or length of a race; those that are fed excess carbohydrates such as bread or high carbohydrate (cereal) based dry foods; Greyhounds that are dehydrated due to excitement, barking and long-distance travelling that results in fluid and body salt loss; and anaemic Greyhounds with reduced oxygen-carrying capacity as a result of a poor diet or blood loss due to heavy worm or flea infestation.

Management: Ensuring that a Greyhound is fit, properly hydrated and prepared for the distance of the race will reduce the risk of muscle acidosis.

Warming up prior to racing by brisk walking and warming down after racing will help minimise the incidence. Supplementing the diet with iron, potassium and alkaline body salts, as well as regular worm and flea control, is also recommended. The severe form, where a Greyhound is acutely muscle sore, dehydrates and rapidly loses body weight, must be referred to a vet for emergency treatment. Refer to Azoturia, Cramping, Exertional Rhabdomyolysis.

ACCESSORY CARPAL BONE INJURY: Most common conditions include bruising of the bone surface and fracture of the accessory carpal bone behind the wrist joint in racing Greyhounds.

Signs: Swelling behind the wrist (carpus) with lameness and reduced stride in the affected limbs. Fracture of the bone can result in tearing of the tendon where it inserts on to the bone, with downward collapse of the wrist and extreme lameness.

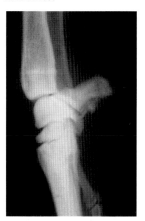
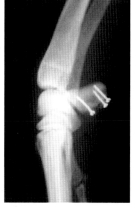

X-ray image of a fracture of accessory carpal bone (stopper bone) behind the wrist, illustrating the stress lines and detachment of fragments of the bone.

This X-ray was taken after the bone was repaired using bone screws. The Greyhound returned successfully to racing.

Causes: The accessory carpal bone lies under the stopper pad behind the wrist. As it is prominent, it is prone to bruising as the wrist flexes downwards when a Greyhound is galloped on a hard track. Fractures usually occur due to sudden overload of the tendon as a result of a fall, loss of footing, or long-term race stress with demineralisation and loss of bone strength. Fractures can also result from structural bone weakness when a racing Greyhound is fed on low-calcium diet.

Management: Bruising of the bone surface can be managed by kennel rest, ice packing morning and evening for 2-3 minutes combined with elastic and pressure bandaging overnight for 5-7 days. In long-term cases, the skin may become devitalised and infected. It may split open during galloping to form an open, thickened swelling, often forcing retirement in chronic cases. Fractures are diagnosed on the extent of swelling and pain and confirmed by X-ray of the wrist. They need to be immobilised in a plaster cast or repaired by surgery under veterinary supervision. The diet should include supplementary calcium and Vitamin D to facilitate fracture repair. Magnetic field therapy for 15-20 minutes twice daily for 3-4 weeks may be beneficial to assist healing of the bone fracture. Serious or repeated fractures will force retirement from racing.

ACHILLES TENDON INJURY: A serious racing injury caused by overload strain of the Achilles tendon (calf muscle tendon bundle) that attaches to the back of the hock (tarsus) joint.

Signs: Severe lameness, with rapid swelling resulting from internal haemorrhage and inflammation within the strained or torn tendon. Upper tears may be felt as a pea to marble-sized hard fibrous lump in the lower calf muscle area, and lower tears as a gap in the tendon strap.

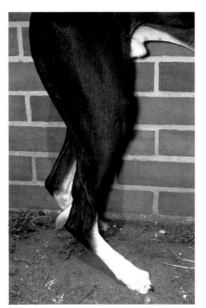

Rupture of the Achilles tendon causes rapid swelling and lameness, with downward collapse of the limb as it bears weight.

Causes: Overflexion of the hock on an uneven or loose track surface, or fatigue of repeated racing, may weaken tendon fibrils, especially those originating from the gastrocnemius or the larger, more powerful, calf muscle of the tendon bundle.

Management: Surgical repair gives the best chance of return to racing, complemented by support bandaging and kennel rest for 14-21 days. Physiotherapy such as 20-30 minutes daily of magnetic field therapy, with careful manual flexion (bending) of the hock for 1-2 minutes twice daily. Initial daily exercise provided by walking on a lead for 14-21 days and a stepwise return to straight galloping over 5-6 weeks are often beneficial.

AGGRESSION: Properly cared for and handled Greyhounds are normally placid, controllable animals. Aggression is usually exhibited by turning the head or fighting during a race. Refer to Fighting. Certain types of testicular or ovarian cancers may result in elevated male hormone levels that increase aggression in older retired Greyhounds. Refer to Testicular Tumours.

ALABAMA ROT: A severe, spreading skin disease, first reported in 1985 in the USA, that appears to specially affect Greyhounds. At present, it is confined to the North American continent and has been reported on most tracks. It is also known as Greentrack disease, as it was first reported at the Greentrack Greyhound raceway in Alabama. It is medically termed Idiopathic Cutaneous and Renal Glomerular Vasculopathy as severe forms are associated with rapid kidney failure and death.

Signs: The first signs usually develop on the skin surface of the hindlimb below the hocks. Initially tissue fluid (oedema) accumulates and the skin swells. The devitalised skin then starts to rot, leading to ulcerated areas up to 100 mm (4 inches) in diameter on the lower limbs. The skin under the chest and in the groin may also be affected and occasionally on the muzzle. Affected Greyhounds exhibit fever, swelling, drooling, depression, vomiting and dark diarrhoea. Death from acute kidney failure can occur within 24 hours. Some Greyhounds develop kidney failure without obvious skin ulceration.

Causes: The cause is unknown. Although Staphylococcus germs (Golden Staph) were initially blamed, it is often secondary infection to the initial stage of skin devitalisation. Infection is more likely when Greyhounds are housed under damp, humid conditions, or when kennels, turn-out areas or yards are highly contaminated with droppings and urine. Recent evidence suggests a possible link between a specific strain of E. coli gut bacteria, which produces a toxin that has a similar skin devitalisation effect in humans. Greyhounds in the USA are routinely given uncooked 3-D and 4-D salvaged meat that could be contaminated with these bacteria, increasing the risk of skin invasion when a Greyhound sits on its haunches or its chest.

Management: Early recognition and diagnosis is absolutely essential. It should be considered as an emergency condition, with rigorous treatment commenced immediately because of the potential for rapid, severe toxic damage to the skin, vascular system and kidneys. The ulcerated areas usually heal in 10-30 days when cleaned and dressed with water-soluble antibiotics to control secondary infection and iodine to control fungal colonisation. Ulcerated areas are best bathed twice daily in an iodine-based antiseptic solution, with clean bedding and regular changes of dressings. Greyhounds with signs of renal failure require intensive fluid and kidney protective therapy. In severe cases, the Greyhound will usually die within 12-48 hours of the initial signs.

ALLERGIES: Greyhounds can suffer from a number of allergic conditions related to diet (red meat allergy), systemic and contact allergies of the skin (allergic dermatitis), airway and lung allergies (asthma), flies and fleas (fly bite and flea bite skin allergies). Allergic reactions are more likely in young Greyhounds. They usually result from an excessive or intense immune mediated reaction or hypersensitivity to a foreign protein or non-protein substance that does not cause a reaction in older Greyhounds. Refer to individual conditions – Red Meat Allergy, Allergic Dermatitis, Asthma, Fly Worry and Flea Bite Allergy.

ALLERGIC DERMATITIS: A term used to describe skin irritation due to hypersensitivity to a food or contact with bedding, heavy flea infestation, or specifically to the skin of the webbing between the toes. Very young and aged,

retired Greyhounds appear to be more susceptible to skin allergies.

Signs: Reddening, swelling and itching of local skin areas are common initial signs. The most common form is inflammation and reddening of the webbing, with small eroded and abraded areas after galloping on a grass track.

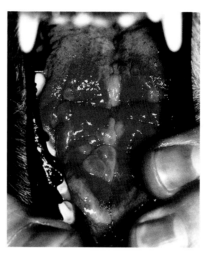

Tongue blisters in this young Greyhound were a result of an acute contact allergy caused by licking the residues of a kennel disinfectant.

Causes: Allergies to red meat, in particular to horsemeat if it is suddenly introduced to the diet, can result in diarrhoea and skin rashes, usually on the underbelly and groin areas. Refer to Red Meat Allergy. Allergy focused on the skin of the webbing is attributed to certain types of cut grass on the track surface and to kennel-cleaning soaps and disinfectants. These can cause an allergic and irritative skin reaction of the webbing, foot pads and contact points on the thighs, chest and joint prominences.

Management: A course of a systemic antibiotic and topical cortisone cream usually helps reduce clinical signs and risk of continued infection and weakening of the webbing over a 5-7 day period. A change of the type of bedding, trying an alternative formulation of antiseptic or detergent for kennel cleaning, and galloping on a different grass or sand surface should be considered if the allergy persists. It may take up to 7-10 days for the contact allergic reaction to settle down after these changes.

ALOPECIA: Loss of hair from the rear and sides of the thighs and chest is a relatively common condition in racing Greyhounds. Refer to Bald Thigh Syndrome. Loss of hair along the top of the nose and around the eyes is usually caused by demodectic mange. Refer to Demodectic Mange. As Greyhounds age, often the hair coat thins, with increased hair loss and dandruff in the coat.

ANAEMIA: Anaemia is not a disease as such, but a condition in which the red blood cell count, or haemoglobin content of the red cells, is lower than normal and therefore transports less oxygen to the muscles and other tissues.

Signs: When raced, affected Greyhounds lack stamina, speed and staying ability. Greyhounds of all ages will develop pale gums and eyelid membranes (more white than pink), exhibit lethargy and tiredness, and often have a dull, rough coat.

Causes: The underlying cause is most commonly due to chronic blood loss from heavy hookworm or flea infestations, infection with the Babesiosis blood parasite, bone marrow depression due to

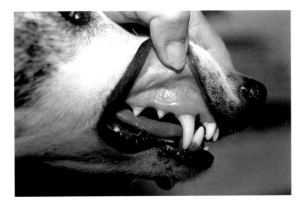

Loss of red blood cells resulting from severe hookworm or flea infestation is the most common cause of anaemia in a racing or aged greyhound. A healthy Greyhound has pink gums (above) compared to the pale membranes of a severely anaemic Greyhound (below).

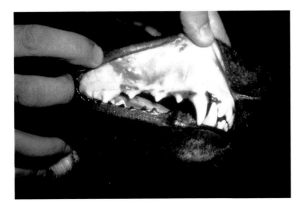

stress or disease, low grade infection, or diets based on white meats, such as chicken or fish without adequate supplementation with iron, an important trace-mineral. In aged Greyhounds, internal bleeding of intestinal cancers can lead to anaemia.

Management: A sample of fresh stools can be checked for hookworm and other worm eggs by a vet. Greyhounds with heavy worm infestation should be wormed out twice 3-4 weeks apart, then at 6-8 week intervals. Manure build-up in the kennel and yards should be removed to avoid recontamination with worm eggs and larvae. Damp dirty yards should be drained and the top 150mm (6 ins) of soil replaced with clean soil in the heavily contaminated areas. Control of flea infestation on the Greyhound and in its bedding should be carried out and maintained on a regular 4-6 week basis. The diet should be evaluated, containing at least 400g (14.1 oz) of red meat, and in racing Greyhounds a daily supplement of iron of up to 40mg daily for 2-3 weeks will provide essential iron for haemoglobin synthesis. Short sprint gallops will demand extra oxygen carrying capacity and increase the red cell numbers in the blood, and assist recovery in racing Greyhounds.

ANAL GLAND PROBLEMS: Greyhounds, and other dogs, have small scent secreting glands on each side of their anal ring. Retired Greyhounds, as they age, are more likely to develop anal gland compaction when fed on soft foods as compared to young healthy racing Greyhounds. As the stool is passed when a Greyhound empties out, the glands are squeezed within the bowel wall, coating the stools with the animal's individual scent. Dogs greet and sniff each other's anal areas to identify the scent of newcomers and recognise companions.

Signs: Impacted glands become swollen and cause an obstruction as the Greyhound empties out. The Greyhound attempts to relieve the discomfort by scraping or skidding its hindquarters along a grassy area. (This can also be a sign that the Greyhound has an infestation of the common tapeworm spread by fleas). Severely impacted glands invariably become infected, swollen and painful. They may burst through the skin around the anus, exuding a pungent, foul-smelling, creamy discharge, most commonly in older retired Greyhounds.

Cause: Soft meat diets, even containing dry foods,

result in soft stools that may reduce the natural massage action on the glands as the Greyhound empties out. The full glands are likely to become infected from bacteria in the stools and this results in swelling, discomfort and the urge to skid the hindquarters.

Management: Severely impacted and discharging glands are best removed surgically. In most cases, providing 300g of beef brisket bone once or twice weekly often helps to clean the teeth and to naturally massage the glands as the bone fragments and residues are passed in the stools. However, in aged Greyhounds with poor teeth, bones may not be chewed adequately and form into a compacted mass in the lower bowel, leading to obstruction and blockage with dry hard stools. Raw bones only must be fed. Cooked bones shatter and cannot be digested effectively, and may obstruct the gut. Where brisket bones are not provided regularly, the glands can be carefully squeezed at 6-8 week intervals with the fingers covered in thin latex or plastic gloves on to a cotton wool ball. Your vet may demonstrate the technique to avoid squirting the often foul scent on to your clothing.

ANNULAR LIGAMENT INJURY: The annular ligaments are band or loop-like structures of tendon tissue that help maintain the position of the tendons as they pass down the rear of the lower limbs below the wrists and hocks.

Signs: It is a relatively uncommon condition in racing Greyhounds. Soreness and swelling is exhibited when the rear area of the shins (metacarpal – front limbs, metatarsals – hindlimbs) and toes are examined in a racing Greyhound that is lame or short in its stride.

Causes: Over extension of the lower limb as a Greyhound gallops, particularly on a hard compacted surface, which leads to concussion and bruising of the undersurface (rear) of the limb and ligament bands under the skin surface.

Management: Ice packing for 1-2 mins, at least 2-3 times daily over the initial period of 36-48 hours, will help control the pain and swelling of the bruised or torn annular ligaments. Follow-up twice-daily massage with a warming liniment, 20 minutes of magnetic field therapy or 2-3 minutes of laser therapy daily for 10-14 days is often recommended. Exercise must be confined to lead walking on a soft surface. The injured area should

be strapped to provide support and protection when walking on a lead or when the Greyhound is allowed free exercise in a turn-out yard or outside run.

ARTHRITIS: In simple terms, arthritis describes inflammation within a joint. However, there are a number of forms of arthritis relative to the site, severity, and type of underlying bone and cartilage changes within the joints and joint surfaces. Septic arthritis occurs when a joint becomes infected with bacteria introduced by a puncture wound or a blood-borne infection that localises within a joint. Racing Greyhounds may develop a painful fluid swelling within a joint due to a joint sprain. Ageing, retired Greyhounds have a higher incidence of degenerative arthritis, often resulting in osteoarthritis (bone and cartilage joint deterioration within a joint), particularly those with a legacy of joint injury from their earlier racing career.

Signs: Swelling, warmth and pain due to inflammation, with reduced mobility of the affected joint and pain on flexion are signs of arthritic damage. Usually the Greyhound is reluctant to bear weight on the affected joint or limb. Joint cartilage surface erosion or bony reaction results in degenerative joint disease and osteoarthritis. These changes can be confirmed on X-ray of the joint, which will provide visual evidence of bone outgrowths and spurs within the joint.

Causes: Arthritis may be associated with internal bone fractures, interosseous (bone-to-bone) ligament strains, sprain of the joint due to overflexion or twisting (torsion injury) when galloping and direct concussion to the joint area. Most joints of the front and hindlimbs are prone to these types of injuries, with the shoulder, wrist and toe joints most commonly affected in the front limbs, and the lower spinal joints, hip, stifle, hock and toe joints in the hindlimbs. Certain bloodlines of young Greyhounds develop a polyarthritic syndrome in a number of joints, as a result of an immune reaction or inherited genetic predisposition. Refer to Polyarthritis.

Management: In severe cases in an older Greyhound, retirement from racing is necessary. Therapy depends on the type, degree and internal changes within the joint. It ranges from rest and twice-daily massage and flexion for minor joint discomfort and occasional lameness, to longer term anti-inflammatory medication to control pain and swelling. In more severe cases, injections of hyaluronic acid, cortisone-type compounds or pentosan polysulfate are often used to assist pain control and joint repair in racing Greyhounds. Dietary supplements of cartilage protective agents based on shark cartilage, chondroitin sulphate, glucosamine, vitamin C and manganese may also be helpful in assisting cartilage replenishment, combating joint surface erosion and aiding repair processes. Where internal fractures are present in the wrist or hock joint, surgery or radiation therapy may be recommended. Strapping of the affected joint(s) to provide support and prevent overflexion during exercise or when racing is helpful in chronic osteoarthritic cases. In aged Greyhounds with degenerative arthritis, judicious use of pain relief medications and supplementation with nutritional compounds to improve cartilage health are advocated.

 ARTICULAR CARTILAGE: The apposing bone surfaces that form a healthy moving joint are protected by a well-lubricated, smooth and water-impregnated, shock-absorbing cartilage layer which is not supplied by sensory or pain-feeling nerves.

Signs: Erosion or damage to the joint cartilage surface can lead to contact with the sensitive underlying bone, resulting in pain, reluctance to bear weight and lameness.

Causes: Often the joint is swollen due to an arthritic reaction or infection, which may lead to erosion of the cartilage layer. This can occur where poor quality cartilage is formed in rapidly growing Greyhounds on a calcium or trace-mineral deficient diet leading to the development of a flap of cartilage lifting from the underlying bone surface of the shoulder, hip or stifle joint. (Refer to OCD). There may also be a genetic predisposition to OCD in certain bloodlines of Greyhounds.

Joint cartilage has a high water content, which acts as a hydraulic shock-absorber during exercise. The concussion of repeated racing on hard tracks can lead to increased wear and tear on the joint surfaces, which is exacerbated by arthritic change and loss of moisture content from the joint cartilage. When loaded during exercise, cartilage

deforms and may shear from the underlying hard bone layer (subchondral bone), leading to joint degeneration. Poor nutrition in growing puppies, with overdevelopment and heavy frame size, exacerbated by diets low in calcium, copper, manganese and zinc, may impair the formation of healthy, well-lubricated cartilage surfaces and dense underlying support bone. Polyarthritis in young Greyhounds causes articular cartilage erosion and severe lameness. Arthroscopic examination and X-rays may help confirm cartilage erosion. Refer to Polyarthritis.

Management: Racing Greyhounds with cartilage erosion and lameness in the shoulder, hip or stifle joints must be rested. A range of dietary supplements containing nutrients, including chondroitin sulphate, glucosamine, Vitamin C, copper, zinc and manganese that are necessary for the development and maintenance of cartilage are available and are considered beneficial for repair of joint cartilage. Intra-articular or intravenous injections of protective, nutritional and lubricating compounds based on hyaluronic acid or pentosan polysulfate are also widely used by vets. Where the OCD condition is present in a young Greyhound, surgical removal of the flap of diseased cartilage is essential to ensure rehabilitation and return to racing.

ASTHMA: Racing Greyhounds can develop an asthma condition related to exercise that causes bronchoconstriction (narrowing) of the lung airways and reduced lung ventilation capacity. It may be an inherited condition as some bloodlines and littermates appear to have a higher incidence of wheezing after exercise.

Signs: An individual Greyhound may exhibit wheezing respiratory sounds and a hacking, persistent moist cough, often lasting for 1-2 hours after a hard gallop or race. Many trainers associate post-race coughing with sand in the throat, that is thought to be inhaled into the throat and windpipe as a Greyhound races. However, if the coughing does not dislodge mucus, phlegm or sand and the symptoms of wheezing and heavy breathing are present each time the affected Greyhound races, then the Greyhound may have asthma. Often affected Greyhounds lose speed and stamina in the final stages of a race.

Causes: Allergies in the environment, such as dusty kennels and bedding, ammonia or liniment

If a Greyhound develops a severe 'wheeze' after a hard gallop, medication with a human bronchodilator, with an improvised face mask made from a polystyrene drinking cup, and administered under veterinary supervision, can rapidly relieve symptoms and prevent collapse due to asthma.

fumes in poorly ventilated race kennels may irritate the lower airways and cause an allergic form of bronchoconstriction or airway narrowing. Typically, the condition occurs after galloping, which suggests it is triggered by exercise or inhalation of cold air, particularly when racing in the late evening during a night time race programme. Often, affected Greyhounds appear choked up in the throat, as if the lead collar is too tight, and cough when made to exercise.

Management: The tonsils and throat should be checked for swelling or excess mucus in a Greyhound with an irritating cough. Refer to Tonsilitis and Biley Throat. A careful, visual and stethoscopic examination of the throat, windpipe and lower airways by a vet is essential. To evaluate the degree of relief of clinical wheezing and coughing, a trial medication with a human bronchodilator puffer may be given, followed by a short handslip or sprint about 10-15 minutes later. If the Greyhound improves in speed, or the symptoms are reduced, asthma should be suspected. In a severely affected Greyhound, pre-race medication with a bronchodilating drug may be necessary, but this is often impractical as these medications can be detected in a swab for varying periods of up to 3-4 days, relative to the type of compound. Once retired, the condition usually presents no further problem, unless the susceptible Greyhound is encouraged to exercise at speed.

AZOTURIA: Azoturia is an old term used in horses to describe a severe form of tying-up, or set-

fast, associated with muscle cramping. In Greyhounds, it has been used to refer to an acute, potentially fatal form of stress-related, severely locked-up type of cramping of the backline and hindlimb driving muscles. More recently, it has been referred to as acute metabolic acidosis syndrome, or exertional rhabdomyolysis. The condition is described under Exertional Rhabdomyolysis and cramping to avoid repetition of common signs and predisposing causes.

B

BABESIOSIS: An infection with a blood cell parasitic organism that is a cause of anaemia in 50 per cent of Greyhounds in the subtropical southeastern states of the USA. It has also been reported in other breeds of dogs in North Queensland in Australia.

Signs: Signs of infection are those typically associated with anaemia, including pale gums, weakness, loss of stamina and condition and a dry, dull coat. It is often associated initially with a fever and loss of appetite as the parasitic infection develops. There is an excess number of damaged red blood cells being recycled through the liver, rather than absolute loss, as occurs in bleeding. As a result, the membranes of the mouth and eyes develop a yellow, jaundiced colour due to the accumulation of larger amounts of yellow haemoglobin-breakdown pigment in the blood and liver. Severe infections can result in debilitation, allergic shock and death.

Cause: The dog tick-borne protozoal organism, *Babesia canis*, penetrates into red blood cells, disrupting and destroying large numbers. This, in turn, results in the release of haemoglobin pigment into the blood, which is then broken down in the liver. The body reacts by mounting an immune response against the organism, which, combined with presence of the parasite in smears of red blood cells, and tick infection, can both be used to confirm that the disease is present. In tick-prone areas, two other blood parasites, *Hepatozoan canis* and *Ehrlichia canis*, may be concurrent with Babesiosis, especially in young Greyhounds.

Management: Severely debilitated Greyhounds may require blood transfusions to restore the vital oxygen-carrying capacity of the blood by replacing the depleted red blood cell numbers. Treatment with anti-protozoal drugs under veterinary supervision, combined with tick control to reduce the risk of re-infection and spread to other Greyhounds is necessary to eradicate the infection and enable recovery. Young, growing Greyhounds on breeding farms in endemic areas have the highest incidence of infection, and racing Greyhounds confined to inside kennels have the lowest risk of infection.

BACK MUSCLE INJURIES:

The majority of Greyhound trainers use the common term 'back muscle' when referring to the gracilis muscle on the inside of the groin area. Tearing and other injuries to the major muscles along the backline are rare, with cramping of these muscles being the most common condition. Back muscle injuries are more fully described under gracilis muscle injuries.

BALANITIS:

A term to describe infection of the opening of the sheath or prepuce housing the penis, often seen as a pus-like, oozing discharge from the sheath (prepuce) opening. It is technically referred to as balanoposthitis and is common in male Greyhounds.

Signs: A creamy, brown to yellowish, sticky discharge from the sheath is relatively common in older male Greyhounds. Excess discharge may splash down the inside of the hindlegs. A brown-tinged 'lick stain' may be evident around the muzzle as Greyhounds habitually lick the sheath opening to relieve the irritation and remove the oozing discharge. Occasionally the infection may travel up the urethra into the bladder, leading to bladder inflammation and infection, referred to as cystitis.

Causes: It is considered that infection with a Herpes virus microbe may cause the initial irritation and inflammation, resulting in a discharge. This invariably becomes contaminated with bacterial germs such as Pasteurella as a Greyhound licks his sheath, or secondary infection is spread by flies attracted to the moisture and smell. Although high doses of Vitamin E and wheat germ have been considered to increase sex drive, sheath secretions and incidence of masturbation in male Greyhounds, this association

is not proven. Continued use of anabolic steroids in male racing Greyhounds is also incriminated, causing the penis to partly protrude from the sheath, resulting in secondary infection of the surrounding membranes.

Management: Antibiotic therapy is only partially successful in controlling this form of external infection. Flushing the sheath with weak, non-irritant antiseptic solutions on alternate days over a 2-3 week period will help clear up chronic infections, but the concentration must be monitored under veterinary supervision to avoid further irritation to the sheath membranes. It is recommended to discontinue any form of anabolic therapy, as well as Vitamin E or wheat germ supplements, during the cleansing period. The lick stain on the muzzle may slowly disappear over a 2-month period as new hair shafts replace the stained hair.

BALD THIGH SYNDROME:

This term is used to describe a progressive thinning and loss of hair from the back and sides of the hindlimbs (thighs) of both male and female racing Greyhounds of all ages. It can also be present on the lower belly, chest and elbows of severely affected Greyhounds.

Signs: The progressive loss of hair over the thighs occurs over a period of 4-6 weeks, without any sign of inflammatory, thickening (dermatitis) or other skin disease, itching or other irritation. The skin itself often becomes markedly crinkly, with a leather-like appearance, developing a darker colour as the hair covering thins out. Often an affected

The typical pattern of hair loss on the thighs, chest and elbows of a Greyhound under stress during a hard racing campaign, commonly referred to as bald thighs.

Greyhound progressively loses performance over the training period, developing a chronic low-grade form of dehydration.

Cause: The underlying cause of the bald thigh syndrome (BTS) has currently not been determined. Some Greyhounds of certain bloodlines show signs of BTS even when not in training, so there may be a genetic link to its development. Psychological factors may also result in hair loss in some animals. The stress of kennelling, exercise and environmental conditions during the training programme is known to increase the levels of the natural stress hormones (cortisone) in normal Greyhounds, as well as those subjected to the stress of racing. Some trainers appear to have a higher number of Greyhounds with BTS as compared to other trainers with comparative kennels and performance history. Some authorities believe it may be related to low thyroid gland activity in individual Greyhounds. However, the symptoms of BTS are not consistent with those associated with low thyroid activity, where the skin often thickens. Inadequate bedding, or an abrasive floor surface, can abrade the hair on the thighs as a Greyhound gets up and down. As well, a woven hessian (burlap) mattress covering can trap and break off hair as a Greyhound moves around on its bed. However, in these cases, the skin is not as smooth or discoloured and a stubble, or an after-shaving-like growth, can be felt when the hand is rubbed over the bald area.

Management: A blood test can be used to confirm a stress-related condition. A lay-up from training for 4-6 weeks will usually result in the start of hair regrowth and recovery of lost performance in a severely affected Greyhound. A reduction in lead walking to 20 minutes daily, and spacing out races to 10-14 day intervals, will often help to slow the progressive development of the hair loss. Supplementation with tablets of the thyroid hormone, thyroxine, under veterinary prescription and management over a 3-4 month period may result in regrowth of hair and recovery of performance in some Greyhounds. Supplementing with slow-release tablets of potassium salt and a balanced body salt mix will help avoid dehydration in long-standing cases.

BARKING: Individual Greyhounds often develop a habit of restlessness and excitement, and may start to bark when confined to kennels or when travelling.

Signs: Occasionally, a retired Greyhound, especially one that has a role as a watchdog, will bark at noises, most commonly at night, that previously would not disturb it into action. This often results from a progressive loss of sight and hearing. An excitable racing Greyhound may develop a habit of barking in anticipation when travelling or kennelled prior to trialling or racing. Barking can result in a forcible expulsion of water vapour from the lungs and respiratory tract, leading to dehydration. Prolonged barking also expels larger amounts of carbon dioxide into the expired air, which can lead to a compensatory outflow of body salts from the kidneys, reducing water intake, which further exacerbates the dehydration effect.

Causes: Barking can be a result of excitement, fear, anticipation or restlessness. When confined to a kennel, some solitary Greyhounds will start to bark, due to insecurity or simply to attract attention for companionship.

Management: When a racing Greyhound barks due to excitement and anticipation before track exercise, provision of water and body salts in the feed will help to counteract any dehydration effect. Barking in the kennels can be reduced by fitting an anti-barking muzzle, or by providing company for a solitary Greyhound. Even a radio left on in the kennels to maintain a background of music and voices can reduce the tendency for some Greyhounds to bark. In older retired Greyhounds, an anti-barking muzzle can be fitted when the animal is kennelled. In chronic cases, where permitted, the de-barking operation may be the only effective way of controlling this annoying habit.

BED SORES: Bed sores develop as an ulcerated wound over bony projections on the toes, limbs and pelvic bones of Greyhounds.

Signs: Initially, the compression of the skin results in reduced blood supply as it is squeezed off over a thinly covered bone in contact with a hard bed surface. The devitalised area will then develop into an inflamed, weeping sore. In chronic cases, the damaged skin erodes away to form a discharging ulcer that often becomes infected with bacteria. Severely affected Greyhounds may become lame or develop bone infection (osteomyelitis) or a blood-borne (systemic) infection.

Causes: The lack of an adequate covering or cushion thickness of bedding material over a hard or abrasive bed area or kennel floor is the primary cause. The tops of toes, sides of the wrist, elbows and shoulder joints, hips and hocks are most commonly affected, as well as the stifles if the bed base is hard and abrasive, such as a concrete kennel floor.

Management: A course of antibiotics to control the secondary infection may be necessary in deeply ulcerated and infected sores with associated pain and swelling. Dressing and covering the ulcerated area with antiseptic, drying and healing preparations twice daily, until it heals, is recommended. Provision of an adequate area of thicker, softer bedding, including use of a foam mattress, shredded paper or layers of blankets, will help to protect the susceptible joints and bony skeletal projections on the pressure points. Where a Greyhound develops repeated bed sores, the area often loses hair and may be more prone to redevelopment of pressure sores if an adequate thickness of bedding cushion is not maintained.

BILEY THROAT: A term used to describe the build-up of phlegm, froth or bile in the throat.

Signs: Accumulation of thick, frothy mucus at the back of the throat, most commonly after a race. Affected Greyhounds rarely cough. Some trainers believe the presence of excess mucus reduces airway efficiency and can adversely affect performance.

Causes: There are many theories to explain a 'biley throat'. Some Greyhounds suffer from an allergy-like condition, which results in increased secretion of mucus when they are given milk in their diet. A low-grade viral infection with development of inflammation of the bronchial airways (bronchitis) may cause inflammation of the throat, windpipe and lower airways, often as a follow-up to kennel cough infection. Greyhounds suffering from acute tonsillitis may accumulate mucus and pus-like discharges in the throat. Infection with the tracheal worm (Refer to Tracheal Worm), and Greyhounds suffering from exercise-induced asthma (Refer to Asthma) may accumulate more mucus than is normal in the throat. Both these conditions, however, are

characterised by a moist or hacking cough after exercise.

Management: Withdrawal of milk from the diet often eliminates the problem within 2-3 days. Treatment of acute tonsillitis and tracheobronchitis with antibiotics and oral mucolytic preparations (compounds that liquify mucus) for 5-7 days often helps to reduce symptoms. A small drink of water, or an electrolyte drink, given prior to racing, can help to clear the throat and minimise the amount of frothy mucus that develops as air is mixed with the mucus during fast exercise.

BILING OUT: This refers to the practice of encouraging a Greyhound to vomit so as to involuntarily empty its stomach contents.

Signs: Some Australian trainers link a loss of appetite and reduced interest in racing with an accumulation of bile in the gut and bloodstream, which is claimed to lead to a 'biley throat'.

Cause: There is no scientific explanation to support the practice of biling out a Greyhound. Inflammation of the stomach wall (gastritis) due to concentrated diets may trigger natural vomiting in a Greyhound. However, anecdotal observations implicate low-fat diets and repeated racing with the need to 'bile out' and 'freshen up' a racing Greyhound. Proponents claim a 'biled out' Greyhound will regain appetite and general well-being within 2-3 days. The majority of specialist Greyhound veterinarians do not condone this practice.

Management: Trainers use an emetic preparation, most commonly apomorphine, often after giving a Greyhound a meal of bread and milk, with tablets administered orally or in the lower eyelid. Strong salt solutions are also given by syringe over the tongue to stimulate vomiting. Laxative preparations, such as syrup of buckthorn and powders containing danthron, are given at intervals of 3-4 weeks after a bread and milk meal to stimulate bowel movement in an effort to remove 'bile' and 'toxic' compounds from the digestive system.

BLADDER SHUTDOWN: A psychological and stress-related condition that causes a male Greyhound to retain urine and be

unable to urinate normally after a stressful race.
Refer to Post Racing Dysuria.

BLOAT: A descriptive term referring to the accumulation of excess gas in the stomach. Any distention of the abdomen, caused by overeating or gorging on dry food, is also referred to as bloat. Luckily, this form of bloat is rarely reported in racing Greyhounds on well-balanced racing diets. Older retired Greyhounds that are given predominantly a diet based on dry food have an increased risk, especially if they are fed large amounts at a time, or at irregular intervals.

Signs: Warning signs of bloat include a distended abdomen, with restricted and laboured breathing. If the gas-filled stomach is displaced and twisted by the other abdominal organs as a Greyhound is exercised, the stomach may rotate in a clockwise direction, resulting in severe gastric enlargement (dilation) as the accumulating gas is unable to escape.

Cause: Intake of an excessive amount, or gorging on, dry food is thought to result in rapid fermentation of the cereal starch in the stomach if inadequate gastric acid is secreted to limit fermentation. A ravenous eating action of a young Greyhound when gorging dry food may result in excess air being swallowed with the food, which then becomes trapped and distends the stomach. Exercising any Greyhound after a full meal may result in rotation of the full stomach and risk of the gastric dilation condition.

Management: In all cases, if the abdomen is distended and the Greyhound is having difficulty in breathing, emergency veterinary assistance, which may involve surgery to correct a twisted stomach, must be sought. Prevention is based on restricting a Greyhound's opportunity to gorge dry foods by limiting intake to no more than 75-100g/10kg (2.5-3oz/22lbs) body weight and feeding at a regular time. (Refer to Gastric Dilation).

BLOW-OUT: This is a highly descriptive term used by American trainers to describe the development of an acute gastroenteritis and explosive diarrhoea, or 'scouring' in Greyhounds.

Signs: Rapid onset of an explosive, watery and

A severe attack of gastroenteritis in a large kennel, as a result of feeding meat with high bacterial contamination, requires thorough cleaning and disinfection to avoid cross contamination.

smelly diarrhoea with abdominal discomfort, depression and dehydration. Often a number of Greyhounds in a kennel room are affected, usually overnight after the main mid-morning meal.

Causes: A sudden change in diet, particularly from beef to horsemeat, may cause an allergic gut reaction in some Greyhounds. In most cases, a 'blow-out' in a kennel of Greyhounds is due to a batch of meat that is contaminated with pathogenic bacterial germs, including Salmonella and E. coli. In American kennels, D-grade meat salvaged from dying, diseased, disabled or dead livestock (4-D) with a high bacterial count is a common cause. As contamination levels in the kennel room increase, other Greyhounds may develop milder forms of gastroenteritis.

Management: Any major changes in diet should be introduced over a 7-10 day period, especially when horsemeat is being phased in, as its digestibility is less, and risk of red meat allergy is higher than with beef. Sources of meat should be thoroughly evaluated to ensure that the meat is not off, with an offensive smell. Frozen 4-D meat should thaw out without signs of being bathed in black, smelly fluid. Meat not readily consumed, or left after a meal, must be discarded. In severe cases, fluid and electrolyte replacement therapy, antibiotics and gut calmative medications may need to be administered and recovery supervised by a vet. Strict hygiene practices, including isolation of affected Greyhounds and thorough cleaning and disinfection of the cages, kennel room and turn-out pens, must be carried out to limit spread of the bacterial contamination.

BONE FRACTURES: Racing Greyhounds can sustain a variety of long bone, joint and toe fractures, usually as a result of race falls, collisions or weakened skeletal structures due to diets that are low in calcium. Each type and form of bone fracture is discussed under the individual bones, with the wrist, metacarpal, toes, fibula and hock joint bones having the highest risk of fracture in racing Greyhounds. (Refer to individual bones)

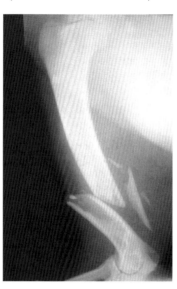

Fracture of the humerus (shoulder bone) is not uncommon. This fracture occurred when two Greyhounds collided in an outside run.

 BOWED TENDONS: Tendons are composed of bundles of fibres consisting of long parallel strands of elastic collagen fibrils or threads. A special type of collagen provides elasticity and load-bearing strength. Tendon fibrils are living tissues that require adequate blood supply and nutrition. They become more elastic and resilient to stretching when warmed up during exercise. They are continuously being repaired and replaced by new fibrils over a 6-12 month period. Tendon fibrils are elastic structures, that not only stretch and elongate when loaded during exercise, but release the 'stretch' energy to give spring to the Greyhound's movement.

Tendons extend from the end of a muscle, usually pass over a joint and insert on to a bone to transfer the muscle power to the lower limb, rather like the strings on a marionette puppet. When unloaded, the collagen fibrils have a crimped structure. On contraction of the muscle to transfer load, the crimp initially straightens and flattens and the tendon is then stretched, using its elastic recoil properties.

If the loading forces are excessive, or the tendon suddenly bears an instant highload force, such as when a limb slips and then grips on the track surface, the already fully loaded tendon can exceed its elastic limit. This can result in partial or widespread rupture of fibrils and blood vessels. Exceeding the elastic limit causes internal disruption, haemorrhage and inflammation within the tendon bundles, seen as a swelling or bow in the normal shape of the tendon.

The term 'bowed tendon' is a common name to describe overstretching and tearing of tendon fibrils within a tendon between its parent muscle and bone anchorage. Tendon injuries are not common in racing Greyhounds because the muscles usually tear first, or the tendon anchorage point to the bone pulls away. Strain and tearing of the digital flexor tendons, or the tendon of the abductor muscle of the fifth digit of the front limb, are the common sites of injury in racing Greyhounds. Tendon injuries in Greyhounds can result in extended downtime from training, and only a 60-65 per cent chance of returning to race soundly for five or more races. Refer to individual conditions.

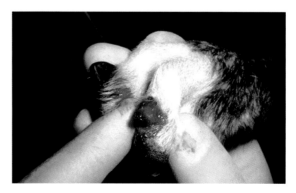 **BROKEN NAILS:** Deformed or chalky nails, and the underlying internal nail bone, may break off at the base of the nail under the cuticle, or toward the point of the toenail, as a Greyhound gallops.

Signs: Loss of all or part of a nail during galloping. Often a chalky stump remains at the broken nail end. The nail appears to be poorly

Soft, chalky nails can break off during galloping, particularly on a hard, track surface. This Greyhound suffered recurring injury and the end toe section was removed – he then returned to race successfully.

formed or weakened. The broken nail end may bleed and the Greyhound will be short in the stride if the sensitive cuticle and nail bed is damaged. Often the nail bed or 'quick' will become infected or inflamed due to trauma after loss of nail or fracture of the internal nail bone.

Causes: Soft, chalky nails that break off readily can be a feature of certain bloodlines, or, in individual Greyhounds during racing, as a result of a low-calcium diet.

Management: Cleaning and disinfecting of the broken nail end with an iodine-based antiseptic is essential, particularly if the underlying nail bone is exposed and likely to become infected. Protection of the nail end by applying a covering of a epoxy polymer or plastic-like glue that sets hard on curing will allow the nail to replace itself over 3-4 weeks. Where the underlying nail bone is broken, the new nail may be deformed or twisted and need regular trimming. Surgery to remove the damaged nail and nail bone is recommended in recurring cases. Supplementing with the vitamin biotin (1mg daily), the amino acid methionine (1000mg daily) and the mineral calcium (2-3 grams daily) may help to strengthen weak or chalky brittle nails, particularly as a Greyhound ages in retirement.

BRUISED NAILS: The seepage and accumulation of blood as a haematoma inside the nail between the quick and the nail bone.

Signs: A red (fresh blood), or dark blue-black (congealed blood), area can be seen where blood collects under the nail surface in lightly pigmented nails. The pressure resulting from the haematoma

Severe bruising of the nail can occur as a result of trauma. This injury was caused when a kennel door was accidentally closed on the Greyhound's toe.

causes acute pain when the nail over the sensitive quick (nail bed) is squeezed between the fingers. Often the Greyhound is short in the stride and lame.

Causes: Catching the nail in a kennel door, striking the nail on a race track railing or a hard stone or other object during galloping, can cause bruising of the fine blood vessels that supply the nail bed and quick under the outer nail. It is similar to a blood blister under the nail of one of your own fingers.

Management: The development of a haematoma in a newly bruised nail is best minimised by applying a block of ice for 2-3 minutes over the bruised area. This will help reduce the intense pain and swelling caused by pressure build-up within the 'quick' or nail bed space. If the nail is long, it is best to trim it back to the tip of the nail bone and quick to prevent it touching the ground. A vet may drill a small hole into the desensitised nail with a dental drill to help relieve the intense pain and release the serum and clotted blood. Where there is a risk of infection, a course of antibiotics, combined with enzyme preparations to disintegrate the blood clot, may also be recommended.

BRONCHITIS: Inflammation, often with increased mucus secretion, of one or both of the large airways (bronchi) as they branch into the lungs.

Signs: Coughing and gurgling are common signs, with repeated gagging and swallowing as the loosened mucus is coughed up. Exercise tolerance and performance is often reduced, with wheezing after galloping. A severe attack of coughing may cause exhaustion and collapse in acute cases.

Causes: An initial infection with a virus or bacterial organism, such as the kennel cough complex, or an allergic reaction to dust or mould particles in the kennel environment and bedding, are both considered common underlying causes. In severe cases, underlying bronchitis may develop into an allergic asthma (refer to Asthma) and chronic tracheobronchitis. Refer to Tracheobronchitis.

Management: The treatment and management programme will be influenced by the underlying cause, the severity and the symptoms. In severe or unresponsive cases, samples of mucus or phlegm may be taken for bacterial culture. Antibiotic, bronchodilation and mucolytic therapy may be necessary to assist airway clearance and drainage. The kennel area and bedding should be thoroughly cleaned and disinfected. Any form of free exercise should be avoided during early morning, or under very cold conditions, as it may irritate the inflamed airway lining and aggravate the wheezing and coughing.

BURSITIS: A condition that describes inflammation of the fluid-filled cushioning sacs over the point of the elbow and hock. The swelling is also referred to as a hygroma.

Signs: A fluid-filled, hot and very sensitive swelling of the normally soft area over the rear of the elbow and hock joints. Some develop within a couple of days, while others enlarge over a 2-3 week period, particularly if they are aggravated by continued bruising of the bony point of the joint as the Greyhound gets up and down from the

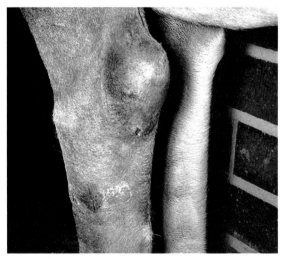

Swelling of the cushioning bursa pouch at the point of the elbow can occur as a result of a hard bed or traumatic injury. Here, the cap of the elbow is infected and requires drainage and anti-inflammatory treatment.

kennel floor or a poorly cushioned bed.

Cause: The common underlying cause is inadequate bedding and traumatic irritation to the bursal sac. It may become permanently hardened or enlarged in some cases due to fibrous invasion into the damaged cushioning pad.

Management: Early cases respond well to ice packing for periods of 2-3 minutes, repeated at least 2-3 times daily for 4-5 days. It is important to provide a thicker, cushioned, foam or rubber bedding mattress and soft bags on the kennel floor. Topical anti-inflammatory ointments and creams, such as DMSO, applied twice daily for 7-10 days, will help limit the swelling and discomfort. Large swellings can be surgically drained and managed by a veterinarian.

C

CALCINOSIS CIRCUMSCRIPTA: A term that describes a hard, bony swelling, which develops on the spine of the shoulder blade or scapula bone.

Signs: The hard, bony non-painful swelling, often up to the size of half a marble, forms on the lower end of the shoulder (scapula bone) spine, sometimes on both shoulders.

Cause: Hard kennel floors, and beds without adequate padding, cause bruising and bleeding of the periosteum (bone-covering membrane) over the thinly-covered bony prominence at the lower end of the scapula spine. A blood clot can form and enlarge when it is continually irritated and bruised as the Greyhound gets up and down.

Management: The bony lump detracts from the Greyhound's appearance, but does not normally interfere with racing form although, in the early stages, the area may be painful. Massaging it with a cooling liniment may relieve any low-grade

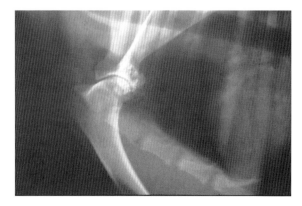

X-ray image of the bony swelling that can develop on the bottom end of the shoulder bone (scapula) spine, referred to as Calcinosis Circumscripta.

swelling. Removal of the lump is a relatively simple surgical operation, which may help improve the animal's appearance. Providing a thicker cushion to the bedding and bags on the floor will help prevent future occurrence.

CALCULI IN THE URINE:

These are chalky deposits commonly referred to as bladder stones or crystals in the urine.

Signs: Many trainers observe a crystal-like deposit when urine dries up. Often a cloudy urine, containing crystals or suspended particles with a gritty, sandy feel, is passed early in the morning after overnight confinement to the kennels. Frequent urination, straining to empty the bladder, and fresh blood in the urine can indicate a build-up of crystals in the urine. Larger crystals, may block the urethra tube from the bladder and restrict bladder emptying, especially in male Greyhounds.

Causes: Dry food diets that are high in protein, as well as calcium, phosphorus and magnesium salts, combined with a low water intake and a high alkaline (pH) reading in the urine, increase the risk of these salts settling out as sedimentary mineral crystals and developing into grit or stones in the bladder.

Management: Crystals can irritate the bladder wall, resulting in swelling (cystitis), discomfort and secondary infection within the bladder wall. Providing up to 70 per cent meat, and a urinary acidifying supplement such as 1500mg methionine or alternatively 500mg ammonium chloride daily in the feed, including electrolytes to encourage water intake and kidney outflow, is recommended. Occasionally large stones can form in the bladder of older retired Greyhounds. Surgery may be required to remove them.

CALCULUS ON THE TEETH:

A chalky, brown, stained deposit, often referred to as plaque, caries or tartar, that forms on the canine and back teeth. As Greyhounds age in retirement, build-up of tartar hastens teeth decay and dental deterioration.

Signs: A hard, brown coating that accumulates initially around the tooth-gum margin. The Greyhound may develop bad breath (halitosis) and reddening of the gums due to a low-grade bacterial infection that resides under the coating due to acid

Greyhounds, particularly aged, retired companion animals fed on soft food diets, often develop a build-up of scale on the tooth-gum margins. This can lead to bad breath and tooth decay.

erosion. If it is not removed, the calculus can build up to a hard scale, or crust, that discolours and decays the teeth as a Greyhound ages.

Causes: Soft, dry food and meat diets leave a residual coating of acidic food around the teeth-gum margin that harbours bacteria, accumulates and hardens into a brown, chalky crust. In severe cases, where gum infection and bad breath results, a secondary tonsillitis may develop, causing coughing and airway restriction. In older Greyhounds, the molar teeth may decay under the coating, with infection of the tooth root, causing toothache as a result of cracked, broken or loose teeth. It may be the underlying cause of premature loss of teeth in an ageing Greyhound.

Management: Small deposits can be controlled by providing abrasive, hard husks or 300g (10.5 oz) of brisket bones or a long ox-bone to gnaw on a regular twice weekly basis. Bones should not be provided within 2-3 days of racing. Large deposits are best removed by the descaling procedure carried out by a vet. The stains, bad breath and early deposits around the gum margins can be controlled by swabbing the margins with 50:50 hydrogen peroxide in water twice daily for 3-5 days, then once weekly as required. Refer also to Gingivitis and Periodontal Disease.

CALF MUSCLE INJURIES:

The gastronemius (lateral and medial muscle portions) and superficial digital flexor muscles form the group of muscles often referred to as the calf muscles, analogous to the calf muscles on the human leg. These muscles are located on the outer

The hamstring group of muscles attach to the Achilles tendon of the hock. Muscle sprain can cause swelling and lameness, with the Greyhound walking and resting on the point of the toes on the injured limb.

side of the hindlimbs behind the stifle joint and their tendons form into the Achilles tendon that attaches to the point of the hock.

Signs: Soft, squelchy swelling due to tearing of the lower end of the calf muscles at the origin of the Achilles tendon. The Greyhound may appear restricted in its hindlimb stride, drag its toes and stand with a partly flexed or bent hock. Pressure over the area with the fingers may cause discomfort. In old injuries, a fibrous scar can be felt and wastage of muscle is apparent.

Cause: Tearing of the lower ends of the muscle where the Achilles tendon attaches, resulting in haemorrhage (diagnosed by a characteristic squelchy feel) and disruption of the muscle structure.

Management: Where haemorrhage occurs, ice packs applied under a firm elastic bandage for 2-3 minutes, at least 3-4 times daily, over the initial 36-48 hours, and kennel rest, will help to limit blood accumulation. In severe injuries, surgical sutures to repair the tear, followed by 14-21 days kennel rest and short lead walks, then 3-4 weeks of physiotherapy, such as ultrasonic or magnetic field therapy, under veterinary supervision, usually gives the best results. Scarring of the tendon attachment area provides a weak point that can rupture at a later date, so use of an injectable sclerosing agent to promote fibrous healing may not give a satisfactory result in this particular injury.

CALLUS ON BONE: The collar, or ring, of thickened bone growth that forms over the site of a bone fracture, or a pulled-away tendon or ligament anchorage to bone.

Signs: Careful examination with the index finger run over the site of a healing or healed bone fracture, such as a metacarpal (shin) bone, often reveals a raised area of thickened bone or a callus.

Cause: The healing process involves increased activity and deposition of calcium under the tissue covering the bone (periosteum) which develops into a raised area. If the fracture of a long bone, metacarpal (shin) or toe bone is not firmly supported to prevent movement during healing, (referred to as being stabilised), the bone collar or callus can become even more enlarged. After healing is complete, the bone surface may remodel by absorbing the excess calcium from the callus to reduce its size. If the callus remains, it can irritate surrounding soft tissue, and rub on tendons that pass over the area, causing irritation, discomfort, inflammation and weakening of the tendon and, in severe cases, increased risk of breakdown and lameness.

Management: Prompt and expert management of fractures and torn anchorages of tendons and ligaments of long bones, toe bones and lower limbs will reduce the risk of formation of an enlarged callus. Proper support of the fractured bone to maintain alignment and stabilisation during healing is essential to reduce the size of the callus. An adequate, but not excessive, intake of calcium and Vitamin D in the diet to enhance bone repair should reduce callus formation in young racing Greyhounds. Magnetic field therapy has been shown to improve the rate of bone healing and, if used, may minimise the size of the callus.

CAMPYLOBACTER INFECTION: Campylobacter microbes are found in the small intestine of otherwise healthy Greyhounds. If they proliferate under suitable conditions they can cause severe diarrhoea, dehydration and debilitation.

Signs: A raised temperature due to infection, followed by a bloody diarrhoea and loss of appetite. Many dogs vomit initially due to a severe toxic intestinal infection. This infection is not common in Greyhounds fed on good-quality, hygienically prepared food.

Cause: Campylobacter bacteria are usually introduced by contaminated chicken meat with the skin attached, or wild bird droppings falling into water containers or food dishes in the kennel or yard area.

Management: Veterinary diagnosis and prompt treatment with oral fluids and anti-diarrhoea mixtures containing a targeted antibiotic is essential. Strict kennel hygiene to clean up the diarrhoea residues and avoid cross-contamination between kennels with shared drainage is important to prevent humans and adjacent Greyhounds becoming infected.

CANINE VIRAL DISEASE: Greyhounds of all ages are susceptible to a number of canine viral diseases. These include: Adenovirus, Canine Coronavirus, Canine Distemper; Canine Hepatitis, Canine Herpes Virus, Canine Parainfluenza and Canine Parvovirus. The following table provides a summary of the causes, signs and management of these viral diseases.

Infection: Adenovirus
Site of Infection: Respiratory tract.
Cause: Aerosol inhalation
Signs: Coughing, with wheezing and laboured breathing due to lower airway inflammation.
Management: Often clears up after 3-7 days, and occasionally secondary bacterial infection can cause pneumonia. Supportive treatment. Vaccination.

Infection: Canine Coronavirus
Site of Infection: Gastrointestinal tract.
Cause: Infection from contaminated droppings.
Signs: Rapid onset of watery orange-coloured diarrhoea and vomiting initially over 24-36 hours, often containing blood. Loss of appetite and gut pain.
Management: Greyhounds usually recover following electrolytes and fluid therapy. Vaccination.

Infection: Canine Distemper Virus.
Site of Infection: A morbilivirus that colonises the respiratory, intestinal and nervous system.
Cause: Infection by aerosol droplets. Common from 3-6 months of age.
Signs: Initial fever, followed by runny eyes and nose, coughing, vomiting, diarrhoea, dehydration and weight loss. Hardening of feet pads and nose leather. Nervous twitches, lack of co-ordination, fits and blindness. Recovery can take up to 2-20 weeks, with severely infected Greyhounds being left with a permanent nervous twitch.
Management: Isolation of infected Greyhounds, especially non-vaccinated Greyhounds that should be immediately vaccinated under vet supervision. It is best to treat symptoms as they occur. Nervous signs may be severe and require euthanasia. All Greyhounds must be vaccinated and given regular annual boosters, even if the disease is not reported for some years.

Infection: Canine Hepatitis Virus.
Site of Infection: An adenovirus type that affects the liver.
Cause: Infection by mouth or inhaled into throat.
Signs: The virus attacks and destroys liver cells. Initial fever, loss of appetite, gut pain, clouding of eyes, coughing and secondary lung infection.
Management: Isolation of infected Greyhounds and supportive therapy. Vaccination.

Infection: Canine Herpes Virus
Site of Infection: A herpes virus affecting the respiratory tract
Cause: Aerosol infection.
Signs: Fever, runny eyes, coughing, sneezing and loss of appetite.
Management: Symptomatic treatment. No vaccination.

Infection: Canine Parainfluenza
Site of Infection: Respiratory tract.
Cause: Aerosol inhalation.
Signs: Coughing and excess mucus due to airway inflammation (bronchitis).
Management: Usually self-limiting due to immune response in 3-5 days. Supportive and symptomatic treatment. Vaccination.

Infection: Canine Parvovirus.
Site of Infection: Gastrointestinal tract.
Cause: Infection from droppings of infected dogs.
Signs: Fever, bloody diarrhoea, severe dehydration leading to vomiting, loss of appetite, death in severely infected Greyhounds within 24-36 hours.
Management: Low-grade infections recover in 2-5 days. Greyhounds with acute infection must be given fluids and electrolytes as well as antibiotics to prevent secondary gut infection. Routine vaccination of all pups and regular boosters in older Greyhounds.

CANKER: Refer to Ear Infections – Otitis Externa.

CARPAL INJURIES: Carpal (wrist) injuries are relatively common in racing Greyhounds. The wrist is constructed of two rows of small bones, aligned and held in position by bone-to-bone ligaments. An accessory carpal bone (stopper bone) protrudes from behind the wrist under the stopper pad. Joint concussion and bruising, bone fractures and ligament sprains can occur when the wrist is fully flattened (extended) when galloping. Retired Greyhounds may develop degenerative osteoarthritis as they age as a result of injuries sustained to the wrists during their racing career.

Signs: The Greyhound will normally pull up lame, holding the wrist off the ground in a bent position, or be reluctant to walk and bear weight. Severe sprain of the distal accessory carpal (wrist) ligament, or a tear-away fracture, will result in swelling and pain when the wrist is pressed or flexed with varying degrees of lameness. Internal sprain of the wrist joint may make a Greyhound reluctant to have its wrist flexed, or reduce flexion when it is bent back (flexed) and squeezed on itself. Chronic, long-term injuries result in osteoarthritis and bony deterioration within the wrist joint.

Causes: Falls, concussion from hard track surfaces, or extreme flattening (hyperextension) of the wrist during weight-bearing when cornering, can cause tearing of internal ligaments, compression of cartilage and bone surfaces, bone chips and fractures of the internal bones. Refer also to Accessory Carpal Bone Injuries.

Management: Depending on the origin of the pain and discomfort, various therapies are used. Internal wrist injuries and joint damage can be treated with injections of anti-inflammatory

A Greyhound with a carpal injury may experience reduced flexion.

cortisone or hyaluronic acid. A number of oral preparations containing glucosamine, chondroitin sulphate, Vitamin C, shark cartilage and trace-minerals to assist in ligament and cartilage repair are available. Refer to Articular Cartilage, Arthritis. Distal accessory and carpal ligament sprains and tears often benefit from topical massage with liniments to reduce arthritic symptoms, and a 2-3 week programme of magnetic field therapy. Strapping the wrist with an elastic support bandage, where legal for racing, may be beneficial to prevent excessive flattening and provide stabilising support to the wrist as the Greyhound gallops.

CARIES ON TEETH: A chalky, brownish coating on the tooth-gum margin areas, also referred to as calculus, tartar and plaque. Refer to Calculus on Teeth.

CARTILAGE EROSION: Apposing joint surfaces are covered with a thin layer of resilient, non-sensory, lubricated cartilage to eliminate wear and provide minimum friction movement and a protective shock-absorbing capacity to the underlying bone. Erosion of the joint cartilage surface can occur due to loss of lubrication fluid, reduction of its water content, concurrent joint infection and damage, or deficiencies of trace-minerals and nutrients that provide the structural resilience of healthy cartilage. Refer to Articular Cartilage.

CATARACTS: The progressive clouding, followed by crystallisation of the lens of the eye into an opaque structure that inhibits the passage of light and reduces sight. Cataracts can eventually result in partial or complete blindness in older, retired Greyhounds.

Signs: An opaque or cloudy appearance, often referred to as 'milkiness' of the lens behind the pupil of one or both eyes. It is usually first noticed as a cloudy disc behind the pupil when a Greyhound with developing cataracts stands in bright light.

Causes: Most common in older Greyhounds due to degeneration of the lens. Cataracts may result from diabetes, or in some breeds, develop as an inherited disorder.

Management: Surgical removal of the lens is possible, but many older ageing Greyhounds that are familiar with their surroundings cope well and can become almost totally blind without running into objects. A full examination by a vet is recommended to evaluate the relative stage of the cataract(s) and the degree of residual sight.

CHERRY EYE: A common term to describe the inflammation and protrusion of the lymphoid (immune protective) gland within the third eyelid.

Signs: A cherry-shaped small lump that develops on the inside corner of the eye(s) nearest to the nose.

Cause: The small lymphoid gland behind the third eyelid can become inflamed due to irritation and allergic reaction to dust, particles of sand or infection within the eyelids. In some Greyhounds, a sudden allergic reaction can develop in the eyes due to dust, pollen from grass when rubbing on lawns or contact with dust from bedding or carpets.

Management: Moistening the eye with human eye drops or ointment can assist in reducing the discomfort and swelling. A cold compress held over the closed eye for one minute can also help to reduce the swelling and discomfort. If the condition persists for 2-3 hours, veterinary advice should be sought as irritation and infection of the cornea may result. Refer to Corneal Ulceration.

CHILBLAINS: Drying and cracking of the skin of the tips of the ears under cold conditions.

Signs: The point and edge of the ear flaps become dry, cracked and may start to bleed if the Greyhound shakes and flaps its ear due to the itchiness and discomfort, or rubs its ears on kennel wire or bedding. In severe cases, the edges may ulcerate, seep blood and attract flies.

Causes: Kennelling under very cold conditions results in reduced circulation on the borders of the relatively thin, sparsely covered ears of a Greyhound.

Management: Early cases will heal when treated for 7-10 days with antibiotic and soothing creams and ointments. The ears must be protected and kept warm. The ears can be pinned against the head by a band of woollen, stretchy football sock

The ear tips are prone to developing chilblains, seen as dry scabby sores on the tips of their ears, when exposed to very cold conditions. The ear tips can be protected from the cold by fitting a woollen sock over the ears as a sleeve.

or stocking, or the sleeve of a cardigan that encircles the top of the head under the throat. Warm, moist foments may be helpful to improve circulation and creams containing vasodilating compounds may be applied under veterinary supervision. Ulcerated borders need specialised veterinary treatment. It is essential that in very cold weather, the Greyhound be housed indoors in a heated room, preferably on a raised bed as the air is coolest at floor level.

COCCIDIOSIS: A cause of diarrhoea due to proliferation of the Coccidia protozoal type organism in the intestinal tract.

Signs: Initial fever, with watery, often blood-tinged diarrhoea, vomiting, dehydration and loss of appetite, occurring most commonly in young puppies. Severe diarrhoea can drain fluids and electrolytes, resulting in dehydration and debilitation. If not treated, it can be fatal.

Causes: Infection with the *Coccidia isopora* organism can occur where the microbe contaminates the soil or is introduced by an infected or carrier Greyhound. The risks of this infection can increase under conditions of overcrowding and poor hygiene on breeding and racing farms, especially in cold, wet, moist conditions or following a stressful period where a Greyhound's immunity may be compromised.

Management: Infection can be confirmed by examination of the droppings for characteristic Coccidia eggs. Infected Greyhounds must be isolated and water and waste cross-contamination within kennels, yards and turn-out pens avoided. Treatment, which may require fluids, electrolytes and anti-coccidial drugs to control the infection, should be supervised by a vet. Antibiotics are not active against protozoal organisms, although sulfonamides may be useful to prevent secondary infection of the irritated intestines. Attention to hygiene and removal of contaminated soil in yards is essential to avoid recurring infections.

COLITIS: An inflammatory disease of the lining of the large intestine.
Signs: The most typical sign is straining to pass small quantities of stools. Greyhounds with colitis often pass droppings covered with a coating of excess slime or whitish mucus film that looks like a skin covering the stools. Occasionally, smears of fresh blood may be noticed on the stools. Some Greyhounds exhibit pain when emptying out, others seek out and eat grass and then may vomit. A few develop a low-grade diarrhoea for 1-2 days before the above signs appear.
Cause: Certain dietary changes, such as a change from beef to horsemeat may cause an allergic type of inflammatory reaction of the colon. Often a sudden increase in the fat and protein content of a dry food, heavy worm infestation, and occasionally a low-grade bacterial bowel infection are also likely to cause a colitis.
Management: A review of diet changes should be carried out, and all new feeds introduced in a gradual manner over 7-10 days to avoid allergy to new food proteins. If the stools are small and concentrated, then extra fibre should be provided in the diet, such as a cupful of steam-cooked vegetables or alternatively 1-2 tablespoons of bran. These may assist the emptying-out action. If symptoms persist, then examination of the stools, internal endoscopic examination and biopsy of the intestinal wall, or a long-term course of a sulphonamide-based antimicrobial preparation and probiotic supplement may be advised by a veterinarian.

COLLAPSED TRACHEAL RINGS: A condition caused by abnormal development of the cartilaginous rings in the wall of the windpipe. The defect is usually within the tracheal rings of the neck area, rather than within the chest cavity. It is also referred to as Segmental Airway Collapse (SAC) by vets.
Signs: On careful examination, a malformation or absence of the windpipe (trachea) cartilage reinforcing rings can be detected along the underside of the neck. Signs of airway restriction are not usually apparent at rest. Affected Greyhounds may cough and wheeze when the windpipe under the collar area is squeezed by the hand or by the collar when walking on the lead. In a racing Greyhound, symptoms of coughing and gasping for air during hard exercise, with a loss of speed after 100-150 metres (130-200 yards) in a gallop, may be a sign to suspect and identify the problem.
Cause: An hereditary disease that results in collapse or flattening of the malformed or missing reinforcement rings (similar to a vacuum cleaner hose structure) of the trachea or windpipe when negative lung pressure is generated on inspiration during exercise. Lengths of 100-150 mm (4-6ins) the windpipe may have inadequate reinforcement due to an absence of cartilage rings in the wall.
Management: Although an operation to insert a plastic implant to strengthen the wall of the windpipe is available, in most cases racing Greyhounds are usually retired early in their race career often without a definite diagnosis of the problem. It is unlikely to cause respiratory distress in a retired Greyhound kept as a companion. Affected Greyhounds should not be bred, as the condition is inherited.

COLLATERAL LIGAMENT INJURIES: The collateral ligaments attach the sides of a bone to the opposing bone, spanning a lower limb joint, such as a toe joint. They are composed of strong bands of fibrous, tendon-like tissue that help align, stabilise and maintain the joint structure against twisting and stretching forces. The most commonly injured collateral ligaments are those on the sides of the toe bone joints. Other collateral ligaments help stabilise the wrist, stifle joint and hock joints.
Signs: Collateral ligaments of the toes in particular can be sprained and stretched (sprung), torn or ruptured along their lengths or pulled away from their bone anchorage points (dislocated). The severity of collateral ligament failure on the toe

joints can be evaluated by gently bending the toe below the affected joint to the right and left. A 'sprung' toe (sprained collateral ligament) will deviate less than 45 degrees to the non-sprained side. A dislocated toe (ruptured collateral ligament), where the ligament is torn apart or away from its anchorage, will hinge sideways at the joint over at least 45-90 degrees. This is a more common injury on the lower joints of the toe.

Cause: Sudden sideways movement on cornering, loss of toe traction, or catching the toe nail in a grass track surface at the gallop can lead to stretching (sprung toe) or tearing/rupture (dislocated toe) of the collateral ligaments on the sides of one or more toes.

Management: Initial ice packing and strapping to keep the 'sprung' toe straight, application of topical inflammatory agents, such as DMSO, application of liniments, and 10-14 days of rest and walking with the toe(s) strapped is usually adequate. Surgical repair of a torn ligament with sutures to replace the ligament is successful in some cases, combined with rest and anti-inflammatory treatment. An injection of a chemical compound (sclerosing agent) to promote fibrous tissue growth is also worthwhile to hasten repair of 'sprung' toes. Dislocated toes with ruptured collateral ligaments may recur and amputation of the lower bone is usually recommended. Once healed, the injured toe can be strapped to its neighbour using a 5mm ($^1/_5$ in) wide rubber band cut from a bicycle inner tube, or conventional elastic adhesive tape.

CONGESTIVE HEART FAILURE: Aged Greyhounds can develop weakness of the right or left side heart muscles, resulting in reduced blood pressure within the body or lung circulation. It is also referred to as Heart Insufficiency.

Signs: Left-Sided Heart Failure: The Greyhound exhibits signs of loss of breath, coughing when resting or exercising (a heart cough), cold lower limbs and a gurgling moist cough when resting at night. In severe cases, fluid build-up referred to as ascites or dropsy in the abdominal cavity, can cause swelling of the abdominal cavity.

Right-Sided Heart Failure: This may be secondary to lung disease, with increased coughing, fluid build-up in the lungs when resting at night and loss of breath when exercised. Infection with adult heartworms may cause reduced right-side heart function.

Causes: Retired Greyhounds may suffer from weakened heart muscles as they age. Acute infection may lead to heart muscle damage causing loss of heart muscle strength and tone. Heart valve damage, disease or failure can cause reduced blood pressure and backflow of blood, leading to a murmur and symptoms of heart insufficiency. Heartworm lodged within the heart can also reduce heart function, leading to a lowering of blood pressure. All conditions can result in fluid build-up under the skin of the lower limbs (oedema) or within the lungs, leading to an unproductive, moist cough.

Management: A careful examination by a vet to check heart sounds, an electrocardiograph (ECG), X-rays of the chest and diagnostic imaging (echocardiograph or ultrasound) will assist in determining the underlying cause. A blood test for heartworm microfilariae (Refer to Heartworm) may be recommended in high-risk areas. Daily medication with drugs to increase the force of heart muscle contraction and the tone and strength of the heart muscle may be combined with a diuretic to remove excess fluid build-up. Routine medication will help the aged Greyhound overcome the symptoms associated with a failing or diseased heart.

CONJUNCTIVITIS: The most common eye condition seen in dogs and Greyhounds.

Signs: The underside lining of the eyelid becomes inflamed, reddened and swollen. It is often itchy, resulting in the Greyhound rubbing its eye with a front paw or the side of its head on bedding etc. The eye is often watery, overflowing at the brim of the lower lid, with tears running down the side of the nose and face. A sticky or crusty build-up of discharge may adhere to the eyelid, or alternatively a strand-like discharge of mucus may exude from the lower inside corner (medial canthus) of one or both eyes.

Causes: Conjunctivitis can often be caused by an allergy to dust, irritation by a hair in the eye, and cold wind in the eyes, all of which can result in inflammation, allergic reaction and swollen eye membranes. Pollen from grasses or lawns in late spring and summer can cause an allergy reaction in retired Greyhounds walked on grass or lying down to rest when confined to yards with grass.

Management: Bathing the eye in normal saline (0.9 per cent salt solution) will help remove allergy inducing dust, pollens, hairs or other foreign matter. An antiseptic and soothing eye ointment carefully instilled into the eye under veterinary supervision will help reduce swelling, discomfort and excess tear production. Chronic cases that do not respond to simple medication must be referred to a vet to help avoid damage to the cornea and risk of ulceration. Refer to Corneal Ulceration.

CONSTIPATION: A commonly used word that describes difficulty in emptying out due to the retention of large or excessively dry stools. As a Greyhound ages, the lower bowel can become less active, with reduced intestinal muscular strength to move the digestive mass through the large intestine.

Signs: Straining to pass stools, or passing large masses of dry stools. In severe cases, the Greyhound may be unable to pass stools. It may become lethargic, lose its appetite and develop acute gut pain.

Causes: Dehydration and inadequate water intake, particularly on diets containing large amounts of dry food, can reduce the moisture content of the stools. Aged Greyhounds may be unable to chew bones into small pieces, resulting in impaction of dry, bone-impregnated stools in the colon or rectum. Prostate gland enlargement as well as cancer (tumour) of the lower intestinal tract in aged Greyhounds may restrict the bowel and result in a build-up of dried-out stools.

Management: A mass of hard stools can be softened by the administration of paraffin oil at 1ml per kg (2.2 lbs) body weight over the tongue, combined with an extra 1-2 cups of water in the food to moisten the stool mass. Ensuring an adequate fibre intake by feeding 1 level tablespoonful of wheat bran per 20kg (44.1 lbs) body weight daily or as required, and feeding wet, but not mushy, feed to increase the fluid content in the diet will reduce the risk of a recurring constipation in racing Greyhounds. In aged Greyhounds suffering from prostate or other tumours, hormonal or surgical treatment may be prescribed by a veterinarian.

CORNEAL ULCERATION: A condition that develops on the surface of the front clear part (cornea) of the eyeball of one or both eyes.

Signs: A pink or white film often spreads over the cornea, with increased tear production and blinking (blephrospasm) and discomfort in strong light. Devitalisation of the outer corneal layers then results in ulceration, with reddening of the eye, severe discomfort and risk of rupture of the internal fluid within the eyeball in acute cases. White scarring of the cornea often develops over the ulcerated or traumatised cornea, restricting sight. This may force retirement in a racing Greyhound.

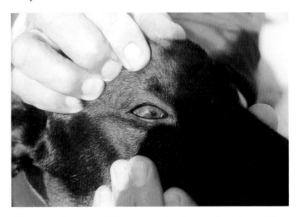

The central area of the cornea is ulcerated with a white scar forming over the central area of sight in this retired Greyhound.

Causes: Corneal ulceration can be caused by infection of the cornea introduced by flies and dust, or traumatic injury to the cornea caused by sand, or other foreign bodies within the eye, or brushing the eye with a paw or scratching by sharp grass awns.

Management: Eye injuries with signs of infection, a film covering the eye or ulceration of the cornea must be treated promptly by a vet and must be regarded as an emergency condition. Careful examination of the eye with fluorescent drops instilled into the eye to highlight any area of ulceration is standard procedure. Aggressive therapy with antibiotic drops, irrigation with saline preparations, control of flies and dust to prevent infection, combined with eyelid and conjunctival suturing to close and protect the healing cornea is standard practice. An Elizabethan collar, or a bucket on the head, to prevent the Greyhound rubbing and causing further trauma is necessary. In cases of severe ulceration, corneal transplants may be considered.

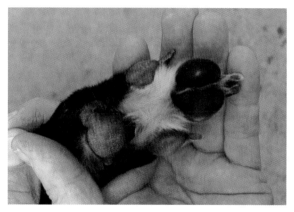

CORNS: Corns develop as an area of sensitive, white fibrous scarring on the pads.

Signs: Corns can be extremely sensitive and painful, causing a shortened stride and lameness. When the area of the corn is pressed, the Greyhound will withdraw the foot, hold the foot off the ground and limp when immediately walked off.

A painful white skin corn developed in the centre of a hindlimb pad after a sharp prickle penetrated the pad.

Causes: The most common cause is an infection by the wart virus (papilloma virus) that localises in the deeper tissue under the pad surface. The corn develops as a cone-shaped lesion with its base on the pad surface and its apex tapering into the pad, which in severe cases, attaches to the underlying tendon tissue under the pad. Often the corn will develop a blood supply and become a permanent and painful lesion within the pad. During exercise the corn is squashed deep into the pad surface, causing soreness and lameness. Cuts to the pad can also result in an area of scar tissue that resembles a corn, but this type of corn is normally shallow and less painful.

Management: Various preparations are available to treat human corns, or thickened sensitive areas on the bulbs of the feet, and these are often used on Greyhounds. They are not usually effective in relieving the discomfort of pad corns in racing Greyhounds, although they may be useful for long-standing corns in older retired Greyhounds. Deep

pad corns are best removed by surgery. The pad heals quickly if kept clean and dry with the wound edges held together with stitches or skin glue. Most Greyhounds can return to training within 12-14 days after surgery. The majority of viral corns that invade the deeper tissues of the pad require extensive surgery and, in severe cases, removal of the affected toe may be considered.

COUGHING: Coughing is a normal reflex action to dislodge mucus or other accumulated or irritating material from the throat, windpipe or lungs. Coughing in an aged Greyhound may be related to a failing heart, with animals developing a moist, unproductive cough when resting at night. Refer to Congestive Heart Failure.

Signs: The type, severity, frequency and duration of coughing are dependent on the underlying cause and its location. In severe cases, coughing can lead to vomiting and respiratory distress.

Causes: Coughing can be 'wet' or 'dry', be productive or unproductive in dislodging mucus and other fluid accumulations from the throat or lower respiratory system. There are many causes of coughing. These include airway disease and inflammation, lung and tracheal parasites, severe heartworm infection with right-side congestive heart failure, allergic asthma and physical irritation. In aged Greyhounds, a chronic cough may develop due to a right-sided or congestive heart failure. Refer to Congestive Heart Failure and Heart Disease.

Management: The treatment and management for controlling a cough is relative to the underlying cause. Where acute respiratory disease is the triggering cause, medications to reduce the cough reflex should not be given, as airway expulsion of accumulated mucus or other material from the airways is suppressed. A full examination of the Greyhound to determine the underlying cause should be carried out by a vet. Refer to Asthma, Collapsed Tracheal Rings, Heartworm, Infectious Tracheobronchitis (Kennel Cough), Lungworm, Pharyngitis, Pneumonia, Tonsillitis, Tracheal Worms.

COUPLING JOINT INJURIES: This is a term used by trainers to describe the location of inflammation and soreness in the lumbosacral joint of the lower back of a racing Greyhound. Chronic arthritis as a result of an earlier racing injury may develop within the joint as a Greyhound ages in retirement.

Signs: The way the Greyhound jumps from the traps or starting boxes, with an awkward exit and noticeable side-to-side wobbling of hindquarters in the final stages of a race can herald the onset of a coupling joint injury. Often the development of a track leg (jack) when racing due to abnormal pelvic movement is also a sign associated with arthritic pain in the lower spine area. The standing animal usually resents downward pressure applied to the midline in front of the pin bones, and in severe cases, the Greyhound will sit down when pressure is applied over the lumbosacral area. In chronic cases, a bitch may be reluctant to squat to urinate due to lower back discomfort and arthritic pain.

A simple test combining rearward manipulation of the hindleg with finger pressure on the spine centrally between the pin bones will cause a pain reaction in Greyhounds with a coupling joint injury.

Causes: The lumbosacral joint allows the hindquarters to slightly rotate to each side around the spinal column when galloping. Injuries usually result from collisions or falls, with muscle injury, sprain of spinal ligaments, and in chronic cases, arthritis of the joint space. In sporting and hunting dogs, narrowing of the spinal nerve canal (stenosis) due to degenerative lumbosacral arthritis and intervertebral disc protrusion as a 'slipped disc' can lead to loss of hindlimb co-ordination, weakness, paralysis of the tail and retention of urine and stools. Aged Greyhounds may develop lower back arthritic conditions that result in lumbosacral stenosis and its symptoms.

Management: Mild cases associated with muscle sprains in young racing Greyhounds respond to rest and twice-daily massage for 3-5 minutes with a warming counter irritant liniment for 5-7 days, or until symptoms subside. Magnetic field therapy, usually 20 minutes twice daily, applied over a 7-10 day period, is often recommended for more serious symptoms. Recurring and chronic cases with pain and loss of speed or developing track leg (jack) are best rested from galloping for 10-14 days. Injections of cortisone and other anti-inflammatory medications into the joint or surrounding muscles may be prescribed under veterinary supervision. Refer also to Lumbosacral Joint Pain, and Track Leg.

CRACKED PADS: All Greyhounds are likely to develop dried-out pads and deep crevice lines in the skin on the pads of their feet.

Signs: Typical signs include thinning of the rough pad surface, which dries out and develops cracks deep into the skin of the pads as they flex and are stretched during exercise. Often the cracked surface becomes infected, inflamed and sore when pressed. It may also weep serum or pus when pressed over the cracked area. When the main pad is cracked and becomes sore, the Greyhound will be lame when walked. In some cases, the thickened rough pads are less flexible and may tear and crack during exercise.

Causes: The natural oils can be leached out during wet weather, or moisture can be lost from the pads when walked on a salted road-way during winter, or under hot dry conditions, causing the pads to dry out, become less pliable and crack as they flex during exercise. Confining young Greyhounds on very dry sandy soil in yards, or walking a Greyhound on bitumen or concrete road surfaces in hot weather, are common causes of dried-out pads. Greyhounds that are galloped on gritty, sandy or dry synthetic race track surfaces, which abrade and dry out the pads, can also develop cracked pads.

Management: When the pads are cracked and sore, any surface infection should be cleaned away and appropriate antibiotics, with topical applications of 10 per cent benzoin ointment (balsam resins or friar's balsam), are also useful to protect and soothe the wound as it heals. The pain can be relieved by the use of local anaesthetic gels, prescribed under veterinary supervision. Bathing the pads twice daily for 5-7 days in a weak iodine-based antiseptic solution will help control further infection. Dry pads can be rehydrated by placing the affected foot in lukewarm water for 2-3 minutes, then applying a soothing, moisturising cream or mixture of fats and oils as a dressing. A mixture of one-third each of neatsfoot oil (very bitter), lanolin or wool fat (absorbs water to rehydrate the skin) and lard (softens the pad) is helpful in conditioning the pads when smeared on twice daily for 5-7 days, then as required on a regular basis. A small foot boot may need to be applied to allow a Greyhound to be walked until the cracked pads soften and heal. Avoid walking a Greyhound on salted road-ways and on hot, dry surfaces to reduce the risk of cracked and dry pads.

 CRAMPING: Cramping is recognised as a sustained muscle contraction of varying duration and severity after fast exercise, particularly in a Greyhound that is unfit for the speed and distance of free-sprint exercise.

Signs: 10 per cent of cramping occurs in the front triceps shoulder area, 30-40 per cent in the muscles along the back and 50 per cent affects the major driving muscle of the hindlimbs in racing Greyhounds. Cramping can occur before, during or 30-60 minutes after a race. A retired, unfit Greyhound may cramp when exercising hard, such as when turned loose, chasing rabbits, balls or running a fence. There are various forms of

A Greyhound should be checked along the major back and hindlimb muscles, if it slows up or fails to chase, during the last half of a race.

cramping that are related to the time of exercise and the duration and the severity of the muscle 'lock-up', often ranging from 30 seconds to 5 minutes.

Subclinical Cramping: Reduced speed and stamina at the end of a race with hard, knotted backline and rear limb muscles that can be felt in the catching area for 15-30 seconds after a race, which free up once the Greyhound is walked off the track and back to the kennels.

Mild Cramping: General stiffness and soreness on recovery after a race, with a feeling of a hard and knotted consistency of affected muscles.

Severe Cramping: Sudden severe muscle lock-up in affected muscles during a race, often in one hindlimb. In severe cases, the Greyhound runs on three legs, falls or stops with limb raised or drags it behind when running.

Acute, Stress-Related Cramping: This severe form develops 24-72 hours after sudden or stressful exercise, with internal muscle damage and lock-up, rapid body weight loss, debilitation and loss of appetite, general stiffness, collapse, kidney failure and severe shock. Also referred to as Exertional Rhabdomyolysis or Acute Acidosis Syndrome. Discomfort, withdrawal of the limb and yelping may result if the cramped muscle(s) are squeezed or pressed.

Cause: Muscle cramping can be caused by a number of metabolic or stress-related conditions. Although it is a relatively common problem in racing Greyhounds, little is known about the cause. The risk of cramping is increased in late-night races under cold conditions or where inadequate warm-up exercise is given prior to a race. In an unfit Greyhound, cramping may be triggered by an increase in L-lactic acid production in the backline and hindlimb muscles during fast, anaerobic exercise. Failure to warm down by walking for 3-5 minutes after a race to clear the acute acid build-up or circulatory inefficiency due to dehydration, may not remove the lactic acid as quickly, resulting in severe muscle damage. Greyhounds that have a nervous, hyperactive temperament may be more prone to cramping, particularly if they are deficient in the body salt potassium and dehydrated when raced. A diet that is low or inadequate in calcium may increase the likelihood of cramping in some Greyhounds.

The risk of cramping appears to be inherited in some bloodlines, either due to poor blood supply to the galloping muscles, or as a result of overheating and stress-related to the inherited condition of exercise-induced malignant hyperthermia. Refer to Exercise-Induced Malignant Hyperthermia or EIMH. High doses of a nervous stimulant, such as caffeine, may induce cramping due to prolonged overactivity. Excess amounts of carbohydrate energy supplied in dry food, particularly bread, may increase the risk of cramping in some Greyhounds as muscle energy stores are broken down by anaerobic pathways. Greyhounds that propel ('drive') themselves with the right hindlimb (5 per cent of all Greyhounds) instead of using the left hindlimb, for a greater part of the race, may cramp in the right hindlimb towards the end of a full circle race.

Management: Cramping is still treated by traditional methods and, because there are many possible predisposing causes, a veterinary examination of a Greyhound that has cramped more than once is recommended. Blood tests to determine calcium and salt balance may be taken. Severe and permanent muscle damage can occur if a Greyhound repeatedly cramps after racing. Stretching, massage and application of a warm, moist towel over the cramped muscles helps to restore circulation and remove harmful metabolites. Once the bulging and knotted muscles relax, the Greyhound can be walked on the lead for a few minutes, and the affected muscles massaged repeatedly between short walks, until the pain and knotting is relieved.

Important: In the event of severe muscle cramping, dehydration, weight loss and shock, the Greyhound should not be walked. It should be confined and emergency veterinary treatment sought. Refer to Exertional Rhabdomyolysis.

Measures to reduce the risk of cramping include the following:

- Check the dietary balance of fats and carbohydrates. Add extra fat as lard or suet at the rate of 12g ($^3/_4$ tablespoon) per cup of high-starch dry food.
- Supplement electrolytes and calcium. Supplements of slow release potassium (600mg/0.106-0.141 oz tablet daily) and calcium (3-4g/0.106-0.141 oz daily) on high-meat diets or in nervy Greyhounds will help to reduce the risk of repeated cramping. An adequate supply of cool clean water must be provided. All meals should be moistened to a soft, but not mushy, consistency to reduce the risk of dehydration.
- Provide supplements of Vitamin E, selenium and Vitamin C. Daily addition of Vitamin E (100iu daily) preferably combined with the trace-mineral selenium (0.03-0.5mg) and Vitamin C (250mg daily) is recommended for a Greyhound that has a history of cramping.
- Ensure an adequate warm-up before galloping. Brisk walking in the kennelling area before a race, or massage of the shoulder, backline and hindlimb muscles to improve circulation and muscle warmth before racing may reduce the risk of cramping in a Greyhound competing in a late-night race.
- Take measures to settle down a nervous temperament. Various medications and calming preparations are available but some may be detectable in after race swabs. They should only be used to help reduce anxiety and excitement over a period of time to allow a Greyhound to develop a more relaxed approach to travelling and racing.
- Ensure and maintain fitness. The training programme must be tailored to the individual Greyhound to achieve fitness for the distance of the race. Refer also to Acute Acidosis Syndrome and Exertional Rhabdomyolysis.

CRUCIATE LIGAMENT INJURY: This injury results from the sprain of the two ligaments that cross over within the knee or stifle joint to stabilise the hinge joint. Cruciate ligament sprains are not a common injury in fit racing Greyhounds as compared to other dogs because support and stabilisation is provided by the large and powerful muscles and a strong tissue sheet surrounding the joint.

Signs: Minor sprains result in slight stiffness and reduced extension of the stifle joint at the walk or when a Greyhound is trotted on the lead. The Greyhound will stand with its stifle joint in a partly bent position with only the tip of its toes touching the ground. The signs do not normally improve with rest and are likely to become more obvious after a subsequent gallop or race. Severe tears of the anterior (forward) ligament will cause pain, lameness and reluctance to bear weight on the affected limb.

Cause: Greyhounds have been selected for racing soundness over many years, and careful breeding to avoid the problem has eliminated weakness of the stifle joints in most bloodlines. Cruciate ligament sprain injury can occur in a young Greyhound as a result of slipping on a loose surface as it jumps from the starting traps or boxes.

Management: Special movements to evaluate cruciate stability will be carried out, along with X-rays if the joint is swollen to ensure there are no bone fractures or surface cartilage defects. In non-racing Greyhounds and young pups, minor sprain injury will usually repair over a 4-6 week period with kennel rest and controlled once-daily walking on the lead so as to avoid free, uncontrolled exercise. Surgical methods have been successful in repairing and stabilising major sprains and tears of the anterior cruciate ligament in breeds of dogs other than Greyhounds. However, in racing Greyhounds, even after surgery is carried out, the extreme forces placed on an already weakened knee joint structure usually result in complete breakdown of joint stability and arthritis in the affected joint, with retirement being advocated in most cases.

CRYPTORCHIDISM: This is a condition where both testicles are retained in the abdomen or inguinal canal of a male Greyhound. In a racing Greyhound, a partially retained testicle is likely to have little effect on performance. Many trainers, however, claim that the testicle is pinched or entrapped during the gallop and can become bruised and sore, reducing a Greyhound's ability to stretch out, or causing difficulty in turning to the side when cornering. In a retired Greyhound, a retained testicle is more likely to develop a tumour condition as the Greyhound ages.

Signs: A smaller than normal testicle or absence of

A young Greyhound with one testicle (monorchid) retained has a higher likelihood of cancer of the retained testicle as the animal ages.

one (monorchidism) or both testicles (cryptorchidism) in the scrotum sac may be noted in growing Greyhounds. One testicle may be present in the scrotal sac, the other smaller one detected in the canal that enters the scrotum in the deep groin area. The dogs have normal male behaviour, with sexual interest and normal libido. Testicles retained inside the abdominal cavity may also twist (torsion) when galloping to cause severe gut pain.

Cause: There appears to be no consistent reason, and often an autosomal genetic predisposition appears to be associated with the condition within a bloodline of related male Greyhounds. Males that have both testicles retained are sterile for breeding. Bitches used for breeding that are related to a cryptorchid dog, are likely to whelp male puppies with retained testicles. If both testicles are retained, they are usually not removed.

Management: If one retained testicle is located in the inguinal canal that enters the scrotum, then treatment with specific male hormones (testosterone) may be attempted, or the small testicle may be removed surgically. Greyhounds with a retained testicle in the abdomen can be treated with male/female hormone mixtures (anabolic hormones) under veterinary supervision to improve their aggression and strength when racing. If a retired male Greyhound is found to have a retained testicle, veterinary advice on removal should be sought, because of the higher risk of cancer in the retained testicle as the animal ages.

CURB: This is an old term used to describe sprain of tendon and ligament structures at the rear of the hock joint about 2.5cm (1 inch) below the point of the hock.

Signs: Common symptoms include swelling with pain when the hock is squeezed between the fingers, or the hock joint is flexed. The swelling is most obvious when viewed from the side of the hock. It is best to compare both hocks to determine the degree of swelling of the curb.

Causes: Bumps or falls during a race, as well as twisting and overextension of the hock joint when cornering, can result in sprain of the superficial digital flexor tendon and ligaments that join the lower hock bone to the metatarsal (rear shin) bones.

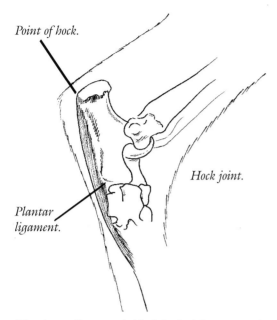

Point of hock.

Hock joint.

Plantar ligament.

The planter ligament behind the hock becomes strained and swells to form a curb.

Management: Initial application of an ice pack under an elastic pressure bandage for 3-5 minutes, 2 or 3 times daily for 3-5 days, will help reduce the inflammation of a new curb injury. A counter-irritant liniment applied twice daily for 5-7 days, or magnetic field therapy twice daily for 7-10 days, combined with lead walking and flexing the hock 10-15 times daily for 4-5 weeks will help to maintain hock mobility and assist healing. Laser therapy is also advocated and may be useful. Physiotherapy, swimming and the use of a support bandage, as well as a plan of a gradual return to short sprints over a 3-4 week period will help strengthen the hocks.

CYSTITIS: A condition that is caused by inflammation of the lining of the bladder wall.
Signs: The condition is most common in racing, breeding and aged bitches. Symptoms include stopping when walking to squat frequently and the passing of small amounts of urine. An affected bitch may exhibit pain on urination, sometimes passing blood, and remaining at the squat after urine stops flowing. Male Greyhounds may exhibit pain on urination, frequently passing small dribbles of urine. Both dogs and bitches may start uncharacteristically to wet in their kennels.

Cause: Common causes of inflammation of the bladder wall include bacterial infection of the bladder lining cells, which is encouraged by excess alkalinisation (pH above 6.5 units) of the urine by alkaline salts contained in diets high in dry food. Common bacteria found in the droppings or on the skin can ascend into the bladder of bitches. In bitches, the common exit of the urethra or tube from the bladder and the vagina allows bacterial germs from licking the vulva to contaminate the exit area. Mineral crystals of salts may form in the alkaline urine and precipitate out, irritating the bladder lining, causing it to bleed. Refer to Calculi in the Urine.

Management: A full examination by a vet is essential to determine the possible underlying cause. A sample of mid-stream urine can be checked for crystals, pH level and presence of blood. Feeding a high-meat (70 per cent by weight) content in the diet, with 1500mg daily of the amino acid methionine, or 500mg ammonium chloride salt, daily is recommended to acidify the urine and avoid recurrence of crystal formation. Acidification of the urine will also have a suppressive action on bacterial infection within the bladder, with mild infections being controlled after 5-7 days of supplementation with an acidifying mixture, especially in aged bitches. If the infection persists, an appropriate antibiotic may be prescribed after urinary culture and antibiotic sensitivity tests. Providing chicken or beef stock flavoured water may help to encourage additional flushing of the bladder, with a higher frequency of urination. The Greyhound should be given only lead work until the condition is controlled.

CUT PADS: Lacerations and cuts, rather than cracks, into the surface layers and deeper structures of the pads are common in Greyhounds walked on roadways and hard stony surfaces.
Signs: Cut surfaces on the toe and main pads that bleed initially. If they are not rested or treated promptly, they will become infected, oozing serum and causing discomfort and lameness.
Cause: Sharp objects such as slivers of glass on roadways, stones, pins or nails can lacerate the hard pad surface and gain entry to the underlying pad tissue.
Management: Greyhounds with cut pads that exhibit pain and are lame should be examined by a

vet and the foot X-rayed to check for embedded sharp objects and foreign bodies. Applications of drying antiseptic lotions and Vitamin A ointment combined with antibiotic powders, as well as padded bandaging, or protection by a foot boot, may be required in severe cases. Any wounds that do not heal quickly or heal and then break open as a festering-type split should be carefully examined for embedded foreign material. Usually at least 7-10 days lead walking and then short distance hand slips over another 7-10 days will be necessary. Cut pads can lead to the development of corns. Refer to Corns.

CUTANEOUS AND RENAL VASCULOPATHY: Refer to Alabama Rot.

D

DANDRUFF: Dandruff describes the presence of dead flakes of skin debris trapped in the haircoat. Also referred to as 'scurfy' coat.
Signs: Skin debris is most noticeable in black-coated Greyhounds as small whitish particles and flakes of dead skin, which are often loosened during grooming. Some Greyhounds naturally shed large amounts of scurf and dandruff.
Cause: Low-grade dermatitis due to skin irritation often related to feed-induced allergies, lack of adequate fat in the diet, heavy flea infestation and a poorly maintained and groomed coat can all result in increased scurf in the coat. Irritation results in

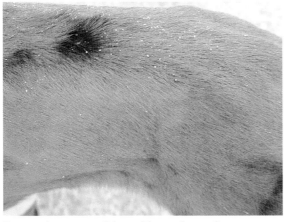

Increased turnover of dermal layers due to dietary deficiencies of vitamins, trace minerals and fatty acids, or use of harsh shampoos – most noticeable in a dark-coated Greyhound.

itching and scratching, which abrades and dislodges more skin debris.
Management: Washing or hydrobathing twice a week with a foaming and deep-cleansing shampoo to remove excess skin debris is a temporary measure if allergic or other skin irritation is present. The addition of 2ml polyunsaturated vegetable oil per 10kg (22 lbs) body weight to the diet will help provide essential fatty acids for skin health. Oils such as sunflower or safflower oils or canola oil are beneficial to skin health. A good-quality higher fat dry food containing linoleic acid, vitamins A, D, zinc, iodine and selenium will often help reduce the problem. A daily supplement of fatty acids, containing gamma linoleic acid (GLA) in evening primrose oil and natural fish oils to reduce skin inflammation, is also helpful to improve skin condition and reduce skin shed. Flea infestation must also be controlled. Refer to Flea Bite Dermatitis.

DEFORMED NAILS: The toenails can become twisted or bent during regrowth of broken or pulled-off toenails.
Signs: Toe nails may regrow with an abnormal flattened out shape, or develop a twisted or hooked end following a broken nail or loss of the nail during exercise.
Cause: Deformed nails can be present at birth and may be inherited in a bloodline on rare occasions. Abnormal nail regrowth is most common following a nail bone fracture, which does not set to a normal shape, thus resulting in a deformed shape as the outer nail regrows over the nail bone. Refer to Broken Nails.
Management: A deformed nail in a racing or retired Greyhound is usually best trimmed or filed every 7-10 days to prevent it interfering with and abrading the adjacent toe, or twisting the toe abnormally when the Greyhound walks or gallops. In most cases, the nail can be trimmed back to the level of the quick, and the end covered with a polymer or epoxy glue mix that hardens on drying, or touched with a hot cautery iron, to seal the exposed end against infection. In severe cases, surgery to remove the nail bone reduces the risk of further nail and toe injury in a racing Greyhound.

DEHYDRATION: This is a common term that describes a reduction in the amount of fluid in the

A severely dehydrated Greyhound may refuse to drink water after a race because it has lost fluid and body salts and is not thirsty. Note the skin folds that are pinched around the neck and tight belly.

blood and tissue cells, usually due to a greater loss of water from the body than can be replaced in food or fluid intake.

Signs: The symptoms of dehydration are common in racing Greyhounds. The degree of dehydration should be evaluated at least once daily, particularly prior to and after travelling or racing. The symptoms of dehydration include a dull dried-out skin and coat, which is slow to return when pinched up over the neck or shoulders. Dehydrated Greyhounds often develop a sticky, dry mouth with a sunken eye, loss of body weight, a tucked-up in the belly appearance, and passing of low volume, highly concentrated urine. Dehydration is one of the most common, everyday problems in racing Greyhounds.

Causes: Common underlying causes include a lack of adequate volumes of cool, clean water to drink, or insufficient moistening of large amounts of dry food prior to feeding. A meat-based diet will provide water, and moistening the dry food portion of the meal will help a Greyhound meet its intake of total water requirement of a litre a day. Many racing Greyhounds are poor drinkers, drinking only 450-500ml (15-17 oz) daily. Electrolyte or body salt imbalances, particularly excessive loss of potassium, can lead to chronic dehydration in racing Greyhounds. Diarrhoea, vomiting, panting during hot weather, stress-related conditions, such as water diabetes or racing thirst, as well as acute acidosis (rhabdomyolysis), also result in severe dehydration due to urinary loss of fluid.

Management: Severe dehydration caused by acute diarrhoea, vomiting or stress conditions may need to be corrected by intravenous fluid therapy and other appropriate medications under veterinary supervision. Refer to Diarrhoea. Mild dehydration from panting, low-grade diarrhoea, or temporary lack of adequate water, can usually be reversed by providing electrolyte mixtures in the feed to encourage water intake and maintain electrolyte balance, complemented by a supply of adequate volumes of cool, clean water to drink. In severe cases, providing 3-4 tablespoonfuls of suet, lard or beef fat trimmings daily in the meal for 5-7 days will help to correct mild forms of chronic dehydration in a racing Greyhound. The animal's body weight must be monitored every second day to avoid excess weight gain. Dampening of dry feed with water, meaty broth or milk/water to a soft, mushy consistency while retaining shape and form will provide additional fluid intake with food consumed. Providing cool, well-ventilated kennels, and reducing walking to avoid unnecessary stress, is helpful to minimise risk of dehydration in all Greyhounds during hot weather.

DEMODECTIC MANGE
(Demodecosis): A skin disease caused by the burrowing skin mite, *Demodex canis (foliculorum)*.

Signs: Demodectic mange may be present as a localised form in young dogs with swelling, loss of hair from the top of the nose, sides of the muzzle, around the eyes and lower front legs. A more widespread condition results in patchy, flaky areas of skin, which often develop a secondary bacterial

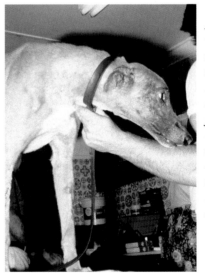

A Greyhound with demodectic mange on the muzzle, around the eyes and a bare patch on the front limbs. In this case, the mange has spread because a lung infection reduced the dog's immune defence.

infection with a greasy skin surface and distinct rancid (oxidised fat) odour.

Cause: It appears that demodectic mange becomes active whenever sickness or stress reduces a Greyhound's immunity. The skin mite *Demodex canis (foliculorum)* can be passed from the skin of a carrier bitch to her puppies as they suck on her teats. The puppies have little immune resistance and, over time, develop the characteristic loss of hair on their muzzles, face and front limbs. Older healthy Greyhounds may harbour the skin mites in the skin glands and hair follicles without signs of skin disease. Retired racing Greyhounds may have their natural immunity weakened due to sickness or as they age, and this allows the latent demodectic mange mites to become active. Stress of weaning, sickness or injury may reduce the immune suppression on the underlying mite population, causing the symptoms to reappear as the mites regain their activity. The mites can be identified by examining scrapings of skin under a microscope.

Management: The application of an effective topical miticide chemical in a skin wash or ointment is usually effective. More generalised infections with secondary bacterial infection (pyoderma) may require a combination of treatments and, in severe cases, a total body clip and removal of the encrusted skin areas may be needed. After the mites have been controlled, the hair will usually regrow within a few weeks. A supplement of vitamins and trace-minerals including Vitamin A and Vitamin E will assist hair, skin regrowth and healing. Infected puppies need to be treated under veterinary supervision if the disease is causing them to lose appetite and fail to thrive.

DERMATITIS: The term that refers to inflammatory conditions of the skin. Conditions such as dandruff or scurf in the coat, eczema and flea bite dermatitis are all forms of dermatitis caused by infection, hypersensitivities to food or environmental allergens or flea infestations.

Signs: Signs vary relative to the underlying cause, the site, extent, depth, severity and duration of the skin reaction, and the degree of self-mutilation by scratching or biting the irritated or inflamed skin area. The skin of the ears, underbelly, feet and above the tail butt are common sites. In most

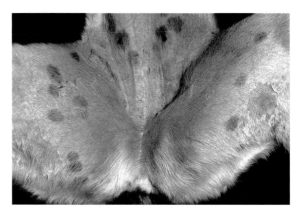

Skin irritation due to dietary allergy or other allergic reaction can cause inflammation, itching and shedding of skin. Contact allergy to bedding, grass or disinfectant residues can cause underbelly dermatitis.

cases, inflammation causes heat, swelling and itchiness of the skin, which leads to the urge to rub, scratch, lick or bite (gnaw) the affected area. Damage to the skin surface encourages secondary bacterial infection and often a more severe skin reaction with weeping, formation of scabs and loss of the protective skin surface to expose the underlying tissue.

Causes: The major cause is related to an allergic or hypersensitivity reaction that causes an inflammatory response. Some breeds of dogs have a genetic predisposition to atopic dermatitis, where antibodies react to allergens, such as foods or preservatives and dust mites and their droppings in house dogs, or allergy to carpets or bedding. This can occur in retired Greyhounds living as indoor companions. Greyhounds have a thin haircoat and generally have a lower allergic response to allergens than other breeds. External parasites such as fleas and mange mites can also cause an intense allergic reaction in hypersensitive Greyhounds. Contact with irritant chemicals in shampoos can cause generalised dermatitis. The webbing and feet may develop intense itching following contact with certain grasses, chemical cleaners, or urine on the kennel floor.

Management: Where severe and long-lasting dermatitis is causing discomfort, diagnosis and treatment by a vet is advised. This may include short courses of antihistamines to reduce the allergic reaction, antibiotics to control skin infection, or cortisone to reduce inflammation and allergy. The cause of allergic skin reactions, particularly atopic dermatitis, should be investigated by eliminating possible food allergies or hypersensitivity to bedding materials, dust or kennel cleaning chemicals. Where dermatitis develops over the tail butt area, rigorous flea control is essential. Refer to Flea Bite Dermatitis. Where increased scurf in the coat or dandruff is the major sign, regular grooming and supplements of essential fatty acids such as gamma linoleic acid (GLA) in evening primrose oil, are recommended. Refer to Dandruff. Refer also to Eczema.

DEWCLAWS: The dewclaw is the common name given to the small fifth digit on the inside of the limb above the other toes.

Signs: A large protruding dewclaw can brush and lacerate the skin of the adjacent limb as a Greyhound gallops, often leading to a swollen, painful dewclaw, due to bruising and inflammation. However, small closely-attached dewclaws with a sharp nail often lacerate the skin causing swelling and lameness.

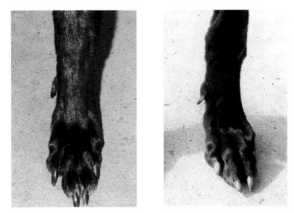

Some bloodlines of Greyhounds have dewclaws that are close to the inside of the metacarpal area (left). These are more likely to rub on the skin to cause soreness. Large dewclaws (right) do not generally rub the skin as they are pulled in as the Greyhound stretches the limb when galloping.

Cause: Prominent dewclaws can brush the adjacent limb or interfere with the stride when galloping. Certain bloodlines may have characteristically large dewclaws.

Management: The nails of the small, closely-attached dewclaws should be trimmed at weekly intervals, or the end of the nail cauterised regularly to keep them short and blunt to avoid laceration of the limb when galloping. Chronically inflamed

dewclaws may need to be removed by surgery if interference recurs when a Greyhound gallops. Applying an elastic wrap around the metacarpal (shin) area will help prevent the dewclaws protruding when galloping. If the front dewclaws of newly-born puppies are prominent, they can be removed surgically during the first week of life, without undue discomfort to the young puppy.

DIABETES: A term used to describe increased thirst and urine output usually resulting from extreme stress. In racing Greyhounds, it is also termed water diabetes syndrome or racing thirst. There are two forms of diabetes in dogs. **Diabetes mellitus** is the form popularly known as sugar diabetes in humans and is caused by decreased or loss of insulin production by the pancreas. This form is not seen in racing Greyhounds, but can develop in aged, retired Greyhounds. **Diabetes insipidus** is the form most related to the syndrome in racing Greyhounds. This form can have a sudden severe onset and develop into a long-term chronic condition. The underlying common trigger appears to be an acute or long term cumulative physical stress. This form is discussed under the term Racing Thirst, as the cause and speed of onset and predisposing causes in racing Greyhounds differ from the typical form of diabetes insipidus found in other Greyhounds. Refer to Racing Thirst or Water Diabetes Syndrome.

DIABETES MELLITUS: Affects retired Greyhounds.

Signs: A progressive increase in volume of weak urine passed on a more frequent basis (polyuria) and accompanying thirst (polydypsia), usually over a period of 1-2 months. Many older Greyhounds may start to wet indoors when confined overnight and may start to dribble weak colourless urine when walked on the lead. In severe cases, the affected Greyhound will become less active, lose weight and develop a chronic form of dehydration, although it eats and drinks adequate amounts of food and water.

Causes: The production of insulin is reduced in the pancreas gland as dogs age, possibly due to hereditary factors or from an acute pancreatic infection (pancreatitis). Refer to Pancreatitis. Normally insulin is released in response to food starches as they are digested after a meal to enable blood sugar to be stored as glycogen in the liver and muscles. When insulin production is reduced, blood sugars are unable to be utilised in the liver and muscle tissues, overflowing into the blood and increasing blood sugar, with excess being excreted via the kidneys (the urine tests positive for glucose). The higher sugar content carries water out of the kidneys with it, resulting in an increased urine output and development of dehydration and thirst for fluid. In severe cases, the rapid depletion of blood sugar between meals may result in hypoglycaemia with muscle weakness and collapse referred to as a diabetic coma.

Management: Any aged, retired Greyhound that develops an unquenchable thirst and an increased urine output should be tested for diabetes. A urine test to check glucose levels and blood tests to monitor blood glucose are required to confirm the condition and monitor the response to therapy. Injections of insulin, usually twice daily, can be given, combined with regular monitoring of blood and urine sugar levels to match the correct dosage of insulin required. A reduction in starch and soluble sugars in the diet, combined with a carefully mapped out exercise programme of walking each day, is essential to obtain the best control in a diabetic dog.

DIARRHOEA: The passage of soft, sloppy stools with a higher water content and in larger volumes than normal. It is also referred to as scours or scouring.

Signs: The signs are related to the severity and the underlying cause of diarrhoea. All forms are notable for frequent passage of watery or loose stools. The odour, frequency of emptying, presence of blood, degree of digestion of the food residues, associated vomiting and gut pain are all related to specific causes. Severe diarrhoea can result in depression, dehydration, debilitation and death in Greyhounds of all ages, with young newly-born puppies and aged Greyhounds at more risk from dehydration and depletion of body reserves.

Causes: There are many causes of diarrhoea. These include feed allergies and intolerances such as an allergy to red meat (often horsemeat) and milk (Refer to Red Meat Allergy and Milk Allergy), malabsorption of food, heavy worm infestation (Refer to Internal Parasites), inflammatory bowel diseases (Refer to Enteritis, Colitis), viral diseases (Refer to Canine Virus Diseases, such as

Distemper and Parvovirus) and bacterial diseases. (Refer to Blow-Outs or Gastroenteritis). In cases of severe diarrhoea, older retired Greyhounds may be weakened, lose weight and suffer an eventual collapse and risk of secondary bacterial infection in the gut or blood system. In aged Greyhounds, reduced digestive activity and certain forms of intestinal cancers may lead to low-grade diarrhoea. Greyhounds that are allowed free-range exercise may eat rotting food and develop diarrhoea over a 24-48 hour period due to bacteria or toxins ingested with the decaying food.

Management: The specific treatment and management of diarrhoea is relative to the underlying cause. A sample of the diarrhoea passed may be checked for parasite eggs, evidence of digestive problems and cultured for bacterial infection. If the Greyhound has a fever, is depressed and dehydrated from an acute diarrhoea over a period of more than 12-18 hours, especially if severe gut discomfort, excessive straining due to intestinal spasms or passage of fresh blood (dysentery) is evident, treatment by a vet is recommended. Initially, food should be withdrawn for 24-48 hours to rest the gut and electrolyte rehydration fluids given in the vein or by mouth to maintain fluid levels and prevent severe dehydration and shock. Where excess doses of antibiotics reduce bowel digestive bacteria, or stress alters their balance, courses of a compounded probiotic containing Lactobacilli acidophilus and other beneficial digestive bacteria are recommended. The Greyhound should be carefully monitored for the following 2-3 days after the diarrhoea has been controlled in case of a recurrence.

DISTEMPER: A highly contagious respiratory and nervous system viral disease of dogs caused by a morbilivirus.

Signs: The incubation period for the virus in the body after infection is 14-21 days, with dogs developing a fever, hacking cough, watery diarrhoea and loss of interest in food. Characteristic thick strands of mucus, often containing pus from secondary infections, hang from the eyes and nose following the initial symptoms of runny eyes and nose. The pads and nose leather may thicken and become hard and less pliable. The disease can be debilitating in young puppies, with brown lines developing within the teeth coating (enamel), which remain throughout its life. As the virus attacks the spinal and other nerves, many dogs develop twitches of the muscles, loss of co-ordination, collapse and paralysis of the hindlegs. Distemper infection can also be a cause of epileptic fits in dogs, often associated with swelling of the brain nervous tissue (encephalitis) as Greyhounds age in retirement. Refer to Epileptic Fits.

Causes: Although the widespread vaccination of all dogs has dramatically reduced the frequency and spread of distemper outbreaks in Greyhounds, complacency and failure to vaccinate to establish and maintain strong immunity can result in outbreaks of the disease from time to time. Stray dogs often act as a reservoir of infection, particularly for Greyhounds walked on roadways or exercised in parklands. If distemper infection is suspected by clinical signs, isolation of the affected dog(s) must be carried out immediately to avoid spread of the viral infection.

Management: Prompt treatment by a vet is essential to treat the symptoms, followed by vaccination. All puppies must be vaccinated with a suitable vaccine and given the full course to establish adequate immunity. Brood bitches can be tested to evaluate their immune levels prior to whelping. All Greyhounds, including retired Greyhounds, should be given routine annual booster vaccinations, or as recommended by a vet.

DROPPED HIP: A deformed hip is an inherited condition in Greyhounds in which the point of the iliac (pin) bone in the foremost upper end of the pelvic girdle is smaller in size, or set lower than normal. It usually is seen on one side only, although in rare cases, both pin bones will be abnormal. The condition does not normally affect a Greyhound's ability to gallop and perform to its potential and has no effect on the action of the hip joint. A knocked-down hip can occur when a young Greyhound hits its iliac or pin bone on a protruding post or object when galloping next to a fence. Severe direct trauma can displace the immature growth plate, resulting in the muscle attachments being deeply bruised and torn. The injury causes displacement typical of a fracture, with bruising, pain and enlargement as it heals. The severity and extent of the muscle wastage, and amount of fibrous tissue during healing, may

adversely influence the performance of the Greyhound. All young Greyhounds should be checked for signs of a dropped-down hip prior to purchase by comparing the location and symmetry of both pin bones from the side and rear view. Young Greyhounds with an obviously displaced pin bone crest may have a less than expected race potential. Refer to Hip Joint Injuries.

DROPPED MUSCLES: The term is used to describe tearing of a muscle from its origin and insertion between two bones in a racing Greyhound. It is also called a ruptured or torn-away muscle. The muscles most commonly affected are those subjected to the most stretching or contraction power during acceleration, galloping and cornering. The most common muscles that drop are the triceps of the shoulder (egg, monkey or pin muscles) or the gracilis muscle in the groin (back muscle). Extensive effort or contraction force, and tension to stabilise the limbs at speed, can result in overstretching of the outer covering (muscle sheath) and tearing or separation of the muscle and ligament fibres away from the bone anchorage points. A dropped gracilis muscle on the inside of the groin is more likely in older racing Greyhounds. Refer to Gracilis Muscle Injury.

Signs: A soft, squelchy consistency due to haemorrhage and fluid accumulation can be felt when the area over the muscle attachment is carefully examined with the fingers. A distinct gap can often be felt between the muscle belly and the anchorage point. In severe cases, the muscle will pull away from its normal position and appear as a limp, bunched-up mass within a squelchy blood haematoma under the skin or muscle sheath. Immediately after a race, the injured muscle will usually have a different texture when examined compared to a normal muscle on the opposite limb. Although the muscle and blood vessels may have torn away, forming extensive bruising, blood clots and serum, the injured area may not have had sufficient time to become inflamed and painful. A sudden loss of speed normally occurs when a muscle pulls away or drops when subjected to contraction force. Within the following 24 hours, lameness and shortness of stride may be noted at the walk. The gait may improve because the muscle is not subjected to loading during walking and the other muscles compensate for it.

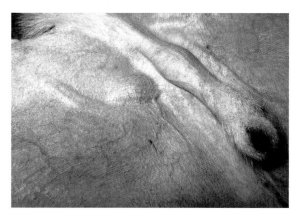

The pectineus muscle in the groin area can occasionally be torn during a race fall or when cornering on a loose surface – evidenced by the swelling and collection of blood (haematoma) over the site of the muscle rupture.

A torn-away or dropped triceps (also referred to as pin, egg or monkey) muscle behind the shoulder, illustrating the build-up of fluid and blood under the skin to form a raised area over the injury, and collection of fluid under the lowest part of the chest.

Cause: The underlying cause is due to a sudden overload of the contracting or fully stretched muscle during acceleration when maximum power or strength is exerted, or when maintaining limb and body stability at speed during cornering and avoidance manoeuvres. Loss of traction on a loose track surface may also result in a sudden overload of a fully stretched muscle when the toes again grip the surface.

Management: Prompt application of cold therapy with an ice pack for 2-3 minutes, combined with support bandaging to help control haemorrhage, will help reduce the inflammatory reaction and replace the torn-away back muscle in its correct position. Repeat the cold therapy 3-4 times during

the first 12-24 hours. Surgical repair to suture the ends of the muscle back to their anchorage points is recommended within the 72 hours following the injury. Muscles subjected to less direct contraction forces heal well following the initial first aid with ice packs and support bandaging. An injection of a chemical to encourage fibrous healing (sclerosing agent) into the torn area may help promote repair and reattachment of the ligamentous attachments to the anchorage points. The Greyhound may need to be confined for 2-4 weeks, with short controlled walks on the lead daily. This should be followed by physiotherapy and longer lead walks daily for 5-7 weeks until healing is complete after 10-12 weeks.

DROPPED TOE: A term to describe the flattening of one or more toes due to flexor tendon damage.

Signs: The arched structure of the toe collapses on the affected toe(s), resulting in the ends of the toes assuming a flattened, collapsed appearance. If both flexor tendons are severed, the toe pad and nail will become elevated, raised and point upwards compared to the normal adjacent toes. The Greyhound may not be obviously lame, except when galloped on a hard track surface, which bruises the underside of the flattened toe(s) and causes inflammation and discomfort.

Cause: Laceration of the tendon structures that attach to the first toe bone under one or more toes, or most commonly, partial or complete severance of the superficial digital flexor tendon. Occasionally, the deep flexor tendon that maintains the arching of the foot will also be damaged and the foot will flatten to contact the ground surface. The tendons are usually damaged or severed by sharp objects such as glass, wire or jagged stones as a Greyhound runs over an exercise area or track surface.

Management: In most cases, the Greyhound is able to gallop and race without being lame or losing speed. However, concussion to the underside of the flattened toe may cause discomfort and a shortened stride on hard, sandy surfaces. A mild counter-irritant liniment applied to the underside of the toe may help strengthen the healing fibrous tissue. Surgical repair using wire sutures to reattach the severed tendon can be carried out, followed by 2 weeks of support bandaging and then 2-4 weeks lead work to strengthen the healing tendon attachment. Removal of the end bone of the toe may be considered if a Greyhound suffers chronic discomfort from the injury. In a retired Greyhound, a dropped toe will normally not cause any discomfort or lameness. However, if the animal is to compete in shows, then surgery to repair the tendon may be necessary to correct the flattened toe appearance.

DRY PADS: Dehydration and cracking of the pad surface. Regular daily applications of a moisturising cream will help maintain the pads in a soft, supple condition, particularly when a Greyhound is walked on abrasive road surfaces, or dry sand under hot conditions. Refer to Cracked Pads.

DYSENTERY: A term historically used to describe the presence of blood in the droppings, most commonly by a Greyhound with severe diarrhoea.

Signs: The motions may contain fresh streaks of blood, or a covering of darker slimy blood that has resulted from bleeding higher up in the intestinal tract. In cases where infection is present, severe discomfort will be apparent as the Greyhound empties out.

Causes: There are a number of underlying conditions that damage the highly vascular intestinal lining. These include infection with bacteria (e.g. Salmonella bowel infection), viruses (e.g. acute Parvovirus) and heavy infestations of blood sucking worms, such as Hookworms. Intestinal infection with the protozoal parasitic organism, *Giardia* species can also occur in Greyhounds housed under damp or wet conditions. Refer to individual conditions.

Management: In severe cases, where blood loss is draining red blood cell numbers and vitality, prompt therapy with fluids, electrolyte salts and even blood transfusions into the vein may be necessary. Cultures of the bloody motions and egg counts for hookworm infection should be performed to determine the underlying cause so that the appropriate treatment can be given.

E

EAR INFECTIONS: The Greyhound has a smooth, short coat, and ears that can be held erect or folded over, in contrast to the pendulous ears of many other breeds of hound. Ear infections and other conditions are not common in Greyhounds. Inflammation of the ear canal is called otitis.

OTITIS EXTERNA: Infection and inflammation of the outer ear canal of one or both ears is the most common form of ear infection, and is referred to as otitis externa or canker.

Signs: The affected ears exude a brownish to tan coloured discharge that coats the inside of the earflap. As a practical guide to diagnosis, bacterial infections generally have a rotting odour, and infections due to yeasts and fungal-type organisms-have a musty smell. Moisture in the ear canal scalds the already irritated skin, causing pain and discomfort. In an attempt to relieve the irritation and pain, the Greyhound will rub or scratch the infected ear(s), further abrading the already inflamed canal.

Cause: Water may be trapped in the ears when a Greyhound is swum or hydrobathed, creating a scalding effect and producing a discharge, which becomes infected with bacteria, fungi or yeasts. Infection with ear mites (Otodectes) may also initiate irritation and scratching, resulting in extra discharge and wax, which can then become infected. Occasionally, grass seeds may lodge in the ear canal of a young Greyhound in an outside yard. This can lead to intense discomfort, with scratching, abrasion and secondary infection of the ear canal.

Management: The soft waxy material and other discharge can be cleaned away from the inside of the ear flap by using a facial tissue soaked in luke warm soapy water. A small amount (2-3 drops) of clean cooking oil squirted into the ear will help soften and remove wax and relieve the intense itching, scratching and rubbing, and soothe the abraded ear canal. The reaction may take 5-7 days to settle down and daily cleaning and use of oil must be maintained during this time. If the animal continues to scratch and rub the ears, a vet should examine the ear for a trapped grass seed or other type of foreign body. Antibiotic and antifungal drops may be prescribed to control infection, or cortisone anti-inflammatory drops to relieve irritation relative to the underlying cause. A full course of treatment must be given to avoid recurrence. If the condition is chronic, surgery to establish permanent drainage of the ear canal may be necessary in older Greyhounds.

OTITIS MEDIA: In severe cases of otitis externa, the infection may invade the middle internal ear (referred to as otitis media) and inner ear chambers. A sharp grass seed can work its way deeper into the ear canal and abrade the canal lining and damage the ear drum. Infection of these chambers can cause the animal to rotate its head downwards on the affected side and walk in a small circle. In severe cases, symptoms of a loss of balance and co-ordination may be apparent. Infection can gain entry to the middle ear chamber from the throat via the (eustachian) connecting tube. Deeper ear infections are serious and must be treated under veterinary supervision with oral antibiotics and other medications. Drainage of the middle ear in severe cases may be necessary, especially if a recurring condition causes discomfort and loss of balance.

EAR MITES: Infection with Otodectes ear mites in the ear canal, most commonly in young Greyhounds.
Signs: Initial irritation and rubbing to relieve the itching of ear mites within the ear canal may cause it to become inflamed and exude a smelly discharge. If not treated promptly, the condition may develop into a canker or otitis externa infection, requiring more extensive and long-term treatment.
Cause: Many Greyhounds harbour the small, whitish ear mites in small numbers within their ear canals without any outward signs. Ear mites can survive off a dog for several weeks, so reinfestation after treatment is common. Ear mites can live on the face, neck and feet, with all these sites providing a potential for re-infection. Older retired Greyhounds with a reduced immune response are likely to harbour larger numbers of ear mites and

Ear mites are often the cause of head-shaking, and these can be seen in the ear canals using an otoscope light.

show symptoms. The moist, warm and waxy environment in the ear canal may encourage ear mites to multiply, leading to intense irritation and itching, and allow bacterial, fungal or yeast infections of canker (otitis externa) to develop as a secondary condition.
Management: Removal of excess wax, and flushing the ear canal with soothing drops containing a miticide preparation, will help to control ear mites living in the ear canal. A weekly wash with an insecticidal shampoo will help control ear mites on the body, and treatment of the bedding and kennel floor is also advised to break the mite cycle. Depending on the extent of the secondary canker condition, other preparations may be prescribed under veterinary supervision.

EAR TIP FLY IRRITATION: An irritation caused by flies settling on and irritating the tips and edges of the earflap.
Signs: Early signs include the development of scabby skin and moist, matted edges of the hair on the earflap, which can eventually become raw on the edges and ooze blood. This then attracts even more flies to compound the problem. The Greyhound may shake its head and rub its ears to relieve the discomfort.
Causes: Common black household flies, mosquitoes and other biting flies are attracted to the broken skin in large numbers, leading to a cycle of fly worry, rubbing, head shaking and ear flapping, scratching and more intense and widespread fly annoyance.
Management: The application of healing and soothing lotions, including drying preparations, will

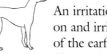

help reduce fly attraction and aid healing. An insect repellent spray or gel applied regularly each morning and evening will help to repel annoying and biting insects. Covering the ears with a sleeve or sock (see Chilblains) also helps reduce fly worry during swarming periods.

EAR TIP CHILBLAINS: Refer to Chilblains.

ECLAMPSIA: A condition caused by the excess loss of calcium from the blood into the milk of a heavily lactating bitch feeding a more than average-sized litter of rapidly growing puppies.
Signs: Initially the bitch may develop a raised temperature and become unsettled and restless. Depletion of blood calcium results in reduced muscle contraction forces, causing weakness, twitching and collapse.
Causes: When puppies, between 2-5 weeks of age, start to grow rapidly and drink larger amounts of milk, the high volume of milk withdrawn may deplete blood calcium reserves in the bitch. An adequate amount of calcium may not be available from the diet, even if supplemented, and calcium is unable to be mobilised from bone stores in sufficient quantities to meet the demand. In some bloodlines, bitches may have a higher incidence of eclampsia and the risk increases in older bitches.
Management: Prompt administration of an injectable form of calcium into the vein is the only effective way of reversing the condition which, if not treated, can result in the bitch lapsing into a coma and dying. Adding extra calcium in the food may not maintain adequate blood levels, as normal parathyroid hormone activity may be suppressed, and not be able to react efficiently to resorb calcium from bone stores to meet demands at the peak of milk production. The best form of management to avoid the condition is to provide a good-quality puppy food to supplement the puppies from 2 weeks of age, especially where a bitch has a litter of 6 or more rapidly growing puppies, thereby reducing the demand for milk and drain of calcium reserves.

ECZEMA: An older term used to describe itching, irritated skin or chronic dermatitis.
Signs: Most skin irritations will cause a Greyhound to scratch, bite or rub the itchy or irritated area leading to further skin damage and risk of secondary bacterial or fungal infection within the outer skin layer.
Cause: Greyhounds may develop an allergy to an individual food or preservatives in a brand of prepared food. In other cases, heavy flea infestation, or skin contact with shampoos, or irritant substances on the kennel floor, or in the soil of yards or turn-out areas, will result in damage to the skin and encourage scratching, biting and secondary infection. A genetic predisposition to allergy dermatitis (called atopy) can also occur in certain bloodlines of Greyhounds.
Management: Because there are many underlying causes of eczema, a diagnosis should be made by a vet so that targeted treatment can be given. A thorough investigation of the animal's diet and environment must be made to determine possible underlying causes. Refer to Dermatitis, Fleas.

ENTERITIS: A term used to describe inflammation of the lining of the small intestine in the upper part of the intestinal tract.
Signs: Signs can be rapid in onset or develop into a low-grade chronic form. More severe symptoms include a raised temperature (fever), watery or runny motions, loss of appetite, dehydration and, in some cases, vomiting, blood in the motions, gut pain and discomfort.
Cause: There are various causes of enteritis ranging from food allergy-induced diarrhoea, heavy roundworm infestation, gastrointestinal infections with bacteria (Salmonella, E coli, Coccidiosis (Eimeria spp)), and viruses (Canine Herpesvirus, Parvovirus and Canine Distemper virus). Refer also to Blow-Outs, Gastroenteritis, and Diarrhoea.
Management: The underlying cause should be investigated by a vet. Low-grade diarrhoea may readily clear up following oral diarrhoea powders or antibiotic-kaolin mixtures. Gut sedatives, antidiarrhoea medications, and antibiotics must only be given under the supervision of a vet. In severe cases, intravenous fluids and supportive vitamins and amino acids may be indicated to correct dehydration. Affected Greyhounds should be isolated if an infectious cause is suspected, and removal of the motions, and disinfection of kennels and floors, must be carried out to minimise cross-infection or re-infection. If a food allergy is linked

to a change in food, then withdrawal followed by a gradual reintroduction once symptoms have settled down, is recommended. Vaccination to minimise the risk of viral causes, especially Parvovirus in young pups, must be considered.

 EPIPHYSITIS: Inflammation of the epiphysis, or growth plate region, at each end of the limb long bones in growing pups.

Signs: Enlargement of the growth plate is most noticeable in growing pups at the end of the forearm bone (radius) above the wrist, often referred to as open wrists, or bumps on the wrist, as well as the toe joints and each end of the tibia below the stifle and above the hock joint. In severe cases, the young Greyhound may experience discomfort and become short in the front limb stride.

Cause: The condition is most common in overdeveloped heavy male pups, or when the joints are subjected to excessive concussion, especially when 3-12-month-old Greyhounds have free access to long runs on dry compacted soil. An inadequate intake or imbalance of either calcium and phosphorus, and other-trace minerals, including copper and zinc, manganese and iodine, as well as a deficiency of Vitamin D in the diet, can reduce growth plate development and lead to abnormal calcification.

Management: The condition is not uncommon in growing Greyhounds, but if the animal develops signs of lameness, particularly after free galloping, then it should be confined to a small yard or kennel for 3-6 weeks. Advice from a vet should be

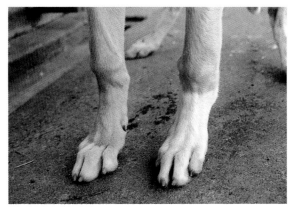

This rapidly growing 5-month-old, heavily built, male Greyhound has marked enlargement (epiphysitis) of the growth plates above the wrist ('knobbly wrists').

sought on the dietary balance. If a Greyhound is grossly overgrown, the food intake can be reduced by 20-25 per cent, but a balanced intake of bone nutrients including calcium, phosphorus, trace-minerals of zinc, copper, manganese and iodine with Vitamin A and Vitamin D must be maintained as a supplement to a meat and dry food based diet. Many dry foods contain Vitamin D and minerals, but these nutrients may not be made available during digestion of the food. A separate supplement containing these nutrients is often recommended. Exercise should be limited, but not discontinued during the corrective period. After confinement, pups should be let out for progressively longer runs to avoid sudden joint and growth plate overload.

EPILEPSY: A nervous seizure, fit or convulsion due to abnormal nerve activity in the brain.

Signs: Seizures last for 30 seconds to 2 minutes. Symptoms vary from being spaced-out and oblivious to surroundings, to foaming at the mouth, rolling the eyes, blinking, head nodding, stiffening of the body muscles, collapse and abnormal movements of the head and limbs. The intense muscle activity during a seizure can overheat the body and result in hyperthermia, extreme fatigue and collapse. Fits are usually first seen prior to, or after, a trial or race, when the Greyhound is excited by anticipation and racing, and after relaxing in the catching area. The fits may become increasingly frequent, intense and of longer duration.

Cause: Fits or epileptic seizures usually have no known cause, and are termed idiopathic fits. There is an inherited link in other breeds of dogs but a genetic predisposition has not been established in Greyhounds. Injury to the head during a race collision or fall, or brain damage due to a developing tumour (brain cancer) may trigger the start of seizures. Infection with the Distemper virus should always be considered, although a Greyhound with a long-term muscle twitch or a 'tic', may not always develop a seizure. Lead poisoning in old kennels painted with lead enamel paints is thought to be a possible triggering cause.

Management: It is best to keep the animal as quiet as possible, preferably away from noise in a darkened area, until it recovers. If it collapses and overheats, then prompt first aid by applying cold wet towels to its body and massaging the body to stimulate blood flow is essential. Placing it in front of a fan or air-conditioner will help cool the body until its temperature returns to normal. A thorough neurological examination, including a full history of the animal's health, including falls, head injuries, viral infections and other abnormal behaviour should be carried out by a vet. X-rays of the head may be necessary if an earlier injury is suspected as a predisposing cause. If a Greyhound has an isolated seizure, and appears normal for a period greater than 6-8 weeks after a fit, drug therapy is usually not given. A number of drugs are available to control seizures, but they must be withdrawn prior to racing. A Greyhound suffering repeated fits should be retired from racing for safety reasons.

EXERCISE-INDUCED BRONCHOSPASM: Refer to Asthma.

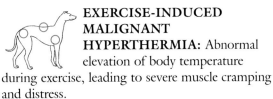

EXERCISE-INDUCED MALIGNANT HYPERTHERMIA: Abnormal elevation of body temperature during exercise, leading to severe muscle cramping and distress.

Signs: Acute symptoms of heat stress with a very high temperature, rapid panting and severe muscle cramping within a few minutes after racing. Affected Greyhounds stagger from the catching area and may develop acute stiffness, soreness and knotting in the shoulder, back and hindlimb muscles.

Cause: Although a relatively uncommon condition, it may be inherited, as some bloodlines of Greyhounds with a nervous, active disposition have a higher incidence. These Greyhounds are likely to develop severe overheating, may collapse and die. In other Greyhounds, it is considered to be a complex form of muscle cramping, resulting from a high temperature and peak muscle lactic acid levels after all-out galloping, especially under hot, humid conditions. Nervy, hyperactive Greyhounds that 'run their race before the start', overachievers or unfit Greyhounds are more prone to this condition.

Management: The affected Greyhound should be carried off the track, and rapidly cooled by immersing in a tub or bath of cold water for 30-45 secs. The muscle cramping should be managed as

for Exertional Rhabdomyolysis under veterinary supervision. Where the inherited form is suspected in a bloodline of Greyhounds, line breeding should be curtailed.

EXERTIONAL RHABDOMYOLYSIS: A severe form of muscle cramping, damage and deterioration associated with hard, stressful exercise.

Signs: There are various forms of exercise-related muscle damage, related to speed of onset and severity of the symptoms. Although cramping is one of the clinical signs often associated with the condition, much more severe muscle damage and acute metabolic stress occurs.

A severely cramped Greyhound should be given intravenous fluids to correct dehydration and prevent kidney damage. This Greyhound suffered an acute cramp and toxic shock event 6 weeks previously, which resulted in severe muscle wastage along the back and hindlimbs. The Greyhound was retired.

Severe form (Hyperacute): Often called acute acidosis syndrome. Severe muscle soreness and swelling, or 'blow up' due to rapid accumulation of lactic acid and water in the backline and hindquarter muscles. The Greyhound is reluctant to walk, becomes distressed and is unable to lie or sit down comfortably. The Greyhound may dehydrate rapidly losing 1-1.5 kg (2-3 lbs) body weight in 12-24 hours, and pass dark port-wine coloured urine. Kidney failure can occur within 48-72 hours.

Less Severe Form (Acute): Stiffness when walking, with pain when the backline and hindlimb muscles are pressed.

Cause: Racing an unfit or dehydrated, easily-stressed Greyhound is the underlying cause of both forms. The severe form is thought to be a result of muscle enzyme, protein and salt loss from cells with leakage of myoglobin pigment into the blood, due to high lactic acid build-up during fast exercise. The less severe form is considered to be caused by electrolyte shifts, potassium deficiency and leakage from muscle cells, high body temperatures and dehydration.

Management: Prompt medical treatment by a vet is essential – it is an emergency condition. If a Greyhound dehydrates, loses weight and the backline muscles remain swollen, extremely sore, and melt away over 12-18 hours, and begins to pass dark urine, prompt intravenous fluid therapy and supportive treatment is essential to save the Greyhound's life or give it a chance of returning to racing. Less acute forms can cause severe muscle damage if left untreated. The preventative management is similar to severe cramping. Attention to a balanced diet, electrolyte supplementation with potassium, ensuring a Greyhound is well hydrated and fit for the distance to race, warmed-up well prior to racing and settling nervy, hyperactive Greyhounds before racing are the main preventative measures. The severe form is more common during hot weather or when a Greyhound has been stressed by racing, or has not had 2-3 days to recover from a previously stressful race or trial. Refer to Cramping.

EYE INJURIES: Accidental abrasions, bruising and lacerations to the eye, the surrounding conjunctiva and eyelids can occur in Greyhounds as a result of falls and sand particles flicked into the eyes during racing. As well, eye injuries can be caused by yard and kennel injuries from sharp pieces of wire, or from the toe nails of other Greyhounds during play or fighting. As the eyes are very sensitive structures and are important for vision when racing, these forms of injury should be referred to a vet for examination and treatment. Greyhounds are prone to other genetic diseases that affect the eyes, as well as conjunctivitis. Refer to Cherry Eye, Conjunctivitis, Corneal Ulcers, Keratitis, Pannus, Progressive Conjunctivitis, and Retinal Atrophy.

EYE ULCERS: Refer to Keratitis.

F

FAILING TO CHASE: A condition in a racing Greyhound that causes it 'not to try', or fail to chase the lure during a race. Also referred to as a non-chaser.

Signs: Lack of effort and keenness in chasing the lure from the start or during a race, often falling back to the rear of the field, or stopping in some cases.

Cause: There are a number of possible causes. Poor initial education during schooling or breaking in; soreness and pain that overrides the inherent willingness to recklessly chase a moving object; poor sight in night racing due to eye disease or inadequate lighting; loss of a direct line of sight obscured by other dogs; a small lure bunny that cannot be easily seen; a history of a severe injury, check or being squeezed by other Greyhounds in a race; illness and sickness; inherited lack of keenness during competitive racing; psychological problems; training off and souring in an individual Greyhound, and a poor standard of lure-driving to maintain an enticing distance in front of the Greyhounds. Many trainers believe that lack of a live kill on a regular basis reduces keenness and interest in the chase.

Management: Reschooling may be effective in an otherwise fit, willing and keen Greyhound. Running the Greyhound in a group that has about the same performance potential may overcome a loser's fear when racing. A thorough checkover by a vet to check for muscle or other soreness, or the possibility of eyesight and eye diseases is a wise precaution. Arranging a couple of solo trials so that the Greyhound can sight and concentrate on a well-driven lure bunny is also helpful in some cases, or changing to a straight track with a centreline drag lure may improve and restore keenness and competitiveness. A stimulant preparation, such as 60-100mg caffeine given about 40 minutes before a trial may increase willingness, alertness and focus on the chase. Caffeine is a prohibited stimulant and must not be used within 7 days prior to racing or within the time interval recommended, to avoid detection. Acupuncture has also been used in an attempt to improve racing focus in a non-chaser, with varying success. In severe cases, psychological problems may be difficult to treat and the Greyhound may best be retired from racing.

FALSE PREGNANCY: The common name used to describe the maternal behaviour pattern, milk gland enlargement and milk secretion that develops in bitches of all breeds, including Greyhound bitches in training in the 9 weeks subsequent to being in season, although they are not mated and are not in whelp. Technically, it is termed Pseudo-pregnancy.

Signs: Most non-pregnant bitches produce milk about 6-8 weeks after being on heat or in season. Weight gain, swelling of the abdomen and maternal behaviour, including motherly aggression, bed-making and uncharacteristic excitability are often noticed. After 7-8 weeks, the milk glands enlarge, often culminating in milk being able to be squeezed from the teats.

Cause: A normal healthy bitch is subjected to the same cycle of hormone changes after her season that occur whether she is pregnant or non-pregnant. Both pregnant and non-pregnant bitches develop a hormone-secreting tissue mass, called a corpus luteum, in their newly-ovulated ovary after ovulation. This tissue body produces the progesterone hormone of pregnancy and the majority of bitches then progress through the clinical signs of pregnancy. In Greyhound bitches in training, the stress of training often suppresses the signs of a false pregnancy.

Management: A reduction in the energy and protein intake to two-thirds by changing to a dry food with a lower energy and crude protein content, combined with limited access to water, without causing the bitch to dehydrate, for 5-7 days, is often effective in reducing early milk gland development in a bitch in training. If a bitch develops enlarged glands and starts to secrete milk, she should not be galloped hard, as the pelvic ligaments may relax under the influence of hormones. Relaxation of the pelvic structures can increase the risk of lower back and hindlimb muscle and ligament injuries. A course of a diuretic medication, monitored by a vet, for 3-5 days to eliminate extra body fluid, will help reduce milk production and assist the bitch to dry up. She can then be returned to full training and racing.

FIBULA FRACTURES: Stress fracture of the thin long fibula bone on the outside of the tibia just above the hock joint, most commonly on the left side hind limb, although a fracture can develop in both hindlimbs.

Signs: Shortened stride in the left hindlimb at the walk becomes apparent after a couple of hard runs on a circle track in a young Greyhound being schooled or broken in. There is no obvious lameness, but often a history of a loss of speed on the bends and running wide. Muscle checks usually reveal an absence of injury or soreness. Pressure applied on the upper part will usually cause discomfort if the fibula is pulled-away or is broken just below the stifle. The very thin lower end, which runs under the prominent vein (saphenous vein) that passes on the outside just above the hollow of the hock in front of the Achilles tendon, is a more common fracture site in a young Greyhound. As the fracture heals, movement

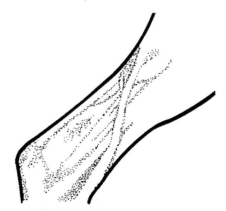

Photo 1   *Photo 2*

An X-ray of a fibula fracture (Photo 1) and a bent fibula bone (Photo 2). Lower fibula fractures are located under the area of the saphenous vein. These are most common on tracks with banked turns, with a higher incidence on the left hindlimb.

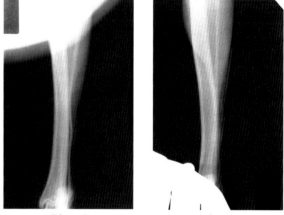

Location of saphenous vein.

during exercise results in a small pea-sized lump, or flat callous, developing on the bone; this causes discomfort if the area is pressed for 10 seconds and the Greyhound is then walked off. Usually the Greyhound will be reluctant to bear weight on the limb, and limp for a few steps after the fracture site is pressed.

Cause: Concussion of the limb caused by a compacted dry race track surface, or a sudden blow, or twisting forces on the immature, very thin fibula bone that follows on the outside of the tibia bone from the stifle to the hock, is the underlying cause in a young Greyhound. Slipping and falling on a hard surface, such as a kennel floor, can cause a direct trauma and fracture to the upper part of the fibula bone.

Management: The size and severity of the fracture and stage of healing of the fracture should be determined by a vet with the aid of an X-ray if necessary. In most cases, both high and lower (non-displaced) fibula fractures heal well if the Greyhound is rested in its kennel for 4-6 weeks, with training resumed in a gradual walking programme, combined with physiotherapy to maintain flexion in the hock. The fracture area should be strapped with tape and massage must be avoided as it can interrupt the bone healing process by moving the fine bone. Magnetic field therapy and a calcium and Vitamin D supplement daily will also help enhance healing over a 3-4 week period. If the fracture is pulled-away or misaligned from the tibia, a rest period of 2-3 weeks is usually adequate prior to a gradual return to training.

FITS: Greyhounds can develop fits, seizures or convulsions related to epilepsy. Refer to Epilepsy.

FLATULENCE: Passage of increased volumes of smelly gas escaping or vented from the anus.
Signs: An unpleasant, strong faecal smell when the Greyhound is kennelled or travelled in a vehicle.
Cause: Very smelly flatulence with 'rotten egg gas' can be a side-effect of feeding more than four eggs a day due to excess sulphur in the diet. An excess intake of vegetable carbohydrate or protein in high cereal-based dry food diets or when vegetables are fed, can also ferment to gas in the large intestine.
Management: Limiting eggs to no more than 2 eggs daily is recommended. Eggs should be cooked by cracking into a cup of newly-boiled water and allowing to stand for 1-1.5 minutes until the white

partially thickens. Reduction in the amount of dry food or vegetables, especially from pea or bean source protein is helpful. Excess milk in the diet can increase fermentation processes, so milk should be limited in an attempt to reduce symptoms.

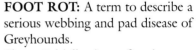

FOOT ROT: A term to describe a serious webbing and pad disease of Greyhounds.
Signs: Initially, signs of moist inflamed and devitalised webbing and pad tissue develop, with hair loss between the toes. Softening of the webbing and pads can result in their tearing when galloping. Pain caused by cracking and splitting of the webbing and pads and low-grade foot soreness can occur in severe cases.
Cause: A soil-borne fungal organism is considered initially to invade the skin of the feet in Greyhounds housed under damp, contaminated conditions. Secondary infection with bacteria may develop, leading to exudate and discomfort. It is not as severe and debilitating as Alabama Rot or Greentrack disease that occurs under humid, tropical conditions. Refer to Alabama Rot.
Management: Bathing of the webbing and pads in a weak PVP based ('tamed') iodine solution to control surface fungal infection twice daily for 3-4 weeks, combined with antibiotics and soothing creams to reduce secondary bacterial infection and moisturise the devitalised tissue, helps control symptoms and clear up the surface rot. In severe cases, bathing in an antifungal preparation may be required to control the underlying infection. Improved kennel and yard hygiene, including replacing contaminated soil to 150mm (6 ins) depth with new soil, will help reduce the risk of recurrence or spread of the underlying fungal infection.

FLAT FEET: A term describing flattened-out toes on all four toes of all feet. Also called hare feet or splayed feet.
Signs: The bones of the toes on all four feet are aligned in a collapsed, flat formation, rather than having the arched form of a normal foot. The wrist may also flex downwards and flatten in severe cases.
Causes: Flat feet are often inherited in a Greyhound bloodline due to weakness of the flexor muscles that pass down the back of the metacarpals

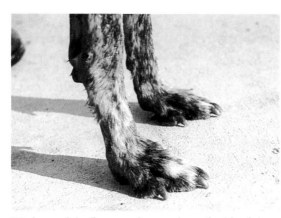

Weakness of the flexor tendons on the underside of the toes can result in splayed or hare feet, which, in this case, was apparent in all four feet.

and maintain the toes in an arched formation. One or more toes on one foot are referred to as dropped toes, which are usually caused by damage and severance of the flexor tendons on the underside of the toes. Refer to Dropped Toes.

Management: Early recognition and physiotherapy to strengthen and develop the flexor muscles in young Greyhounds is successful in some cases. Weakness in older Greyhounds cannot be corrected and, as it is an inherited condition, the bloodline should not be selected for breeding.

FIGHTING: A term to describe aggressive behaviour by a Greyhound during a race. It is also referred to as 'turning the head' during a race.

Signs: Aggressive behaviour during a race, turning the head to the side with attempts to bite or push an adjacent Greyhound to one side as they run together during a race.

Cause: There are a number of possible causes for aggressive, masculine highly competitive behaviour in a Greyhound. Muscle soreness or other injuries that cause pain may make a Greyhound aggressive, as well as imbalances of hormones that result in increased levels of circulating male hormone. Use of an anabolic steroid or male hormones, now banned worldwide, commonly caused aggressive behaviour in excess dosages. Greyhounds that fail to chase, or those that become bored in a race, may turn their head in play, without true aggression or intent to fight. Bitches appear to turn their heads in play, rather than aggressively fight, in many cases.

Management: The Greyhound should be examined for a muscle injury or other cause of pain

that could make it aggressive when racing. Courses of hormone therapy, based on male hormone (testosterone) to bitches and female hormone (progesterone) to dogs may be successful, especially if a dog is highly competitive when racing. However, under racing conditions, hormone use can contravene the drug medication rules. Courses of a stimulant such as 60-100mg of caffeine, given 40 minutes before a trial under strict veterinary supervision, may increase alertness and keenness when trialing to prevent a Greyhound losing interest and 'failing to chase'. The Greyhound may increase its keenness and forget about turning its head to fight or play. Other methods, such as acupuncture and herbal therapy, are of possible benefit. Refer to Failing to Chase. A dog that repeatedly fights in an aggressive manner will be barred from racing and is best retired.

FLEAS: Fleas are wingless insects that can live separate from the dog, but need to ingest fresh or dried blood to breed and multiply.

Signs: Fleas live on the skin surface of a dog, especially in areas where the animal is unable to scratch to disturb or dislodge them, such as on the rear of the hindquarters and tail butt area, or the sparsely covered lower belly and the inside of the back legs.

Cause: Fleas bite the dog to suck blood, contaminating the skin layers with saliva which results in an acute allergy in some Greyhounds, with itching, scratching and biting and gnawing of the inflamed skin, especially above the tail butt. In severe cases, the skin develops purulent scabs and sores and the hair thins out over the irritated area. Heavy flea infestations, which develop under moist, warm conditions, can suck enough blood within 2-3 weeks to cause anaemia, with pale gums, rough coat and lack of stamina when racing. Fleas only live on a Greyhound for a short period each day, with the breeding population harboured in bedding and warm moist, mulched areas in outside runs, yards or turn-out pens.

Management: Regular washing of a Greyhound with insecticide washes, or courses of oral flea control drugs, which will help to control fleas on the animal's body, are recommended. Many preparations contain chemicals that prevent flea breeding and kill larvae of fleas harboured in the bedding and kennel area. Rigorous and regular control of fleas in the environment is the only effective, long-term means of breaking the life-cycle and preventing heavy infestations under warm, moist conditions. This involves removing and destroying, or washing bedding in an insecticidal wash, and spraying crevices or cracks in the wooden bases of kennel beds with a flea-control agent. Where a Greyhound is anaemic, a course of iron and other blood forming nutrients may be prescribed over a 3-4 week period to assist recovery.

FLY BITE DERMATITIS: Refer to Ear Tip Fly Worry.

G

GASTRIC DILATION: A condition where the stomach rotates within the abdominal cavity and enlarges due to accumulated gas. In severe cases, it causes circulatory shock and, if not surgically corrected, can result in stomach rupture and a rapid and painful death. It is also referred to as Volvulus or Bloat. Refer to Bloat.

GASTRO-ENTERITIS: Gastritis is inflammation of the stomach wall, which often co-exists with inflammation of the intestine, or enteritis. Refer also to Blow-Outs, Colitis, Diarrhoea and Enteritis.
Signs: The gastritis component usually causes abdominal discomfort and vomiting, with the ensuing enteritis leading to diarrhoea.
Cause: There are a number of causes including acute digestive upset due to ingestion of contaminated food, viral infections (such as parvovirus), licking irritant topical medications from the skin, kidney failure, liver disease and bacterial diarrhoea.
Management: Withdrawal of food for one or two meals and, once the vomiting is controlled, water can be given to maintain fluid levels. Where enteritis is present, medication with Kaolin and gut sedative preparations, under veterinary supervision, helps to resolve the inflammation and excessive intestinal movement. In acute cases, fluid therapy to correct dehydration and electrolyte loss is paramount to avoid debilitation and possible

shock. The underlying dietary, toxic or infective cause should be investigated by a vet.

GINGIVITIS: Inflammation of the gums around the gum-tooth margins, often associated with development of periodontal disease.
Signs: Although it is more common as a dog ages, pups and racing Greyhounds can develop gum disease, with reddening, discomfort and bleeding around the gum-tooth margins. Often a foul breath (halitosis) develops due to proliferation of bacteria. The bacteria, harboured in the inflamed area, ferment trapped food particles between the teeth or gum margins. In severe cases, swelling of the tonsils (tonsillitis) can result.

Swabbing the tooth-gum margins twice daily with 1 part hydrogen peroxide (3%) in 2 parts water, applied with a cotton bud helps aerate the gum edges and reduce low-grade infection associated with gingivitis.

Cause: A build-up of calculus, tartar or plaque harbours bacteria, which results in low-grade infection and inflammatory reaction. Soft diets, without hard husks or bones to chew, allow food particles to be trapped between the teeth, which encourages bacteria and gum irritation. Regular teeth descaling is necessary.
Management: Refer to Calculus on the Teeth for guidelines on management and prevention. In severe cases, antibiotics may need to be given initially to control the underlying infection prior to descaling to prevent ongoing inflammation. Where the gums are reddened and sensitive, the teeth will need to be descaled under a general anaesthetic to avoid discomfort and allow better control of bleeding during the cleaning procedure. Twice-daily swabbing with a mixture of 1 part hydrogen

peroxide (3%) to 2 parts water, applied with a cotton bud, for 5-7 days will help clean and aerate the tooth-gum margins to control any anaerobic infection.

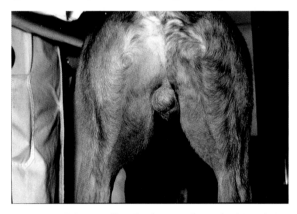

GRACILIS MUSCLE INJURY: The gracilis muscle is commonly referred to as the Back Muscle on the inside of the groin. It acts to stabilise the hip and hock joints and prevent the hindlimbs splaying apart when galloping.

Signs: Minor bruising and internal tearing of the muscle will be exhibited by swelling and pain in the muscle once the Greyhound cools down. The Greyhound is usually reluctant to extend its hip and hock, with a reduced stride length at the walk. Tearing of the muscle (dropped muscle) from the midline pelvis bone origin on the inside of the groin area may not affect straight-line performance.

Rupture of the gracilis ('back') muscle on the left side is often obvious after a race, although the Greyhound may not be lame.

It is often not detected until the muscle sags downwards on the inside of the thigh, with collection of blood under the skin and soreness.

Cause: Injury to the gracilis muscle is not common in a young Greyhound, unless the track surface is very loose on the corners and the legs splay apart and overload the muscle when cornering or avoiding a fall or interference during a race. The incidence of gracilis tears, and pull-away from its origin as a dropped muscle, increases by up to three times in Greyhounds over three years old, especially those running on loose surface sand tracks.

Management: Prompt first aid in severe tears and pulled-away (dropped) gracilis muscle is paramount to increasing the chances of healing. The muscle should be pushed back into its normal position and held in place by a small ice pack to prevent continued bleeding, and overwrapped by an elastic bandage. The injury should be evaluated by a vet within 12-24 hours. Mild tears are best injected with an anti-inflammatory or muscle-healing preparation, combined with 14-21 days' rest and walking on the lead while supported by an elastic bandage. Although a dropped muscle is often stitched back into place within 24 hours of the injury occurring, holding the muscle back in position with support bandages has an almost equal chance of healing over a 6-8 week period to enable a return to racing.

GREENTRACK DISEASE: Refer to Alabama Rot.

GROWTH PLATE ABNORMALITIES: Refer to Epiphysitis.

GUM DISEASE: Refer to Gingivitis.

H

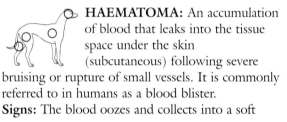

HAEMATOMA: An accumulation of blood that leaks into the tissue space under the skin (subcutaneous) following severe bruising or rupture of small vessels. It is commonly referred to in humans as a blood blister.

Signs: The blood oozes and collects into a soft

Muscles can pull away from their attachments to bone with haemorrhage and haematoma (blood blister) formation, as occurred in the rupture of the deep 'belly' muscle in this Greyhound.

swelling, relative to the tightness of the skin and the size of the blood vessel(s) that are damaged.
Causes: In racing Greyhounds, haemorrhage into muscle tissue, as a result of bruising and blood vessel rupture, forms an internal haematoma or bruise. The blood clots and separates, and the collection of serum fluids interferes with healing. Another common location for a haematoma is on the inside of the hindlimb above the hock, when the outside of the elbow brushes or strikes the area as it passes through between the hindlimbs when galloping. The skin is tight over the area of underlying bone and the bruising results in the development of a small soft blood sac, referred to as a track leg or jack. Refer to Track Leg for details of this injury. Occasionally a Greyhound will bruise the earflap when shaking its head and striking the ear on the kennel wall, or as a result of a fall, or running into a fence. This can cause a large sac of blood, referred to as an aural haematoma, to form between the cartilage core layer and the skin.
Management: A cold compress applied to the ear will reduce the size of the blood sac. The affected ear will droop downwards due to the weight of the collected blood. If the blood is not drained out between 4-7 days after the haematoma forms, shrinkage of the fibrous blood clot will cause disfiguration and drooping of the earflap, to form a distorted ear shape, sometimes referred to as a cauliflower ear.

HALITOSIS: A term used to describe very smelly breath in a Greyhound.
Signs: A strongly rotting odour in the breath that is detected when the Greyhound pants after exercise, or when the mouth is examined.
Causes: The accumulation of scale on the teeth, severe gum disease (gingivitis) or food particles trapped between the teeth encourages bacterial and yeast build-up and fermentation to produce a strong odour. Greyhounds that lick themselves (sheath or vulva) may also increase the level of bacterial contamination in the mouth. Aged Greyhounds with decayed and diseased molar teeth may also suffer from halitosis, especially when fed on soft, mushy diets that become trapped in the larger gaps between the eroded teeth.
Management: In severe and persistent cases, the Greyhound's teeth should be thoroughly descaled

and examined for gum disease and decay. Refer to Calculus and Gingivitis. Swabbing the gum-tooth margins with a mix of 1 part hydrogen peroxide (3%) and 2 parts water twice daily for 5-7 days often help to freshen the breath.

HARE FEET: A common term used to describe flattening of the four main toes on all four feet. It is considered an inherited conformation weakness. The condition is also termed flat feet or splayed feet. Refer to Flat Feet.

HEART DISEASE: The healthy heart pumps blood around the body, through the lungs, to offload carbon dioxide and pick up oxygen in the red cells, then pressurises the blood to circulate it to the muscles, gut organs and body. A Greyhound's heart beats about 100-140 times per minute at rest. When excited before racing, it elevates to 130-180 beats/min, and during racing it pumps at 250 beats/min to maximise blood pressure and delivery volume for oxygen transport during exercise. There are a number of primary and secondary diseases that affect the heart. These can lead to reduced efficiency of blood delivery to the working muscles which, in a racing Greyhound, can directly affect stamina and speed. Primary heart disease can be related to conditions that affect the electrical transmission of the nerve and heart muscle contraction impulse, physical trauma and bruising to the heart muscle when a Greyhound falls or collides with another Greyhound in a race, and infection of the sac, or pericardium, around the heart that protects and lubricates the beating heart. Retired Greyhounds may develop a weakened or diseased heart as they age, which can reduce their level of activity and lifestyle. Secondary heart disease is most commonly caused by infection with the large heartworm spread by mosquitoes in tropical and subtropical countries. Refer to Heartworm Disease.
Signs: Common signs of an underlying heart condition include poor stamina, loss of speed, low exercise tolerance with shortness of breath, rapid panting, severe distress after exercise, dark tongue and membranes in the mouth, and weakness and collapse after a race due to reduced oxygen transport from the lungs to the muscles and body.

Where the blood pressure is lowered due to heart muscle injury or disease, fluid may collect in the lungs and chest which results in a moist, muffled cough, particularly after a Greyhound has been resting. The lower limbs may swell (oedema) due to fluid retention in the tissues, and, in severe cases, fluid accumulates in the abdominal cavity.

Cause: A puppy may be born with a diseased or weak heart muscle, heart nerve abnormalities, or valve deformities and weakness of the heart chamber walls. The heart muscle can also become infected by bacterial or viral organisms in severe systemic infections. This results in endocarditis, with severe discomfort and risk of heart failure. The large canine heartworm (*Dirofilaria immitis*) develop and live as adults in the right ventricle chamber of the heart, which can restrict blood delivery to the lungs. Refer to Heartworm Disease.

Management: The diagnosis and management of heart disease involves listening to the heart beating using a stethoscope to detect abnormalities, X-rays to evaluate heart size and position, an ECG to monitor heart nerve and muscle activity, as well as blood tests to determine heart muscle enzyme levels and presence of heartworm larvae (microfilariae) in countries where heartworm infection occurs. Management includes restriction of exercise, with medication to treat the underlying cause or assist in improving heart function and strength to remove secondary fluid build-up and to promote improved circulation. In older retired Greyhounds that are overweight, dieting to control weight is an important part of management. Where the underlying cause is heartworm blockage, specialised treatment will be necessary.

HEARTWORM DISEASE:

Infection with a species of long thin worm that specifically colonises the right side chambers of a dog's heart. It is the most common cause of heart disease in racing Greyhounds in countries where the parasite is present.

Signs: History of loss of performance, lack of stamina, distressed and rapid breathing, muddy, dark or 'blueness' of the tongue vessels and mouth membranes (cyanosis) during recovery after racing. In advanced cases, a moist, muffled, cough may develop as fluid accumulates on the lungs due to restriction of blood flow to the lungs and reduced blood pressure, combined with a soft 'pitting'

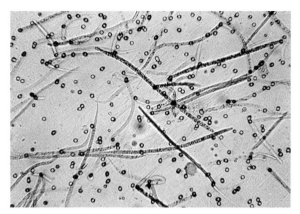

Microfilariae or the blood borne living stages (magnified) produced by the adult female heartworm (Dirofilaria immitis) resident in the right chambers of the heart. The small, round bodies are red blood cells. The blood was centrifuged to concentrate the microfilariae for this photograph.

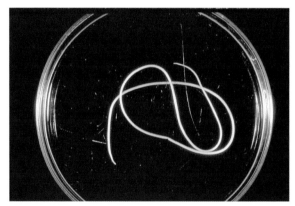

An adult heartworm (Dirofilaria immitis) retrieved from the heart of an infected Greyhound, measuring 25 cm in length and 3 mm in diameter.

swelling (oedema) of the lower limbs.

Cause: There are two species of heartworm parasite that colonise the right ventricle chamber of the heart. The most common species that causes clinical disease in Greyhounds is *Dirofilaria immitis*. It is endemic in southern USA, the northern and eastern coast of Australia, and is spread by several species of mosquitoes. Mosquitoes suck blood containing minute larvae (microfilariae) circulating in the blood of a Greyhound or other dog harbouring adult, sexually mature heartworms. The microfilariae are deposited under the skin, develop into an infective stage in 3 months in a small cyst, then travel in the blood to the heart, and colonise the right ventricle chamber, developing to adults in 3 months. Mature heartworms are thin, thread-like worms, up to 30 cms (12 ins) in length. As many as 200 may lodge and develop in the heart, projecting into the right atrium and lung arteries and reducing right side valve and heart efficiency. Heartworms may live for many years and large infections will result in chronic heart failure in Greyhounds of all ages. The other heartworm, *Dipetalonema reconditum*, is a smaller heartworm that appears not to cause major health related problems in dogs. It is spread by fleas.

Management: Diagnosis of heartworm is made by listening for heart valve failure on the right side of the heart as it pumps blood to the lungs. Blood tests to detect microfilariae, and X-rays to evaluate heart size and shape, also aid diagnosis. As heartworms live in the heart, treatment to kill them must be carefully supervised and monitored by a vet. Shock, and severe blockage of the lung, can occur as dead worms fragment and are carried in the circulation. Preventative drugs are available to control microfilariae in the blood and are very effective when given on a regular programmed basis. Preventative therapy must only be commenced after a Greyhound has been tested negative for heartworm microfilariae. A negative test will help to avoid untoward allergic reaction to the antiparasitic drug, which could result in circulatory shock and death. Steps to control mosquitoes in the kennels are helpful, but do not constitute a reliable preventative measure in endemic areas.

HEAT STROKE/HEAT STRESS: A term to describe a critically elevated body temperature as a result of rapid overheating and inability to lose excess heat efficiently by panting.

Signs: Overheated Greyhounds develop a rapid, distressed panting, increased heart rate and a warm, dry skin. In severe cases, the Greyhound may vomit, become incoordinated and delirious, then convulse and collapse into a coma within 5-10 minutes.

Cause: Hard exercise in an excitable, dehydrated Greyhound, under hot, humid conditions when evaporative cooling efficiency from panting is decreased, is the most common cause in a racing Greyhound. It can also occur during confinement to hot, poorly ventilated kennels, or in outside yards without shade under humid conditions with no air movement. Dehydration, with a reduction in airway and lung moisture to evaporate when panting, increases the risk. Hydrobathing a Greyhound with warm water in an enclosed room or kennel area during hot humid weather can cause acute symptoms of heat stress within 5-10 minutes. Greyhounds left unattended in vehicles or trailers with the windows or vents closed, particularly when hot after a trial or race, can rapidly over heat in 5-10 minutes, collapse and die due to acute heat stress. Exercise-induced malignant hyperthermia is an inherited disease, which can result in overheating, distress and cramping. Refer to Exercise-Induced Hyperthermia.

Management: Prompt first aid and cooling is essential to prevent debilitation and death. Hose the Greyhound with cold water for 2-3 minutes, towel to dry off, then repeat until the distress of panting is reduced. Sponge cold water on the tongue and mouth to help cool the blood and reduce body temperature. Greyhounds that are in a collapsed state should be immersed in a bath of cool water for 30 seconds, then towel-dried and sponged, or hosed off with cool water as recommended. It is important not to leave the coat saturated with water after washing or bathing a heat-stressed Greyhound, as the trapped water will retain heat. Always towel dry, and if available, direct a fan on to the body to increase evaporative cooling. Monitor the body temperature at 5-10 minute intervals until it stabilises below 39.0 degrees C (102 degrees F) for at least 30 minutes and the Greyhound is settled and resting. Fluids and body salts should be given to correct dehydration.

HIP JOINT INJURIES: The major injury is fracture within the joint and associated arthritis that can cause pain and discomfort as a Greyhound ages in retirement.

Signs: The Greyhound is reluctant to bear weight on the affected hindlimb. Swelling over the hip, with discomfort displayed when the hindlimb is moved or rotated. Older injuries progress to an arthritic stage with reduced stride and freedom of movement, and chronic lameness.

Cause: Fracture of the hip joint socket (acetabulum) can occur spontaneously during a race, sometimes without a history of a fall or collision.

Management: Diagnosis can be confirmed by X-ray of the pelvis and hip. Surgery to repair the fracture and associated tissue damage increases the chance of return to racing. Although it helps to stabilise the fracture, not all Greyhounds retain their previous form, and often develop arthritic change in the joint. The hip support muscles may waste away, weakening the hip structure. This results in a loss of speed and recurring injuries when a Greyhound runs on a circle track, especially if the right hip is injured. It is best to race the Greyhound on a straight track in this case.

HIP SUPPORT MUSCLE INJURIES: Hip support injuries are often associated with sprain or tearing of the muscles that provide the stability and movement to the hip joint, pelvis and hindlimb. These include the biceps femoris, sartorius, rectus femoris, and the lateral vastus muscles.

Signs: When one or more muscles in the left hip support group are sore, the Greyhound will drive up the straight with the left hindlimb, changing alternatively to the right limb during galloping. This results in a wobbling, side-to-side line of galloping when viewed from the rear when racing. Right-sided soreness results in loss of power and ability to hold and balance on cornering as the Greyhound uses its right hind leg to straighten up out of a corner, often causing it to deviate and run to the outside. Right-side injury has a higher incidence on sand tracks. Recurring right-sided problems are often associated with an increased risk of track leg or jack, on the inside of the left hindlimb, especially when combined with lumbosacral joint (coupling joint) and left shoulder muscle injuries. Swelling, discomfort and attempts

Right side hip support muscle injuries bulge out to the side when viewed from the rear, compared to the normal muscle symmetry on the left side.

to withdraw the limb when manipulated can be detected when the injured muscles are examined. When viewed from the rear, the injured side appears swollen out, rather than concave, as on the normal, unaffected side of the hip area.

Cause: Overload sprains, or tears of the muscles, can occur during acceleration, particularly if there is a short straight to the first bend. Incidence is doubled on a sand track as a result of slippage on the corners due to an uneven or loose surface compared to a similar grass or compacted loam surface. Bumping and interference in a race can overload the hip support muscles as a Greyhound attempts to regain stability at speed, especially when cornering and using the right hindlimb to help steer itself around the corner.

Management: Mild sprains and soreness may respond to massage and ultrasound therapy over a 5-7 day period, followed by short, straight line handslips on alternate days for 10-14 days. Use of magnetic therapy, injections of cortisone and muscle repair mixtures are recommended. When combined with kennel rest for at least 10-14 days, these provide a greater chance of the Greyhound returning to form. In the more serious form of injury, with tearing and haemorrhage, chronic soreness and loss of muscle function, a longer rest and physiotherapy rehabilitation period is necessary. If the injury recurs, racing up a straight track may be successful. Alternatively, it may be necessary to retire the Greyhound from racing.

HOCK INJURIES: Injuries within the hock result from sprain and strain of the internal ligaments and dislocation and fracture of the small tarsal bones that form the hock joint. Up to 96 per cent of hock bone fractures occur in the right hock, ranging from single fragment to multiple fractures within the bones.

Signs: Swelling, reluctance to flex the hock or bear weight are common signs of internal ligament sprains. Fracture or dislocation ('popping') of the central tarsal bone of the right hock causes instability of the joint as the animal walks, with a prominent swelling on the inside of the joint. In most cases, the animal will hold the limb off the ground after popping its hock, or sustaining other forms of severe hock injury. Dislocation of the hock joint can also occur, with swelling, lameness and joint instability.

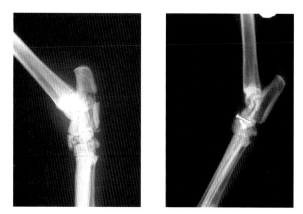

X-ray of a 'popped' hock (left) showing dislocation of the central tarsal bone. It was pushed back into place and secured by a thick, elastic bandage over a 5 week period to enable a successful return to racing. The X-ray (right) is of a similar injury which was screwed to assist repair with excellent results.

Cause: Most hock injuries occur as a result of a fall or interference in a race, where the Greyhound suddenly changes direction or brakes at full speed. Fracture of the central tarsal bone of the right hock is most common on poorly-banked turns with a shifting surface on a race track, as the right limb is subjected to increased compression force and rotational stress when cornering on a loose surface.

Management: Hock injuries can be related to poor conformation and weakness within the hock joint. Prompt first aid to immobilise the injured joint is paramount to success in treating hock fractures. The use of cold compresses and pressure support strapping applied to the hock will increase the chances of repair. Hock injuries are best evaluated by examination and X-ray to confirm the type, location and severity of the fracture. Surgical repair, or even the application of a strong rubber sleeve as a stabilising bandage for a fracture of the central tarsal bone, provide the best chance of return to racing. As the hock is a vital and flexible joint, joint active medications to assist in repair, such as hyaluronic acid, glycoaminoglycans and cortisone therapy may be beneficial to reduce inflammation and improve repair processes. Refer to Arthritis, Articular Cartilage.

HOOKWORM INFECTION: Hookworms are an internal parasite of dogs that colonise the small intestine. There are two species of hookworm – *Ancylostomum* and *Uncinaria* species. The prevalence of each varies from country to country.

The *Ancylostomum* species of hookworm suck blood and are distributed in moderate-to-warm countries, and regions within a country. The *Uncinaria* species is most common in cold countries and is found in Greyhounds in the UK, northern USA, and southern Australia's cooler regions. *Uncinaria* hookworms damage the intestinal wall as they feed, leading to protein loss.

Signs: Heavy infeststions of *Uncinaria* species of hookworms result in nutrient and protein loss, evident as a dull coat, poor general condition and lack of vitality. Even relatively mild infestations of *Ancylostomum* hookworm can lead to blood loss, with symptoms of anaemia, including lack of stamina, pale gums and reduced performance. Severe infections cause internal intestinal bleeding, evidenced by smelly, dark stools. Heavy infestations in pups can cause severe anaemia, with debilitation, weakness and death within 10-14 days of becoming infected with the hookworm larvae. Dermatitis can develop between the toes, as hookworm larvae, hatched from eggs passed in the droppings of an infected Greyhound, penetrate the webbing and skin of the lower limbs as a Greyhound stands on the contaminated ground or wash bay surface.

Cause: Both species of hookworms can be taken in as larvae on contaminated food, or by direct penetration through the webbing and skin of the lower limb. Greyhounds are most likely to be infected when standing on a damp communal wash area at a track, or when confined to heavily contaminated yards, runs or turn-out pens. Puppies are more severely affected, and have fewer reserves, with a heavy infection likely to cause severe anaemia and death.

Management: Effective control of hookworms requires a combination of regular worming, with efficient and targeted preparations in all Greyhounds, complemented by strict kennel and yard hygiene. Routine measures include picking up the droppings twice daily, close mowing of grass in yards in which Greyhounds empty out and, if necessary, regular 6-monthly replacement of the top 150mm (6 ins) of sand or soil in contaminated yards, runs and turn-out pens. Anaemic Greyhounds must be treated with blood-building supplements, and, in severe cases of debilitation, blood transfusions may be necessary. A vaccine is available to stimulate immunity against hookworm and it provides protective antibodies to young growing pups when used under veterinary supervision.

HOT SPOTS: A term used to describe moist, inflamed areas of skin on the sides and backline of a Greyhound. They are also commonly referred to as Milk Sores or Pustules.

Signs: Juicy, inflamed and ulcerated circular areas from 5mm to 20mm (^{1}/5-^{4}/5 ins) in size develop over a period of 3-10 days on the skin over the ribcage, backline, the inside thighs, and above the tail of a Greyhound. A single animal, or a group of Greyhounds in the kennel, may be affected.

Cause: Insect bites from biting flies, mosquitoes and even fleas, are thought initially to cause an allergic reaction in the skin, which raises above the skin surface, pushing the hair up around the borders of the lesion. Invariably, the bites become infected with bacteria, including *Staphylococcus* species (Golden Staph variety), causing a pus-filled, inflamed and ulcerated sore that does not heal. Many trainers also associate hot spots with a rich diet and the development of hives, often as a result of large amounts of milk being fed (hence milk sores), vitamin supplements and high protein feeds. The lesions are more common under hot, humid conditions when biting insects are more active.

Management: When a number of scattered juicy sores develop on a Greyhound, a course of a suitable oral antibiotic may be prescribed by a vet. Bathing the hot spot area with a PVP (tamed) iodine wash to control skin bacteria and drying the ulcers with a paint-on iodine antiseptic, twice daily for 7-10 days, is helpful to promote healing over the following 10-14 day period. Control of biting insects by repellents and fly screens in the kennel, as well as rigorous flea control during warm humid weather, will help prevent further lesions. Many trainers discontinue milk, vitamin supplements and high protein dry foods in an effort to prevent any possible hive-type reaction, caused by a rich diet, while the lesions heal. A Greyhound should be prevented from licking the sores on the body by fitting a muzzle with the front taped over, a light rug, or in severe cases, a large-size Elizabethan collar or 10 litre (2.2 gallons) plastic bucket secured to its collar. Careful attention to kennel hygiene, and thorough cleaning and disinfection of the floor and bedding, will help to reduce the risk of milk sores. Refer to Dermatitis.

HUSK: A term widely used in the UK, Ireland and USA to describe an irritating, often unproductive, cough.

Signs: A moist cough, which is aggravated by breathing in cold air early in the morning, or when racing late at night under cold conditions. These symptoms have been outlined under coughing, and underlying causes include tracheitis, tracheobronchitis, exercise-induced asthma and allergic coughing. Refer to Coughing, Asthma, Tracheitis and Kennel Cough for specific causes and management.

HYGROMA: A soft, fluid sac that develops on the bony prominences of the elbow and hock. The terms Bursitis or Capped Elbow or Capped Hock are also commonly used by trainers. Refer to Bursitis.

HYPERTHERMIA: An acute, extreme, life-threatening elevation of the body temperature, usually exceeding 41-42 degrees C (106-108 degrees F). The terms heat stroke, heat stress, and exercise-induced malignant hyperthermia are used to describe specific causes of hyperthermia. Refer to Heat Stroke/Stress and Exercise-Induced Malignant Hyperthermia.

HYPOTHYROIDISM: A condition related to lower than normal activity of the thyroid gland or production of the thyroid hormone (thyroxine). Greyhounds characteristically have a lower circulating level of thyroid hormone (thyroxine) than other breeds of dogs. However, studies in the USA on 100 racing Greyhounds, indicated that low thyroxine was not associated with poor racing or breeding performance.

Signs: Common signs that have been linked to low thyroxine levels (hypothyroidism) include inconsistent and poor performance, tiredness and listlessness, form reversal and failure to chase. Some Greyhounds have a history of multiple muscle injuries from which they did not recover fully, despite physiotherapy and other treatment. A poor, dull, lifeless coat with scurf (dandruff) and itching have been linked to low thyroid function.

Cause: It is well documented that low thyroid

activity is associated with infertility in bitches and stud dogs, with a loss in libido and a low sperm count, especially in young stud dogs less than 5 years of age. The condition of bald thigh syndrome in racing Greyhounds is also often considered to be responsive to courses of thyroxine hormone. Diets deficient in iodine can result in lower thyroid function and blood thyroxine levels. Cortisone release as a consequence of stress during hard training may suppress thyroid gland function and be the underlying cause for the lower thyroxine levels in racing Greyhounds, although adequate levels are present to maintain health and performance.

Management: A blood test to determine the level of thyroxine hormone will confirm if thyroid function is lower than normal, although the interpretation must consider the normally lower levels found in Greyhounds as compared to other breeds of dogs. Responses to thyroid hormone supplements have been observed in racing Greyhounds, by way of improved condition and reversal of the hair loss associated with bald thigh syndrome. However, research has not been able to demonstrate a definite response as evidenced by improved performance to replacement therapy with thyroxine in controlled studies in racing Greyhounds. Refer to Bald Thigh Syndrome. Where a Greyhound exhibits many of the symptoms associated with hypothyroidism, particularly where low blood thyroxine levels are combined with a history of poor, inconsistent racing performance, a 10-14 day course of thyroxine tablets may be prescribed and the response, if any, evaluated.

I

ICTERUS: The term used to describe yellowish discolouration of the mouth and eye membranes and, in severe cases, the skin and body fluids caused by accumulation of excess bile pigment in the blood. It is commonly referred to as jaundice. Refer to Jaundice.

INFECTIOUS TRACHEOBRONCHITIS: See Kennel Cough.

IMMUNOSUPPRESSION: A descriptive term used when referring to the syndrome related to lowered immune defence in the blood and tissues. It is not a disease as such, but is caused by a variety of infectious, physical, chemical and other agents, including pain and stress that act to suppress the immune system. In some cases, the immune system can be deliberately suppressed by chemical and drug medications in treating auto-immune-related diseases where the body develops immunity against its own cells, as well as the uncommon condition of leukaemia in Greyhounds.

Signs: Depression of the immune system decreases the antibody and white blood cell mediated immunity against infectious disease, parasite invasions (such as roundworms and demodectic mange), and some skin conditions. The Greyhound may also be slow to recover from a normally short-term infection or disease.

Causes: Many of the commonly used drugs to relieve pain and inflammation of joints and musculo-skeletal injury, such as phenylbutazone and cortisone-type drugs, as well as certain antibiotics used to treat skin itches and infections, have an immunosuppressive side-effect. High doses, or prolonged medication, can reduce the natural immune defence against bacterial, viral and fungal diseases that the animal would normally have developed, or the stronger build-up of long-lasting immunity acquired from specific vaccinations. The immune response can be suppressed by long term training programmes, which may make the Greyhound more susceptible to bacterial skin diseases, demodectic mange and fungal conditions of the skin, pads and webbing. Refer to Demodectic Mange. Some viral diseases, such as canine distemper and parvovirus, act to suppress the body's immunity. Many drugs used to control leukaemia in older Greyhounds act to reduce the immune cell production by the bone marrow. In some cases, such as occurs with the Polyarthritis syndrome in young Greyhounds, and certain skin diseases, the over-active immune response, or auto-immune reaction, can be suppressed by controlled doses of cortisone and other chemotherapy medications to assist in managing the disease and its harmful effects. Refer to Polyarthritis syndrome.

Management: Whenever high dose rates, or long courses of potentially immunosuppressive drugs, or other medications, including antibiotics and painkillers, are prescribed, they may reduce the immune response to viral, bacterial and fungal infections. Appropriate quarantine and hygiene should be adopted to reduce the risk of concurrent disease, or infection during, and for sometime after, the immunosuppressive side-effects of these medications. The dose rate and duration of treatment should be monitored under veterinary supervision. If a Greyhound is suffering from the stress of over-racing, and develops symptoms of weakened immunity, it should be rested for 4-6 weeks or longer to regain full function of its immune system. Vitamin A and Vitamin E and the trace-minerals of copper, manganese and selenium are often prescribed to assist immune recovery.

INFECTIOUS DISEASES: Infectious diseases are those that can be spread from one Greyhound to other Greyhounds. Greyhounds in contact with an infected animal, or in the same area, are susceptible to a number of infectious diseases caused by canine specific viruses and bacterial germs. Even infection with certain internal parasites can be classed as an infectious disease when spread by eggs or larvae, particularly in young Greyhounds. Infectious diseases can be spread by already infected animals, or 'carrier' animals that harbour the disease, usually a virus, but do not show any symptoms themselves. Infectious diseases can be introduced to the body by inhalation of aerosol droplets, such as occurs in canine distemper, by eating food containing the organisms shed in the stools or body fluids of an affected Greyhound, such as parvovirus and Salmonella bacteria, or as a result of being bitten by an insect carrying the infective stage of a disease, such as heartworm or babesiosis.

The control of infectious diseases relies on early recognition and isolation of the sick Greyhound, with prompt and targeted treatment, combined with strict hygiene and proper disposal of infected discharges and droppings. Measures should be taken to limit the risk of spread by the isolation and quarantine of all new Greyhounds to ensure they have no signs of disease before being introduced to the kennel area. Regular booster vaccinations will help ensure that maximum immunity is maintained against common viruses in new and resident Greyhounds. Refer to Specific Diseases such as Canine Viral Diseases, Diarrhoea and Babesiosis for more information.

INTERDIGITAL DERMATITIS: A condition that results from inflammation of the skin of the webbing between the toes and pads and the under parts of the pastern that contact the ground.

Signs: Depending on the underlying cause, symptoms can range from acutely inflamed and reddened skin, with discomfort when squeezed, to a dry or chronic moist condition. Greyhounds may lick their feet and webbing, softening the skin and, in some cases, slowing the natural rate of recovery. In severe cases, the Greyhound will be lame when walking, especially when more than one foot is affected,.

Causes: Primary causes include fungal colonisation of the webbing and skin, usually contracted under wet conditions in contaminated yards, runs or turn-out pens. Greyhounds with light skin pigment are commonly considered more likely to develop interdigital dermatitis under wet, contaminated conditions. Skin contact with chemicals in cleaning and disinfectant solutions used on kennel floors can cause a surface irritation or allergic reaction of the delicate skin of the webbing. The skin of the webbing and pads may also be penetrated by the burrowing larvae of hookworms (called transcutaneous migration) that cause irritation and dermatitis between the pads. Refer to Hookworms and Dermatitis.

Management: It is important that a proper diagnosis is made, relative to the underlying cause, as management and treatment must be coordinated to ensure efficient and complete control. Antibiotics, anti-allergy medications and soothing, moisturising preparations may be prescribed. In all cases, clean, dry bedding should be provided to reduce the continued contamination. The yards and turn-out areas should be cleaned up to reduce the level of contamination. In recurring cases, the top 100-150mm (4-6 ins) of surface soil of a turn-out pen, or day yard, should be either replaced or, alternatively, dusted with lime or a non-irritant disinfecting and drying chemical. Where hookworm skin larval migration is suspected, topical application of an antiparasite preparation, combined with antiseptic dressings, is recommended. As well as a thorough worm treatment, the Greyhound's turn-out yard should have the top 150mm (6 ins) of soil removed to reduce egg and larval populations in heavily contaminated areas. Refer to Hookworms.

INTERDIGITAL CYSTS: These are seen as small, closed or open nodules on the webbing between the toes or in the space between the main pads. This type of cyst is not common in Greyhounds.

Signs: Small, raised, cauliflower-shaped nodules that develop on the edges of the webbing between the toes over a 7-10 day period. The cysts often become inflamed and infected with bacteria, bursting to weep a mixture of blood and pus (serosanguinous) or a cheese-like discharge when squeezed. Many are sore when squeezed and may lead to a shortened stride, particularly if more than one cyst is present on the same foot. Cysts located between the main pads, particularly on the hind feet, are usually obviously painful when the Greyhound is walked on a hard surface. One, or more feet, may develop cysts.

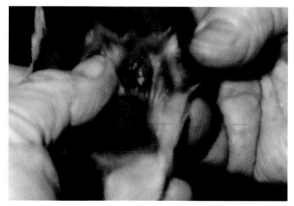

A large and painful interdigital cyst on the webbing between the toes. It was removed by electro-cauterising the cyst with a hot blade. The area was then allowed to heal as an open wound over a 14 day period before the Greyhound returned to training.

Cause: It is considered that the *Papilloma* virus (or wart virus) invades the abraded edges of the webbing and develops into an inverted sac of infected fluid and cells (a cyst) within the skin of the webbing. A type of cyst can also develop when small, sharp prickles, or burrs, penetrate the skin to form a festering, weeping raised cyst-like sore.

Management: Although an uninfected, cauliflower-like cyst can be squeezed to remove its cheesy core, it is unwise to squeeze to express an infected cyst, as bacterial contamination will be forced into the surrounding tissue. In this case, the lesion may enlarge and become more infected and painful, resulting in lameness. Surgical removal of the cysts by electrocautery will usually allow the webbing to heal within 14-21 days. During this period, the wound can be treated as an open wound, with application of a topical iodine-based antiseptic and drying preparation. The webbing should be allowed to stretch naturally to regain its pliability as it heals, encouraged by walking the Greyhound on the lead. A dressing, and waterproof bandage on the foot, will keep out soil, water and other contamination to prevent the wound becoming re-infected.

INTERNAL PARASITES: Greyhounds are susceptible to all the internal parasites or worms that are common to other breeds of dogs. However, because racing Greyhounds are required to perform as athletes, even relatively low infestation of intestinal worms may reduce their performance.

The common worms include

Common Name: Hookworms.
Species: *Uncinaria stenocephala* (Intestinal irritation).
Site of infection: Small bowel.
Prevalence: All Greyhounds.
Species: *Ancylostoma caninum.* (Blood-sucking)
Site of infection: Small bowel
Prevalence: Puppies mainly.

Common Name: Roundworms.
Species: *Toxacaris canis, Toxascaris leonina.*
Site of infection: Caecum and large bowel.
Prevalence: Growing and adult Greyhounds.

Common Name: Whipworms.
Species: *Trichuris canis, Trichuris vulpis.*
Site of infection: Large bowel.
Prevalence: All Greyhounds.

Common Name: Tracheal Worms.
Species: *Filaroides osleri.*
Site of infection: Lower windpipe and bronchi.
Prevalence: Mainly Adult Greyhounds.

Common Name: Tapeworms.
Species: *Taenia species.*

Site of infection: Large bowel.
Prevalence: All Greyhounds.
Species: *Dipylidium caninum*
Site of infection: Large bowel
Prevalence: All Greyhounds

Common Name: Heartworm.
Species: *Dirofilaria immitis.*
Site of infection: Right side of Heart.
Prevalence: Greyhounds older than 3 months.

Although a number of other worms have been reported in Greyhounds, including lungworms (*Capillaria spp*) and intestinal threadworms (*Strongyloides spp*), these worms are incidental infections and are susceptible to most worming compounds (anthelmintics) used to control the common internal parasites. Refer to Heartworm Disease, Hookworms, Toxacaris, Tapeworms, Tracheal worms, Roundworms and Whipworms.

J

JACK: A term used by North American trainers when referring to bone surface reaction and a haematoma (blood blister) that forms on the inside of the hindlimbs above the hock. In Australia and other countries, it is referred to as a 'track leg', which is the term used in this book. Technically, it is termed medial tibial periostosis, or inflammation of the periosteum covering the inside of the tibia bone above the hock. The swelling is most common on the inside of the left hindleg and often becomes a regular, chronic injury in a racing Greyhound. It is due to bruising of the skin over the hard bone surface when the outside of the elbow on the front limb on the same side brushes or strokes it during racing. Refer to Track Leg.

JAUNDICE: An abnormal, yellow discolouration of the mucous and eye membranes, body tissues, blood and urine, due to retention of excess bile.

Signs: Jaundice is not a disease as such, but an indication of an underlying disease process, usually involving the liver, with retention of excess bile pigment in the blood, tissues and body fluids.

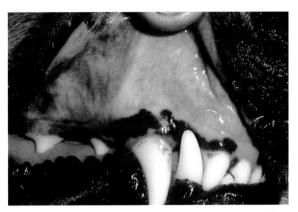

A yellowish to 'muddy' colour of the tongue, gums and mouth membranes is a sign of jaundice. In this case, it was associated with severe gastroenteritis with concurrent dehydration.

Faint yellow tinges of the whites of the eyes and gum tissues are often the first signs of jaundice. If the underlying cause develops further, to an acute or severe form, the bare skin on the belly and inside of the rear legs, the urine and, eventually, a yellowing of the droppings becomes apparent.

Causes: Jaundice is not a common clinical condition in Greyhounds, except in areas where babesiosis and leptospirosis infection occurs. However, mild forms can develop following severe infection, resulting in excessive blood cell breakdown and certain types of liver disease. Blockage of the bile duct into the small intestine can cause retention of bile and its pigments in the liver, with overflow into the blood and accumulation in the tissues.

Management: The Greyhound should be examined by a vet, who will invariably require a blood test and liver function tests to determine the underlying cause. By the time symptoms of jaundice are noticeable, a relatively severe disease condition may have developed. Because diseases such as leptospirosis (Refer to Leptospirosis) are infectious to humans, isolation from other Greyhounds should be enforced until a definite diagnosis is available. Targeted medication must be given to treat any microbial or parasitic infection, as well as the concurrent liver disease. A complete recovery must be assured before treatment is withdrawn.

JOINT INJURIES: As an athletic, high-speed racing animal, the limb joints of racing

Greyhounds are subjected to overflexion (bending backwards) and overextension (bending forwards) due to high compression, added momentum (straight line) and centrifugal (cornering) loading at racing speeds. Concussion on hard track surfaces and rotational (twisting) and lateral (sideways) forces are also imposed during directional changes and track surface slippage as a Greyhound gallops at maximum speed.

Individual front limb loading at maximum speed in a straight line has been measured at 2.4 times the animal's bodyweight, which places high compressive and weight-bearing forces on the limb structure, including the joints. The joints are subjected to repeated wear and tear each time a Greyhound gallops. The speed of galloping and the instability of the track surface imposes the risk of joint injury each time a Greyhound accelerates, corners, changes direction and sprints during a race.

Remarkably, the overall incidence of joint injury is not as high as muscle injury. Muscle injuries can usually heal in the short term if rested and managed correctly; however, joint injury is usually more chronic in nature due to slow repair of the ligament, bone and cartilage structures, with risk of long-term arthritic change and degeneration. The most common joint injuries occur in the shoulder joint, carpal joints (wrist) of the front limb, lower back lumbosacral joint (coupling joint), the stifle and hock joints of the hindlimb, and toe joints of all limbs. The inside two toes on each limb next to the rail have a higher risk, due to lateral and twisting forces when cornering, than the outer adjacent toes.

The upper neck joints are occasionally injured in falls or when a Greyhound hits the inside of the lid of the starting box or trap, as well as a result of head-on collisions with other Greyhounds. The hip support joint can develop fractures of the pelvic socket (acetabulum), but the incidence is low compared to the lower limb joints. The main joint injuries are outlined under each individual joint. Refer to Shoulder Joint, Carpal (Wrist) Joint, Hip Joint injuries, Coupling Joint, Stifle Joint, Hock Joint, and Toe Joint Injuries. Other underlying conditions such as Polyarthritis, Articular Cartilage Injury and Arthritis are discussed under their respective alphabetical listing.

JUVENILE BONE DISEASE: The term used to describe abnormal development of bone and joints in a young, growing Greyhound, which can lead to weakness and increased risk of breakdown injuries in the animal's future racing career. These conditions are technically known as juvenile osteodystophy (weak bone formation), rickets (abnormal joint formation), metaphyseal osteopathy (growth plate injury) and epiphysitis (inflammation and enlarged growth plates on the ends of bones). In horses, the condition is referred to as developmental orthopaedic disease, which is a complex joint disease interrelated to hereditary influences, nutrition and exercise.

Signs: There are a number of visible, and not so outwardly obvious, signs associated with juvenile bone disease. Swelling of the epiphysis, or growth plate, area is visible as big or lumpy joints (big joints) above and below the wrist, hock and toe, which, in severe cases, can lead to intermittent lameness, deformed joints and limb and joint breakdown. Bone weakness has no visible outward signs, but can increase the risk of bone fracture and joint deterioration in both the growing and adult racing Greyhound. Although rickets is a term used to describe abnormal bone and joint development, it is not as common in Greyhounds compared to larger breeds of dogs.

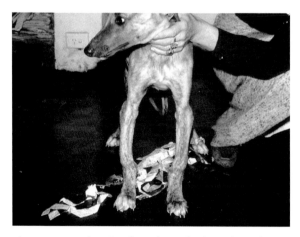

A young, growing Greyhound can develop enlarged, lumpy wrists due to abnormal growth rate (refer to Epiphysitis). In severe cases, poorly balanced diets can lead to 'rickets' and bowed out legs due to low calcium, high calcium, low Vitamin D or other imbalances between these nutrients.

Causes: The most common cause is related to excess or inadequate nutritional energy intake; a diet that is imbalanced or deficient in calcium; phosphorus and trace-mineral intake on an all-meat or all-cereal diet; low or excess Vitamin D in the diet; and sudden overloading exercise (or even insufficient exercise) in a grossly overdeveloped pup or weaner. Other predisposing influences are genetic, hormonal and conformational abnormalities of the limbs.

Management: The common condition of growth plate enlargement is discussed under Epiphysitis. Although genetic and environmental influences can result in juvenile bone disease, hereditary influences have been minimised over the years by selective breeding of Greyhounds to avoid joint and bone problems. The greatest influence is related to a combination of nutrition and exercise, both of which are controlled by the breeder or owner as the pups are raised to racing age.

Most proprietary diets formulated for growing pups are balanced, but recent evidence suggests that Vitamin D and calcium in cereal-based dry foods may not be efficiently absorbed due to binding (calcium) and loss of potency (Vitamin D), with subsequent development of a rickets-like bone and joint abnormality. Overfeeding of home-made diets, consisting of high intakes of meat or dry food, should be avoided, as excess energy intake can promote rapid growth and a risk of trace-mineral deficiencies that hamper joint development.

The calcium and phosphorus balance should be maintained between 1.2-1.4 parts of calcium to 1.0 part of phosphorus, complemented by an adequate intake of trace-minerals including copper, zinc and manganese and Vitamin D provided by a well-formulated supplement. Growing Greyhounds must be provided with the opportunity for yard and long run exercise for at least 15-20 minutes daily, preferably during daylight hours, relative to weather conditions. As epiphysitis is often the first obvious sign of juvenile bone disease, advice should be sought from a vet or canine nutritionist regarding the adequacy and balance of the young Greyhound's diet and the frequency, level and type of exercise suitable for the young, growing Greyhound. Refer to Epiphysitis.

K

KENNEL COUGH: An infectious respiratory disease caused by a combination of bacterial and viral germs, often associated with an introduction of a Greyhound carrying or harbouring the infection to the racing or home kennels. It is technically referred to as Infectious Bronchitis or Infectious Tracheobronchitis, although the symptoms of Tracheobronchitis are often lingering and more chronic in nature.

Signs: A persistent, harsh non-productive cough, often with bouts of coughing, with gagging or retching if the animal becomes excited during exercise, or distressed due to frequent coughing. Initially, the Greyhound may have a fever, lose its appetite and be less active. Often the cough appears as if the Greyhound is trying to clear an object caught in its throat. Excitement or intake of cold air when walking or galloping will initiate a coughing bout. As the condition progresses, brownish or grey-coloured mucus will often strand from the nose and mouth. Occasionally, the infection will spread to the lungs causing pneumonia, particularly if the Greyhound continues to be raced.

Causes: In most countries, the infectious respiratory diseases or viruses, Parainfluenza virus and Adenovirus Type 2, appear to be required to initiate the respiratory condition. The bacterial germ, Bordetella bronchiseptica, is often present in the airways. Although its activity is suppressed in healthy dogs, it can become active and multiply in the lining of the damaged airways. This secondary invader results in inflammation, irritation and increased airway mucus production and outflow. The incubation period is 5-7 days, and once infected, a Greyhound can retain the bacteria in its airway lining cells for 90-100 days or longer, shedding them into the environment as a carrier of the disease. Another airway bacterial germ, Streptococcus zooepidemicus, which is also present in healthy airways, has been associated with an acute respiratory disease with internal lung bleeding and pneumonia in Greyhounds in North America. Infection with these bacteria can cause severe debilitation and death.

Management: All infected Greyhounds should be isolated from healthy Greyhounds that do not have the symptoms. The course of the disease can last for 2-3 weeks or longer, relative to the degree of secondary infection, the level of stress in the Greyhound and the severity of lower airway and lung involvement. The Greyhound should be kept as quiet as possible to avoid excitement, as a coughing bout may cause respiratory distress and spray the infectious organisms into the air. A cough suppressant can be administered under veterinary supervision if the coughing is causing loss of sleep or distress in the initial stages of the disease. A course of a targeted antibiotic that can penetrate the thick mucus discharge to control the underlying infection, often in combination with a mucolytic preparation to make the mucus more liquid and easier to transport out of the lower airways, is required. This can assist the normal cleaning action of the cilia cells in the airways to clear the lungs. The Greyhound must not be galloped or raced during the recovery period and a veterinary check to ensure the airway disease is clearing up should be carried out before the Greyhound is put back into training. A number of types of vaccine are available, in single or combined inoculations, to prevent the disease. Regular boosters to new Greyhounds entering the kennels are essential to deter an ongoing risk of infection and help prevent carrier animals acting as a source of further sporadic outbreaks. Refer also to Coughing, Tracheitis.

KERATITIS: A term to describe inflammation of the cornea, or clear window surface, of the eye external to the pupil. The condition is often referred to as pannus by Greyhound trainers, but this term is used to describe an immune-related keratitis condition.

Signs: Initially, the Greyhound will be observed to be blinking the affected eye more frequently than normal, with overflow of tears and attempts to rub the painful eye. The cornea may develop an initial hazy film, due to water uptake, with the surface becoming white and cloudy, often developing an inflamed zone around the edges. An ulcerated area with thinning of the cornea will also develop at the site of infection. If left untreated, small blood vessels will grow across the surface of the eye (called neovascularisation), with a dark pigment being deposited in the corneal layers. In severe cases, ulceration of the cornea can lead to rupture

and blindness in the eye, even if the cornea heals with an obvious scar.

Causes: Keratitis is usually associated with some form of trauma to the cornea, such as a particle of sand hitting the eyeball during a race; a small piece of grass or hair caught in and adhered to the cornea; rubbing the eye with the paw and accidentally scratching it; or a Greyhound rubbing its head to relieve an itchy ear. If the eye dries out excessively under hot dusty conditions, or the drying effect is created by very bright sunlight, this can result in a protective inflammatory reaction of the cornea. Secondary infection of an initial surface injury to the cornea can result in scarring and restricted vision. Refer also to Pannus.

Management: Early recognition and diagnosis, with prompt treatment, is essential to avoid permanent scarring of the clear cornea area. Greyhounds with eye injuries should be kennelled in subdued light on non-dusty bedding. A vet can check the cornea for ulceration using a strip of fluorescein (fluorescent) dye. The type of medication with eye drops must be carefully selected and combined with antibiotics to control infection. If necessary, cortisone drops or ointment should be used to reduce irritation and risk of rubbing the eye and causing further injury. Cortisone medications must not be used indiscriminately, as the drug can reduce the immune defence of the eye and conjunctiva, and lead to severe infection, delay of healing and further damage to the cornea. A bucket may need to be secured to the animal's head to reduce the irritation from light. In severe cases, the conjunctiva membranes that encircle the eyeball can be used as cover over the ulcerated area to protect it, with the eyelids stitched together to prevent blinking and protect the healing ulcer. An injection of a small volume of an appropriate antibiotic into the conjunctival membranes inside the eyelid is used to provide a slow release form of medication in the tears to control surface infection as the cornea heals.

KIDNEY DISEASE: It is a common belief among trainers that racing Greyhounds suffer from a number of kidney ailments. However, young, healthy Greyhounds of racing age have a very low incidence of kidney diseases, accounting for less than 5 per cent of the problems that affect a racing Greyhound. Kidney diseases are more common in older Greyhounds, particularly aged brood bitches and retired Greyhounds. The kidneys carry out the vital function of filtering the blood of waste and other toxic metabolic products. When galloping, the blood is directed to the contracting muscles and blood flow through the kidneys decreases to 20 per cent of its normal rate. At rest, up to 25 per cent of the total blood flow passes through the kidneys, with the entire blood volume circulating through the kidneys each hour. The kidneys also control the acid-base balance and levels of body salts and fluids within the body cells, tissue and blood. They also monitor the tissue demand for oxygen and the level of blood haemoglobin by releasing a natural hormone, erythropoietin (EPO) that stimulates bone marrow function to accelerate red cell and haemoglobin synthesis. This will lead to improvement in the oxygen-carrying capacity to meet oxygen needs in the muscles when galloping. The two most common problems that can affect the function of the kidneys are nephritis, or inflammation of the kidneys, and the water diabetes syndrome or racing thirst, where the control of urine concentration and volume is reduced or lost in the 12-24 hours following extremely stressful exercise. Refer to Nephritis and Water Diabetes Syndrome.

KNEE JOINT INJURIES: The knee joint or stifle joint is a hinge joint consisting of the large major thigh bone, or femur, and the tibia to form the stifle joint. A small bony kneecap (patella) moves in a groove at the front of the joint to provide stability and allow movement of the tendon of the hindlimb quadriceps muscle group over the joint. The stifle joint in a racing Greyhound is a robust, strong structure. Most injuries in young Greyhounds result from accidental falls and twisting forces during cornering, or avoidance manoeuvres at speed when playing or running in a group. A separation fracture of the tibial crest, termed an avulsion fracture of the tibial crest, is a relatively common injury in young Greyhounds running in outside yards. Other knee injuries include patella fractures, which are relatively uncommon and, even less frequently, cruciate ligament sprain in young puppies. Refer to Cruciate Ligament Injury, Patella Fractures, and Tibial Crest Fractures.

KNOCKED-UP TOES: A term to describe the elevation of the last toe bone (digit), pad and toenail off the ground surface when the Greyhound stands.

Signs: The last segment of the toe develops a flattened appearance, with the toenail raised off the surface and, in severe cases, the toe rests on the back of the pad or on the under part of the toe.

Causes: When the deep digital flexor tendon that attaches under each toe is cut or sprained it weakens or tears internally. In severe cases, it may be pulled off its anchorage point to the bottom of the last toe (third digit or phalange). The toe is no longer held in contact with the ground surface. This results in the extensor tendon on top of the toe maintaining its pull, raising the toenail and the tip of the toe above the surface.

Management: When the toe nail is lifted upwards by a finger, it readily bends upwards as there is no stability provided by the deep flexor tendon on the underside of the toe. There is little that can be done to repair a knocked-up toe, as a surgical approach to repair the deep flexor tendon is difficult. Keeping the nail trimmed so that it cannot catch on grass or bedding, thereby risking damage to the toe joint by overextension, is helpful. Removal of the toe, pad and the last digit is recommended if the pad and toe are badly knocked-up.

L

LARYNGITIS: A term that describes inflammation of the throat and larynx, or voice box, which produces the dog bark sound.

Signs: A change in the barking sound, often with a choking, gurgling or squeaking-type of higher-pitched sound when a Greyhound barks.

Causes: Greyhounds that are barkers in the kennel may become hoarse from laryngitis. Laryngitis and laryngo-tracheitis may also be a complication of a respiratory disease, such as kennel cough, which may persist for 2-4 weeks after the initial infection. A Greyhound that pulls hard on the lead and compresses the larynx in the throat area may develop throat inflammation and symptoms of laryngitis.

Management: The underlying cause of the

inflammation or infection is best treated with anti-inflammatory drugs and antibiotics as prescribed by a vet. Syringing 10ml (0.325 oz) of honey or glycerine over the tongue twice daily may also help relieve irritation and assist recovery. If the Greyhound is a barker, then an anti-barking muzzle may be helpful to reduce ongoing irritation as the condition is controlled.

LEPTOSPIROSIS: An infection causing liver and kidney damage due to Leptospira bacteria, which can affect humans. It is not common in well-managed kennels.

Signs: Yellowing of the gums, tongue and eye membranes are usually the first signs (Refer to Jaundice), followed by a high temperature, loss of appetite, depression, vomiting and diarrhoea. In severe cases, non-pigmented skin will also develop a jaundiced colour and it may be fatal, due to acute liver, kidney and blood vessel destruction.

Causes: Rats and mice are the carriers of the Leptospira bacteria and infected dogs can also harbour the infection, excreting the bacteria in their urine. Contaminated rat, mouse and dog urine can build-up bacterial levels in the porous or cracked cement of kennel floors, the soil of yards and turn-out pens, and surface run-off water collected in stagnant canals, pools, dams and ponds. The thin, spring-shaped Leptospira germs can penetrate the skin, webbing and softened footpads. Leptospira can also contaminate food and water. Urine samples can be examined to identify the characteristic bacteria.

Management: An early diagnosis, combined with isolation and treatment of sick Greyhounds with high doses of penicillin injection over a 5-7 day period under veterinary supervision is necessary to control the spread of infection and prevent more severe liver and kidney damage. Strict hygiene when handling and nursing sick Greyhounds is essential, as Leptospira germs can infect humans. All bedding must be replaced, rats and mice controlled and, if an outbreak is severe, the top 150mm (6 ins) of soil in yards and turn-out pens removed and replaced with clean soil. Contaminated water should not be used to wash kennels or hose yards, and all drinking water from dams or ponds should be boiled if chlorinated mains or clean rainwater is not available.

LICE: Skin lice are occasionally harboured on young Greyhounds living in outside runs.

Signs: Dog lice are small, white skin insects about a quarter of the size of an adult flea. The eggs are visible as white dots adhering to the hair along the edges of the ears, forehead and around the elbows where lice usually congregate. The surface-feeding species of lice will cause Greyhounds with sensitive, thin skin to itch and scratch incessantly, resulting in trauma and inflammation of the skin and hair loss. Other, less sensitive, Greyhounds rarely scratch and the lice infestation may not even be noticed.

Causes: Heavy infestations of blood-sucking lice can cause anaemia. Infestation with lice is most common during the cooler months in young Greyhounds in outside yards, as the thicker haircoat is more protective to the lice, which complete their life-cycle on the Greyhound. Spread of lice within the group occurs in shared kennels and outside shelters.

Management: Lice infestation can be confirmed by collecting a few in a glass jar for identification by a vet. Treatment of all Greyhounds in a group with two insecticidal washes at a 14-day interval will break the life-cycle. Bedding should be replaced to avoid recontamination, as lice eggs are often resistant to insecticidal sprays.

LIGAMENT INJURIES: Ligaments span the distance between two adjacent bones that form a joint in the spinal column, limb or toes and the bones within a joint, such as the wrist and hock. Internal ligaments within the shoulder, hip and stifle (such as cruciate ligaments in the knee) improve the stability of these joints. Bruising, overstretching or strain and tearing of joint ligaments are a common form of injury in racing Greyhounds.

Signs: The degree of swelling, pain, joint instability and lameness is relative to the severity of the ligament injury and its position. Minor strains may cause localised swelling and discomfort on movement or flexion of a joint. Tearing of a ligament will result in swelling, severe pain and instability of a joint, such as occurs in a sprung or dislocated toe. Tearing of the ligament from its anchorage point on the bone will result in swelling and, often, healing with a bony reaction due to disruption of the bone surface layer (periosteum) with calcification of the attachment points to form a bony lump, such as occurs in a curb of the hock. The major ligament injuries that occur in racing Greyhounds are described under each specific condition. Refer to Annular Ligament Injuries, Collateral Ligament injuries, Cruciate Ligament Injuries, Curb, Dislocated Toes, Sprung Toes and Sesamoid Ligament Injuries.

LIVER PROBLEMS: The liver is a vital organ involved in food utilisation, metabolic processes, and the secretion of bile stored in the gall bladder attached to the liver and released after each meal, that acts as a fat emulsifier in the small intestine. As well, the liver stores certain vitamins and trace-minerals, makes a dog's supply of Vitamin C (from glucose), is vital in the process of drug metabolism and detoxification functions, protein and blood recycling activity and elimination of wastes in the bile. Diseases of the liver cause clinical signs such as debility, vomiting and jaundice. The liver cells (hepatocytes) have a unique property of being able to replace and regrow sections of damaged liver after toxic or traumatic damage. As the liver is a large organ, it can suffer minor toxic or even cancerous damage without showing outward signs. The liver can be affected by many infectious diseases, such a Canine Viral Hepatitis, toxic damage and in older retired Greyhounds, tumours or cancer of the liver cells. Refer also to Jaundice.

LUMBOSACRAL INJURIES: Falls and collisions during racing can result in trauma and unnatural rotational stress on the lumbosacral

Lower back and lumbrosacral pain can be assessed by pressing down on the backline just in front of the hips – moving back to the rump area.

joints (or junction). Anatomically, the junction is positioned where the lumbar spinal column of the lower back forms a joint with the sacral bone body within the pelvic girdle of the hindquarters. This junction is commonly referred to by trainers as the 'coupling joint'. The joint has limited rotational movement to allow flexion and twisting during galloping and turning. Concussion to the vertebral joint, and strain of the collateral ligaments, can cause inflammation and pain, developing into arthritis in more chronic cases. The common signs, causes and management are discussed under the topic of Coupling Joint Injuries. Refer to Coupling Joint Injuries.

LUMBAR VERTEBRAL FRACTURES: There are two fractures associated with the upward bony projections (called dorsal spines) or processes of the lumbar or lower back vertebrae that form the spinal column. The most common injury is caused by tearing of the ligaments and a stress fracture of the spinal process at the last lumbar vertebra. The other, more serious, fracture can occur within any of the last 2-3 lumbar vertebra of the back. Also refer to as Lumbar Spine Injuries.

Signs: Lower lumbar vertebral fractures result in intense lower back pain, arching of the back as the back muscles are held in tension to support the fractured vertebrae. Within 12-24 hours, the area around the fractured vertebra swells and often the Greyhound develops symptoms of hindlimb incoordination and paralysis as a result of trauma and squeezing of the spinal cord as it passes through the fractured, unstable vertebra. Signs associated with ligament tearing and overload (stress) fracture of the spinal process of the last lumbar vertebra include discomfort when the lower back is pressed downwards in front of the pin bones, with more intense pain and movement of the spinal process when they are manipulated to the side. Affected Greyhounds are much slower to accelerate out of the boxes or traps and fall behind or run wide when cornering.

Causes: Fracture of a lumbar vertebral body can be caused by a serious fall on cornering or a side-on collision with another Greyhound when recovering from interferance or a 'check' in a race. Stress fracture of the spinal projection on the last lumbar vertebra in front of the lumbosacral joint

can occur as a Greyhound jumps from the boxes or traps, and powers off under full acceleration propelled by the backline and hindlimb muscles.
Management: Fractures of a lower back lumbar vertebra usually cause spinal cord compression trauma, resulting in incoordination and, in severe cases, dragging of one or both hindlimbs. Fractures can be confirmed on X-ray. Unfortunately, treatment is often unsuccessful and euthanasia is a humane way of preventing the poor quality of life of a disabled Greyhound. Ligament tearing and stress fracture of the spine of the last lumbar vertebra usually responds well to rest and physiotherapy, including magnetic field therapy for 15-20 minutes twice daily over a 3-4 week period. If the bone does not heal, surgical removal of the spinal process can be carried out, followed by at least a 2-month lay-off from racing to allow healing. However, often the Greyhound loses speed and may develop lumbosacral arthritis.

LUNG PROBLEMS: Greyhounds have been selected and bred for a large lung capacity to ensure a maximum area for oxygen uptake during racing. The lungs also provide a large vascular area for evaporative cooling of the blood during exercise as a Greyhound breathes and pants after exercise, or when hot. The lungs are highly vascular, non-muscular organs that inflate due to the negative pressure created in the chest cavity as the muscular diaphragm contracts back towards the gut cavity at each breath. The ribcage provides the structural support to withstand the crushing pressure of the outside air pressure during inhalation, and protect the soft lung tissue from injury. The average Greyhound has a lung capacity of about 1.5-2 litres (3-4 pints) when the thousands of air sacs are fully inflated. The air is delivered into each lung by the large bronchi and smaller bronchioles that supply the air-sacs (alveoli) in a similar structure layout to the stem and branches that form a bunch of grapes.

Lung diseases are most commonly related to upper respiratory tract viral and secondary bacterial infections that are drawn down, or settle in, the lower airways and air-sacs of one or both lungs. Inflammation of the bronchi is a relatively common condition, with infection, inflammation and fluid accumulation in the lower airways and airsacs which, in severe cases, results in symptoms of pneumonia.

Several species of internal parasites or worms can

be harboured in, or migrate through, the lower airways and the air-sacs, leading to irritation, inflammation, infection and coughing. Between 10-15 per cent of Greyhounds haemorrhage into their lungs due to high capillary blood vessel rupture generated when racing, causing a 'bleed' into the air-sacs and airways. In severe cases, this form of exercise-induced pulmonary haemorrhage, which occurs commonly in racing and performance horses and also in racing camels, reduces speed and stamina in the final stages of the race. Occasionally, a Greyhound will cough up blood after a hard, fast race and veterinary advice should immediately be sought.

LUNGWORMS: Lungworms are small, roundworms that colonise the windpipe and bronchi, rather than the lung tissue and airsacs. There are a number of species of worms that are harboured in the airways and lungs during their developmental life-cycle.
Signs: Lungworms invariably cause symptoms of chronic coughing, often with increased mucus and airway inflammation which, in severe cases, can affect racing performance.
Causes: Greyhounds have the highest incidence of lungworm of any breed of dog. Poor racing performance is a common side-effect. Various types of worms, or their eggs, can be found on examination of sputum, or by using a flexible fibreoptic bronchoscope to examine the windpipe and bronchi leading into the lungs. The most common species are summarised below:

Species: *Capillaria aerophila* (Lungworm).
Location: Lung airways – eggs into airways.
Side-effect: Chronic coughing, wheezing and distress after racing.

Species: *Angiostrongylus vasorum* (A species of Heartworm) Very low incidence in UK.
Spread by snails.
Location: Eggs develop to larvae in lower airways.
Side-effect: Coughing and reduced airway function. Worms travel through air-sacs to enter the right side heart chamber and pulmonary artery.

Species: *Filaroides osleri* (Tracheal Worm).
Location: Harboured in nodules at the base of the windpipe where it branches to bronchi.

Side-effect: Coughing after exercise, reduced performance. (Refer to Tracheal Worm).

Species: *Toxacaris species* (Canine Roundworm).
Location: Migrating developing larvae from small intestine travel through diaphragm and lung tissue into airways and are coughed and swallowed to complete development life-cycle.
Side-effect: Coughing and inflammation of airways. Most common in growing puppies. (Refer to Roundworm).
Management: Diagnosis in a Greyhound with a chronic cough is either by identifying eggs in sputum samples, or by examination of the airways with a bronchoscope. Treatment with a specific worming compound will control the worms, followed by mucolytic and other medications to clean up the excess mucus and exudates in the airways.

LYMES DISEASE: See Ticks.

LUMBOSACRAL INJURIES: A severe race fall or collision can lead to inflammation of the lumbosacral joint area and eventual arthritis of the joint, with lower back pain and loss of agility, racing performance and risk of a track leg or jack. Refer to Lumbar Spinal Injuries, Coupling Joint Injuries, Track Leg.

M

MANGE: Mange is the common name that describes loss of hair and the skin disease associated with infestation by three species of parasitic skin mites.
Signs Inflammation and reddening of the skin, itching and abrasion of skin due to scratching. Abrasion to the skin results in weeping of blood fluid or serum, with crusting and scale formation on the skin. The loss of hair on various locations is relative to the type and number of mites.
Causes: Burrowing skin mites are the common underlying cause. The three species are Demodectic mites, Sarcoptes mites and ear mites (Otodectes species). Refer to Demodectic Mange, Sarcoptic Mange, Ear Mites.
Management: Specific insecticides to control skin

mites are available, relative to the type of mite. All animals in the kennels must be treated to break the mite life-cycle and prevent spread of the mange condition.

MASTURBATION: It is common for male dogs to develop penile erections and protrude the penis from the sheath. Occasionally, a male Greyhound will lick its penis or mimic a pelvic thrusting action, which results in an ejaculation. Once the reflex condition is enjoyed, the Greyhound may develop an annoying habit, fouling its kennel and bedding. An occasional masturbation does not affect race performance. Management to discourage the habit includes fitting a corset-type band around the lower belly, isolating the dog away from bitches in the kennel, therapy with female hormones and castration in long-term, intractable cases.

METABOLIC ACIDOSIS: A term used to describe the rapid accumulation of lactic acid in rapidly contracting muscles during anaerobic energy metabolism at maximum speed when racing. It is more common in Greyhounds that are unfit for the speed or distance of a race. The build-up of lactic acid can lead to premature muscle fatigue, symptoms of muscle soreness and cramping and, in the severe form, extensive muscle damage, dehydration, dark urine, kidney failure and death. Refer to Acidosis, Exertional Rhabdomyolysis.

METACARPAL INJURIES: The metacarpal bones are thin, long, slightly arched bones that form the upper part of the lower limb below the carpus (wrist) on each of the four toes, corresponding to the bones from the wrist to the first knuckle on the human hand. They are also commonly known as the shin bones. Injury to the metacarpal bones, including inflammation of the bone surface (called metacarpal periostitis) in young Greyhounds, and stress fractures, are relatively common in racing Greyhounds running on circle race tracks. Refer to Metacarpal Fractures, Metacarpal Periostitis (Shin Soreness)

METACARPAL FRACTURES:
The metacarpal bones are subjected to high loading forces at race speeds. Centrifugal forces, which are generated on cornering, greatly increase the loading and bending forces on the inside two metacarpal bones next to the rail on each front foot, as a Greyhound leans over to the left when cornering in a trial or race. Metacarpal fractures are usually associated with weakening or development of stress lines into the bone surface or structure from circle racing, and acute or chronic metacarpal periostitis (shin soreness) in young Greyhounds. A metacarpal bone can develop either a hairline fracture, a complete failure with a spiral or fragmented fracture, or a separation of the growth plate on the lower end of the bone.

Signs: *Metacarpal Hairline Fractures:* The affected Greyhound will pull up limping, or be reluctant to stand on the affected limb, after a circle gallop.

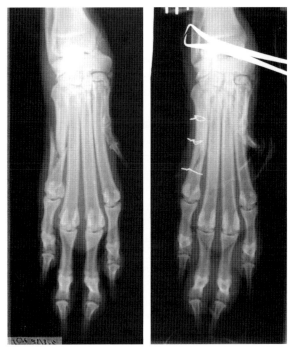

Photo 1   *Photo 2*

The outside metacarpal (shin bone) on the left front limb (left metacarpal 5) and inside on the right front limb (right metacarpal 2) are prone to twisting and extreme sideways bending forces during cornering. The X-ray image is diagnostic of a metacarpal bone midshaft stress fracture before repair (Photo 1) and after repair (Photo 2) using wire. The Greyhound returned to race successfully in a straight run 8 weeks later.

The animal will resent backward flexion of the wrist on the affected foot and may show lameness for 2-3 days, improving with rest. When each of the metacarpals is pressed downwards with the thumb and index finger along its length, signs of pain and withdrawal will be shown on the cracked bone. If a hairline fracture has been present for some time, a roughening of the surface of the bone under the skin, due to bone reaction and callus formation, will be detected when a finger is run up and down the length of the affected bone.

Complete Metacarpal Fractures: These are complete fractures, with the bone ends causing a gritting sensation when examined, resulting in severe discomfort, warmth, swelling and lameness on the affected foot. The outside bone on the left foot (left metacarpal 5) and inside bone on the right foot nearest the rail (right metacarpal 2) have the highest risk and incidence of fracture.

Causes: Both hairline fractures, and complete fractures, are the result of overloading and excessive downward and sideways bending forces generated when cornering at the gallop. In most cases, a fast, heavy-shouldered young Greyhound, that has not been conditioned on a circle track to allow time to model and strengthen the shin bones, is more prone to complete fracture when raced on a compacted track with poor banking and small radius bends. Usually, there is a history of the Greyhound having developed a metacarpal periostitis or shin soreness as a bone reaction following one or more gallops around a tight circle, poorly banked racetrack. The bone surface can develop a series of stress or fatigue-like cracks. More details relating to the progressive bone reaction and weakening due to overloading stress is provided under the discussion relating to metacarpal periostitis (shin soreness). Refer to Metacarpal Periostitis.

Management: Careful examination and X-rays of both front feet by a vet is necessary to confirm the severity of a hairline fracture or degree of loss of density, malalignment, fragmentation and involvement of the wrist or toe joint in a complete metacarpal fracture. In some cases, the two bones of the left foot nearest the rail will be fractured or develop varying degrees of hairline cracks. Occasionally, both feet will show bone stress changes in a young Greyhound.

Hairline Fractures: Hairline fractures can be managed conservatively, with strapping support, magnetic field therapy and warming liniments applied to help stimulate bone repair over a period of 4-6 weeks. If the X-ray of the bone(s) show loss of density and decalcification, then calcium and Vitamin D supplements, combined with carefully chosen and controlled anabolic steroid therapy, may be prescribed. Repeat X-rays may be taken to confirm healing, or the degree of bone calcification, before returning the Greyhound to light training in a gradual manner over 3-4 weeks. It is important that the wrist and the joints are flexed a number of times daily to maintain full joint movement.

Complete Fractures: Simple fractures can be stabilised by a thick padded bandage applied to the foot, a splint cast or a plaster cast and confining the Greyhound to a kennel for 3-4 weeks. Repeat X-rays will determine the extent of healing after this time, with another 4 weeks of physiotherapy to allow the healing bone to strengthen. Surgical repair using pins or plates may be necessary where multiple fragmentation and malalignment is present. There is a 60 per cent chance the Greyhound will return and race competitively. Up to 3 months rest may be required before the Greyhound can be returned to training. Where two metacarpal bones are shattered, a return to racing is unlikely.

Growth Plate Separation Fractures: These occur on the bottom end of the two metacarpals of the middle toes in young, immature Greyhounds. X-rays are usually necessary to distinguish growth plate separation as compared to a lower shaft fracture. Where the growth plate is still aligned on the bone, heavy strapping of the foot and use of physiotherapy such as magnetic field therapy, combined with confinement and calcium and Vitamin D supplements are standard treatment methods. Unfortunately, if the injury is not detected for a few days after the growth plate disruption, healing may not be complete and a repeat fracture may occur.

METACARPAL PERIOSTITIS:

Inflammation and reaction of the membrane (periosteum) covering the metacarpal (shin) bones of the front limbs. It is commonly referred to as 'shin soreness', which is analogous to cannon bone overload in young, fast, thoroughbred racehorses.

Signs: The signs are relative to the degree of overload and bone inflammatory change. The two inside metacarpal bones next to the rail on each front foot are more severely affected.

Early Signs: Early signs include shortening of the stride and loss of speed in a young Greyhound following a fast trial gallop or race on a circle track. Discomfort will be shown when the wrist is tightly flexed and the metacarpal bones are squeezed as a group in the hand. Accumulation of inflammatory fluid about midway along the surface of the affected bone(s) may be present. In a subsequent race, the Greyhound may be able to stride out along the straights, but on the approach to a turn, the stride may shorten and slow down, the head lift and the tail whirl as the Greyhound drifts out wide on the corner.

Advanced Signs: In more severe cases, the Greyhound may limp on a front limb when caught after a race, and hold the affected leg, usually the left fore, off the ground for a minute or so after the run. Flexion of the wrist(s) will usually cause discomfort over a 24-48 hour period after a race. Discomfort and soreness will be noted on the 'railing' bones closest to the running rail. A fluid swelling may take 2-3 days to appear after a circle race, with increased resentment when the individual metacarpals are pressed with the thumb and index finger.

Long-Term Changes: In more advanced cases, a ridge of thickened bone will develop on the top surface of the affected metacarpal bones along the entire length of the bone. There may be little soreness or active inflammation at this stage. Small microfractures may radiate into the bone from the surface and the weakened bone may develop a hairline or complete fracture during a subsequent race.

Cause: Metacarpal periostitis usually develops in a young, fast Greyhound when it is trialled or raced before the bones have time to model and thicken to withstand the increased loading forces imposed at the all-out gallop. The centrifugal force imposed when cornering is partially offset by leaning into the rail, but downward forces up to 10 times the normal straight line loading causes flexing of the immature metacarpal bones. This leads to minute stress fractures that radiate into the surface and cause inflammation and bone reaction. Centrifugal force is proportional to:

$$\frac{(\text{Body weight of Greyhound}) \times (\text{Velocity/Speed})^2 \, (\text{Squared})}{\text{Radius of the bend/circle}}$$

A heavier, more well-developed, fast, young, immature Greyhound galloping on a tight, inadequately banked turn is more likely to develop metacarpal soreness if pushed too fast, too early before the bones can thicken and adapt to the increased loading forces. Equal weight is shared by the four metacarpal bones during straight line galloping, but when cornering, the inside metacarpals (metacarpals 4 & 5 on the left front and metacarpals 2 & 3 on the right front) nearest the rail are subjected to sudden, dramatic increases in loading. Bone modelling can occur to strengthen the areas subjected to increased loading and flexing stress, but this is a slow process that takes weeks to complete. X-rays of both front pasterns will show a thickening or 'milkiness' of the bone cavity of the 'railing' bones as compared to the adjacent bones. Metacarpal soreness can also develop in older Greyhounds, particularly those that have been rested for some time and then subjected to a hard and shorter training schedule to try and get them fit in the shortest possible time for a particular race.

Management: Careful management and a gradual introduction to circle galloping will help to avoid metacarpal soreness and stress changes in young racing Greyhounds. It is essential to recognise and treat the condition in its early stage. Initially the inflammation, fluid build-up and soreness can be reduced by a cold compress applied to each foot for 2 minutes, 3-4 times daily, initially for 5-7 days. A daily supplement of calcium, phosphorus and Vitamin D should be provided to help the calcification and modelling processes reinforce the weakened bone. Magnetic field therapy for 20 minutes twice daily, combined with mild counter-irritant liniments applied daily for 2-3 weeks, may also be useful to encourage bone repair and reduce swelling. Ultrasound therapy under ice-cold water for 5-7 minutes twice daily for 7-10 days is also beneficial.

Initially, the Greyhound should be rested until the inflammation settles down. After this time, the Greyhound can be galloped 2 or 3 times weekly for 2-3 weeks up a straight track over 200 metres and, if available, allowed free galloping or short handslips to maintain fitness. Once introduced back to a circle track, it is best to allow the Greyhound to gallop around only one end circle from a handslip start on the outside of the circle. Repeat 2-3 times, then handslip from along the

back straight and allow the Greyhound to gallop around one end circle. Allowing a young Greyhound to handslip 2-3 times each week over 150 metres from the start of training may encourage modelling and strengthening of the metacarpals, followed by a gradual introduction to circle galloping over increasing distances until the Greyhound is fit for racing.

MILK SORES: A term used to describe raised, juicy and pus-filled lumps on the skin of the shoulder, back and rib cage that were historically considered to be caused by feeding milk to racing Greyhounds. They are also commonly referred to as 'hot spots' that develop on the skin of Greyhounds. Refer to Hot Spots.

MILK ALLERGY: An allergy reaction to milk protein (casein) and milk sugar (lactose) in an individual greyhound.

Signs: Development of skin bumps, a hive-type reaction on the skin, often along the neck, rib cage and between the hindlegs. The Greyhound may also develop a 'frothy throat' due to excess mucus build-up following exercise.

Cause: It is considered that individual Greyhounds may develop a reaction in the pharyngeal and upper airways, resulting in increased phlegm. Others develop excess mucus in the airways, which is difficult to cough up. Air mixes with the mucus during exercise producing 'froth in the throat'.

Management: Management to exclude milk from the diet is the first consideration. Initially the amount of milk can be halved, and the result observed over 7-10 days, and then eliminated from the diet if necessary. Milk is often given as a source of fluid and calcium, however, it provides only 300mg of calcium per cupful (250ml or 8ozs) but a Greyhound requiries from 5-7 grams of calcium per day. Supplementation with a small amount of calcium powder will provide the major source of this important bone and muscle mineral.

MITES: Small insects that commonly cause mange and ear mite infestations. Refer to Demodectic Mange, Sarcoptic Mange, and Ear Mite Infestations.

MONKEY MUSCLE INJURY:
A common term used to describe sprain or tearing the triceps muscle group on the rear of the shoulder blade. Also referred to as the egg or pin muscle. Refer to Dropped Muscles, Muscle Injuries.

MUSCLE INJURIES: Muscle Injuries are the most common cause for downtime from training or lost racing opportunities in racing Greyhounds. Up to 50 per cent of Greyhounds suffer some degree of muscle injury each time they race, resulting in a chronic pain state and risk of more serious injury developing in subsequent races. One or more muscle injuries may be sustained in a race.

Signs: Muscle injuries are normally graded from Grade 1 to Grade 3 relative to type, position, degree and severity of the injury and the estimated time for recovery. Most muscle injuries do not cause an obvious initial lameness, but soreness and changes within the muscle may be detected after cooling down, particularly when examined on the morning after a race.

Grade 1: Minor bruising, overstrain, soreness, stiffness and minimum damage to the muscle structure or anchorage points. These types of injuries are common, but often not identified in the early stage.

Grade 2: More distinct internal damage to the muscle sheath and fibres, with tearing of the sheath and separation of fibres, often accompanied by localised bleeding and swelling over the injury site.

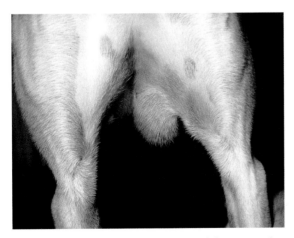

This retired Greyhound with a ruptured deep pectoral (chest) muscle was active and free of pain or discomfort.

Grade 3: These are the most serious forms, involving tearing and separation of fibres, usually in the major muscles used to maintain body stability and steering when cornering at speed. On examination, a squelchy feel due to internal bleeding, gaps and holes in the sheath and fibre bundles, pain and swelling after cooling down and lameness and loss of speed are common diagnostic signs.

Causes: The major propulsion muscles of the front limb, backline, hindquarters and hindlimbs exert high contractile power on the limbs during acceleration and cornering when racing. High loading forces are concentrated on certain muscle groups, commonly referred to as stress pathways on the limbs, which are specific to each side of the body as a Greyhound gallops around bends on circle tracks. The major areas that develop injuries include the deltoid and triceps muscle groups on the left front limbs, and the sartorius and vastas groups of the left hindlimb in straight line galloping. The deltoid and biceps muscle groups of the right front limb, and hip support group of the right hindlimb, have a higher incidence of strain overload injuries as a Greyhound corners, particularly on a sand track with a loose surface on the bends. Often low-grade soreness is overlooked, or not given adequate physiotherapy or sufficient time to heal before the Greyhound is galloped again in a trial or race.

Other factors, such as excessive body weight, particularly in male Greyhounds, with lack of adequate fitness, sharp corners, loose surfaces on racetracks, Greyhounds with poor conformation and movement, checking and deviations during racing and insufficient warm-up prior to racing all increase the risk of Greyhounds developing muscle injuries. Greyhounds weighing above 33kg (72lbs) have a 55 per cent higher risk of sustaining musculo-skeletal injuries when racing.

Management: The type of therapy, downtime from training and long-term prognosis is relative to the grade, position and number of muscle and associated bone and joint injuries sustained in a race. Greyhounds should be thoroughly checked over before and after trialling or racing and, most certainly, on the morning following racing. An examination by an experienced person or a Greyhound vet may be necessary to identify and evaluate the type, grade and relevance of muscle injuries. Initially, therapy for Grade 2 and 3 muscle injuries should include complete rest, application of ice-cold compresses for 2-3 minutes, 3-4 times daily for the first 24-48 hours to control pain, confine the injury and constrict bleeding vessels.

In severe muscle tears, surgical repair is recommended to minimise scarring and reduce downtime from training. After the first 24-48 hours, a number of forms of physiotherapy can be used to aid blood flow into the damaged muscle tissue. These include the use of simple massage, heat lamps and ultrasound to improve blood flow once the internal bleeding has stopped. Magnetic field and laser therapy is widely used for bone and tendon/ligament injuries, but muscle repair is less responsive. A planned gradual reintroduction to training is necessary to help rehabilitate muscle injuries to enable a Greyhound to return to competitive racing.

MYOCARDITIS: Inflammation of the heart or cardiac muscle.
Signs: Initial fever, associated with shallow breathing, rapid heart rate, a weak pulse, cold feet and lower limbs, with risk of collapse and death during exercise. In acute cases, where severe heart muscle damage occurs, collapse and death can occur within a few hours.
Causes: The most common cause is a certain strain of parvovirus infection that targets the heart muscle of young pups from 2-10 weeks of age. Often parvovirus infection also causes acute diarrhoea. See Parvovirus Disease.
Management: In most cases, symptoms are not noted before extensive heart muscle damage has occurred and the puppy is found dying or dead. In acute cases, rest and specific medication to aid circulation and fluid replacement is often given by trainers. All bitches should be given a booster vaccination early in pregnancy. Puppies should be given vaccinations for parvovirus after 6 weeks of age to boost their immunity. Refer to Parvovirus.

MYOSITIS: A term used to describe inflammation of muscle tissue, often associated with muscle injury or severe cramping. Refer to Muscle Injuries.

MYOGLOBINURIA: A term to describe the passing of dark pigment in the urine following development of severe muscle acidosis. Myoglobin, the oxygen storage pigment in muscle cells, escapes

A range of urine samples indicating common urinary changes in Greyhounds. From left to right:
1. Normal, yellowish urine of a healthy Greyhound.
2. Urine containing calcium and phosphate crystals in suspension imparting a 'gritty' feel to the urine.
3. One of a number of large bladder stones removed from the bladder of an old, retired Greyhound.
4. Urine from a Greyhound that has suffered severe cramping, with retained acids in the muscles, resulting in severe muscle damage and myoglobin pigment being leached out from red blood cells.
5. Urine collected from a Greyhound suffering from acute cramping with severe muscle damage, releasing myoglobin in the blood and urine.

into the blood fluid (plasma) following severe muscle injury or acidosis (cramping). The pigment is released into the blood and excreted out through the kidneys, imparting a dark colour to the urine. Bleeding into the bladder from injury, severe cystitis, leptospirosis or cancer in the bladder wall in aged Greyhounds may result in breakdown of blood cells in the acid urine. This causes a darker colouration in the urine and requires investigation by a vet. Refer to Acidosis, Cramping.

N

NAIL PROBLEMS: Racing Greyhounds can suffer from brittle, easily broken or split toe nails, pulled-away nails and infected nail beds (paronychia). Some individual Greyhounds have inherently soft nails that bruise easily and wear away and do not grow fast enough to maintain adequate nail length. The types of common nail injuries are outlined under each specific condition. Refer to Broken Nails, Deformed Nails, Nail Bed Infection, Sand Toe, Soft Nails, Split Nails.

NAIL BED INFECTION: Bacterial infection and inflammation of the nail growth band or cuticle at the base of a toe nail. It is technically referred to as paronychia.

Signs: Swelling and pain around the hairline of one or more nails and in severe cases, a pus-like discharge may be weep from the enlarged cuticle area. The nail may be pulled off or shed if the infection weakens the nail bed.

Causes: Muddy conditions in outside yards and wet, heavily contaminated, muddy or sandy turn-out pens, may allow bacteria to gain entry to the nail bed, especially if the cuticle is softened by the moisture or abraded by sharp sand or gravel. In racing Greyhounds, a spike of grass or sand carrying bacteria may be forced under the cuticle as the toe nails dig into the track surface for traction, abrading the soft tissue and allowing infection to establish. The outside toe on the left hindlimb next to the rail is most commonly affected. This form is commonly called sand toe. Refer to Sand Toe.

Management: Where the cuticle is inflamed due to embedded sand or mud, squirting warm saline under the enlarged cuticle and gently hooking any grit out with an old soft toothbrush will remove it. Applying a drawing poultice of magnesium sulphate overnight is also helpful to remove deeply embedded particles of fine sand. An antiseptic, drying agent containing weak iodine or, in severe cases, a course of antibiotic or DMSO drops may be prescribed by a vet. Refer also to Sand Toe.

NECK INJURIES: Injuries to the upper neck are associated with strain of the associated ligaments and traumatic damage to the vertebral joints. They are often referred to as cervical or poll injuries.

Signs: Stiffness, resistance due to muscle spasm and discomfort when the head is carefully rotated from side to side and the muzzle is pushed down toward the chest during a routine after-race check. Acute injury will often result in slow acceleration from the start. In chronic cases, the Greyhound may have a distinct elevated head carriage as it jumps from the boxes or traps and appear to have a high-stepping gait with its front limbs. It may also develop left-side wrist pain due to the altered gait when cornering, although it does not have a primary wrist injury.

Causes: Hitting the lid of the starting box or trap, head-on collisions, falls at the start or other race falls may compress the neck vertebral joints or twist the head abnormally. This results in ligament strain between the vertebral bones and concussion to the neck spinal joints. Often the rotation joint (atlas bone) at the base of the skull and the second joint (axis bone) commonly show most discomfort on manipulation.

Management: A thorough check and, in severe cases, X-ray of the base of the skull and upper neck may be required to evaluate joint or bony damage. Rest, combined with physiotherapy, such as liniment massage, hydrobathing and magnetic field therapy for 2-3 weeks, may be prescribed to relieve muscle spasm and arthritic discomfort, with a lay-off from racing relative to the severity of the injury.

NEPHRITIS: A term that refers to inflammation of the kidney tissue, which results in severe kidney damage in acute cases. It is relatively common in racing Greyhounds and the incidence increases as Greyhounds age in retirement.

Signs: The deterioration of kidney function and kidney (renal) failure is often a slow, insidious process in ageing Greyhounds. Over time, there is a reduction in the volume, colour and consistency of the urine relative to the underlying cause. The Greyhound's urine will develop a strong odour and the animal may develop a urine smell to its breath as nitrogen wastes build up in the blood. As the blood carries higher levels of metabolic wastes that cannot be filtered through the failing kidneys, the Greyhound may vomit its food up, lose appetite and body weight. Acute nephritis is usually associated with an elevated temperature, depression, loss of appetite, vomiting, severe back pain, often with an arched back and low or no urine output. In a racing Greyhound, the animal will become lethargic, lose appetite and performance and exhibit pain when the kidneys are examined.

Causes: Blood-borne infections, such as E. coli bacteria, can localise in the kidneys and cause inflammatory damage. Severe acidosis after a hard, stressful gallop when the Greyhound is dehydrated, can cause kidney cell damage and secondary inflammation. Although Leptospira bacteria are a cause of nephritis under conditions of poor hygiene and sanitation, it is not common in racing Greyhounds. A diagnosis is usually made by blood and urine tests taken from sick Greyhounds.

Management: As there are varying degrees of nephritis, it is usually best to rest a Greyhound from racing, relieve the stress situation and control the underlying infection with antibiotics. Nephritis is a potentially fatal disease and prompt recognition, treatment with fluids and pulsed antibiotic doses, combined with urinary antiseptics, may be prescribed. Refer also to Kidney Disease.

NERVE INJURIES: (See illustration) Nerve injuries can interfere or block sensation and the impulses that activate muscle contraction. This results in paralysis of the affected muscles. Specific nerve injuries are not common in racing Greyhounds.

Signs: Injury to the nerves of the spinal cord and hindlimb can lead to lack of muscle control in the hindlimbs and, in severe cases, paralysis of the hindquarters. This can occur in an aged Greyhound with a painful back injury that results in a vertebral disc protrusion (slipped disc) which presses into the spinal cord and cuts vital nerve pathways. Refer to Vertebral Joint Conditions.

Causes: Race falls are the most common cause of spinal cord and vertebral injuries that can affect muscle control and sensory function. Injury to the sciatic and femoral nerves of the hindlimbs can occur when the point of a needle stabs the nerve when a deep intramuscular injection is given into the thigh. Muscle wastage on the affected side of the hindlimb may result from a misplaced intramuscular injection.

Management: A careful examination by a vet using sensory tests and X-rays will determine the location and severity of the nerve damage. Physiotherapy may be helpful to aid recovery from a bruised or pinched nerve. Intramuscular injections should be given by a vet, avoiding the side of the hindlimb along the path of the femoral nerve. Surgery to repair a slipped disc is possible in Greyhounds, giving a chance of a good recovery in early cases of mild hindlimb paralysis.

NERVOUS BEHAVIOUR: Excitement and anticipation prior to racing, or crowd-shy behaviour, may affect individual Greyhounds and adversely influence race-day performance.

Signs: Overexcitement with restlessness, barking, drooling and pulling on the lead are common signs. Overexcitement and anticipation may cause a Greyhound to 'run its race before the start', risking fatigue and dehydration. Some immature Greyhounds may exhibit crowd-shyness, with shivering, shaking and cowering for protection when taken to a race track.

Causes: Certain bloodlines may have a reputation for nervous temperament and excitable behaviour. Immaturity, poor education and training may also cause a Greyhound to become nervy and crowd-shy.

Management: In some cases, schooling in a group of Greyhounds will settle crowd-shyness linked to a lack of confidence. As well, taking the young Greyhound on a lead into a crowded area at a trial track to mingle with other Greyhounds and their handlers may help settle the condition. High doses of supplementary Vitamin E and Vitamin B1 may be beneficial in settling a nervous temperament. Courses of mild sedatives, or a calmative herbal preparation, may be prescribed by a vet to settle an excitable temperament. Replacement of lost fluid and electrolytes from barking and panting due to pre-race excitement and travelling is important prior to racing. A rehydration fluid drink should be offered prior to travelling and kennelling to replenish body fluids and salts.

NON-CHASERS: A term to describe a Greyhound that fails to chase the lure or put in full effort, keenness and interest when racing. Refer to Failing to Chase.

NUTRITIONAL OSTEODYSTROPHY: An intermittent lameness condition in an ageing Greyhound that is caused by abnormal and weak bone and joint development in the growing dog. Affected Greyhounds become lame after exercise, with pain in the limbs and along the back, with reluctance to move. In the young Greyhound, a deficiency or imbalance of each nutrient, or a combination of calcium, phosphorus and vitamin D in the diet, can lead to poor musculo-skeletal development and long-term unsoundness in the adult Greyhound. Refer to Juvenile Bone Disease.

O

OBESITY: The polite term used to describe an overly fat or overweight Greyhound, particularly in a retired Greyhound.

Signs: Excessive body fat accumulation, reluctance to exercise, often leading to an inability to walk and an overload lameness on the limbs and joints.

Causes: In most cases, it is caused by overfeeding a high carbohydrate or fat diet, or full-time access to snacks of dry food, exacerbated by a lack of adequate exercise to maintain fitness and utilise excess energy. This is often a result of confinement in a small yard. Older Greyhound bitches in particular are more likely to put on weight.

Management: In severe cases, management of the Greyhound's diet and exercise programme by a vet is advised to avoid any deficiencies or risk of exercise-induced heart or limb problems. Obese animals should be restricted to 3-4 small meals a day and be given regular exercise. The opportunity to steal other animals' food at mealtime, table scraps and snacks must be curtailed. As obesity is often an early sign of developing diabetes, a urine check for diabetes should be carried out on a regular basis.

OLECRANON FRACTURES: Fracture and displacement of the olecranon process of the ulna bone that forms the bony prominence at the point of the elbow occurs most commonly in young Greyhounds.

Signs: Swelling, severe pain, weight-bearing discomfort and aggressive resentment when the rear of the elbow is squeezed or an attempt is made to flex the joint.

Causes: Detachment of the growth plate of the olecranon process in young Greyhounds can result from a fall. In older Greyhounds, the triceps muscle, which attaches to the point of the elbow, may detach from the olecranon process in a race fall or during acceleration.

Management: X-rays are usually taken to confirm the position and severity of the fracture, which may also involve the small ulna bone. Surgical stabilisation of the fracture and reattachment with

bone pins or plates is recommended. A long rest period and diet containing adequate calcium, phosphorus and Vitamin D will enable bone healing. Most fractures heal without developing arthritis or affecting performance in a Greyhound of racing age.

OSTEOCHONDRITIS DISSICANS (OCD): Inflammation, devitalisation and detachment of the joint cartilage, often in the shoulder joint, of a growing Greyhound.

Signs: Weight-bearing lameness on the affected joint or, in severe cases, the joint on both limbs, where the cartilage layer has lifted and resulted in bone-to-bone contact with sensitive underlying bone. The shoulder joint has the highest incidence in racing Greyhounds, but the knee (stifle), elbow and hock joint can also be affected.

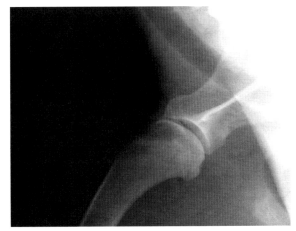

An X-ray of a shoulder joint of a young, heavily-built Greyhound with a history of front limb lameness. The cartilage defect is on the front of the joint area, causing pain and discomfort as the greyhound extends the joint during its stride.

Causes: The condition appears to be prevalent in certain bloodlines of Greyhounds, especially those with heavy bodyweight and signs of over development. Although it often develops between 3 to 9 months of age, usually the lameness is not apparent until the Greyhound is schooled on the circle or encouraged to run freely in a long yard. The cartilage of the joint grows quickly and appears to outstrip its underlying blood supply, or the cartilage is compressed by excess body weight.

The open joint clearly shows the reddened area with loss of a cartilage flap associated with a painful OCD lesion.

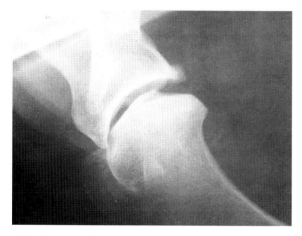

The 'flap' of cartilage can be clearly seen in an X-ray image of another lame young Greyhound.

Poor cartilage development may be a result of a diet deficient in calcium, phosphorus, copper, zinc and manganese in a rapidly growing young Greyhound. This results in lack of adequate nutrition for development, with devitalisation and detachment of the cartilage layer, which then lifts and allows contact with the underlying bone.

Management: An injection of anaesthetic into the joint will relieve pain and an X-ray will confirm the severity of the condition. Surgery should be undertaken to remove the dead cartilage flap. Then injections of joint repair preparations and oral supplements of chondroitin sulphate, glucosamine, copper, zinc and manganese, as well as Vitamin C, will help to facilitate the joint repair process. In young pups, a 60-80 per cent recovery rate can be expected, but the chances are reduced if more than

one joint is involved or the condition is not treated early.

OSTEOARTHRITIS: The most common form of bone reaction, joint degeneration and arthritic change following joint injury in racing Greyhounds. Osteoarthritis develops as a result of initial arthritis with inflammation and deterioration of the internal joint environment. The joint responds by laying down new bone in place of damaged or eroded cartilage, and the sensory joint capsule and internal membrane thickens, resulting in reduced movement and joint pain. This is normally termed degenerative arthritis, particularly in an ageing, retired Greyhound. In severe cases, the joint may become immobile (or ankylose) due to a bony growth within and surrounding a joint. Osteoarthritis can be initiated from joint wear and tear, concussion and overflexion of a joint. It may also develop secondary to an internal joint fracture, such as following wrist or hock injury, osteochondritis or ligament rupture in a joint. X-rays of the affected joint can determine the extent of the arthritic change. Refer to Arthritis.

OTITIS EXTERNA: Inflammation caused by trauma or infection of the outer ear canal, affecting one or both ears. Refer to Ear Problems.

P

PAD INJURIES: The foot pads of racing Greyhounds are subjected to high distortion and shearing forces when galloping. The pads can be lacerated when walking on rough areas, pierced by sharp objects and thorns, or torn when galloping. The pads may dry out and crack, become infected, bruised and weakened, and tear due to being too soft under wet conditions. Corns can develop on the pad surface. The pad surface may also become thickened following infection with the distemper virus. Pad injuries invariably cause lameness and often require an extended lay-off from training to heal if they become lacerated or badly infected. Daily care of the pads is essential to check for injuries and to apply conditioning or drying preparations relative to the state of the pads to maintain their suppleness and resilience. Specific pad injuries are discussed under individual conditions. Refer to Corns, Cracked Pads, Cut Pads, Dry Pads, Foot Rot, Soft Pads and Torn Pads.

PANCREATIC DISEASES: The pancreas is a gland which secretes essential digestive enzymes into the small intestine to digest carbohydrates, proteins and fats. It also produces insulin that is vital for the control of blood sugar levels. Diseases of the pancreas are rare in racing Greyhounds. Pancreatic insufficiency syndrome and, occasionally, pancreatitis are diagnosed in racing and retired Greyhounds. Sugar diabetes or, technically, Diabetes mellitus, resulting from production of inadequate insulin hormone, occasionally affects aged breeding and retired Greyhounds. Refer to Pancreatic Insufficiency and Pancreatitis.

PANCREATIC INSUFFICIENCY: Lack of adequate enzyme formation essential for the digestion of sugars, proteins and fats.

Signs: Pancreatic insufficiency causes a Greyhound to appear undernourished, lose condition, become thin and lack stamina, despite being given extra food. Affected Greyhounds fail to put on condition, become 'poor doers' and are unable to maintain an adequate and stable racing condition and weight when in training. Large volumes of pale grey or fatty yellowish stools, which float in water, are passed. The overload of sugars and proteins normally digested in the small intestine into the large intestine leads to smelly flatulence and stools, gas distension of the bowels and often low-grade diarrhoea.

Causes : The underlying cause is related to genetic abnormalities or a previous bout of pancreatitis.

Management: Diagnosis is made by the physical appearance of the stools and a blood test. In racing Greyhounds, the inconvenience of providing daily medication usually forces retirement of the animal. A range of pancreatic enzymes is available, but they should be given in a coated tablet to prevent stomach acid damage and reduced potency before reaching the small intestine. They must be given with every meal for best results. Small meals given 3 times daily will assist digestion. A low-fat diet can be provided, with extra fat given as palm or coconut oil, which contain a type of fat which is absorbed directly into the bloodstream without the need for pancreatic lipase enzyme.

PANCREATITIS: Inflammation of the pancreas gland is very rare in well-fed and managed Greyhounds.

Signs: Sudden illness, a high fever, restlessness, severe abdominal pain with arching of the back and reluctance to move, excess salivation and repeated vomiting, fluid loss, jaundice and shock. The condition may be fatal if not recognised and treated promptly.

Causes: Trauma and bruising of the pancreas following a race fall, infection introduced from the pancreatic duct, or blockage of the duct. A high-fat diet may increase the risk in older Greyhounds. Pancreatic function may be reduced after recovery.

Management: Immediate attention by a vet is essential. Antibiotics, surgery to correct a blocked duct and treatment for shock may be required. Food should be withdrawn and fluids and electrolytes given via the mouth only. On recovery, a low-fat diet as outlined under Pancreatic Insufficiency should be given.

PANNUS: A condition of the cornea of the eye due to an auto-immune related condition. It is technically known as Superficial Stromal Keratitis (SSK).

Signs: Eye irritation with weeping and clouding of the cornea is usually noticed initially which, if not treated, progresses to a more advanced stage. Over a period of 2-4 weeks, a web-like growth of fine

A severe pannus covering the eye of a retired Greyhound.

red blood vessels slowly spreads across the cornea from the sides of the eyeball. Pannus can develop from 1-2 years of age, with a vascular form (pinkish eye), which matures to a granulated or scarred appearance, often with a dark pigment covering a large area of the eye. Scarring of the cornea can result in impaired vision and forced retirement from racing.

Causes: The condition is thought to be an auto-immune-related reaction in which the immune system attacks the cornea. It is possibly inherited in certain bloodlines of Greyhounds. The risk may be increased by exposure to high levels of ultraviolet light in Greyhounds housed in outside yards.

Management: Pannus must be treated under the supervision of a vet. Eye drops containing corticosteroid drugs, applied 3-4 times daily, will suppress the immune reaction and the growth of the web-like vessels. A long-acting corticosteroid preparation can be injected under the conjunctiva to provide longer-term suppression. Other medications have been used experimentally to assist corneal repair and lubrication. Affected Greyhounds should be housed indoors out of the direct sunlight.

PANTING: Describes increased and forced respiration. Greyhounds do not sweat to cool themselves, and rely on panting to inhale cool air over the lung surface and expel air warmed by the transfer of heat from the blood flowing in the highly vascular, thin walled lung capillaries. Panting relies on the exchange of air across the lung air-sac surface and evaporation of moisture to cool the blood. Panting is an efficient mechanism used to cool the brain under hot conditions. Where respiratory disease or hot, humid conditions reduce the efficiency of heat loss, overheating of the body and Heat Stress can rapidly occur. Refer to Heat Stress, Respiratory Disease.

PAPILLOMAS: The Papilloma virus is a common cause of warts on the lower limbs and corns in the foot pads of Greyhounds. Refer to Corns, Warts.

PARASITES: Greyhounds can harbour a number of internal and external parasites. Internal parasites use the Greyhound's gut and internal organs as a source of nourishment and lodging, sapping vital nutrients, blood and food. External parasites use the protection of the animal's haircoat or hair follicles, or the deeper layers of the skin, feeding on the skin or its blood supply, causing irritation, allergic responses or loss of blood. Over the last 20 years, better knowledge and understanding of the life-cycles of these parasites, and the development of highly effective drug or chemical treatments, have reduced the incidence and the severity of harmful effects of parasites to a minimum in well-managed kennels.

Internal Parasites: Refer to Roundworms, Hookworms, Whipworms, Tapeworms, Heartworm and Tracheal Worms.

External Parasites: Refer to Fleas, Ticks, Mites and Lice.

PARONYCHIA: Refer to Sand Toe.

PARVOVIRUS: Canine Parvovirus was initially reported at almost the same time in many countries in the late 1970s. It is a highly infectious viral disease specific to dogs, which results in debilitation and mortality of pups and all breeds of dogs, including Greyhounds. It can cause severe diarrhoea and persistent vomiting, with dehydration and death within 24-48 hours in puppies. There are two strains, CPV1, which causes mild diarrhoea, and CPV2, which results in acute heart failure and diarrhoea. Refer to Canine Viral Diseases, Infectious Diseases – Parvovirus.

PATELLA FRACTURES: Fracture of the cartilage-covered kneecap or patella can occasionally occur in the left hindlimb of a Greyhound.

Signs: Swelling and pain on the front aspect of the stifle joint next to the flank. The Greyhound may be reluctant to put the affected limb, usually the left hindlimb, to the ground or bear weight for 1-2 days after the injury, often standing with the stifle turned outwards to ease the discomfort.

Causes: Trauma to the front of the stifle joint as a result of hitting the inside rail (hence the left limb has a higher incidence), the frame of the starting box or trap or, occasionally, a gate post when squeezing through a gate into a yard with a group of other Greyhounds.

Management: Surgical repair is the only form of

treatment that will provide an opportunity for the fracture to heal. A 5-6 week course of physiotherapy to maintain muscle tone, flexing the joint to prevent adhesions, with preparations to provide nutrients to promote bone and cartilage repair, are part of the recuperative management. However, despite adequate healing of the fracture, arthritic changes commonly develop in the stifle joint and only about 20 per cent of Greyhounds will return to racing.

PELVIC FRACTURES: Pelvic fractures mainly involve the socket or acetabulum rim that forms the hip joint with the thigh bone (femur). They can occur spontaneously during a race, or as a result of a fall or collision with the rail, or another Greyhound. Refer to Hip Joint Injuries.

PEMPHIGUS: A technical term that refers to a rare auto-immune disease resulting in the loss of the toe nails.

Signs: Shedding of one nail initially, followed by others, and within 10-14 days, the nails on all four feet are progressively lost. Each nail appears to swell and, over a week or so, lose its vitality. Often a secondary infection within the dying quick and nail bone oozes a smelly discharge and pus. The nails fall off, exposing the porous devitalised nail bone. When galloped, affected nails will be torn off.

Causes: A non-heritable auto-immune condition in individual Greyhounds that results in a progressive reduction of the blood supply to the nail bed and quick.

Management: Early recognition and treatment by a vet is essential. Cortisone drugs are used to suppress the immune reaction and antibiotics to limit the risk of infection. Although healthy nails will regrow, the cortisone medication must be maintained to suppress the immune reaction, otherwise the nails will be shed again. The Greyhound cannot be raced while on cortisone medication.

PERICARDITIS: Inflammation of the outer lining membranes around the heart due to an infection. It is very uncommon in Greyhounds.

Signs: Initial fever, discomfort when lifted under the chest, an elevated and muffled heartbeat and collapse when exercised. The veins on the ears and limbs become distended and the gums often develop a dull, bluish colour due to reduced oxygenation.

Causes: Certain types of systemic (blood borne) infections can localise in the pericardial tissue, a race fall can cause bleeding into the pericardial sac, or a chest infection following a severe virus with pneumonia, may introduce bacterial infection. X-rays can help confirm the distended sac around the heart.

Management: As pericarditis usually involves infection within the chest cavity, concurrent antibiotics and drainage of the chest are necessary. The long-term lung and heart damage usually forces retirement in racing Greyhounds.

PERIODONTAL DISEASE: A term to describe inflammation and infection of the gums and the deeper tooth root membranes in the surrounding bony jaw socket.

Signs: Periodontal disease is a common problem in older Greyhounds initially caused by inflammation and infection of the gum-tooth margins. (Refer to Gingivitis). The gums may recede, exposing the tooth root, which allows infection to spread into the deeper membranes that anchor the teeth in the jaw. Bleeding and reddening of the gums will cause discomfort, which increases as the tooth root also becomes infected. If a severe toothache develops, the dog may be reluctant to chew its food and will eat very slowly trying to avoid discomfort. In advanced cases, the teeth may loosen and require removal. The dog may develop bad breath due to fermentation of food trapped around the teeth. Refer to Halitosis.

Causes: Build-up of calculus or plaque on the teeth, which harbour bacteria, cause pressure on the gums, which then recede, exposing the deeper periodontal membranes to infection.

Management: Antibiotics may initially control the periodontal infection, combined with a thorough descaling of the teeth. Cleaning of the teeth and massaging the gums, as described for gingivitis, is necessary to prevent further problems.

PHANTOM PREGNANCY: The state of exhibiting the signs and behaviour of pregnancy without being pregnant with or without mating in bitches. Also referred to as false pregnancy, pseudopregnancy. Refer to False Pregnancy.

PHARYNGITIS: Pharyngitis is the medical term for a sore and inflamed throat. Although pharyngitis can be caused by licking or eating chemical irritants, in most cases it is associated with tonsillitis and upper respiratory tract viral diseases. Management should be adopted as outlined for tonsillitis. Refer to Tonsillitis.

PHYSITIS: Inflammation of the growth plate at each end of a long bone, usually the forearm (radius) and shank (tibia). It is usually referred to as epiphysitis or physitis of the end of the bone. Refer to Epiphysitis.

PNEUMONIA: A commonly used term to refer to inflammation of the solid areas of the lung tissue, often in conjunction with inflammation of the lower airways and pleural membrane (pleurisy). It is technically called pneumonitis.
Signs: Initial fever, loss of appetite, shortness of breath when walking, progressing to a fast, shallow panting form of respiration, severe pain and discomfort shown when coughing, bluish colour (lack of oxygen) of the tongue and throat and, occasionally, a nasal discharge. A louder than normal rasping sound may be heard on stethoscope examination of the chest cavity.
Causes: Viral respiratory diseases and secondary bacterial infection result in inflammation of the lung tissues surrounding the airways, restricting inflation and the efficient oxygenation of the blood. Kennel cough can cause pneumonia if not treated promptly in the severe form and accidental inhalation of water, milk or food invariably results in pneumonia. Pneumonitis may also be caused by inhalation of irritant gases and dust that causes an allergic reaction in the airways and air-sacs.
Management: Evaluation and diagnosis, often including X-rays, must be carried out by a vet without delay. Courses of specific antibiotics, complemented by medications to assist airway drainage and, in acute cases, using a mask to deliver oxygen, may be required. Careful nursing

to ensure that the animal is kept warm and regains its appetite will greatly assist recovery.

PNEUMOTHORAX: A term used to describe the accumulation of air outside the lungs and trapped within the chest (pleural) cavity on either side of the lungs. It is a very rare condition in racing Greyhounds. To enable the lungs to inflate and inhale air as the diaphragm contracts, a negative pressure (vacuum) has to be maintained within the chest cavity. Refer to Lung Problems.
Signs: Shallow, rapid breathing with respiratory distress, during only light exercise. The lungs will fail to function and the Greyhound will collapse if the air continues to enter the chest cavity. In some cases, where a puncture wound has pierced the chest cavity, a pocket of air may build-up under the skin and at the entrance of the windpipe into the chest.
Causes: In most cases, severe bruising and rupture of the lung airways or tissue, as a result of a race fall or collision or concurrent pneumonia, can result in leakage of air into the surrounding chest cavity. Accidental puncture wounds between the ribs can introduce infection and allow air to be drawn into the chest cavity.
Management: Diagnosis can be confirmed by X-ray. In mild cases, at least 3-4 weeks of kennel rest, taking care to avoid excitement, will give time for the air to be slowly absorbed back into the lung surface. Concurrent lung infection, or other traumatic damage from a fall, should be treated promptly. Drainage of the air from the chest cavity using a fine needle inserted through the ribs and applying suction under surgical conditions may be necessary.

POISONING: Occasionally a Greyhound will eat rat baits and have contact with other potentially toxic preparations such as chemical cleaners and disinfectants in the kennel environment. Poisoning should be suspected in an otherwise healthy Greyhound that develops signs of severe depression or drowsiness, incoordination, vomiting, a nervous condition or bleeding from the gums and mouth. It is important to keep the animal comfortable, i.e. if it is cold, wrap a blanket around it to keep it warm. The animal must be examined by a vet as soon as possible.
First Aid: If a Greyhound is known to have

recently swallowed a poison bait, undertake the first aid directions on the package. If vomiting is recommended, give 2 teaspoonful of hydrogen peroxide or, alternatively, 1 teaspoonful of baking soda in water over the tongue by syringe as a first aid measure. Always ensure mouse and rat baits, snail baits and flea control preparations are kept out of reach of Greyhounds. Do not place baits on the floor outside kennels, in outside runs or on the top of cages where they may be dislodged and fall into the kennel. Dead rats and mice killed by the baits should be removed promptly from the kennel area.

POLYARTHRITIS: Polyarthritis refers to the development of arthritis in a number of joints. (Refer to arthritis). However, a specific polyarthritis condition can develop in the young Greyhound. This specific form is regarded as an auto-immune disease, with an inherited predisposition, resulting in swelling and progressive destruction of major limb joints in young Greyhounds. It was initially reported in Australia in 1976 and more recently in the United States. It is also referred to as Erosive Polyarthritis, or polyarthritis syndrome.

Signs: The signs of arthritis are outlined under Arthritis. The condition of Erosive Polyarthritis is most common in young Greyhounds from 3 to 30 months of age and often a number of litter mates are affected over a period of time. Initially, one or two joints will develop a puffy, hot, painful internal fluid swelling, often in the wrists or hocks, but the shoulder, elbow and stifle joints may also be affected. The toe joints can be involved in severe cases. The Greyhound may, initially, have a raised temperature which is often presumed to be an

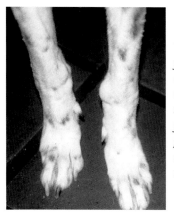

The wrists and toe joints of the front limbs of this young Greyhound are swollen with extra joint fluid due to polyarthritis. The left hock joint was also affected.

infection, with successive and progressive pressure swelling within the joints, with discomfort on flexion, reduced mobility and lameness when walking. The Greyhound may lose its appetite and become depressed at the onset of the disease. In some cases, the arthritis will settle down in one joint, but another joint will then develop symptoms and the arthritic signs may reappear in the initial joint at a later date. As the disease progresses, the joints erode and collapse, resulting in severe pain and lameness.

Causes: Although various bacterial, viral and other microbial infections are thought to trigger the condition, it is considered to be an auto-immune reaction to the animal's own joint tissue. Recently, a mycoplasma microbe has been isolated from the joints of an affected Greyhound. A number of bloodlines appear to have an inherited tendency, in which one or most of a litter will be affected, sometimes as late as 2 years of age when in race training. However, there is often a history of intermittent lameness in a growing pup, which settles down, the symptoms not being apparent until they rapidly flare up again 6-12 months later.

Management: Confirmation of erosive polyarthritis by a vet is based on age, breeding, history of earlier joint swelling and, in lame Greyhounds, examination of joint fluid for the characteristic elevated white cell count. Treatment of erosive polyarthritis in young Greyhounds with cortisone and other medications to suppress symptoms has been found to be consistently ineffective and, in most cases, the affected Greyhounds are humanely destroyed.

POST RACING DYSURIA: This is a term to describe the inability to urinate freely after a race, seen only in male Greyhounds. It is commonly referred to as bladder shutdown by trainers and stranguria by vets.

Signs: There are 3 stages relative to the severity of the bladder shutdown.

Severity	Time after racing
Typical Signs	

Stage 1	2 to 12 hours
Stand to urinate, with a delay of 10-30 seconds, urine passed in a thin stream.	

Stage 2	2 to 48 hours

Delay in opening bladder more than 30 seconds. Urine passed in a thin, pulsing stream or only a few drops are produced. The bladder remains full and painful.

Stage 3	2 to 48 hours

Complete shutdown, no urine produced. Bladder distended. Urine collected often contains blood.

Causes: The condition is most prevalent in young, nervous, excitable male Greyhounds. It develops following stressful conditions such as waiting in the kennels before a race, schooling and the excitement of racing. It may develop before the Greyhound is exercised. The nervous control of the bladder sphincter (exit valve) muscle ring and bladder muscles are interrelated. The nervous control of the bladder exit valve muscle overrides the nervous impulses to contract the bladder wall muscles to enable urine to flow out. Excitement increases the muscle tone in the outflow (urethra) tube as well, narrowing the tube diameter and resulting in urine being passed in a thinner stream. In severe cases, complete constriction of the bladder sphincter and the urethra will result in an inability to pass urine.

Management: Stage 1 symptoms can often be reduced by avoiding stress and keeping the dog quiet. Although it may take time to empty the bladder after a race, full urine flow is usually restored in 24-48 hours. Stages 2 and 3 require treatment with drugs that help to relax the bladder sphincter and urethra tube. In severe cases, the bladder may have to be catheterised with an indwelling tube and allowed to drain continuously over 2-3 days until the condition resolves. When returned to training, special care to avoid over-excitement and stress helps to prevent recurrence.

PSEUDOPREGNANCY: The state of exhibiting the signs and behaviour of pregnancy without being pregnant with or without mating in bitches. Refer to False Pregnancy

PROGRESSIVE RETINAL ATROPHY: There are two forms of retinal degeneration in dogs. Both are inherited conditions that result in progressive loss of sight and daylight blindness in both eyes. Greyhounds can develop a form known as central progressive retinal atrophy.

Signs: First signs of poor eyesight are noticed when a Greyhound runs poorly in twilight meetings or on dimly lit tracks at night. The Greyhound begins to lose sight of the lure, developing a reputation for running erratically, often in the midfield of a race. As the light-sensitive retina at the rear of the eyeball degenerates, the pupils dilate to compensate and let in more light, even in sunlight. Eventually, the eyes appear as bright, green, glowing circles if the animal looks toward the light, or a torch beam is directed into the dilated pupils.

Causes: The condition may become apparent in young Greyhounds when being schooled, but is usually not noticeable until the Greyhound is 2-3 years of age. It is considered that progressive degeneration of the blood supply to the light sensitive retina occurs, with shrinking of the optic nerve area and a reduced clarity of vision in daylight.

Management: Examination of both eyes by a vet using an ophthalmoscope will confirm the condition. There is no treatment, and affected Greyhounds should not be bred.

PROSTATE INFLAMMATION (PROSTATITIS): Inflammation of the prostate gland, which is located at the exit to the bladder surrounding the urethra in male dogs. The inflammation is technically known as Prostatitis.

Signs: It is not a common disease of the male racing Greyhound. The prostate gland can become inflamed and enlarged around the urethra. Signs include discomfort and difficulty during urination, passing short spurts of urine. It should not be confused with the inability to urinate after a race, which is described under post racing dysuria.

Causes: Although rare, most cases are due to ascending infection from chronic balanitis of the sheath (prepuce). It is most likely to develop in stud and retired male Greyhounds.

Management: Diagnosis by a vet using careful internal pelvic examination is necessary to estimate the size of the prostate enlargement. A course of an appropriate antibiotic will assist in controlling any residual infection. Treatment of chronic balanitis to prevent recurrence in older Greyhounds is recommended. In retired Greyhounds, an examination and biopsy to ensure the condition is not cancerous should be carried out.

PYODERMA: A term used to describe bacterial infection associated with build-up of pus and increased fatty secretions within the layers of the skin.

Signs: Pyoderma most commonly develops in the outer (superficial) layers of the skin and, occasionally, deeper within the skin. The superficial form appears as areas of reddened skin, with a rash-like surface, covered with a greasy, rancid film of fat and small erupting pus-filled lumps. Some areas are itchy and may encourage rubbing and scratching. Often the condition is concentrated around the eyes, muzzle and under the front limbs, with loss of hair in severe or chronic forms. The skin often feels soft and spongy with pus oozing when pressed.

Causes: The most common cause is skin invasion by Streptococcus and Staphylococcus bacteria, especially if the skin has a lowered immunity. It may also be associated with Demodectic mite infestation around the muzzle and eyes as a result of low immunity against the mange mite in younger dogs and an associated secondary bacterial infection in the skin.

Management: Skin scrapings may be required to check for Demodectic mites in young Greyhounds, and swabs to determine the type of bacteria, in order to select the appropriate antibiotic. A prolonged course of antibiotics and skin cleansing washes are usually effective. Cleaning the kennel environment, washing blankets and rugs, and overall improved hygiene, is paramount to help prevent other dogs developing the condition or recurrence in previously affected Greyhounds.

PYOMETRA: Pyometra is a term that describes infection and collection of fluid within the uterus (womb). It may occur in racing bitches up to 8 weeks after a heat cycle.

Signs: Owners of bitches should be alerted to the typical signs of a pyometra after a season cycle in a bitch. Initial signs include a fever, loss of appetite and an increased craving to drink. As the infection and fluid accumulates in the uterus, toxins absorbed into the bloodstream may result in vomiting, depression and toxic collapse. If the entrance to the womb (cervix) is open, discharge may be seen dribbling from the vulva, with the bitch frequently licking the area.

Causes: When associated with a false pregnancy, increases in progesterone hormone levels lead to a build-up of secretion and fluid in the womb. These can become infected either by bacteria entering through a relaxed cervix (womb opening to the vagina) or from the bloodstream. Rapid build-up of infection and white cells (pus) will cause vomiting and severe debilitation. The pressure in the womb will cause leakage of fluid through the cervix, with a discharge appearing at the vulva within a few days. Racing bitches that are given excessive doses of testosterone hormones to keep them from coming into season may develop a swollen, puffy vulva and an enlarged clitoris.

Management: Prompt diagnosis and treatment is essential to avoid toxic build-up and risk of debilitation, collapse and death. The uterus may need to be drained and flushed with antibiotics and fluids to clean out the infection, complemented by high doses of systemic antibiotics. In severe cases, the infected uterus may be removed surgically to resolve the condition and prevent recurrence.

Q

QUADRICEPS MUSCLE INJURY: The Quadriceps femoris muscle is a deep layer thigh muscle at the rear area of the hindlimb. It is attached to the pelvic bones and, through the quadriceps tendon, attached to the patella (kneecap) provides muscle power to the lower limb in the forward stride action.

Signs: The quadriceps femoris muscle may become overloaded during acceleration, resulting in internal tearing with pain, swelling and haemorrhage (bruising) and reduced length of the hindlimb stride.

Causes: Fast acceleration and slippage on a loose surface increases the load demand on the Quadriceps muscle through the patella to the front of the fibia (shank) bone, particularly on the right hindlimb.

Management: Cold therapy with ice packs to reduce internal bleeding and swelling should be applied for an initial 36-48 hour period after the injury. This should be followed by massage, ultrasound and muscle stimulation (Faradic) therapy.

QUADRICEPS TENDON: The Quadriceps tendon attached to the patella (kneecap) can be bruised and develop a strain injury following a fall or trauma to the patella, resulting in weakness and lameness of the lower hindlimb and dragging of the toes, particularly on the left hindlimb. Physiotherapy will assist repair of the tendon over a 3-4 month period, combined with flexion of the limb to retain movement and a gradual return to walking and a straight line galloping programme for at least 4-6 weeks. Refer to Patella Fractures, Tibial Crest Avulsion.

QUARTER BONE SORENESS: Refer to Metacarpal Periostitis.

QUICK PROBLEMS: The quick is the name given to the folds of sensitive vascular tissue (called lamellae) that bond the inside of the nail shell to the underlying nail bone or last digit bone forming the toe nail. The condition is often referred to as sore quicks.
Signs: The nail is highly sensitive when squeezed and, in severe cases, the Greyhound will be reluctant to walk on a hard surface.
Causes: The quicks can be infected if the nail splits to allow bacterial infection to establish under the nail, or torn away if the nail becomes trapped in the track surface (usually a matted grass track surface). If this happens, the quick can become bruised and sore. The quick can be devitalised by an immune or toxic reaction that weakens the nail-to-bone attachment, resulting in shedding of the nail, a condition referred to as pemphigus. Refer also to Nail Injuries, Pemphigus.
Management: Where the quicks are sore when the nail is squeezed, a careful examination to check for splits and underlying infection is necessary. Infected quicks are best treated with antibiotic preparations and the nail cleaned and dipped in an iodine (PVP 'tamed' iodine) solution to minimise surface infection. If the quick appears devitalised and the nail shell is loose or has been shed, then careful cleansing, antibiotic therapy, and wrapping the toe in a protective bandage, are standard treatment methods. Rest from training for 5-7 days, relative to the severity of the injury, may be necessary.

R

RABIES: A disease caused by infection with a rhabdovirus microbe that attacks the nervous system of dogs and all warm-blooded animals, including bats. The disease results in extreme hyper-excitement and invariably death. It is endemic in North America and Europe, although the strain that affects foxes is not as dangerous to dogs.
Signs: A Greyhound or other dog with the 'furious' form of rabies will show various degrees of brain damage, with aggressive behaviour, restlessness and seizures and excitement. The affected animal will attack and bite animals and humans. The so-called 'dumb' form is less specific, resulting in progressive nerve paralysis, drooling of saliva and loss of the swallowing action and inability to eat, with death due to respiratory paralysis usually occuring in 3-6 days.
Causes: The virus is spread by bites, infected saliva, and wound contamination with urine.
Management: The chances of recovery are poor to hopeless. Greyhounds with confirmed rabies should be humanely euthanised. All Greyhounds in risk areas should be vaccinated to protect them and prevent spread of the disease.

RACING CONDITION: A term used to describe a lean body condition with distinct 'condition lines' along the body. As a guide, a Greyhound in racing condition should be well and firmly muscled, covered over the pin bones and ribs with the last 3 ribs visible. The belly should be firm and taut, without being tucked-up. A good indication is the presence of 'condition lines' along the ribcage and flank, with a ridge or muscle tuck on the lower flank border.

RACING THIRST: A term used by American and UK trainers that describes the excessive thirst and desire to drink water, with the passing of large volumes of weak, diluted urine. The condition is related to extreme stress imposed by a hard race, often in a dehydrated Greyhound. It is also referred to as Water Diabetes in Australia and other countries.
Signs: The condition is usually classified into

acute, sub-acute and chronic forms. Invariably, a trainer finds the water bowl empty and the kennel floor flooded with weak urine, referred to as polyuria. In the acute form, a Greyhound will develop excessive thirst (called polydypsia) within 1-4 hours after a stressful, hard race. The animal can lose 5-10 per cent of its body weight in 36-48 hours, becoming severely dehydrated with panting, depression and loss of appetite. The sub-acute form has a slower onset over 4-24 hours after a stressful race. The Greyhound may drink 2-4 litres (up to a gallon) of water daily and even its own urine. Greyhounds with the chronic form drink 1-2 litres (up to half a gallon) of water daily, which is excessive for a Greyhound that normally only drinks between 500-1000ml (1-2 pints) of water each day.

Causes: The release of antidiuretic hormone (ADH) which acts to limit urinary output, is reduced or prevented by stress and associated cortisone hormone interaction. Invariably, racing thirst is associated with a hard race, or other stress situations. These include a noisy or dirty kennel environment; low-protein diets; chronic pain of racing injuries; nervous excitable temperament; suddenly changing weather, especially racing under hot conditions; racing too frequently or over excessive distances; a chronic dehydrated state or kidney infection; a deficiency of potassium in the diet; high doses of painkillers and cortisone drugs to treat an injury; excess electrolytes and diuretics (kidney tonics) and concurrent disease. Often it occurs following a hard, fast race in which a Greyhound falls and attempts to catch the field, or escapes the catching area and runs an extra lap of the track.

Management: Diagnosis is confirmed by clinical signs and tests for specific gravity of urine. The extent and type of treatment depends on the relative severity of the condition. In mild forms limiting, but not withdrawing, water intake for a few hours helps to readjust the ADH hormonal control on the kidney tubules and assists in overcoming the problem in 12-24 hours. It is important to ensure that the Greyhound does not dehydrate and is allowed to rest in a darkened, quiet, warm kennel. Acute cases should be given fluids and electrolytes into the vein, as well as drugs to replace or mimic the action of the ADH hormone. A course of antibiotics to prevent kidney infection, with complete kennel rest and a

moist diet with electrolytes, vitamin C and thyroid hormone, is also beneficial to aid recovery. Greyhounds that are excitable have less chance of recovery to full racing potential. Measures to improve the kennel environment and avoid stressful conditions are essential to prevent recurrence in susceptible Greyhounds.

RADIUS BONE INJURY: The radius is the major long bone of the forearm between the elbow and wrist. The ulna, a thinner bone on the inside of the limb, is located to the rear of the radius. Fracture of the radius bone is the most common form of injury, with the majority involving the lower third of the bone above the wrist and, in most cases, the accompanying ulna bone as well. In young Greyhounds, fractures due to falls or collisions when running in long yards usually occur in the mid-shaft area. X rays are normally taken to determine the severity and degree of misalignment of the bone fracture. Complete bone fractures are usually repaired by a bone plate, to ensure best stability, chances of healing and return to competitive racing. Over recent years, a new form of stress injury to the right radius bone has been recognised as a cause of a specific type of lameness in racing Greyhounds.

Signs: Right Medial Radius Stress Microfractures: Typical signs include lameness for 2-3 days after a race in a heavy-weight (above 33kg (70lb)) adult male racing Greyhound, which is raced on the same track a few times at intervals of 7-10 days. The Greyhound usually reacts to thumb pressure applied to the inside of the radius bone about a third of the way down its length over an area of about 20mm in diameter.

Causes: This type of bone fracture which appears as small cracks in the bone, has been reported in heavy, male Greyhounds running on tracks with poorly-banked and uneven bends, with changing radius of circle.

Management: Diagnosis is often difficult, as the fatigue-induced microfracture lines cannot be seen on X-ray. Best results are obtained by a reduction in galloping for 3-4 weeks, avoiding the track on which it has occurred, and returning the Greyhound to straight line gallops and races for a further 3-4 weeks. Supplements of calcium and vitamin D and daily applications of physiotherapy with magnetic field therapy are advocated to help the bone repair during the lay off period.

RED MEAT ALLERGY: Individual Greyhounds, and certain bloodlines of Greyhounds, may develop a gastrointestinal intolerance or allergy to red meat. It is reported most commonly in the German Shepherd breed and other large breeds of dogs.
Signs: The allergy results in low grade diarrhoea ranging from frequent passage of soft, watery stools to more intense gut pain and irritated bowel syndrome with non-infected gastro-enteritis. If the feeding of red meat is continued, the Greyhound will start to lose condition due to poor absorption of its food.
Causes: The symptoms have been linked to diets, which are based on red meat, with a higher incidence reported on horsemeat diets. It can affect puppies, racing Greyhounds and retired Greyhounds as they age.
Management: The low grade looseness and malabsorption condition often clears up over 3-4 days once red meat, especially horsemeat, is removed from the diet. Alternative 'white' meats such as pork, chicken or fish can be provided or the diet changed to a minimum residue, high-energy dry food.

If 'white' meats are substituted, then a supplement of 20-30mg iron should be given daily to racing Greyhounds to provide this essential blood mineral. Changing to an alternative red meat, such as from horsemeat to beef, may help reduce the individual allergy, or even boiling the meat to cook it as a stew may reduce the risk of gut allergy in sensitive Greyhounds.

RETAINED TESTICLES: Retention of one or both testicles within the inguinal canal or abdominal cavity is common in all dog breeds, including Greyhounds. It is considered to be an hereditary condition due to an autosomal recessive gene, and therefore hard to eliminate in Greyhounds. In a retired ageing Greyhound, a retained testicle has a higher risk of developing a cancerous condition, and it should be surgically removed as a safeguard against tumour development. It is also referred to as monorchidism (one testicle retained) and cryptorchidism (both testicles retained). Refer to Cryptorchidism.

RETINAL ATROPHY: Refer to Progressive Retinal Atrophy.

RESPIRATORY DISEASES: Greyhounds are susceptible to a number of respiratory viral and other upper and lower respiratory tract disorders. Greyhounds have a large lung capacity to provide oxygen for elite athletic performance, so any condition that affects the efficiency of oxygen uptake has an adverse affect on speed and stamina. Mechanical obstruction of the larynx at the entrance to the windpipe by an elongated soft palate occasionally occurs in racing Greyhounds.
Signs: Elongated Soft Palate: Affected Greyhounds have a history of noisy, fluttering, respiratory sounds and snoring when sleeping. Obvious grunting or choking sounds when breathing in at the gallop are caused by the soft palate being sucked over the laryngeal opening, obstructing the intake of air into the lungs. The Greyhound may collapse due to respiratory distress.
Management: Surgery to shorten the soft palate is advocated and enables return to competitive racing. Other major respiratory diseases are outlined under the individual conditions. Refer to Asthma, Canine Viral Disease, Coughing, Distemper, Exercise-Induced Bronchospasm, Husk, Kennel Cough, Lung Problems, Panting, Pharyngitis, Pneumonia, Pneumothorax, Rhinitis, Sinusitis, Tonsillitis, Tracheitis, Tracheobronchitis, Tracheal Worms.

RHABDOMYOLYSIS: A term to describe inflammation and disintegration (lysis) of muscle fibres, usually as a result of an acute acidosis build-up with cramping following extreme exertion. Refer to Acidosis, Cramping, Exertional Rhabdomyolysis.

RHINITIS: The condition caused by inflammation and swelling of the nasal passage lining, often with partial obstruction of the nasal passage. It is most common in young Greyhounds that develop an acute allergy to straw bedding.
Signs: Symptoms include sneezing, face rubbing, snuffling, noisy breathing and a nasal discharge. If it is an allergic condition, the eyes will often water and overflow with tears.

Causes: There are a number of causes of infectious rhinitis that can be spread within a group of Greyhounds, including bacterial, viral and parasitic diseases. In individual Greyhounds, allergies to inhalation of dust, dust mites in bedding, pollens from flowers and fungal spores may result in rhinitis and respiratory distress. Infection with lung worms (*Capillaria* (*Eucoleus*) *aerophilia*) have been associated with rhinitis in Greyhounds, often resulting in chronic narrowing of the nasal passages.

Management: The underlying cause must be identified and, in the case of lungworm infection, appropriate treatment given. Reducing dust in bedding by using shredded paper, linen bed covers and regular cleaning of the kennel area will help to minimise the allergic form of rhinitis in susceptible Greyhounds.

RIB INJURIES: Injuries to the ribs are usually a result of a fall or collision with the track rails or fences during a race.

Signs: Bruising of a rib or ribs due to trauma will usually cause discomfort when breathing, with a haematoma, collection of fluid or painful inflammatory reaction under the skin at the site of the injury. Evidence of abrasion or a wound may be present. A cracked fractured rib(s) may have similar signs, but in severe depression fractures, the animal will have difficulty in breathing and, occasionally, the chest cavity lining will be punctured by the end of the broken rib, leading to pneumothorax or collection of air inside the chest. Refer to Pneumothorax.

Causes: Rib fractures can occur in young pups when they collide when playing in a yard. The ribs can be bruised or fractured in race falls, collisions or other mishaps when galloping at speed.

Management: Examination by a vet is mandatory if the site of injury is very painful or the Greyhound has blood or fluid collection under the skin, or difficulty in breathing. X-rays may be necessary to determine the severity of a cracked or fractured rib under these circumstances. In most cases, there should be a lay-off from training, with kennel rest initially, and then lead walking resumed once the swelling has decreased and the soreness overcome. Refer also to Spare Ribs.

RINGWORM: Ringworm is a skin condition due to infection with a fungal organism that invades the skin. The common name used is misleading, as the condition was historically thought in humans to be a worm parasitic disease that was manifested by circular lesions on the skin. It is most common in younger Greyhounds, and sick or aged Greyhounds with lowered skin defences, especially under wet conditions.

Signs: The ringworm growth has a number of signs, ranging from small scurfy areas with hair loss, to more inflamed lesions that enlarge as the fungal organism spreads. The fungus can also gain entry to the nail bed and cause loss of the nails, resulting in the condition referred to as pemphigus.

Causes: A fungal organism that resides in the root of hair follicles, often in young Greyhounds that have poor immunity against skin infections. It can spread from dog to dog on hair shed on to the bedding. Aged Greyhounds may also develop the infection because of lowering immunity.

Management: The fungus lives deep in the hair root area and skin layers. Topical medications are usually not very effective in Greyhounds. Ringworm can be diagnosed by scanning the skin with an ultraviolet light source (Woods lamp) to identify the fluorescent fungal growths. Daily skin washes, based on PVP (tamed) iodine for a 2-3 week or longer period, combined with antibiotics to control secondary infections, may be necessary. The type of ringworm that affects Greyhounds does not spread to humans, although isolation of infected Greyhounds, improved hygiene and cleaning standards and avoidance of shared kennels with a Greyhound harbouring the condition are important measures to limit its spread. Refer also to Pemphigus.

ROUNDWORM: The species of roundworm that colonises the small intestine of dogs is shared with Greyhounds, with parasitic infection most common and potentially a health problem in young and growing pups up until 12 months of age.

Signs: The overall signs in puppies are a pot-bellied appearance, less than optimum growth rate and poor general health. When a pup has a heavy infestation of roundworms, diarrhoea can develop, leading to dehydration and debilitation. Severe infections can also cause puppies to cough as the immature worms migrate from the bowels through the liver and lungs to be coughed up and swallowed to complete their development phase prior to colonising the small intestine.

Causes: The common species of roundworms are Toxascaris and Toxocara, although other worms with a round, tubular appearance such as hookworms, whipworms and tracheal worms are classified as roundworms or nematodes. Infective roundworm larvae can be passed to puppies through the bitch's membranes, in her milk and in eggs that contaminate her teats and the rearing area. Children can ingest roundworm eggs by licking their fingers or eating food after playing with infected puppies and not washing their hands. Migrating roundworms can cause abdominal problems in children as they burrow through the gut organs, a phase which is termed visceral larval migrans. After the age of 12-15 months, healthy growing Greyhounds develop immunity against roundworms and adult dogs are less susceptible, although many act as carriers with about 12 per cent passing eggs in their stools. Aged Greyhounds in retirement, due to the warning of their imune defence system, may develop infestations that can affect their health.

Management: Very effective worming preparations are available to safely control and treat roundworms in young puppies, starting at 2 weeks of age and repeated every 10-14 days until the puppies reach 12-14 weeks of age. A bitch should be treated after 6 weeks of pregnancy on a regular fortnightly programme until her puppies are born. Adult Greyhounds should be treated every 4-6 months, especially if they have contact with young growing Greyhounds in the kennel or yards, as a natural management routine to control all worms.

S

SAND BURN: A condition caused by abrasion of the webbing between the pads, most commonly on the hind feet, when running on sand tracks. It is also referred to as sand rash, which is often a lesser form of the injury.

Signs: Abrasion and loss of hair, reddening and inflammation of the webbing between the toes and around the main pad. In severe cases, full thickness abrasion and tearing of the webbing with a bleeding and weeping moist surface may develop. Inflammation and moist discharges due to secondary infection with soil bacteria may be present on the edges of the webbing.

Causes: Sand under grass or an especially dry sandy track surface with coarse, sharply-fragmented sand particles can scuff and abrade the webbing as the Greyhound accelerates out of the starting boxes or traps, or as it corners at speed.

Management: Medications to dry the abraded areas and control surface infection will aid healing within 7-10 days. In severe cases, the foot should be bandaged to protect the webbing as it heals. Keeping the webbing pliable, but not soft, by application of a glycerine-based soothing ointment daily may reduce the risk in a flat-footed Greyhound. It is essential that the wound heals before the Greyhound returns to racing. The webbing may be hardened by the daily application of iodine, surgical alcohol or balsam ointments, especially if the skin is naturally thin and easily abraded. If the lesion recurs, the split should be surgically repaired. Refer to Split Webbing.

SAND RASH: An alternative term used to describe abrasion of the webbing by sand, often referred to as sand burn. Refer to Sand Burn.

SAND TOE: A term used to describe inflammation and infection of the cuticle and deeper nail bed as a result of collection and impaction of sand. It is also technically referred to as paronychia, but sand toe is often regarded as a specific form of more severe cuticle and nail bed infection in racing Greyhounds.

Signs: Although it can occur on any toe, it is most common on the outside toe (5th toe) of the left hind foot and the inside toe (2nd toe) of the right hind foot. Greyhounds with white feet and lightly pigmented skin will have a higher incidence. Initially, the condition starts as a mild inflammation and infection of the cuticle, which becomes enlarged and flares out around the hairline rim of the nail as sand collects under the cuticle rim. In severe cases, such as occurs on the outside toe of the left hind foot, the cuticle is

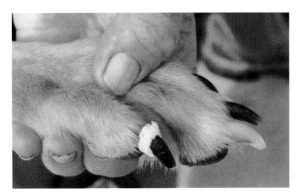

There are various methods of preventing sand toe and severe paronychia. Bands or protective covers of adhesive tape can deflect or prevent sand being forced under the cuticles during galloping.

painful to touch, weeps pus-like fluid and may abrade and bleed if not attended to prior to racing.

Causes: At the gallop when cornering, as sand particles are forced along the nail, they abrade and embed under the cuticle, separating the cuticle from the nail at the hairline border. The collection of sand increases the gap between the cuticle and nail to the depth of the nail bed, causing flaring of the hairline rim, which then collects more sand.

Management: Sand toe is a more severe form of paronychia. Management includes cleaning the sand away from under the cuticle, treating the secondary infection and drying and hardening the cuticle. The hair over the cuticle must not be trimmed back as it increases the risk of sand abrading the cuticle. Various measures can be taken to prevent sand from collecting under the cuticles on the susceptible toes of the hind foot. A deflector, or spoiler, can be applied around the nail using a 2-3mm wide piece of adhesive elastic tape encircling the toenail about 3-4 mm ($^{1}/_{4}$ ins) in front of the hairline on the problem nails. It can be applied, if approved for racing, before kennelling and should be protected with an overwrap of elastic tape applied around the end of the toe, when waiting in the kennels prior to racing.

SARCOPTIC MANGE: A type of mange caused by a mite, Sarcoptes scabei, which burrows in tunnels into the skin to feed, develop and lay eggs.

Signs: Intense irritation, itching and scratching is caused by mites burrowing into the skin surface, especially on thin-skinned areas such as the chest, belly, borders of the ears and elbows. The dog bites itself to relieve the itch, with abrasion and loss of hair patches. Biting may cause sores that become infected with bacteria under the crusts and scabs, often developing into a greasy, pyoderma skin condition. Refer to Pyoderma.

Causes: The small circular mange mite, Sarcoptes scabei, when introduced by an infected dog, spreads to other Greyhounds as they rub against each other, taking 8-10 weeks for the mange condition to develop. The mites cannot live for more than 2-3 days off the host dog. Although the mite may establish an itchy skin irritation under the armpits and elbows of humans handling infected dogs, a different type of mite causes scabies in humans. The irritation caused by the opportunist dog mite is self-limiting in humans.

Management: Diagnosis is confirmed by skin scrapings to identify the mites or their eggs, although a number of scrapings around the edges of the lesions are often needed to make a positive link to the Sarcoptes mite. Insecticidal skin washes at weekly intervals for 3-5 weeks will control the mites as they burrow within the skin surface. All Greyhounds in the kennel, whether in contact or not, should be treated. If left untreated, the condition can affect a Greyhound for years.

SARTORIUS MUSCLE INJURIES: The sartorius or whip muscle is a thin muscle bordering the flank on the front outline of the hindlimb between the pin bone and stifle joint. In racing Greyhounds, the muscle sheath can tear when overloaded during galloping, especially on slippery or loose track surfaces. The injury responds well to massage and ultrasound therapy for 10-14 days. Refer to Muscle Injuries, Spare Rib Problems.

SCAPULA BONE INJURIES: The flat scapula or shoulder blade has a narrow, raised bony ridge for attachment of the powerful shoulder muscles on each side. It can fracture along the base of the ridge, leading to lameness.

Signs: A hairline fracture along the base of the bony ridge shows minimal discomfort when the shoulder is flexed backwards, but the Greyhound is reluctant to bear weight. A complete fracture is much more obvious, with swelling and pain over the shoulder, which becomes progressively worse within 2-3 days.

Causes: A glancing blow to the shoulder, such as when a Greyhound hits the frame of the starting boxes or traps, or collides with the running rail or outer fence during a trial or race. Fractures can occur when a Greyhound pulls up quickly at the end of the race using its powerful shoulder muscles.

Management: Diagnosis by X-ray may be required to identify the fracture. Conservative therapy with kennel rest, magnetic field therapy and supplements of calcium and Vitamin D usually promote healing within 4-6 weeks. However, often the spine attachment is weakened and fractures may recur when accelerating and pulling up after a race.

SEGMENTAL AIRWAY COLLAPSE: Refer to Collapsed Tracheal Rings.

SEIZURES: Refer to Epilepsy.

SESAMOID BONE INJURIES: The sesamoid bones are small rounded bones located within the tendons that pass over the top (one sesamoid) and bottom (two sesamoids) of each toe joint.

Signs: Fracture of a sesamoid bone causes a grating sensation in the joint as the toes are flexed. Because the sesamoids have a vital function within the tendons as a pulley over the joint, damage to the sesamoids can reduce the strength of the tendons and risk long-term injury. They often cause long-term lameness and toe joint arthritis that can plague a racing Greyhound for the remainder of its career. In retired Greyhounds, sesamoid injuries can lead to painful arthritis of the affected toe joints as the animal ages. Surgical removal of the segments of the toe may be an option to reduce the discomfort in an aged Greyhound.

Causes: The sesamoids increase the surface area and redirect forces within the tendons over the toe joints. Inflammation of the sesamoids (sesamoiditis), fractures or dislocation of the sesamoids and tearing of the sesamoid ligaments are not a common injury in racing Greyhounds, but they can occur when the toes are subjected to extreme torsion forces during cornering at the gallop.

Management: X-rays can help to identify sesamoid injuries and, in long-standing cases, the sesamoid bones may erode away. Unfortunately, treatment of sesamoid injuries is not often successful. Sesamoiditis usually responds to cold therapy, anti-inflammatory medications and rest, with strapping of the affected toes. Applying a splint to the affected toe for 6-8 weeks will help new fractures to heal, but eroded, long-term fractured bones do not heal and often cause joint arthritis and reduce the chance that the Greyhound will return to competitive racing.

SHEATH ABNORMALITIES: The sheath of the penis of male dogs commonly develops a chronic low-grade bacterial infection, referred to as balanitis. Characteristically, it has a thick, creamy-yellow purulent discharge. Refer to Balanitis.

SHIN SORENESS: Refer to Metacarpal Periostitis.

SHOULDER INJURIES: The shoulder joint in a Greyhound is a relatively strong structure, which forms a joint with limited mobility between the shoulder blade (scapula) and the shoulder bone (humerus). Most injuries are related to falls, severe interference and collisions, or hitting the starting box, or trap frame, or the running rails during a race. Very few injuries are related directly to strain of the strong muscle groups that surround the shoulder joint. The major problems are related to joint cartilage deterioration, fractures of the shoulder blade spine and bone reaction due to injury. Arthritis of the shoulder joint may develop as a Greyhound ages in retirement, as a legacy of its racing career. Refer to Arthritis, Cartilage Erosion, Calcinosis Circumscripta, Joint Injuries, Osteochondritis Dissicans (OCD), Scapula Bone Injuries.

SINUSITIS: The air-filled sinus spaces shield the front area of the brain cavity and connect the upper jaw tooth root area to the nasal passages. Inflammation and build-up of infection of the lining membranes can lead to sinusitis. Sinusitis is not a common nasal condition in racing

Greyhounds, but it can occur in older retired Greyhounds due to tooth root abscesses and fungal infection within the sinuses.

Signs: Difficulty in breathing from the nose, with a nasal discharge due to build-up of infection and excess purulent mucus.

Management: The nasal discharge may be swabbed and a culture grown to identify the type of infection. Medications given to reduce the thick mucus build-up and allow it to drain, complemented by targeted antibiotics against the specific type of infective organism, is the standard therapy combination. Treatment may need to be continued for 10-14 days to clear up persistent infections. If the sinuses are blocked by thick mucus resulting from fungal (Aspergillus species) colonisation, surgery to open and drain the sinuses is necessary. In older Greyhounds with an upper tooth root abscess, the affected tooth will need to be removed to allow effective drainage and treatment.

SKIN DISEASES: Greyhounds have a thin skin and a short haircoat and generally suffer from very few skin diseases. Dermatitis, or inflammation of the skin, skin manges, flea irritations and localised surface sores (hot spots, staphylococcus dermatitis, milk sores) can develop. The skin of the webbing and pads are prone to infection under damp, poor hygiene kennel conditions. Refer to Abscesses, Allergic Dermatitis, Alopecia, Bald Thigh Syndrome, Bed Sores, Chilblains, Demodectic Mange, External Parasites, Foot Rot, Fleas, Lice, Hot Spots, Milk Sores, Mites, Sarcoptes Mange, Pad Injuries, Urticaria, Viral Papillomas, Warts.

 SKIN CANCERS (TUMOURS): Older retired Greyhounds can develop skin tumours. In most cases, they are benign or localised, non spreading skin cancers. However, if a skin tumour enlarges quickly, or the surface skin erodes and develops into a surface sore, then veterinary advice should be sought. A biopsy sample of the tumour can help identify the type of tumour and its state of malignancy. Removal by surgery may be necessary and is often successful. Even for benign tumours, surgery is usually cosmetically desirable. Tumours of the mammary glands in aged bitches are not uncommon, and any lumps in the glands should be evaluated as early as possible to determine the type, and potential malignancy, of the tumour.

SOFT NAILS: Individual Greyhounds may develop soft, flaky toe nails that crumble and break-away on the ends.

Signs: One or more toenails may appear soft and 'cheesy' on the under surface, which chip easily and crumble on the cut ends.

Causes: Certain bloodlines have a higher incidence of soft or weak nails. Aged Greyhounds often develop soft nails. Low-calcium diets may lead to reduced nail hardness and strength. Severe toxic diarrhoea, or distemper infection, may result in subsequent growth of soft, flaky nails.

Management: Soft nails should be trimmed to maintain about 2mm (^{1}/10 ins) gap between the point and a hard surface when standing. Cheesy nails can be disinfected with weak iodine solution (2.5 per cent) daily for 5-7 days to limit any underlying infection in the nail bed or quicks. Various human nail preparations can be coated on to the surface to harden the nails. The nail ends can be protected against chipping by applying a polymer or epoxy adhesive preparation after swabbing with surgical spirit. Once the polymer sets, the hardened points can be filed back to shape. A daily supplement of 1mg Biotin, a B group vitamin, combined with a calcium additive, will help to harden all the nails over a 4-6 week period. Refer also to Broken Nails, Bruised Nails.

SPARE RIB PROBLEMS: The spare rib is the last (13th) rib of the ribcage that is often small and does not join in the rear border arch of the ribs along the front of the flank area. It is also referred to as a floating rib.

Signs: A Greyhound may run wide on a corner due

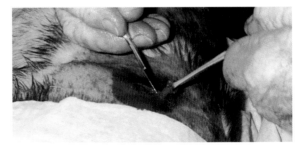

A simple operation to remove the left spare (13th rib) or the small vestigial, often sharp, backward angled rib on the left side, is considered to assist Greyhounds with swelling and pain over the point of the rib to better negotiate bends on the racetrack.

to the stabbing action of a sharp spare rib as the body flexes to the left. When pressed, the tissue over the rib may be sore and inflamed.

Causes: In some bloodlines of racing Greyhounds, the vestigial rib is sharp and pointed backwards. It is thought to be a cause for soreness in the flank and adjacent upper hindlimb muscles, such as the sartorius (whip) muscle, in Greyhounds running on tight circle tracks.

Management: The removal of sharp spare ribs is controversial in Greyhound veterinary practice. However, there is anecdotal evidence that suggests that removal of a sharp rib under local anaesthetic often restores a Greyhound's cornering speed after 10-14 days recuperation, enabling an improvement in some cases of up to 10 lengths in race speed.

SPINAL PAIN: A painful reaction to downward pressure applied along the spine and backline is a common problem in racing Greyhounds.

Signs: The Greyhound has a history of not stretching out, running with a more rigid back, jumping poorly from the traps and running erratically on the corners. When the backline of a Greyhound with spinal pain is pressed downwards in a springing action using the palms of the hand, the spring is reduced, the back held in a more rigid arch and signs of discomfort are displayed.

Causes: The underlying cause can be related to wear and tear of the intervertebral spaces and pressure on associated nerves and muscles. This syndrome is referred to as a spinal mobility fault, which affects the spinal nerve. Referred pain can be

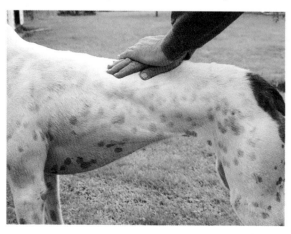

The spinal column and associated muscles can be checked for spinal pain by a 'spring' test on the backline.

detected in the muscles of the front and hindlimbs.

Management: Diagnosis and therapy must be carried out under specialist veterinary supervision. Chiropractic manipulation, ultrasound, acupuncture and magnetic field applications of physiotherapy have been used with success. Physiotherapy and rest periods usually range from 5-7 days for minor spinal faults after chiropractic manipulation, to more regular therapy sessions in long-standing, recurring spinal problems. Also refer to Lumbosacral Injuries.

SPLAYED TOES: A common term used to describe flattening and separation of the toes when the Greyhound is standing.

Signs: One or more toes of the foot may lose their arched form, collapsing to become flattened in appearance and often spreading apart. The wrist joint is often lowered or has a dropped-down appearance. Lameness is relative to the cause and degree of the flexor tendon damage.

Causes: The condition is caused by sprain, rupture, laceration and severance of the flexor tendons, which attach to the underside of the toes to maintain the arched appearance. The tendons may be severed on one or more toes by sharp objects, such as glass, when the Greyhound is walked on roadways, or in the sand on a race track.

Management: The flexor tendons may repair or reunite when the toes are supported and the Greyhound is rested, but there is a high risk of recurring sprain and lameness. Strapping the weakened toe to an adjacent toe, to help maintain its support function and prevent them splaying apart when exercising, is helpful. If the wrist is also dropped, then the Greyhound is best retired from racing. In the aged Greyhound, splayed toes can lead to arthritis in the toe joints and wrist if it is weakened. Also refer to Flat Feet.

SPLIT NAILS: The toenails may split from the end, allowing grit, sand and accompanying infection to enter the underlying quick and nail bed. Split nails are often brittle or soft and may break along the cracked area. After any infection has been treated, cauterising the ends with a hot point will fuse and close over the ends to prevent further splits. Management to overcome other nail problems, such as soft nails and nail bed infection, should be adopted as warranted. Refer to Broken Nails, Bruised Nails, Nail Bed Infection, Soft Nails.

 SPLIT WEBBING: The webbing which stretches between the toes to prevent them separating excessively when galloping, is reinforced by a strong layer of fibrous tissue within the skin.
Signs: The webbing can tear or split apart between one or more toes during galloping. The lacerated webbing bleeds and collects sand, which invariably leads to bacterial infection of the wound. Splits can vary from 1-2mm (^{1}/10 ins) up to a complete webbing tear finishing at the end of the V-shape between the toes. These tears can be up to 2 cm (almost 1 inch) long. Unfortunately, the webbing heals slowly due to its fibrous content and at least 3-4 weeks rest and treatment is often necessary.
Causes: Excessive stretching of the webbing flap when cornering can cause it to reach its stretch limit, tear and split apart. The webbing can be lacerated by sharp objects, increasing the risk that it will split if the Greyhound continues to be galloped.
Management: Small splits at the front of the webbing can be healed as an open wound by dressing with antiseptic cream and protecting the wound by bandaging the feet. Despite careful nursing and wound treatment of large splits, the webbing will usually split again once the animal is galloped. Partial removal of the lacerated edges along the sides of the toes, or removing the webbing tissue as far back as possible, is necessary so there is no tension on the webbing when the toes are spread apart and gives the best long-term result. The wound can be sutured or allowed to heal as an open wound to encourage it to stretch and reduce tension as the fibrous tissue shrinks on healing. After surgery to stitch the webbing together, a Greyhound can often run again after 3-4 weeks, but if the splits are allowed to heal naturally it may take up to 5-6 weeks until the webbing is strong enough to withstand tension when galloping. Refer also to Webbing Problems.

 SPRUNG TOES: The toes of racing Greyhounds are subjected to high loading, torsional and stretching forces during galloping. The collateral ligaments on the side of each toe

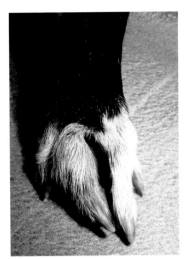

Tearing or stretching of the ligaments on the side (collateral) of one or more toe joint results in a sprung toe.

that hold the adjacent digits in apposition to form the joints can be stretched, torn or pulled off their anchorage points. Refer to Collateral Ligaments.
Signs: A sprung toe joint will be swollen and painful on the side of the sprained or stretched collateral ligament. The toe will be able to be deviated to the opposite side by up to a 45-degree angle, with signs of discomfort and withdrawal. A dislocated toe, in which the collateral ligament is completely ruptured or torn away, will be swollen, painful and when manipulated, will hinge sideways up to 90 degrees (at a right angle) away from the side of the ruptured ligament.
Causes: A sprung toe is a result of overstretching and sprain of the collateral ligaments. Excessive stretching and rupture results in complete sideways instability of the toe joint, referred to as a dislocated toe. Sprung toes are more common when Greyhounds are run on grass tracks, as the toes are more likely to become caught in longer or matted grass surfaces. Similar damage can occur in a retired Greyhound that turns or stops on a grassy surface when free galloping.
Management: *Sprung Toe:* Cold therapy using crushed ice under an elastic pressure bandage wrapped around the joint for 3-4 mins will help reduce swelling and discomfort. It should be repeated every 2-3 hours for the initial 12 hours and then, once the swelling is reduced, twice daily for a further 48 hours. DMSO and muscle liniments applied over the injured area will reduce the swelling and assist healing. Injectable sclerosing agents, deposited under the skin over the torn ligament, may be prescribed by a vet. Strapping the injured toe to its neighbour with tape or a

wide, lightly-tensioned rubber band, (e.g. a ring made of 5mm ($^1/_5$ ins) wide racing bicycle inner tube) will help support the toe when walking. A programme of daily walking for 2-3 weeks will assist in healing. After this period of time, short straightline handslips over 100 metres (110 yards) for 10-14 days can be given with a return to full training provided the joint is stable and pain-free. *Dislocated Toes:* First aid application as recommended for sprung toes for the first 12 hours. Surgical stabilisation with strong sutures to replace the ruptured ligament will provide a lattice for fibrous tissue and ligament regrowth. A longer rest period may be necessary. If the toe end joint is dislocated, then removal of the toe to the next joint may be the best option, as recurrence is high in racing Greyhounds. Strapping the toe to its neighbour when galloping is recommended. In retired Greyhounds, a bony growth around the joint may develop into arthritis. Refer to Arthritis.

STIFLE INJURIES: Stifle, or hindlimb knee injuries, are not common in racing Greyhounds, but can occur as a result of collisions with the running rail or fence during a race.
Signs: The stifle joint will usually swell around the joint when external support tissues are bruised, overstretched or rupture of the collateral ligaments on the side of the stifle occurs, leading to severe joint instability and lameness. Refer to Collateral Ligaments. Internal joint conditions involve the articular cartilage or meniscal layers of the joint with severe weight-bearing lameness, but in most cases it is associated with collateral ligament injury. A clicking sound may be heard due to the damaged meniscus cartilage when the stifle is slowly flexed, but the absence of a 'click' does not eliminate meniscal damage as an underlying cause. The tendon of the long digital extensor muscle that extends the toes and flexes the hock may be subject to strain during acceleration out of the starting traps or boxes. The cruciate ligaments that provide internal joint stability may be ruptured in older Greyhounds as they turn or twist when galloping, with a higher incidence in bitches. Osteochondritis dissicans (OCD) can also develop in the stifle joint of overgrown, under exercised young Greyhounds. Refer to Osteochondritis and OCD. The patella or kneecap may fracture and cause arthritic changes. Refer to Patella fractures.

Causes: The stifle joint is subjected to torsional and high loading forces when transmitting the power of the upper hindlimb muscles to the tibia and lower limb, especially during acceleration, cornering and braking when pulling up after a race. An uneven track surface or loose sand surface will increase the risk of stifle injury.
Management: There are many possible causes for stifle injury and associated lameness, so that a thorough examination, often combined with X-rays, joint blocks with local anaesthetic and arthroscopic examination may assist in establishing a diagnosis. Minor injuries to ligaments and associated instability often resolve and repair under a programme of lead walking for 4-6 weeks, swimming and daily full-joint flexion. Surgical repair of the ligaments, using grafts and tissue tucks around the joint to improve its stability, are now available to assist repair processes and improve joint stability. Magnetic field therapy, laser therapy for ligament repair and acupuncture have been used with varying success. Cartilage, and especially meniscal layers, are very slow to repair and regrow. Intra-articular arthroscopic surgery to remove damaged cartilage and meniscal layers to allow regeneration, complemented by injectable joint treatment and oral chondroitin, glucosamine and trace-mineral supplements have been found to assist repair. Rest and lead walking for 2-3 weeks is necessary to allow joint cartilage regeneration after arthroscopic surgery. Refer to Arthritis, Articular Cartilage, Joint Injuries.

STOPPER PAD INJURIES: The accessory carpal foot pad behind the wrist is often referred to as the stopper pad. Laceration and tearing of the stopper pad can occur on loose, rough or dry track surfaces when the wrist is flattened to touch the ground surface.
Signs: The pad(s) may be cracked, lacerated, split on the pad surface and torn away from the underlying tissue. These conditions become inflamed and painful and invariably become infected with bacteria from contamination with soil or sand from yards and turn-out pens, especially under wet conditions. A torn pad may be peeled back, exposing the sensitive underlying tissue, resulting in swelling, infection and lameness.
Causes: Laceration and tearing is due to trauma and concussion to the normally resilient pads. Cuts

from glass, synthetic track surfaces and abrasions from dry coarse sand cause soreness and lameness. Very dry pads are less resilient and more likely to tear if deflected or stretched to the limit.

Management: Cut or lacerated pads must be thoroughly cleaned and disinfected using a preparation such as a PVP (tamed) iodine solution. Topical Vitamin A, zinc cream and antibiotic-based ointments can be applied to the lacerated pad to help moisturise and assist healing. An over-wrap of elastic padded bandage will protect the pad during lead walking exercise. Laser and magnetic field therapy have been used with reported success. Torn away pads can be sutured back in place, but often the underlying tissue is devitalised and the success of reattachment is variable. Rest and lead walking for 2-3 weeks is usually required to ensure the pad(s) heal and regain strength and resilience.

STOPPER TENDON INJURIES: The stopper tendon is the common name for the flexor carpal ulnaris muscle and its tendon insertion on to the accessory carpal bone behind the wrist.

Signs: After tendon sprain, swelling and discomfort may take 12-24 hours to develop. In severe cases, swelling develops after cooling-out from a race. A piece of bone may be pulled off the accessory carpal bone at the site of the tendon attachment, with swelling and acute lameness within 12-24 hours. When the wrist is flexed back upon itself, the animal will display increased discomfort as the inflamed fibres are displaced and

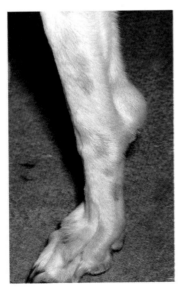

Rupture of the flexor tendon that attaches to the accessory carpal bone under the stopper pad can occur when galloping on a rough or uneven track surface. This injury necessitated long term therapy and eventual retirement.

squeezed by the restriction behind the wrist.

Causes: Extreme downward extension or flattening of the wrist during galloping reaches the stretch limit of the tendon structure, which can be overloaded by rough track surfaces with 'cup-outs' or holes from previous races and a shifting sand surface. Fatigue in muscles increases the risk of tendon overstretching.

Management: Prompt first aid with cold packs for 3-4 minutes under an elastic pressure bandage will help reduce swelling, pain and further disruption to tendon fibres. Repeat every 30 minutes over $1^1/2$-2 hours, then support with an elastic pressure bandage, wrapped to include the wrist. If the swelling remains, an X-ray to check for bone damage is indicated. Physiotherapy with warming liniments, magnetic field therapy, laser therapy and Faradic treatment are useful. Swimming for 2-3 minutes twice daily will help maintain fitness. A 12-16 week or longer healing time may be necessary for severe tendon injuries.

STRESS INDUCED CONDITIONS: Physical and mental stress can have an effect on both the health and performance of a racing Greyhound.

Signs: Signs of stress include loss of vitality, reduced appetite, poor recovery from racing and training, increased risk of disease resulting from lowered immunity, anaemia, a dull rough coat and loss of condition. Excitable and nervous, as well as timid, Greyhounds suffer from the direct effects of stress.

Causes: There are many causes of stress, which can include hard or inconsistent training methods; nutritional inadequacy; changing environmental conditions; long-distance transport, excess noise and fear of race-day spectators. Stress results in the release of cortisone hormones, which can have a direct influence on metabolism, psychological balance, bone marrow function and the immune response to disease.

Management: Attempts to minimise stress by adopting careful and considerate training methods to match the temperament of a particular Greyhound; maintaining comfortable kennel conditions, especially warmth in cold weather; providing an adequate and balanced diet and ensuring comfort when travelling. Supplements of Vitamins A, E and C and probiotics may assist the body in combating the effects of stress.

SUNBURN: Greyhounds with lightly-pigmented skin on the topline of the nose, ear tips and white body patches of skin and hair can suffer sunburn damage to the skin when housed in outside yards.

Signs: Typical reddening, soreness and swelling of the skin surface. Within a few days, the damaged skin flakes off, exposing underlying layers of reactive, sore skin. Mild sunburn may lead to serum exudates and scabs attached to the underlying skin. In mild conditions, the hair will fall out to leave reactive and unprotected skin.

Causes: Excess exposure to ultraviolet light when daytime levels are high under summertime conditions.

Management: Soothing ointments and creams containing zinc oxide and sunscreen agents will help reduce risk when applied prior to exposure to high ultraviolet levels. Alternatively, the Greyhound should be kept in the kennel during critical periods and let out early in the morning and late in the afternoon. In severe cases, antibiotic medication may be required to control secondary infections.

SUPERFICIAL STROMAL KERATITIS: Refer to Pannus.

SYNOVITIS: Synovitis, or inflammation of the synovial membrane or joint capsule lining, occurs as a result of joint damage and early arthritis. It results in fluid swelling of the joint, with pain and inflammation due to fluid pressure. Synovitis is a defensive response to joint cartilage wear and tear, concussive injury or joint infection. Refer to Arthritis, Joint Diseases.

T

TAIL INJURIES: Greyhounds have a long, thin tail which can fracture relatively easily in a race fall or collision, or when caught accidentally in the starting trap door. The end of the tail can become abraded by wagging and striking it on the walls of the kennel or yard fences.

Signs: *Fractures:* Fractures are easily identified because the tail swells and deviates to one side at the fracture site. The tail is often limp below the

Chronic tail waggers often develop severely abraded, split or devitalised areas on the point of the tail. A protective bandage, or a plastic mesh hair-curler can be used to cushion the tail end to prevent further trauma and abrasion.

fracture area if the nerves are bruised or damaged.

Tail End Trauma: The tip of the tail becomes bruised and abraded due to trauma resulting from wagging and striking it on rough or hard walls or fences. The skin becomes abraded, exposing the underlying flesh around the end of the tail. In severe cases, the tip of the tail bone may be exposed, oozing blood and serum. The tail end becomes sore and inflamed, but tail-bashing often continues unabated.

Causes: Tail-base fractures at the origin of the tail can occur when a Greyhound runs into another from behind during a race. The tail is pushed vertically upwards and snaps the vertebrae or between the joint at the base, as it is forced over the animal's back. The partly-raised tail can be broken when a frightened or inexperienced Greyhound leans back heavily on the rear door of the starting traps. Mid-tail fractures along the length of the tail are caused by excessive bending or compression when a Greyhound falls in a race. Catching the tail in a door or fence can dislocate the tail joints or fracture the small bones in the bottom third of the tail. Tail End Trauma occurs due to striking the tip of the tail on rough or hard walls when wagging it in a confined kennel space.

Management: Fractured tails do not heal quickly, even if they are well strapped or splinted. Often the nerve and blood supply has been compromised. Amputation at the level of the fracture is the best option. Greyhounds can race successfully with a shorter or fully amputated tail. Tail-base fractures will heal satisfactorily if the tail is taped and tied between the hindlimbs to prevent it being wagged. Usually 3-4 weeks rest and lead walking will enable tail-base fractures to heal.

Tail End Abrasion: Dressing the abraded area with soothing and antiseptic preparations and protecting it against further trauma is essential. In severe cases, surgical removal of the damaged area may be necessary. The tail tip can be protected by a plastic mesh, like a haircurler, fastened on to the end segments with adhesive tape. Tying the tail between the hindlegs also helps to prevent it being wagged. However, the animal will have to be taken out at least 3-4 times daily to pass stools and in bitches, to enable them to urinate with dignity and prevent discomfort and urine scalding of the tail. Hanging bags, old bed quilts etc. over the kennel walls to cushion the trauma to the tail end in a habitual tail wagger is recommended.

TAPEWORMS: Greyhounds are hosts to species of common tapeworms, which are spread by eating raw meat or offal of the specific carrier animal, or by fleas.
Signs: Tapeworm infection may cause low-grade intestinal irritation. Slimy mucus-coated stools are produced due to tapeworm irritation and inflammation of the large intestinal wall. Heavy infestations may cause loss of weight and a dull lifeless coat. Other tell-tale signs include licking the anal area and skidding the buttocks along the ground to relieve the itch caused by mobile and migrating segments of *Dipylidium caninum*, the common tapeworm that is spread by fleas.
Causes: Three species of tapeworms inhabit the large intestine of dogs.

Species: *Taenia* spp. (Flat tapeworm).
Appearance: Flat white segments.
Spread by intermediate host: Meat of infected cattle, sheep, deer, rabbits, rats, mice.

Species: *Echinococcus caninum* (hydatid tapeworm).
Appearance: Small stumpy segments.
Spread by intermediate host: Offal and intestines of infected sheep, goats or deer.

Species: *Dipylidium caninum*.
Appearance: Cucumber-shaped, white, mobile segments.
Spread by intermediate host: Dog fleas.

Management: Tapeworms are controlled only by specific worm preparations at regular 8-week intervals. Faecal contamination of yards does not spread tapeworms. Infection can be prevented by avoiding offal and non-inspected sources of beef and sheep meat. Rigorous flea control will help reduce the incidence of the flea tapeworm, *Dipylidium caninum*. Refer to Fleas.

TARSAL INJURIES: The tarsus is the anatomical name for the hock joint. Sprains, fracture and arthritic conditions can occur in racing and retired Greyhounds. Refer to Hock Injuries.

TARTAR ON TEETH: Tartar is a crusty or hard shell-like accumulation of food material on the canine and back teeth. It is also referred to as calculus, plaque and caries. Refer to Calculus on Teeth, Gingivitis, Periodontal Disease.

TENDON INJURIES: Strain and tearing of the tendons of the Flexor carpi ulnaris muscle (stopper tendon) behind the wrist and the Achilles Tendon above the hock can occur in racing Greyhounds. Tendon injuries usually result from overloading of the tendon during galloping, falls during a race, loss of traction on the track surface or accumulative tendon strain of repeated racing and during long preparation. Tendons are composed of bundles of elastic collagen strands (fibrils) that travel the full length of the tendon from its muscle origin to the point of attachment. Tendons are elastic structures that store a reserve of kinetic energy as a spring-like effect during locomotion, helping to add power and spring to the gait. They have a poor blood supply and heal and repair very slowly, with replacement of a less elastic type of collagen fibre following tearing or rupture.

Tendons are more elastic and able to absorb overload when warmed up during exercise, generating their own heat from elastic kinetic energy, reaching temperatures 2-3 degrees C (4-5 degrees F) above normal body operating temperatures during exercise. When tendon fibres are torn or ruptured, the accompanying fine blood vessels stretch and break, flooding blood into the damaged fibre bundles, forming a blood clot. The resultant intense inflammation caused by fibre ruptures, combined with blood, accumulation, results in further misalignment of the thin fibrils and fibre bundles, which delays the repair and reuniting processes. Prompt first aid with cold therapy and pressure bandaging helps to control the collection of inflammatory fluid and blood, which reduces the overall damage to the tendon and improves the chances of a successful, although lengthy, repair and strengthening process. Refer to Stopper Tendon Injuries, Achilles Tendon Injuries.

TESTICULAR ABNORMALITIES: The failure of one or both testicles to descend into the scrotal sac from the abdominal cavity in young puppies results in the condition of monorchidism (one testicle retained) or cryptorchidism (both testicles retained). The condition appears to have an hereditary predisposition in certain bloodlines of Greyhounds. Refer to Cryptorchidism. The testicles can also become cancerous, especially the smaller retained testicles subjected to the constant heat of the abdominal cavity. Testicular tumours often result in a change in behaviour relative to the type of hormone produced in the cancerous cells. Some Greyhounds become very aggressive if male hormone (testosterone) production is increased by the specific cancerous cells, others lose their male behaviour if the female hormone (oestrogen) is predominant as a result of the tumour cells. Removal of the testicular tumour, often requiring abdominal surgery, is the only way to avoid long-term complications and spread of certain forms of malignant testicular cancer.

TETANUS: A usually fatal toxin produced by the soil-borne bacterial microbe, Clostridium tetani. The toxin produces nerve and muscle spasm. Fortunately, this disease is not common in well-cared-for Greyhounds.
Signs: Initial fever and loss of appetite, progressing to stiffness in gait and inability to drink and eat due to jaw muscle lock-up (commonly referred to as lock-jaw). Excitement increases the symptoms of severe muscle (tetanic) spasm. Death is usually caused by respiratory muscle spasm and inability to breathe.
Causes: The spores of *Clostridium tetani*, an anaerobic microbe, are passed in the droppings of many animals, with the highest levels in horse manure. Dogs can become infected when the spores contaminate deep anaerobic puncture wounds, especially in farm environments. The incubation period is from 3-21 days. Dogs are some 360 times less susceptible to tetanus than horses. The potent toxin produced travels along nerves to cause progressive nerve paralysis and muscle spasm.
Management: A dog with tetanus requires intensive nursing, with tube feeding, antibiotics and muscle-relaxant therapy. The major preventative measure is to ensure that all wounds from piercing objects or bite injuries are cleaned with 50:50 hydrogen peroxide in water (provides oxygen which inhibits tetanus spore growth) and antiseptics. Courses of penicillin will eliminate the bacteria from the wound. Routine vaccination is normally not advised.

THYROID CONDITIONS: The major condition related to thyroid function in Greyhounds is hypothyroidism or low production of thyroxine, a metabolic control hormone. Low thyroid production in retired Greyhounds may result in tiredness, reduced activity and weight gain although the appetite is curtailed. Muscle weakness and a tired, wrinkled expression may be apparent on the dog's face. Refer to Hypothyroidism.

TIBIAL CREST AVULSION: A term that is used to describe fracture of the growth plate on the front of the tibia bone where it forms part of the stifle joint. The lower end of the patella (kneecap) ligament anchors on to the tibial tuberosity or crest at the front of the tibia, with the growth plate held by cartilage to the underlying bone in young Greyhounds. The injury can occur in young Greyhounds due to traumatic injury in outside runs from falls, or collisions with fences, or their companions. Twisting and turning at speed also increases the loading on the patella through the quadriceps femoris muscle tendon which attaches to the tibial crest. The fracture can be identified on X-ray to determine the severity of the crest displacement. In Greyhounds up to 21 months of age, it is exhibited as swelling and lameness in front of the damaged stifle joint. Some develop a long-term fracture zone from an earlier

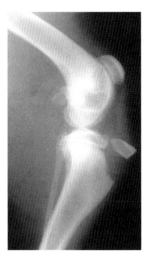

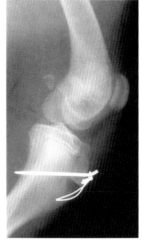

The front section of the joint at the growth plate junction can be fractured and dislodged by trauma of young Greyhounds playing in outside runs.

The tibial crest can be repositioned by a stabilising wire, and usually heals well without further complications.

injury. A plaster cast will help to immobilise new non-displaced fractures. Surgery to insert a pin to reattach the displaced growth plate, combined with restriction of hindlimb movement by support bandaging, ensures better long-term healing and freedom from stifle instability in racing Greyhounds.

TICKS: There are a number of species of blood-sucking ticks that can affect Greyhounds in various countries and localities. Ticks affect farm animals and wildlife and can attach to Greyhounds as an alternate host. Some ticks spread infectious and potentially fatal diseases.

Signs: Ticks are small insects that attach close to the skin and engorge blood to enlarge into a visible, soft, wart-like lump. They cause skin irritation and itching as they burrow their head into the skin and anaemia can result when heavy infestations are harboured. Once engorged, the female tick detaches and lays eggs in ground debris.

Causes: Ticks crawl into the haircoat of a Greyhound when it comes in contact with forest or farm environs inhabited by host carrier animals. Some ticks carry diseases such as Lyme disease (Borreliosis), which are infectious to animals and humans. These ticks are prevalent in the UK and USA. Lyme disease results in a high fever, loss of appetite and arthritis in one or more joints. It can be treated with antibiotics. The paralysis tick (*Ixodes holocyclus*), that parasitizes bandicoots on the east coast of Australia, produces a potent toxin that causes nervous paralysis, a high-pitched bark, depression and weakness of the limbs. If the tick is not removed, the toxin it produces causes respiratory paralysis and death. Antiserum is available to combat this potent neurotoxin.

Management: Ticks should not be pulled off, as the head and mouth parts will detach and remain embedded in the dog's skin leading to infected sores, and in the case of *Ixodes holocyclus*, continued release of toxin. Ticks should be swabbed with a suitable insecticide or washed in an insecticidal shampoo. Flooding the skin area around the tick's body with a few drops of vegetable cooking oil will make removal easier by suffocating the tick within 1-2 minutes. In tick-prone areas, the skin and haircoat of Greyhounds should be carefully examined every day to check for ticks.

TOE INJURIES: The toes of Greyhounds are subjected to extreme concussion, rotation and torsion forces during galloping. The toes are composed of three small bones, corresponding to the human finger, with the last bone pointed to carry the toe nail. The major injuries are related to overstretching and strain of ligaments that form the structural stability of the toe joint, resulting in conditions such as sprung toes and dislocated toes. These conditions are more common in Greyhounds racing on grass race tracks, accounting for up to 8 per cent of race day injuries. Refer to Dislocated Toes, Sprung Toes. Injuries to the pads, nails and webbing are related to the high stresses imposed at racing speeds, abrasive track surfaces, changes in moisture content of the pad skin covering, and bacterial and fungal infections of the skin and nails. Sand can be forced under the cuticle edge of the inner toe nails on the hindlimbs, leading to chronic inflammation and soreness, which is termed paronychia or sand toe. Refer to Paronychia, Sand Toe. Laceration or cuts to the pads and webbing when walking on roadways can damage the underside support tendons of the toes and result in wounds, webbing splits and pad corns that can plague a Greyhound during its racing career. Refer to Nail Problems, Pad Injuries, Webbing Problems.

TONSILLITIS: A well-known term that describes inflamed, sore and enlarged tonsils in the roof of the throat, often associated with a sore throat or pharyngitis.

Signs: The outward signs include a slight fever, picking at feed, discomfort when swallowing, occasional gagging, and coughing if the tonsils become infected. When the mouth is opened and the tongue depressed, the inflamed tonsils appear swollen and red with engorged blood readily visible, often protruding out of the small fold of membrane or crypt on each side of the roof of the throat. If touched with the finger tip, the engorged tonsils may ooze blood and this will result in a coughing due to blood irritating the throat. Often the throat (pharynx) is also inflamed.

Check the tonsils of a Greyhound that picks at its food, froths at the mouth after a gallop or has a cough when exercised. The tonsils of an affected dog will appear red and swollen.

Causes: The tonsils act as a first line of immune defence as a lymphoid gland against infection in the mouth and throat. When challenged, they enlarge to provide immune protection against infection entering the body. Inflammation can be caused either by viral respiratory disease or increased bacterial contamination of the throat due to heavy calculus on teeth, severe gingivitis and licking the sheath or vulva. Often, the Greyhound has a brownish stain around the lips and muzzle if it has been licking the sheath or vulva. Refer to Balanitis, Calculus on Teeth, Gingivitis. Tonsillitis is most common in young Greyhounds returning to the kennels after schooling and breaking-in where changes in climate, stress and virus

infections cause the tonsils to react. Inhaling cold air without adequate warm-up before galloping can also cause reactive tonsils.

Management: A course of antibiotics will control any primary or secondary bacterial infection, combined with mucolytic preparations to reduce phlegm build-up. If the teeth are coated with heavy tartar, they should be cleaned. Refer to Calculus on Teeth. Measures should also be taken to discourage sheath or vulva licking by fitting a 10 litre (2.2 gallons) plastic bucket to the collar overnight in the kennel to prevent licking, while the infection is being treated. Refer to Balanitis. Feeding soft, moist foods and dampened dry food will make swallowing more comfortable. A mouth-wash containing 2 drops of weak iodine solution (2.5 per cent) mixed in 10ml (two teaspoons) of glycerine and squirted on to the tongue twice daily for 5-7 days often assists in reducing contamination levels in the throat and allows the tonsils to revert to their normal size. If a Greyhound suffers a number of bouts of tonsillitis, then surgical removal of the tonsils may be necessary.

TONSIL ENLARGEMENT: Also referred to as Tonsillar Hypertrophy. Chronic recurring tonsillitis may result in permanent enlargement of one or both tonsils.

Signs: The tonsil(s) when examined does not appear inflamed or different in colour to the throat tissue, but simply enlarged and elevated out of the tonsillar crypts. The animal eats well, but when made to gallop over distances exceeding 400 metres (437 yards), it may suffer respiratory distress and reduction in speed and performance due to partial obstruction of the throat airway. During recovery from a gallop, the animal may cough as if choking, with noisy breathing and an extended time to regain its wind after racing.

Causes: Repeated challenges to the immune lymphoid tissue in the tonsils results in its growth and the development of fibrous tissue around and internally within the tonsil(s).

Management: The best method of treatment is to surgically remove the enlarged tonsil(s), with feeding of a soft diet for 10-14 days until the base of the tonsil area heals. Often electrocautery is used to remove tonsils and minimise bleeding. The Greyhound can usually return to full training within 6-8 weeks, depending on the rate of healing. Because the upper airway obstruction is removed, a full return to performance is achieved.

TRACK LEG: A common term used in Australia and the UK to describe a defined raised area of bruised tissue that usually develops on the inside of the left hindlimb above the hock. In the USA it is referred to as 'jack'. Technically, it is known as Medial Tibial Trauma Syndrome.

Signs: A soft tissue swelling develops within 2-6 hours after a race above the hock, usually on the inside of the left leg and occasionally on the right

A track leg or 'jack' swelling on the inside of the tibia due to trauma by the outside of the elbow during the galloping action. The collection of blood was drained, ice-packs were applied with an anti-inflammatory cream.

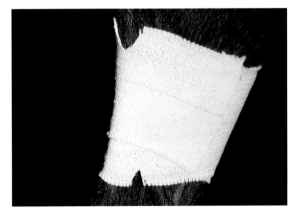

Protective taping and greasing of the inside of the hindlimb and outside of the elbow help to reduce the trauma to the tibia and continued bone surface reaction. The bandage must be applied in a clockwise direction on the left limb (anti-clockwise on the right limb) to pull the track leg 'lump' back into the tendon groove. The adhesive bandage should be split, as shown, to allow the limb to move freely.

side. The Greyhound may not be lame, but the swelling enlarges to a soft blood blister (haematoma) as a result of tissue bruising. If not treated, the blood will clot, forming a hard fibrous and calcified lump, increasing the risk of it being struck again and creating ongoing reaction and soreness.

Causes: An altered running gait due to injury causes the outside border of the elbow to strike the inside of the hindlimb midway between the stifle and hock. This usually happens at the gallop, as the Greyhound corners to the left. The most common predisposing injuries that alter the gait are lumbosacral and right hip support soreness. Injury to the left shoulder is not a common cause, although right shoulder injury may alter the flight path of the left front limb to the outside during galloping. A higher incidence occurs on tracks with tight corners and lack of banking. The traumatic injury causes bruising, blood vessel rupture and bony reaction (periosteal reaction) on the inside of the tibia bone.

Management: Prompt first aid with an ice pack held in place with an elastic pressure bandage for 2-3 minutes will limit bruising and haemorrhage. If a fluid-filled (serous) lump forms, it can be drained and injected with a long-acting cortisone preparation, then rebandaged to maintain elastic pressure for 4-7 days until the swelling subsides. Anti-inflammatory creams may be applied to reduce pain and swelling. A thorough check of the back and hindlimbs must be carried out to identify any underlying injury that could alter the gait, followed up by appropriate physiotherapy if necessary. If it is unsure whether a Greyhound is hitting itself, a smear of red lipstick on the outside of the point of the elbow can be useful to mark the track leg (jack) area if the dog is trialled on a circle. The injured area can be taped to protect it against trauma, or a rubber patch glued over the area to provide a cushioning effect when galloping. Both the outside of the left elbow and the injury area should be liberally greased with handcream or petroleum jelly, although sand will adhere to the latter, when galloping on sand tracks. In chronic, recurring cases, surgical removal of the bony lump may be necessary to prevent ongoing trauma and lameness. If, despite exhaustive therapy, it is not possible to prevent the Greyhound striking itself, then the animal should be run on a straight track to reduce the risk of recurrence of the injury.

TRACHEAL WORM: A thread-like worm, *Filaroides osleri*, that colonises the lower end of the trachea, or windpipe, and upper division of the bronchial tubes.

Signs: A persistent rasping cough, aggravated to a distressed state following exercise that activates the worms, occurring most commonly in young Greyhounds. Infected Greyhounds have excess mucus (phlegm) in the throat with tracheobronchitis. Refer to Tracheobronchitis.

Causes: Tracheal worms or Windpipe worms have been reported in Greyhounds in most countries but the incidence is not known, except in the UK where two surveys found that 18 per cent of Greyhounds harboured the parasite. Adult worms live in nodules and raised areas of the lining of the lower windpipe and origin of the bronchi. The adult female worm lays eggs which are coughed up in mucus and phlegm, are swallowed and passed in the stools as infective larvae. Puppies of a carrier bitch become infected by eating droppings or by the bitch licking her puppies. An infection takes 2 months to establish in the puppies as they grow.

Management: An accurate diagnosis can be made by observing worms in the nodules and collecting airway mucus for eggs using a bronchoscope. Although wormers are available, control of the tracheal worm is inconsistent. Rearing puppies in isolation away from infected Greyhounds will help to reduce the spread of this disease.

TRACHEITIS: A term that describes inflammation of the lining of the trachea, or windpipe. In most cases, the inflammation extends down into the bronchial airways, resulting in the tracheobronchitis condition and symptoms of kennel cough.

Signs: Initial fever, loss of appetite, wheezing and coughing, with a mucoid discharge from the nose, lasting a few days to several weeks if not treated. Often tonsillitis and a pharyngitis (inflamed throat) are also present. If caused by the tracheal worm, the infected Greyhound exhibits a moist cough after exercise. Refer to Tracheal Worm.

Causes: An excessive amount of dust from bedding and dry, dusty outside runs can cause tracheal inflammation and a rasping cough in young Greyhounds. An infection with a canine respiratory virus, such as Parainfluenza Type 2,

Adenovirus Type 2, Distemper and herpes virus may initiate upper respiratory tract inflammation which extends into the trachea. *Bordetella bronchiseptica*, a bacterial germ that is normally present in the nose and throat, initiates inflammation of the windpipe and the viral/bacterial combination often leads to the symptoms of kennel cough. Refer to Kennel Cough. The tracheal worm, which resides in nodules in the lower windpipe, also causes a localised tracheitis. Refer to Tracheal Worms.

Management: Tracheitis of viral or bacterial cause is usually only a short-term condition, resulting in coughing and developing into tracheobronchitis. Low-grade tracheitis often responds to antibiotic therapy to reduce secondary bacterial infection combined with mucolytic preparations to liquify and allow expulsion of excess mucus and secretions. Uncomplicated tracheitis clears up within 5-7 days, but if it develops into kennel cough, recovery may take 4-6 weeks. Refer to Kennel Cough. Low dust bedding such as shredded paper in place of straw or hulls is preferred. Dust in outside yards can be settled by spraying with water. Refer also to Tracheal Worm.

TRACHEOBRONCHITIS: Upper airway respiratory disease often develops into an inflammatory and reactive condition in the windpipe and branching bronchi in the lungs. It is often involved in the kennel cough condition, in which case it is referred to as infectious tracheobronchitis. Puppies and growing Greyhounds, as well as racing and retired Greyhounds are all susceptible, especially in crowded kennel conditions.

Signs: Early signs are similar to those for tracheitis, developing into a more persistent condition with husking cough, often ending in a gurgling moist cough as mucoid accumulations are loosened in the bronchi, commonly described as phlegm in the throat. Symptoms can last for a few days to several weeks. Refer also to Kennel Cough. Exercise tolerance is reduced due to airway inflammation and blockage with mucus. Strands of thick mucus may stream from the mouth and cling to the left side of the body as the Greyhound gallops on a circle track.

Causes: Often a combination of viral and bacterial contamination with *Bordetella bronchiseptica* create an inflammatory mucoid condition in the windpipe and lower branching airways. The tracheal worm can also cause similar symptoms. Refer to Tracheal Worm.

Management: The treatment and management plan as described for kennel cough will assist in clearing up tracheobronchitis. Refer to Kennel Cough. Aggressive therapy and management will help avoid symptoms of chronic respiratory disease which, if not controlled, can result in long-term impairment of lung function and reduced performance in racing Greyhounds.

TRAINING-OFF: Training-off is a term used by trainers to describe loss of keenness, alertness and interest in racing, often accompanied by reduced appetite, weight loss, dehydration, apparent tiredness and slower recovery from trialling or racing. Many trainers believe that these symptoms are associated with metabolic and toxic stress to the liver during a hard or extended racing programme. Often, a blood count indicates changes due to physical stress. Supplements of the amino acid dl-methionine (1000mg (.353oz) daily), a range of B group vitamins and Vitamin C (250mg (.008825oz) daily) are given to assist detoxification and metabolic processes in the liver. This is usually combined with a lay-off from training and a moist diet of stewed meat supplemented with body salts for 5-7 days, to overcome liver depression, dehydration, improve the appetite and vitality and freshen up the Greyhound's vitality and keenness. Although there is no scientific evidence to support this practice, it is possible that a short lay-off and change in diet may help overcome the mental, metabolic and physical symptoms associated with the stress of long-term training and repeated racing.

U

ULNA FRACTURES: The thin ulna bone adjacent to the forearm or more robust radius bone, may fracture in 3 sites. Fractures of the shaft of the radius and/or ulna are the most common type of broken long bone above the wrist and hock of racing Greyhounds.

Fracture Site: Olecranon Process:
Signs: Acute lameness with swelling and haemorrhage. Refer to Olecranon Fractures.

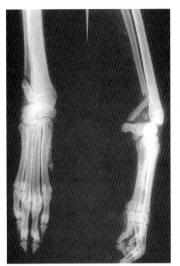

Fracture of the ulna and dislocation of the wrist (carpal) joint occurred as a result of a race fall. The fracture was surgically repaired and the Greyhound regained normal limb function in retirement.

Fracture Site: Mid Shaft:
Signs: Swelling, severe pain, weight bearing discomfort and aggressive resentment when the joint is flexed. In severe cases, bone fragments protrude through the skin.
Fracture Site: Styloid Process (bottom end)
Signs: Slowing up when negotiating bends in a race, with mild lameness in the limb on recovery. May develop into a chronic non-union fracture site.
Causes: The radius and ulna have the highest incidence of upper limb fractures in racing Greyhounds. Fractures result from race falls, collisions and overload stress during racing.
Management: X-rays are usually taken to confirm the severity of the fracture. The best chance of a Greyhound returning to racing is achieved when the fractures are stabilised by bone plates and given 6-8 weeks to heal, depending on the severity of the fracture and degree of associated tissue damage. A diet containing adequate calcium, phosphorus and vitamin D will enable bone healing, complemented by daily magnetic field therapy. A gradual return to full training, including physiotherapy to strengthen weakened muscles, over a 4-5 week period, usually ensures a Greyhound can return to competitive racing.

UMBILICAL HERNIA: The navel in a normal puppy heals to a flat, fibrous scar in the midline of the central abdomen.
Signs: A hernia is a soft lump, up to the size of a marble, usually first seen in a puppy under a week old and persisting as the puppy grows to

adulthood. The lump can usually be gently pressed back into the abdominal cavity with the fingers, where the midline muscle layers do not form normally around the umbilicus.

Causes: Occasionally a newborn puppy will develop signs of a hernia after the umbilical (navel) cord detaches after whelping. Some authorities consider it an accidental occurrence, others believe it is an inherited prevalence in certain bloodlines of Greyhounds.

Management: The lump of a hernia is formed by the collection of abdominal fat poking through a defect in the midline muscle layers. The chances of an umbilical hernia trapping abdominal contents, and causing them to be pinched off, are relative to the size of the hole in the midline and the amount and type of gut content trapped within the hernia. Large hernias will require surgical intervention to suture the midline muscle layers at the umbilicus.

URINARY TRACT DISORDERS: The urinary tract includes two kidneys, a tube from each kidney to the bladder (uretor), the muscular expandable bladder and the exit tube to the penis or rear of the vagina (urethra). Many trainers focus on their Greyhound's kidneys as a source of major concern, discomfort and ailment. The majority of diseases are caused by ascending infection introduced via the urethra into the bladder. Bladder infections result in inflammation of the bladder wall (cystitis), which causes discomfort and scalding pain on urination, with discoloured, high-ammonia and cloudy urine which has sharp mineral crystal sedimentation. Cystitis is most common in bitches because of the risk of infection entering from the floor of the vagina adjacent to the external vulval opening. Refer to Cystitis, Calculi in the Urine.

Note: Many trainers observe, and become concerned by, yellowing of the urine when high doses of minerals and vitamins are given. This is often caused by excretion of excess Vitamin B2 (Riboflavine), which has a strong natural yellow colour.

Inflammation of the kidneys, or nephritis, is relatively common in racing Greyhounds, with the incidence increasing as a Greyhound ages. Blood-borne infection and acid urine can localise within the kidney and damage the kidney cells. Refer to Nephritis. The problem that is referred to as post

racing dysuria or, commonly, bladder shut down, can occur in nervy hyperactive male Greyhounds. In this condition, the urine is passed in fine pulsed streams, if at all, after a delay of up to 4-48 hours after a hard strenuous race. Refer to Post Racing Dysuria.

URTICARIA: The medical term used to describe a skin condition, often caused by a rapid allergic response, causing a number of soft fluid lumps, hive-like bumps or weals to collect under the skin. The often itchy reaction can be caused by insect bites or eating certain food in a sensitive individual, which is referred to as hives. As well, contact with chemical irritants in the kennel environment can result in an allergic dermatitis. Refer to Allergic Dermatitis.

V

VAGINITIS: Vaginitis, or inflammation of the vaginal canal in a bitch, is a relatively common condition in Greyhound bitches of all ages.

Signs: Up to 10 per cent of bitches will develop a vaginal infection during their lifetime, but it is more common following a season cycle, when a bitch is bred or after whelping. Young racing bitches may lose performance if the vaginitis persists. A low-grade vaginal bacterial infection does not always result in an obvious vaginal discharge, but the vulva may become reddened due to excessive licking from vaginal irritation. A vaginal infection may spread to the uterus, which results in higher volume discharge. Refer to Pyometra. It may also be a predisposing cause of cystitis if infection ascends into the bladder. Refer to Cystitis.

Causes: The primary causes are common bacteria such as *E. coli*, *Streptococcal* and *Staphylococcal* species that are present in the kennel environment and contaminate the buttocks area. Medication with anabolic steroids in a racing bitch, to prevent her coming into season, can increase the risk of vaginal infections due to a change in the normal protective and immune secretions within the vagina.

Management: In most cases, a low-grade vaginitis will clear up without treatment in an otherwise healthy bitch with a strong immune system. If the infection develops into an obvious discharge, then referral to a vet is necessary. The vet will take a swab from the vagina and select an appropriate antibiotic course to control the specific type of bacteria causing the condition. Fitting a muzzle with the front taped over may discourage licking of the vulva. Improving the standard of hygiene in the kennel, yards and turn-out pens may help to reduce the overall risk of contamination and subsequent vaginitis.

VERTEBRAL JOINT CONDITIONS: The Greyhound has a very flexible spinal column that enables it to arch its back during the galloping motion to provide extra power and a longer stride length. The spinal column can also flex sideways and has limited rotational movement at the lumbosacral junction. The major conditions relate to injury to the powerful backline muscles surrounding the spinal column and mechanical faults between the vertebrae that result in spinal pain and reduced performance. Refer to Spinal Pain. Arthritic changes can develop, primarily in racing Greyhounds in the upper neck area and the lumbosacral joint. In aged retired Greyhounds, arthritis in the joint spaces between the vertebrae causes back pain and reduced mobility. Refer to Coupling Joint Injuries, Lumbar Vertebral Fractures, Lumbosacral Injuries, Neck Injuries.

Older Greyhounds may also sustain compression injuries to the soft, fluid-filled cartilage discs that provide shock-absorption and cushioning between the vertebral bones of the lower back. This is often referred to as a 'slipped disc', or more accurately, vertebral disc protrusion. As a Greyhound ages, the intervertebral disc becomes less flexible and, in some cases, starts to deteriorate due to wear and tear and arthritic changes from earlier injuries to the lower back when racing. The vertebral disc can rupture when squashed in the vertebral space, with the disc material protruding upwards into the spinal cord canal. This can cause pressure and damage to the spinal cord, resulting in intense pain and, in severe cases, varying degrees of back and hindlimb paralysis relative to the degree of the rupture and damage to the spinal cord and its branching nerve structure.

VIRAL PAPILLOMAS (WARTS): A papilloma is the medical term for a wart, which is a rapidly growing raised growth on the skin surface. Warts are caused by a virus.
Signs: Warts occur as white, cauliflower-like, skin growths, usually on the lower limbs and in the webbing between the toes. Warts often occur in groups, taking 6 weeks to develop into a fleshy growth. They can be knocked during exercise, exposing a juicy surface, and larger warts may bleed. Warts on the nail cuticle are especially prone to abrasion and can become sore and cause lameness.

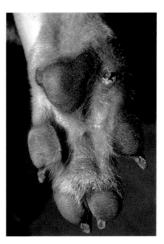

'Cauliflower' or 'cabbage' warts develop on the sides of the foot pads, webbing or on the toe cuticle. This large wart next to the main pad was removed by electrocautery and the Greyhound returned to training 21 days later.

Causes: The *Papilloma* virus gains entry to the skin via abrasions, cuts and sand burns. When mature warts on Greyhounds are abraded, they shed the virus into sand, floors and bedding. An outbreak of warts on the webbing and cuticles can occur in a group of Greyhounds when sand or grass wash bays at race tracks become contaminated with the virus from warts that are abraded during a race.
Management: Mature warts on the skin of the pastern and toes can be removed carefully by thoroughly disinfecting the skin with PVP (tamed) iodine wash. Then squeeze the wart to express the juicy core, holding a swab to control bleeding and follow up with the application of an iodine antiseptic twice daily to the residual growth until it dries up and heals. Warts on the nail cuticles should be referred to a vet for removal using local anaesthetic. After removal, the wart growth must be destroyed to prevent spread of the virus. In the event of an outbreak of warts, swabbing the Greyhound's feet in a PVP iodine wash twice daily will help prevent infection.

VOLVULUS: The technical name that refers to gastric dilation, gastric torsion syndrome or, commonly, the condition referred to as bloat. Refer to Bloat, Gastric Dilation.

VOMITING: Dogs fortunately have a very well-developed reflex action that enables them to vomit food that causes stomach irritation (gastritis), is too cold or when meat is off due to a heavy bacterial count or when kept under poor storage conditions. However, vomiting may also be caused by other toxic conditions, or stimulated by nausea and consumption of green grass.
Signs: Vomiting after eating is most common. Often the regurgitated food mass may be slimy and have an acidic smell following partial digestion in the stomach. A blockage of the small intestine, or a foreign body in the stomach, will cause vomiting soon after eating. If vomiting occurs on a regular basis after eating, or the Greyhound has a fever, is depressed or has diarrhoea from gastroenteritis, then it should be investigated by a vet. Occasionally, vomit will contain other foreign bodies such as plastic, sticks or pieces of bone, suggesting that a retired Greyhound with free run of the home is scavenging for food, or chewing wood when bored and confined to a small yard without a companion.
Causes: Vomiting is most commonly a reflex reaction to stomach irritation or gastritis. This can be caused by poor-quality or contaminated food; food that is fed cold directly from a refrigerator, or gorging food too quickly in a very hungry, greedy Greyhound, or one that is competing for food with others. Toxic conditions such as kidney and liver disease can cause nausea and vomiting, as can certain bacterial and viral diseases. If the vomiting is associated with a fever or depression, nervous signs or other signs of illness, the underlying cause should be investigated by a vet. When nauseated, Greyhounds will eat green grass to stimulate vomiting and empty their stomach contents as a natural purging action. If the animal appears healthy and consumes its next meal without vomiting, it is often a short-term gastric irritation problem. Also refer to Biling Out.
Management: A simple case of stomach upset can be resolved by withdrawing food for 12-24 hours and discouraging the eating of grass that causes retching and further discomfort. The Greyhound should be given only small quantities of cool, clean water until the nausea settles down, and then small meals until it recovers fully. Where the vomiting is frequent and distressful to the animal, medications to suppress the vomiting, control gastric acid production and protect the gastric lining can be prescribed, along with fluids to prevent dehydration.

W

WARTS: Warts are skin outgrowths caused by the *Papilloma* virus, which localise on the lower limbs below the wrist and hock. Refer to Viral Papillomas (Warts).

WATER DIABETES SYNDROME (WDS): A term to describe the symptoms of intense thirst and intake of large volumes of water (polydypsia) with outflow of diluted urine (polyuria) through the kidneys. It is caused by the extreme physical stress of overachieving in a race, often under adverse conditions, with suppression of antidiuretic hormone that helps concentrate and limit urine outflow. It is also referred to as Racing Thirst. Refer to Racing Thirst.

WEBBING PROBLEMS: The skin between the toes that prevents the toes from spreading during exercise and galloping is referred to as the webbing. When the Greyhound gallops on an abrasive sand track surface, the webbing can be abraded and worn away with inflammation, surface infection and lameness. Refer to Sand Burn. The webbing can also become lacerated by sharp objects, or tear and split under the extreme stretching forces endured when galloping, especially around corners on a race track. Refer to Split Webbing. A number of bacterial, viral and fungal organisms resident in the soil, yards and turn-out pens can gain entry to the skin of the webbing, establishing an infection that results in inflammation, weakening and erosion of the webbing. Refer to Foot Rot, Interdigital Cysts, Interdigital Dermatitis, Viral Papillomas. Contact with irritant, and potentially allergenic, chemicals used in cleaning or disinfecting the kennels, yards or turn-out pens may cause a hypersensitive form of dermatitis. Very young and aged retired Greyhounds appear to be more susceptible.
Note: It has been popular to spray diesel (fuel oil) on to the surfaces of yards to control dust and on to race tracks to prevent the surface freezing during the

The webbing of this hindfoot was split during a race. The edges were trimmed and allowed to heal as an open wound without recurring web injury.

winter months. Chemical burns from diesel can cause interdigital inflammation to the pads and webbing and an increased incidence of paronychia. Heating elements embedded into the track surface eliminate the need to use fuel oil. Refer to Allergic Dermatitis.

WHIPWORMS: Whipworm is a roundworm that colonises the large intestine of dogs.

Signs: Heavy infestation of whipworms can cause weight loss, anaemia and, in severe cases, diarrhoea and gut discomfort. The diarrhoea is often slimy or mucus-coated and may contain fresh or partly digested blood. Heavy infrstations can reduce growth in young Greyhounds and performance in racing Greyhounds.

Causes: Whipworm, or *Trichuris vulpis*, attaches to the lining of the large intestine, sucking nutrients and causing blood leakage in heavy infestations. Mature adult worms take from 6-10 weeks to develop following ingestion of infective eggs on contaminated food or soil. The eggs can survive in the yard environment for years.

Management: Regular worming every 6-8 weeks with a targeted worming preparation is necessary to control whipworm. Strict hygiene to prevent re-infection is essential, with rigorous cleaning and disinfection of kennels, yards and turn-out pens to prevent build-up of infective eggs.

WRIST INJURIES: The wrist, or carpal joint, in the front limbs is subjected to extreme downward loading and risk of over extension or complete flattening of the wrist, particularly when leaning into a corner at racing speed. The wrist is prone to internal ligament sprain, bone compressive fractures and tendon strain. Arthritic change can develop, leading to reduced wrist flexion and lameness, particularly as Greyhounds age in retirement. Refer to Arthritis, Articular Cartilage Injury, Carpal Injuries, Joint Injuries, Polyarthritis, Stopper Tendon injuries.

WOUNDS: Wounds on the skin of Greyhounds are usually caused by lacerations and cuts to the feet and lower limbs on fencing or when being walked on

This wound was caused by a sharp object on a track, developing a 'button ulcer' on the rear of the pastern, which became an infected, crusty sore.

roadways. Body wounds can be caused by falls or striking the rails during a race. All wounds should be thoroughly cleaned and an appropriate topical medication applied to reduce surface infection and aid healing. Large wounds are best sutured to speed up closure and minimise scarring. Greyhounds, like all dogs, have an innate habit of licking wounds to soothe them, introducing infection and excessive moisture that can delay healing. Dressings may need to be applied to prevent licking, but, if a wound is itchy, the animal may tear off the bandage, risking further injury. A muzzle with the front taped over, an Elizabethan collar, or a 10 litre (2.5 gallon) plastic bucket attached to the collar may be necessary to prevent the animal licking body, limb and foot wounds. Regular feeding and drinking times must be allocated if licking is curtailed by these methods. Refer also to Cut Pads, Split Webbing.

X Y Z No entries

ACKNOWLEDGMENTS

The author, John Kohnke, acknowledges the photographs supplied by Greyhound veterinarians, including the late Dr Reg Hoskins, Dr Phil Davis, University of Sydney and Dr Brian Daniels, Quakers Hill Veterinary Surgery, NSW, Australia. Lola and Merven Burgess, and Barry and Sheila Allison of Vineyard NSW Australia are also acknowledged for their help in providing Greyhounds for photographs.